Theoretical and Practice Frameworks for Agent-Based Systems

Yu Zhang
Trinity University, USA

Information Science
REFERENCE

Managing Director:	Lindsay Johnston
Senior Editorial Director:	Heather A. Probst
Book Production Manager:	Sean Woznicki
Development Manager:	Joel Gamon
Development Editor:	Development Editor
Acquisitions Editor:	Erika Gallagher
Typesetter:	Jen McHugh
Cover Design:	Nick Newcomer, Lisandro Gonzalez

Published in the United States of America by
Information Science Reference (an imprint of IGI Global)
701 E. Chocolate Avenue
Hershey PA 17033
Tel: 717-533-8845
Fax: 717-533-8661
E-mail: cust@igi-global.com
Web site: http://www.igi-global.com

Library of Congress Cataloging-in-Publication Data

Theoretical and practice frameworks for agent-based systems / Yu Zhang, editor.
    p. cm.
  Includes bibliographical references and index.
  Summary: "This book tackles these real problems and issues pertaining to agent-based systems, bringing the theoretical research of intelligent agents to researchers and practitioners in academia, government, and innumerable industries"--Provided by publisher.
  ISBN 978-1-4666-1565-6 (hbk.) -- ISBN 978-1-4666-1566-3 (ebook) -- ISBN 978-1-4666-1567-0 (print & perpetual access) 1. Multiagent systems. 2. Intelligent agents (Computer software) I. Zhang, Yu, 1974-
  QA76.76.I58T54 2012
  006.3--dc23
                                    2012002102

British Cataloguing in Publication Data
A Cataloguing in Publication record for this book is available from the British Library.

All work contributed to this book is new, previously-unpublished material. The views expressed in this book are those of the authors, but not necessarily of the publisher.

Table of Contents

Section 1
Resource Allocation and Scheduling

Section 2
Agent Collaboration

Section 3
Social Simulation

Section 4
E-Business Simulation

Section 6
Simulation in Ecosystem

\

Detailed Table of Contents

Section 1
Resource Allocation and Scheduling

Chapter 1

The objective of Resource Allocation and Monitoring System is to make the procedures involved in allocating fund resources to competing clients transparent so that deserving candidates get funds. Proactive and goal directed behaviour of agents make the system transparent and intelligent. This paper presents design of Multi Agent Systems for Resource Allocation and Monitoring using Agent Unified Modelling Language (AUML) and implementation in agent based development tool. At a conceptual level, three agents are identified with their roles and responsibilities. The identified agents, functionalities, and interactions are also included and results show that multi agent technology can be used for effective decision making for resource allocation and monitoring problem.

Chapter 2

Decision making in models of activity and travel behaviour is usually individual-based and focuses on outcomes rather than the decision process. Using agent-based modelling techniques and incorporating interaction protocols into the model can assist in modelling decision-making in more detail. This paper describes an agent-based model of social activity generation and scheduling, in which utility-based agents interact with each other to schedule activities. Six different protocols are tested. The authors show that the model outcomes reflect minor changes in the protocol, while changing the order of the protocol leads to significantly different outcomes, hence the protocol plays a large role in the simulation results and should be studied in more detail.

In this paper, the authors demonstrate the use of software agents to extend the role of humans in a collaborative work process. The extended roles to agents provide a convenient means for humans to delegate mundane tasks to software agents. The framework employs the FIPA ACL communication protocol which implements communication between agents. An interface for each agent implements the communication between humans and agents. Such interface and the subsequent communication performed by agents and between agents contribute to the achievement of shared goals.

Chapter 4

Sign-based stigmergic methods such as the ant colony optimization algorithm have been used to solve network optimization, scheduling problems, and other optimization problems that can be visualized as directed graphs. However, there has been little research focused on the use of optimization methods based on sematectonic stigmergy, such as coordination through collective construction. This paper develops a novel approach where the process of agent-directed stigmergic construction is introduced as a general optimization tool. The development of this new approach involves adopting previous work on stigmergic construction to a virtual space and applying statistical mechanics–based techniques to data produced during the stigmergic construction process. From this a unique procedure for solving optimization problems using a computational procedure that simulates sematectonic stigmergic processes such as stigmergic construction is proposed.

In this paper, the authors propose software architecture to monitor elderly or dependent people in their own house. Many studies have been done on hardware aspects resulting in operational products, but there is a lack of adaptive algorithms to handle all the data generated by these products due to data being distributed and heterogeneous in a large scale environment. The authors propose a multi-agent classification method to collect and to aggregate data about activity, movements, and physiological information of the monitored people. Data generated at this local level are communicated and adjusted between agents to obtain a set of patterns. This data is dynamic; the system has to store the built patterns and has to create new patterns when new data is available. Therefore, the system is adaptive and can be spread on a large scale. Generated data is used at a local level, for example to raise an alert, but also to evaluate global risks. This paper presents specification choices and the massively multi-agent architecture that was developed; an example with a sample of ten dependant people gives an illustration.

> *Kristen Lund, Trinity University, USA*
> *Yu Zhang, Trinity University, USA*

This paper studies the concept of tolerance in dynamic social networks where agents are able to make and break connections with neighbors to improve their payoffs. This problem was initially introduced to the authors by observing resistance (or tolerance) in experiments run in dynamic networks under the two rules that they have developed: the Highest Rewarding Neighborhood rule and the Highest Weighted Reward rule. These rules help agents evaluate their neighbors and decide whether to break a connection or not. They introduce the idea of tolerance in dynamic networks by allowing an agent to maintain a relationship with a bad neighbor for some time. In this research, the authors investigate and define the phenomenon of tolerance in dynamic social networks, particularly with the two rules. The paper defines a mathematical model to predict an agent's tolerance of a bad neighbor and determine the factors that affect it. After defining a general version of tolerance, the idea of optimal tolerance is explored, providing situations in which tolerance can be used as a tool to affect network efficiency and network structure.

> *Rajiv Kadaba, The University of Texas at Austin, USA*
> *Suratna Budalakoti, The University of Texas at Austin, USA*
> *David DeAngelis, The University of Texas at Austin, USA*
> *K. Suzanne Barber, The University of Texas at Austin, USA*

Entities interacting on the web establish their identity by creating virtual personas. These entities, or agents, can be human users or software-based. This research models identity using the *Entity-Persona Model*, a semantically annotated social network inferred from the persistent traces of interaction between personas on the web. A *Persona Mapping Algorithm* is proposed which compares the local views of personas in their social network referred to as their Virtual Signatures, for structural and semantic similarity. The semantics of the *Entity-Persona Model* are modeled by a vector space model of the text associated with the personas in the network, which allows comparison of their Virtual Signatures. This enables all the publicly accessible personas of an entity to be identified on the scale of the web. This research enables an agent to identify a single entity using multiple personas on different networks, provided that multiple personas exhibit characteristic behavior. The agent is able to increase the trustworthiness of on-line interactions by establishing the identity of entities operating under multiple personas. Consequently, reputation measures based on on-line interactions with multiple personas can be aggregated and resolved to the true singular identity.

> *Yu Zhang, Trinity University, USA*
> *Maksim Tsikhanovich, Bard College, USA*
> *Georgi Smilyanov, Bard College, USA*

Diffusion is a process by which information, viruses, ideas, or new behavior spread over social networks. Traditional diffusion models are history insensitive, i.e. only giving activated nodes a one-time chance to activate each of its neighboring nodes with some probability. But history dependent interactions between people are often observed in the real world. This paper proposes the History Sensitive Cascade Model (HSCM), a model of information cascade through a network over time. The authors consider the "activation" problem of finding the probability of that a particular node receives information given that some nodes are initially informed. In this paper it is also proven that selecting a set of k nodes with greatest expected influence is NP-hard, and results from submodular functions are used to provide a greedy approximation algorithm with a $1-1/e-\varepsilon$ lower bound, where ε depends polynomially on the precision of the solution to the "activation" problem. Finally, experiments are performed comparing the greedy algorithm to three other approximation algorithms.

Chapter 9

Wagdi Alrawagfeh, Memorial University of Newfoundland, Canada
Edward Brown, Memorial University of Newfoundland, Canada
Manrique Mata-Montero, Memorial University of Newfoundland, Canada

Norms have an obvious role in the coordinating and predicting behaviours in societies of software agents. Most researchers assume that agents already know the norms of their societies beforehand at design time. Others assume that norms are assigned by a leader or a legislator. Some researchers take into account the acquisition of societies' norms through inference. Their works apply to closed multi-agent societies in which the agents have identical (or similar) internal architecture for representing norms. This paper addresses three things: 1) the idea of a Verification Component that was previously used to verify candidate norms in multi-agent societies, 2) a known modification of the Verification Component that makes it applicable in open multi-agent societies, and 3) a modification of the Verification Component, so that agents can dynamically infer the new emerged and abrogated norms in open multi-agent societies. Using the JADE software framework, we build a restaurant interaction scenario as an example (where restaurants usually host heterogeneous agents), and demonstrate how permission and prohibition of behavior can be identified by agents using dynamic norms.

Section 4
E-Business Simulation

Chapter 10

Radu Burete, University of Craiova, Romania
Amelia Bădică, University of Craiova, Romania
Costin Bădică, University of Craiova, Romania
Florin Moraru, University of Craiova, Romania

Trust is a very important quality attribute of an e-service. In particular, the increasing complexity of the e-business environment requires the development of new computational models of trust and reputation for e-business agents. In this paper, the authors introduce a new reputation model for agents engaged in e-business transactions. The model enhances classic reputation models by the addition of forgiveness factor and the use of new sources of reputation information based on agents groups. The paper proposes an improvement of this model by employing the recent con-resistance concept. Finally, the authors show how the model can be used in an agent-based market environment where trusted buyer and seller agents meet, negotiate, and transact multi-issue e-business contracts. The system was implemented using JADE multi-agent platform and initially evaluated on a sample set of scenarios. The paper introduces the design and implementation of the agent-based system together with the experimental scenarios and results.

Chapter 11

Bireshwar Dass Mazumdar, Banaras Hindu University, India

Swati Basak, Banaras Hindu University, India

Neelam Modanwal, Banaras Hindu University, India

Multi agent system (MAS) model has been extensively used in the different tasks of E-Commerce such as customer relation management (CRM), negotiation and brokering. The objective of this paper is to evaluate a seller agent's various cognitive parameters like capability, trust, and desire. After selecting a best seller agent from ordering queue, it applies negotiation strategies to find the most profitable proposal for both buyer and seller. This mechanism belongs to a semi cooperative negotiation type, and selecting a seller and buyer agent pair using mental and cognitive parameters. This work provides a logical cognitive model, logical negotiation model between buyer agent and selected seller agent.

Chapter 12

Deborah Lim, Universiti Malaysia Sabah, Malaysia

Patricia Anthony, Universiti Malaysia Sabah, Malaysia

Chong Mun Ho, Universiti Malaysia Sabah, Malaysia

The introduction of online auction has resulted in a rich collection of problems and issues especially in the bidding process. During the bidding process, bidders have to monitor multiple auction houses, pick from the many auctions to participate in and make the right bid. If bidders are able to predict the closing price for each auction, then they are able to make a better decision making on the time, place and the amount they can bid for an item. However, predicting closing price for an auction is not easy since it is dependent on many factors such as the behavior of each bidder, the number of the bidders participating in that auction as well as each bidder's reservation price. This paper reports on the development of a predictor agent that utilizes Grey System Theory GM (1, 1) to predict the online auction closing price in order to maximize the bidder's profit. The performance of this agent is compared with an Artificial Neural Network Predictor Agent (using Feed-Forward Back-Propagation Prediction Model). The effectiveness of these two agents is evaluated in a simulated auction environment as well as using real eBay auction's data.

Chapter 13

Robert Somogyi, Paris School of Economics, France

János Vincze, Corvinus University of Budapest and Institute of Economics of the Hungarian Academy of Sciences, Hungary

The phenomenon of infrequent price changes has troubled economists for decades. Intuitively one feels that for most price-setters there exists a range of inaction, i.e., a substantial measure of the states of the world, within which they do not wish to modify prevailing prices. Economists wishing to maintain rationality of price-setters resorted to fixed price adjustment costs as an explanation for price rigidity. This paper proposes an alternative explanation, without recourse to any sort of physical adjustment cost, by putting strategic interaction into the center-stage of the analysis. Price-making is treated as a repeated oligopoly game. The traditional analysis of these games cannot pinpoint any equilibrium as a reasonable "solution" of the strategic situation. Thus, decision-makers have a genuine strategic uncertainty about the strategies of other decision-makers. Hesitation may lead to inaction. To model this situation, the authors follow the style of agent-based models, by modeling firms that change their pricing strategies following an evolutionary algorithm. In addition to reproducing the known negative relationship between price rigidity and the level of general inflation, the model exhibits several features observed in real data. Moreover, most prices fall into the theoretical "range" without explicitly building this property into strategies.

Section 5
Simulation in Health Sciences

Chapter 14

In agent-based modeling (ABM), an explicit spatial representation may be required for certain aspects of the system to be modeled realistically. A spatial ABM includes landscapes in which agents seek resources necessary for their survival. The *spatial heterogeneity* of the underlying landscape plays a crucial role in the resource-seeking process. This study describes a previous agent-based model of malaria, and the modeling of its spatial extension. In both models, all mosquito agents are represented individually. In the new spatial model, the agents also possess explicit spatial information. Within a landscape, adult female mosquito agents search for two types of resources: aquatic habitats (AHs) and bloodmeal locations (BMLs). These resources are specified within different spatial patterns, or landscapes. Model verification between the non-spatial and spatial models by means of docking is examined. Using different landscapes, the authors show that mosquito abundance remains unchanged. With the same overall system capacity, varying the density of resources in a landscape does not affect abundance. When the density of resources is constant, the overall capacity drives the system. For the spatial model, using landscapes with different resource densities of both resource-types, the authors show that spatial heterogeneity influences the mosquito population.

Chapter 15

Malaria is a vector-borne illness affecting millions of lives annually and imposes a heavy financial burden felt worldwide. Moreover, there is growing concern that global climate change, in particular, rising temperature, will increase this burden. As such, policy makers are in need of tools capable of informing them about the potential strengths and weaknesses of intervention and control strategies. A previously developed agent-based model of the *Anopheles gambiae* mosquito is extended, one of the primary vectors of malaria, to investigate how changes in temperature influence the dynamics of malaria transmission and the effectiveness of a common malaria intervention: insecticide-treated nets (ITNs). Results from the simulations suggest two important findings. Consistent with previous studies, an increase in mosquito abundance as temperature increases is observed. However, the increase in mosquito abundance reduces the effectiveness of ITNs at a given coverage level. The implications and limitations of these findings are discussed.

Vector-borne diseases account for 16% of the global infectious disease burden (WHO, 2004). Many of these debilitating and sometimes fatal diseases are transmitted between human hosts by mosquitoes. Mosquito-targeted intervention methods have controlled or eliminated mosquito-borne diseases from many regions of the world but regions of constant transmission (holoendemic areas) still exist (Molineaux et al., 1980). To eliminate these illnesses, researchers need to understand how interventions impact a mosquito population so as to identify potential avenues for new intervention techniques. This paper presents a software architecture that allows researchers to simulate transgenic interventions on a mosquito population. The authors present specifications for a model that captures these transgenic aspects and present a software architecture that meets those needs. The authors also provide a proof of concept and some observations about sterile insect technique strategies as simulated by this architecture.

Section 6
Simulation in Ecosystem

In this paper, the authors present a computational model of a fundamental social phenomenon in the study of animal behavior: the foraging. The purpose of this work is, first, to test the validity of the proposed model compared to another existing model, the flocking model; then, to try to understand whether the model may provide useful suggestions in studying the size of the group in some species of social mammals.

Preface

Agent-based systems serve as a foundation for a new breed of computer modeling and simulation technologies that act as virtual laboratories for scientists in many disciplines such as health sciences, social sciences, and ecosystem. One of the fundamental questions of agent-based systems has traditionally been how should agents make decisions given they inhabit an environment where their actions may have unforeseen or unpredictable effects on others? This question often raises interesting points about the extent to which the individual autonomy of agents should be sacrificed for global needs and desires of society. Volume 3 (2011) of the *International Journal of Agent Technologies and Systems* presents a contribution to solving this question. By employing realistic models based off of recent advances in decision-making and social interaction, we are able to reproduce realistic behavior based on rational agents.

AGENT AND MULTI-AGENT SYSTEMS

An *agent* is defined as a mapping from perceptions to actions (Russell, 1995). It can be achieved via hardware (e.g. robotics) or software systems. The agent resides in the environment, behaves autonomously, purposively, and flexibly; it may have sensing, adaptive, social, and emotional capabilities (Wooldridge, 1995). The capabilities of a single agent are limited by its knowledge, its computing resources, and its perspective. Particularly, when interdependent problems arise, agents in the system must coordinate with one another to ensure that interdependent problems are properly managed. Thus, they form *multi-agent systems*. In a multi-agent system, multiple agents that cooperate towards the achievement of a joint goal are viewed as a *team*. *Teamwork* is a cooperative effort by a team of agents to achieve a joint goal (Tambe, 1997; Cannon-Bowers, 1997).

AGENT-BASED SYSTEMS

Agent-Based Systems integrate the technologies of modeling and simulation and agent systems; and consists of three distinct, yet related, areas that can be grouped under two categories, as follows (Yilmaz & Ören, 2006):

- **Simulation for Agents (agent simulation):** simulation of agent systems in engineering, human and social dynamics, military applications, etc.

- **Agents for Simulation (which has two aspects):** *agent-supported simulation* that deals with the use of agents as a support facility to enable computer assistance in problem solving or enhancing cognitive capabilities; and *agent-based simulation* that focuses on the use of agents for the generation of model behavior in a simulation study.

On one hand, agent-based systems allow us to use agents to develop domain-specific simulation; on the other hand, it supports the use of agent technology to develop simulation techniques and toolkits that are subsequently applied either with or without agents. The real world problems are complex and there is no single agent-based abstraction that can solve every problem. The integration of simulation and agent technology can help us better understand complex real world problems and improve our capability in developing autonomic simulation systems with robust decision making in real-time for these problems.

ADVANCES IN AGENT TECHNOLOGIES AND SYSTEMS SERIES

The *Advances in Agent Technologies and Systems Series* is an annual journal summation volume published by IGI Global. As one of the premier platforms to the synergy of agent modeling and simulation technologies, the *International Journal of Agent Technologies and Systems* attracts enthusiastic responses every year, and has an impressive Editorial Board (http://www.igi-global.com/journal/international-journal-agent-technologies-systems/1109).

The Volume 3 in 2011 published 18 papers from 8 countries. Every paper was assigned to an associate editor and was reviewed by three referees. Every paper was revised at least one round based on referees' comments and resubmitted for final acceptance.

It is worth noting that part of the published papers in this volume were selected and extended from the Agent-Directed Simulation Symposium at the SpringSim Multiconference in Boston, April 4-5, 2011. The Agent-Directed Simulation Symposium is an annual conference as part of the Spring Simulation Multiconference (SpringSim) sponsored by the Society for Modeling and Simulation International. A further round of call for papers was sent to all accepted papers. Authors were asked to significantly expand and improve their ADS paper in order to make a submission to the *International Journal of Agent Technologies and Systems*. All submissions were reviewed by three referees. Finally, we accepted six to published in the journal.

This volume investigates six different research domains in agent-based systems: Agent System Design, Agent Collaboration, Social Simulation, Simulation in E-Business, Simulation in Health Sciences, Simulation in Ecosystem. The volume also includes a Book Review. We believe that this volume provides the most recent developments in these selected topics and will be an important source of information for researchers in the area of agent-based systems.

The following sections present all papers in this volume in the six research domains and the book review.

AGENT SYSTEM DESIGN

The design of agent systems deals with building interaction and collaboration in distributed and dynamic domains, where each autonomous agent works cooperatively to solve a part of a problem in parallel.

However, a team of agents is more flexible and efficient than a group of single agents only when a flexible and efficient means of coordinating the agents exists. In many ways, the agent system design problem is similar to that of parallel computing: doubling the number of processors used in a computation usually will not double the speed with which the solution is found. The extra processing power does not become an advantage until a sophisticated means of cooperative processing is found. This challenge inspires many design patterns and rule definitions.

In agent literature, Jennings first emphasizes that coordination is a key property that guarantees better multi-agent team performance (Jennings, 1993). Without coordination, a multi-agent system can become a collection of incohesive individuals. He developed a model of coordination, whose two central concepts are (joint) commitment and (social) convention. Jennings views a commitment as a promise to take a certain action, and conventions as rules for monitoring these commitments. He argues that "all coordination mechanisms can ultimately be reduced to joint commitments and their associated social conventions".

In this volume, the chapter titled "Design of Multi Agent System for Resource Allocation and Monitoring" by Manish Arora and M. Syamala Devi proposes to use the Agent Unified Modeling Language to design a multi-agent system for resource allocation and monitoring. The objective of Resource Allocation and Monitoring System is to make the procedures involved in allocating fund resources to competing clients transparent so that deserving candidates get funds. Proactive and goal directed behaviour of agents make the system transparent and intelligent. This chapter presents design of Multi Agent Systems for Resource Allocation and Monitoring using Agent Unified Modelling Language (AUML) and implementation in agent based development tool. At a conceptual level, three agents are identified with their roles and responsibilities. The identified agents, functionalities, and interactions are also included, and results show that multi agent technology can be used for effective decision making for resource allocation and monitoring problem.

Next paper is titled "The Effects of Different Interaction Protocols in Agent-Based Simulation of Social Activities" by Nicole Ronald, Theo Arentze, and Harry Timmermans. Decision-making in models of activity and travel behaviour is usually individual-based and focuses on outcomes rather than the decision process. Using agent-based modelling techniques and incorporating interaction protocols into the model can assist in modelling decision-making in more detail. This chapter describes an agent-based model of social activity generation and scheduling in which utility-based agents interact with each other to schedule activities. Six different protocols are tested. The authors show that the model outcomes reflect minor changes in the protocol, while changing the order of the protocol leads to significantly different outcomes, hence the protocol plays a large role in the simulation results and should be studied in more detail.

AGENT COLLABORATION

Back in 1992, a group of Australian researchers propose planned team activity in the logical and practical design of rational agents cooperating in a team (Kinny, 1992). This is a pioneer work in agent collaboration. In present time, the practices presented in this work, such as common knowledge, still guides the research in agent collaboration. Kinny et al. suggest that joint plans (common to all agents) that specify the means of satisfying joint goals are supplied in advance, rather than being generated by the agents. Their argument is that the agents embedded in a dynamic environment can respond rapidly to important events by adopting applicable plans. The joint plans are represented by concepts of skills and team members' roles. These plans usually will be qualified by preconditions that specify under what circumstances they are applicable. The plan execution for each agent consists of the selection and hierarchical expansion of these plans.

To achieve the planned team activity, common knowledge necessary for coordination and synchronization of agents' activities is imposed on the agents. The common knowledge that includes mutual beliefs about the world and about each other's actions places strong requirements upon agents' observation. Kinny et al. propose that the common knowledge can be achieved alternatively by communication between agents. This approach implies the need of effective communication. The assumption that the plans of individual agents are known at compile time might enhance the team's proactivity by the possibility of reasoning in advance about which team members potentially can achieve certain goals.

In this volume, "A Collaborative Framework for Multiagent Systems" by Moamin Ahmed, Mohd Sharifuddin Ahmad, and Mohd Zaliman M. Yusoff demonstrates the use of software agents to extend the role of humans in a collaborative work process. The extended roles to agents provide a convenient means for humans to delegate mundane tasks to software agents. The framework employs the FIPA ACL communication protocol, which implements communication between agents. An interface for each agent implements the communication between humans and agents. Such interface and the subsequent communication performed by agents and between agents contribute to the achievement of shared goals.

The next chapter is titled "Initial Formulation of an Optimization Method Based on Stigmergic Construction" by Aditya C. Velivelli and Kenneth M. Bryden. Sign-based stigmergic methods such as the ant colony optimization algorithm have been used to solve network optimization, scheduling problems, and other optimization problems that can be visualized as directed graphs. However, there has been little research focused on the use of optimization methods based on sematectonic stigmergy, such as coordination through collective construction. This chapter develops a novel approach where the process of agent-directed stigmergic construction is introduced as a general optimization tool. The development of this new approach involves adopting previous work on stigmergic construction to a virtual space and applying statistical mechanics-based techniques to data produced during the stigmergic construction process. From this, a unique procedure for solving optimization problems using a computational procedure that simulates sematectonic stigmergic processes such as stigmergic construction is proposed.

SOCIAL SIMULATION

In multi-agent simulations, when agents communicate with each other or work together on a common goal, agents are often organized into *networks*. While the value of simulation as a tool in the natural sciences has been realized for quite some time, its potential in the social sciences is only beginning to be explored. A class of simulation used to study social behavior and phenomena is known as *social simulations*. One particular type of social simulation is known as *agent based social simulation*. Here agents are used to model social entities such as people, groups, and towns. One purpose of these models is to reproduce realistic behavior in the simulation, which is then used to draw conclusions about the corresponding real world entities. If realistic behavior can be reproduced then researchers in the social sciences can be given virtual laboratories from which they can experience the same benefits received by the natural sciences. Such a framework for modeling realistic behavior needs to reproduce both internal decision-making as well as social interactions. This is certainly not an easy task as entire fields are founded in researching both of these questions.

The applications of human behavioral simulations could be applied to investigate social phenomena. They could be used to make predictions about how people will act in complex situations. For example, these simulations could be used to investigate emergency evacuation plans, or for military purposes where they can test various strategies in a safe environment (Brooks, et al., 2004; Christensen & Sasaki, 2008). They could even be used for entertainment purposes, as in various simulation-based video games (Aylett, Louchart, & Pickering, 2004).

In this volume, the chapter titled "Meta-Monitoring Using an Adaptive Agent-Based System to Support Dependent People in Place" by Nicolas Singer, Sylvie Trouilhet, and Ali Rammal proposes software architecture to monitor elderly or dependent people in their own house. Many studies have been done on hardware aspects resulting in operational products, but there is a lack of adaptive algorithms to handle all the data generated by these products due to data being distributed and heterogeneous in a large scale environment. The authors propose a multi-agent classification method to collect and to aggregate data about activity, movements, and physiological information of the monitored people. Data generated at this local level is communicated and adjusted between agents to obtain a set of patterns. This data is dynamic; the system has to store the built patterns and has to create new patterns when new data is available. Therefore, the system is adaptive and can be spread on a large scale. Generated data is used at a local level, for example to raise an alert, but also to evaluate global risks. This chapter presents specification choices and the massively multi-agent architecture that was developed; an example with a sample of ten dependant people gives an illustration.

Next chapter is titled "Simulating Tolerance in Dynamic Social Networks" by Kristen Lund and Yu Zhang. This chapter studies the concept of tolerance in dynamic social networks where agents are able to make and break connections with neighbors to improve their payoffs. This problem was initially introduced to the authors by observing resistance (or tolerance) in experiments run in dynamic networks under the two rules that they have developed: the Highest Rewarding Neighborhood rule and the Highest Weighted Reward rule. These rules help agents evaluate their neighbors and decide whether to break a connection or not. They introduce the idea of tolerance in dynamic networks by allowing an agent to maintain a relationship with a bad neighbor for some time. In this research, the authors investigate and define the phenomenon of tolerance in dynamic social networks, particularly with the two rules. The chapter defines a mathematical model to predict an agent's tolerance of a bad neighbor and determine the factors that affect it. After defining a general version of tolerance, the idea of optimal tolerance is explored, providing situations in which tolerance can be used as a tool to affect network efficiency and network structure.

Researchers Rajiv Kadaba, Suratna Budalakoti, David DeAngelis, and K. Suzanne Barber study agent virtual reality. Their paper is titled "Modeling Virtual Footprints," which presents a persona mapping algorithm to compare an individual's view to their virtual signatures vs. the view of it in their social network. Entities interacting on the web establish their identity by creating virtual personas. These entities, or agents, can be human users or software-based. This research models identity using the Entity-Persona Model, a semantically annotated social network inferred from the persistent traces of interaction between personas on the web. A Persona Mapping Algorithm is proposed which compares the local views of personas in their social network referred to as their Virtual Signatures, for structural and semantic similarity. The semantics of the Entity-Persona Model are modeled by a vector space model of the text associated with the personas in the network, which allows comparison of their Virtual

Signatures. This enables all the publicly accessible personas of an entity to be identified on the scale of the web. This research enables an agent to identify a single entity using multiple personas on different networks, provided that multiple personas exhibit characteristic behavior. The agent is able to increase the trustworthiness of on-line interactions by establishing the identity of entities operating under multiple personas. Consequently, reputation measures based on on-line interactions with multiple personas can be aggregated and resolved to the true singular identity.

The paper titled "History Sensitive Cascade Model" by Yu Zhang, Maksim Tsikhanovich, and Georgi Smilyanov introduces a history dependent diffusion algorithm for social network. Diffusion is a process by which information, viruses, ideas, or new behavior spread over social networks. Traditional diffusion models are history insensitive, i.e. only giving activated nodes a one-time chance to activate each of its neighboring nodes with some probability, but history dependent interactions between people are often observed in the real world. This chapter proposes the History Sensitive Cascade Model (HSCM), a model of information cascade through a network over time. The authors consider the "activation" problem of finding the probability of that a particular node receives information given that some nodes are initially informed. In this chapter, it is also proven that selecting a set of k nodes with greatest expected influence is NP-hard, and results from submodular functions are used to provide a greedy approximation algorithm with a $1-1/e-e$ lower bound, where e depends polynomially on the precision of the solution to the "activation" problem. Finally, experiments are performed comparing the greedy algorithm to three other approximation algorithms.

The last chapter in this section is titled "Norms of Behaviour and Their Identification and Verification in Open Multi-Agent Societies" by Wagdi Alrawagfeh, Edward Brown, and Manrique Mata-Montero. Norms have an obvious role in the coordinating and predicting behaviours in societies of software agents. Most researchers assume that agents already know the norms of their societies beforehand at design time. Others assume that norms are assigned by a leader or a legislator. Some researchers take into account the acquisition of societies' norms through inference. Their works apply to closed multi-agent societies in which the agents have identical (or similar) internal architecture for representing norms. This chapter addresses three things: 1) the idea of a Verification Component that was previously used to verify candidate norms in multi-agent societies, 2) a known modification of the Verification Component that makes it applicable in open multi-agent societies, and 3) a modification of the Verification Component, so that agents can dynamically infer the new emerged and abrogated norms in open multi-agent societies. Using the JADE software framework, we build a restaurant interaction scenario as an example (where restaurants usually host heterogeneous agents), and demonstrate how permission and prohibition of behavior can be identified by agents using dynamic norms.

E-BUSINESS SIMULATION

The first chapter in this category studies an important topic in E-Business—trust. The chapter is titled "Enhanced Reputation Model with Forgiveness for E-Business Agents" by Radu Burete, Amelia Badica, Costin Badica, and Florin Moraru (University of Craiova, Romania). Trust is a very important quality attribute of an e-service. In particular, the increasing complexity of the e-business environment requires the development of new computational models of trust and reputation for e-business agents. In this chapter, the authors introduce a new reputation model for agents engaged in e-business transactions. The model enhances classic reputation models by the addition of forgiveness factor and the use of new sources of reputation information based on agents groups. The chapter proposes an improvement of this model by employing the recent con-resistance concept. Finally, the authors show how the model can be used in an agent-based market environment where trusted buyer and seller agents meet, negotiate, and transact multi-issue e-business contracts. The system was implemented using JADE multi-agent platform and initially evaluated on a sample set of scenarios. The chapter introduces the design and implementation of the agent-based system together with the experimental scenarios and results.

The chapter titled "Multi-Agent Negotiation Paradigm for Agent Selection in B2C E-Commerce" proposes a negotiation rule for B2C business. It is by Bireshwar Dass Mazumdar, Swati Basak, and Neelam Modanwal. Multi Agent System (MAS) model has been extensively used in the different tasks of E-Commerce such as Customer Relation Management (CRM), negotiation, and brokering. The objective of this chapter is to evaluate a seller agent's various cognitive parameters like capability, trust, and desire. After selecting a best seller agent from ordering queue, it applies negotiation strategies to find the most profitable proposal for both buyer and seller. This mechanism belongs to a semi cooperative negotiation type, and selecting a seller and buyer agent pair using mental and cognitive parameters. This work provides a logical cognitive model, logical negotiation model between buyer agent and selected seller agent.

The next chapter is titled "The Performance of Grey System Agent and ANN Agent in Predicting Closing Prices for Online Auctions" by Deborah Lim, Patricia Anthony, and Chong Mun Ho. The introduction of online auction has resulted in a rich collection of problems and issues especially in the bidding process. During the bidding process, bidders have to monitor multiple auction houses, pick from the many auctions to participate in and make the right bid. If bidders are able to predict the closing price for each auction, then they are able to make a better decision making on the time, place, and the amount they can bid for an item. However, predicting closing price for an auction is not easy since it is dependent on many factors such as the behavior of each bidder, the number of the bidders participating in that auction as well as each bidder's reservation price. This chapter reports on the development of a predictor agent that utilizes Grey System Theory GM (1, 1) to predict the online auction closing price in order to maximize the bidder's profit. The performance of this agent is compared with an Artificial Neural Network Predictor Agent (using Feed-Forward Back-Propagation Prediction Model). The effectiveness of these two agents is evaluated in a simulated auction environment as well as using real eBay auction's data.

The last chapter in this category focuses on price-making in game theory. The chapter is titled "Price Rigidity and Strategic Uncertainty: An Agent-Based Approach" by Robert Somogyi and János Vincze. The phenomenon of infrequent price changes has troubled economists for decades. Intuitively one feels that for most price-setters there exists a range of inaction, i.e., a substantial measure of the states of the world, within which they do not wish to modify prevailing prices. Economists wishing to maintain rationality of price-setters resorted to fixed price adjustment costs as an explanation for price rigidity. This chapter proposes an alternative explanation, without recourse to any sort of physical adjustment cost, by putting strategic interaction into the center-stage of the analysis. Price-making is treated as a repeated oligopoly game. The traditional analysis of these games cannot pinpoint any equilibrium as a reasonable "solution" of the strategic situation. Thus, decision-makers have a genuine strategic uncertainty about the strategies of other decision-makers. Hesitation may lead to inaction. To model this situation, the authors follow the style of agent-based models, by modeling firms that change their pricing strategies following an evolutionary algorithm. In addition to reproducing the known negative relationship between price rigidity and the level of general inflation, the model exhibits several features observed in real data. Moreover, most prices fall into the theoretical "range" without explicitly building this property into strategies.

SIMULATION IN HEALTH SCIENCES

This category presents three chapters from the University of Notre Dame in the area of health sciences. The first chapter is titled "A Spatial Agent-Based Model of Malaria: Model Verification and Effects of Spatial Heterogeneity" by S. M. Niaz Arifin, Gregory J. Davis, and Ying Zhou. In Agent-Based Modeling (ABM), an explicit spatial representation may be required for certain aspects of the system to be modeled realistically. A spatial ABM includes landscapes in which agents seek resources necessary for their survival. The spatial heterogeneity of the underlying landscape plays a crucial role in the resource-seeking process. This study describes a previous agent-based model of malaria, and the modeling of its spatial extension. In both models, all mosquito agents are represented individually. In the new spatial model, the agents also possess explicit spatial information. Within a landscape, adult female mosquito agents search for two types of resources: Aquatic Habitats (AHs) and Bloodmeal Locations (BMLs). These resources are specified within different spatial patterns, or landscapes. Model verification between the non-spatial and spatial models by means of docking is examined. Using different landscapes, the authors show that mosquito abundance remains unchanged. With the same overall system capacity, varying the density of resources in a landscape does not affect abundance. When the density of resources is constant, the overall capacity drives the system. For the spatial model, using landscapes with different resource densities of both resource-types, the authors show that spatial heterogeneity influences the mosquito population.

The second chapter is titled "Assessing the Impact of Temperature Change on the Effectiveness of Insecticide-Treated Nets" by Gregory J. Davis. Malaria is a vector-borne illness affecting millions of lives annually and imposes a heavy financial burden felt worldwide. Moreover, there is growing concern that global climate change, in particular, rising temperature, will increase this burden. As such, policy makers are in need of tools capable of informing them about the potential strengths and weaknesses of intervention and control strategies. A previously developed agent-based model of the Anopheles gambiae mosquito is extended, one of the primary vectors of malaria, to investigate how changes in temperature influence the dynamics of malaria transmission and the effectiveness of a common malaria intervention: Insecticide-Treated Nets (ITNs). Results from the simulations suggest two important findings. Consistent with previous studies, an increase in mosquito abundance as temperature increases is observed. However, the increase in mosquito abundance reduces the effectiveness of ITNs at a given coverage level. The implications and limitations of these findings are discussed.

The third chapter is titled "A Framework for Modeling Genetically-Aware Mosquito Vectors for Sterile Insect Technique" by James E. Gentile and Samuel S. C. Rund. Vector-borne diseases account for 16% of the global infectious disease burden (WHO, 2004). Many of these debilitating and sometimes fatal diseases are transmitted between human hosts by mosquitoes. Mosquito-targeted intervention methods have controlled or eliminated mosquito-borne diseases from many regions of the world but regions of constant transmission (holoendemic areas) still exist (Molineaux, et al., 1980). To eliminate these illnesses, researchers need to understand how interventions impact a mosquito population so as to identify potential avenues for new intervention techniques. This paper presents a software architecture that allows researchers to simulate transgenic interventions on a mosquito population. The authors present specifications for a model that captures these transgenic aspects and present a software architecture that meets those needs. The authors also provide a proof of concept and some observations about sterile insect technique strategies as simulated by this architecture.

SIMULATION IN ECOSYSTEM

We present one chapter in simulating ecosystem. The title is "Quasi-PSO Algorithm for Modeling Foraging Dynamics in Social Mammals" by Marco Campenní and Federico Cecconi. In this chapter, the authors present a computational model of a fundamental social phenomenon in the study of animal behavior: the foraging. The purpose of this work is, first, to test the validity of the proposed model compared to another existing model, the flocking model; then, to try to understand whether the model may provide useful suggestions in studying the size of the group in some species of social mammals.

CONCLUSION

Agent-based systems have long eluded the collaboration system, health sciences, business and management sciences, social sciences, and many more disciplines as viable tools. This is in part due to the fact that objects' in the world actions and interactions do not adhere to well defined rules. However, recent advances in studying both decision theory and organization theory have provided insight into the mechanics behind behavior either by human or other creatures. In order to provide these disciplines with a viable tool, agent-based systems must provide a proper computational model of both decision-making and social interaction then these structures and institutions and the cognitive capabilities of the agents that comprise them must be modeled to a level where computational complexity is not sacrificed on the behalf of realism. This volume presents a contribution to this goal. By employing realistic models based off of recent advances in decision making and social interaction, we are able to reproduce realistic behavior based on rational agents.

Yu Zhang
Trinity University, USA

REFERENCES

Aylett, R., Louchart, S., & Pickering, J. (2004). A mechanism for acting and speaking for empathic agents. In *Proceedings of the Autonomous Agents and Multi-Agent Systems Workshop*. Autonomous Agents and Multi-Agent Systems Workshop.

Brooks, H., et al. (2004). Using agent-based simulation to reduce collateral damage during military operations. In *Proceedings of the Systems and Information Engineering Design Symposium*, (pp. 71 – 77). Systems and Information Engineering Design Symposium.

Cannon-Bowers, J. A., & Salas, E. (1997). A framework for developing team performance measures in training . In Brannick, M. T., Salas, E., & Prince, C. (Eds.), *Team Performance Assessment and Measurement: Theory, Research and Applications* (pp. 45–62). Hillsdale, NJ: Lawrence Erlbaum Associates.

Christensen, K., & Sasaki, Y. (2008). Agent-based emergency evacuation simulation with individuals with disabilities in the population. *Journal of Artificial Societies and Social Simulation, 11*(39).

Jennings, N. R. (1993). Commitments and conventions: The foundation of coordination in multi-agent systems. *The Knowledge Engineering Review, 8*(3), 223–250. doi:10.1017/S0269888900000205

Kinny, D., et al. (1992). Planned team activity. In *Proceedings of the Fourth European Workshop on Modeling Autonomous Agents in a Multi-Agent World (MAAMAW 1992)*. Berlin, Germany: Springer-Verlag.

Russell, S., & Norvig, P. (1995). *Artificial intelligence a modern approach*. Upper Saddle River, NJ: Prentice Hall.

Tambe, M. (1997). Towards flexible teamwork. *Journal of Artificial Intelligence Research, 7*(1), 83–124.

Wooldridge, M., & Jennings, N. (1995). Intelligent agents: Theory and practice. *The Knowledge Engineering Review, 10*(2), 115–152. doi:10.1017/S0269888900008122

Yilmaz, L., & Ören, T. (2006). Simulation-based problem solving environments for conflict studies. *Simulation & Gaming Journal, 37*(4), 534–556. doi:10.1177/1046878106292537

Acknowledgment

I thank the Program Committee of Agent-Directed Simulation Symposium for their contributions to enhancing the quality of the papers selected from the symposium. I also acknowledge the support from the *International Journal of Agent Technologies and Systems* editorial board and all reviewers.

Yu Zhang
Trinity University, USA

Section 1
Resource Allocation and Scheduling

Chapter 1
Design of Multi Agent System for Resource Allocation and Monitoring

Manish Arora
DOEACC Society, India

M. Syamala Devi
Panjab University, India

ABSTRACT

The objective of Resource Allocation and Monitoring System is to make the procedures involved in allocating fund resources to competing clients transparent so that deserving candidates get funds. Proactive and goal directed behaviour of agents make the system transparent and intelligent. This paper presents design of Multi Agent Systems for Resource Allocation and Monitoring using Agent Unified Modelling Language (AUML) and implementation in agent based development tool. At a conceptual level, three agents are identified with their roles and responsibilities. The identified agents, functionalities, and interactions are also included and results show that multi agent technology can be used for effective decision making for resource allocation and monitoring problem.

INTRODUCTION

Resource Allocation problem occurs when fixed and limited resources are allocated to competing fund seekers to execute their projects. These resources may be of different types like work force, machine timings, raw material and funds. Fund seekers can submit their project proposals to avail grant to allocating agencies. Projects can be of different nature like R & D projects and social oriented schemes. On receiving the project proposals from fund seekers, funding allocation agencies evaluate proposals technically as well as financially. After the submission of funds request, committee on the behalf of funding agency evaluates request. In some cases, fund seekers are asked to present the project proposal. Based on the recommendation of committee, funds are allocated from 0 percent (no allocation) to 100 percent (full

DOI: 10.4018/978-1-4666-1565-6.ch001

allocation). Factors considered to make decision to allocate funds are classified into quantifiable factors like number of students trained in case of education sector and non-quantifiable factors like impact on society and image of fund seeker.

In India, there are different government agencies giving financial support to different organizations. Education is one such sector, where many funds are given for research and development and to provide quality education. One such organization is University Grant Commission (UGC). UGC receives financial aids from Ministry of Human Resources and Development and disburses the same to universities and colleges all over India. In Information Technology sector, Department of Information Technology, Ministry of Communication and Information Technology has gained software products by granting funds to various institutions who are engaged in development of software products.

Second part of the problem is timely monitoring the utilization of funds. The proper and timely utilization of funds ensures the fulfilment of objective of allocation of funds. An integrated decision making system, Multi Agent System for Resource Allocation and Monitoring (MASRAM) is designed based on above facts.

An Agent in Multi Agent System (MAS) is an autonomous entity that performs a given task using information gathered from its environment to act in a suitable manner to complete the task. Multi-Agent System comprises of multiple agents that interact with one another. Agent acts on the behalf of users / other agents with different goals and motivation. Agents require ability to cooperate, coordinate and negotiate with each other to have successful interaction. The Agents in MAS work in a team to achieve common goal.

Deployment of agent-based systems depends on how well agents are designed and depicted during early phases of agent oriented software development along with their roles and responsibilities (James et al., 2000). AUML is graphical modelling technique that is standardized by Technical Committee of Foundation for Intelligent Physical Agents (FIPA) (Janilma et al., 2005). AUML is the specification technique supporting the whole software engineering process- from planning, through analysis, design and finally to system construction, transition and maintenance. This modelling language is used to design the system. The designed system helps in developing agents using application development platform.

REVIEW OF RELATED RESEARCH

In their study, Jenyl Mumpower and Thomas A. Darling (1991) have discussed three procedures that can be used to resolve Resource Allocation Problem. In Incremental Appropriation, resource allocation begins with no allocation and then allocates small resources. The process is repeated until resources are exhausted. In the second procedure, multiple negotiators give different concessions. Resources are moved from one point to another and utility function is checked. In the third procedure, different negotiators assign different weights to different programmes.

Quantification of non-quantitative indicators is important to make decision of allocation (Jin et al., 2008). The non-quantifiable indicators can be measured through fuzzy comprehensive measurement method. Since non-quantifiable indicators are measured by human, whose knowledge and experiences may not be complete and exact. The probabilistic tools are used to deal with such data. This approach is also used to rank employees' performance using both quantitative and non-quantitative measures.

Multi Criteria Decision-Making (MCDM) helps in making decision of evaluation and selection problems where quantifiable and non-quantifiable factors are used (Mohamad et al., 2007). Non-quantifiable factors deal with vague data and fuzzy system handles such data. Two layered approach is used to assign weights to subjective (non quantifiable) factors and quantifiable factors. Top layer deals with decision making factors leading to overall achievement of goal. Second layer is used to assign the suitable weights (Suresh, 2004).

Monitoring is very important factor to know the utilization of the funds, benefits gained from funding and giving further financial help. According to Department of Foreign and Budget Monitoring (Ministry of Plan Implementation, Sri Lanka) (2006), Project Monitoring is timely gathering on input, output, activities critical for attainment of project objectives with a view to ensure input, work schedule and target outputs are proceeded as planned. Department periodically updates the progress status. Monitoring tools like PERT/Gantt chart are useful for monitoring progress of project.

From review, it has been found that MAS systems are widely used in resource allocation problems such transportation, scheduling, production planning and system resources (Gorodetski et al., 2003; Anthony et al., 1997). Through AUML, actions and roles of agents are mapped to agent based programs (Viviane et al., 2004).

MASRAM MODEL

Three agents have been designed for MASRAM problem. At the abstract level these agents are:

i.   Coordinator Agent
ii.   Fund Seeker Agent
iii.   Fund Allocator and Monitor Agent

Coordinator Agent

Coordinator Agent interacts with three types of users of MASRAM i.e. Fund Seeker user, Fund Allocator user and Reviewer user. Fund Seeker user seeks funds, Fund Allocator user allocates funds and monitors the utilization while Review user reviews the proposal. Coordinator Agent forwards requests received from Fund Seeker user

to Fund Seeker Agent. Coordinator Agent also forwards requests received from Fund Allocator user and Reviewer user to Fund Allocator and Monitor Agent. To summarize, this agent interacts with following agents/users.

i.   Fund Seeker User
ii.   Fund Allocator User
iii.   Reviewer User
iv.   Fund Seeker Agent
v.   Fund Allocator and Monitoring Agent

Fund Seeker Agent

Fund Seeker Agent receives all the requests sent by Coordinator Agent and act accordingly. This agent interacts with Coordinator Agent only.

Fund Allocator and Monitor Agent

Fund Allocator and Monitor Agent in turn evaluates proposal, assigns weights and allocates suitable funds based on allocation procedure. Fund Allocator and Monitor Agent interacts with Coordinator Agent only.

Agents and overview of the interaction among them have been shown is Figure 1.

DESIGN OF MASRAM

The system is completely designed using AUML tool. During the research, each agent has been designed with respect to its roles, responsibilities, interaction, internal behaviour and deployment. The numbers of agents are decided after resolving certain issues. These issues were:

i.   Decomposition of agents
ii.   Coordination among agents
iii.   Responsiveness
iv.   Knowledge availability

Figure 1. Multi agent system for resource allocation and monitoring model

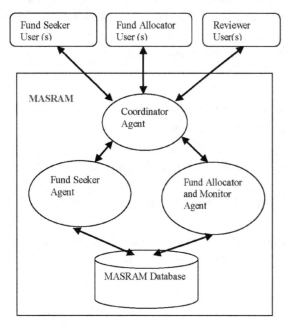

The agents, their responsibilities and interactions have been discussed in this section.

Responsibilities of Agent

Responsibilities of each of three agents identified are discussed below:

Fund Seeker Agent

The responsibilities of fund seeker agent other than getting users' profiles are:

Interactions with Coordinator Agent
  i. To provide list of available sources based on nature of project
  ii. To accept project proposal
  iii. To provide status of proposal
  iv. To accept utilization of funds

Coordinator Agent

The responsibilities are:

Interactions with Fund Seeker User
  i. To provide list of sources based on project nature asked
  ii. To accept project proposal
  iii. To show status of funds allocation
  iv. To get utilization status
Interactions with Fund Allocator User
  i. To get funds availability, criteria for particular nature of project
Interactions with Reviewer User
  i. To provide project proposal for review
  ii. To get values for decision making factors on project proposal
Interactions with Fund Seeker Agent
  i. To forward fund seeker user profile
  ii. To forward changes in seeker user profile
  iii. To request Fund Seeker Agent to provide list of sources based on nature of project
  iv. To forward project proposal for fund allocation
  v. To request Fund Seeker Agent to provide status of proposal
  vi. To inform Fund Seeker Agent the utilization of funds
Interactions with Fund Allocator and Monitoring Agent
  i. To forward availability of funds and criteria
  ii. To get project proposal for review from reviewer user
  iii. To forward values of decision making factors received from reviewers

Fund Allocator and Monitor Agent

Fund Allocator and Monitor Agent interacts with Coordinator Agent and responsibilities are:

Interactions with Coordinator Agent
  i.   To accept availability of funds and criteria for particular nature of project
  ii.   To provide proposal for review from reviewer users
  iii. To allocate funds based on review, weighting factors and criteria
  iv.   To monitor the progress of projects

All the three designed agents have been defined completely in terms of their roles, characteristics, operations to be performed and interaction with other agents. One such designed agent, Funds Allocator and Monitor Agent is shown in Figure 2.

Funds Allocation Procedure

One major function of Fund Allocator and Monitor Agent is to allocate funds. It uses a heuristic algorithm of Weight Based Resource Allocation to allocate funds. The algorithm has been designed based on weight assignment procedure discussed in Review of Related Literature section. The algorithm also takes care of probability of successful execution based on past experience of fund seeker. The algorithm allocates funds to multiple fund seekers from multiple categories (Arora et al., 2009).

Agents' Interaction

In order to achieve goal, agents interact with each other as per their need. Sequence diagram of AUML (adopted by FIPA to express agent interaction protocols) is used to show the interaction among agents. Interaction between two agents, Coordinator and Fund Seeker is shown in Figure

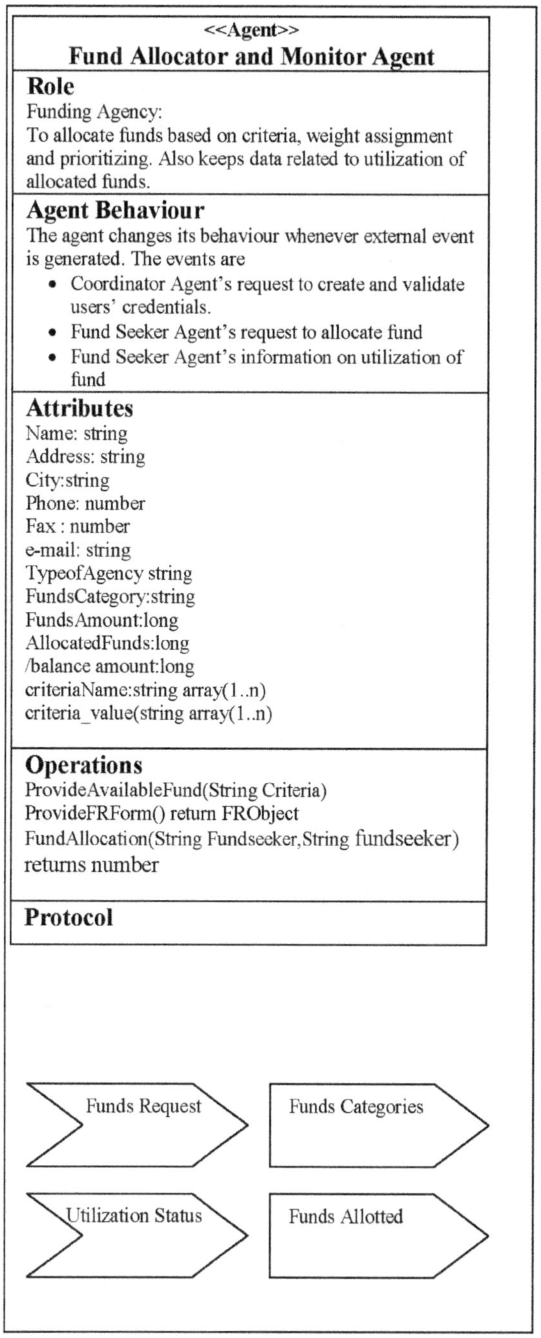

Figure 2. Description of fund allocator and monitor agent

<<Agent>>
Fund Allocator and Monitor Agent
Role
Funding Agency:
To allocate funds based on criteria, weight assignment and prioritizing. Also keeps data related to utilization of allocated funds.
Agent Behaviour
The agent changes its behaviour whenever external event is generated. The events are
• Coordinator Agent's request to create and validate users' credentials.
• Fund Seeker Agent's request to allocate fund
• Fund Seeker Agent's information on utilization of fund
Attributes
Name: string
Address: string
City:string
Phone: number
Fax : number
e-mail: string
TypeofAgency string
FundsCategory:string
FundsAmount:long
AllocatedFunds:long
/balance amount:long
criteriaName:string array(1..n)
criteria_value(string array(1..n)
Operations
ProvideAvailableFund(String Criteria)
ProvideFRForm() return FRObject
FundAllocation(String Fundseeker,String fundseeker) returns number
Protocol

Funds Request   Funds Categories

Utilization Status   Funds Allotted

3. There are five major interactions that take between these two agents. These are request to create profile, find sources, allocate funds, know status of proposal and update status of fund utilization.

Internal Behaviour of Agents

State chart diagram was used to describe the internal behaviour of the agent. This diagram defines all possible states an agent can reach and how it can change its state depending on messages sent to it. As an instance internal behaviour of one of the action, receiving project proposal, of Fund Seeker Agent is shows in Figure 4.

Deployment of Agents

All the three agents will be residing on server side. Two servers are proposed to use agent based application, one as database server and second as agent server. Agent Server hosts all three agents. Three types of users will interact from client machine through Graphical User Interface (GUI) as shown in Figure 5. All the functions of these agents like executing fund allocation algorithm will be performed by agents on server side only.

Goals set for Agent

Each agent has certain goal to achieve in order to complete its task. The goals set for each agent are shown in Table 1.

IMPLEMENTATION

The described design of MASRAM with help of AUML, fund seeker agent, is implemented in agent development platform, JADE (Java Agent Development Framework). JADE is a FIPA compliant development tool to develop multi agent applications. Diagram components shown in designs can easily be mapped onto source code in JADE (Margus et al., 2001). All the agents are mapped in java programs that extend Agent class of JADE. This program has two standard methods, setup() and takeDown(). The actions supposed to be performed by agents are written in JADE as java classes. As an instance, abstract code for fund seeker agent's action to process the request of coordinator agent to find sources and sending back list of available sources funds is shown Table 2.

CONCLUSION

This paper described MASRAM and its decision-making capability using multi agent technology. The complete system was designed using AUML starting from depicting overview of the system to physical deployment of agents. Design covered both conceptual and detailed design. The conceptual design identified three agents and their roles. The detailed design depicted interaction among agents and action to be performed. The ap-

Table 1. Goals to achieve

Agent	Goal
Fund Seeker	Finding Source Creating Profile Evaluating Proposal
Fund Allocator and Monitor	Allocating funds Collecting reviews Ranking proposals
Coordinator	Initiating agent for tasks to perform

Figure 3. Interaction diagram: funds allocation

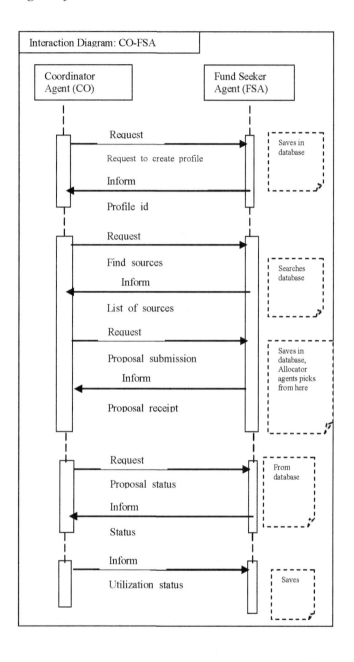

proach outlined here was found more effective in implementing resource allocation and monitoring system in JADE. The manual operations currently being done in resource allocation and monitoring will be taken over by agents of MASRAM.

FUTURE WORK

Plans in this direction include complete implementation of this modelled system in JADE with oracle as backend database. The developed system will be tested on historical data of around 5 years to validate the work done.

Figure 4. Internal behaviour: fund seeker agent

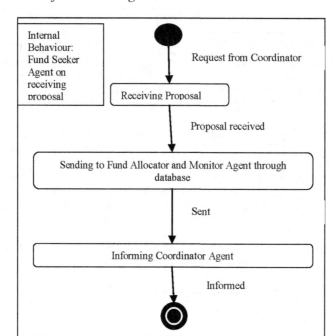

Table 2.Code Abstract

```
public class fundSeekerAgent extends Agent
{ ....
 protected void setup()
  { ...
{     public void onTick()
     {        msg = receive();    ...    }
    private void source_action(Concept a1,String pn)      {
    try    {...
        ContentManager cm = getContentManager();
        ..
ACLMessage reply = msg.createReply();
        reply.setPerformative(ACLMessage.INFORM);
            ...
        send(reply);
    }            ...}protected void takeDown()
{    try { DFService.deregister(this); }
  catch (Exception e) {} }.}
```

Figure 5. Deployment diagram

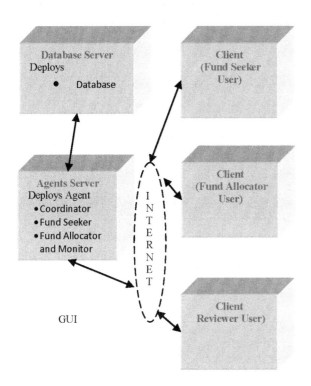

REFERENCES

Arora, M., & Syamala, D. M. (2009). Weight Based Funds Allocation Algorithm. In *Proceedings of the Advance Computing Conference (IACC-2009)* (pp. 413-417). Washington, DC: IEEE.

Chavez, A., Moukas, A., & Maes, P. (1997). Challenger: A Multi Agent System for Distributed Resource Allocation. In *Proceeding of First International Conference on Autonomous Agents (Agent97),* Marina Del Ray, CA (pp. 323-331). New York: ACM Press.

Cheng, J., Bai, H., & Li, Z. (2008). Quantification of Non Quantitative Indicators of Performance Measurement. In *Proceedings of the Wireless Communications, Networking and Mobile Computing (WiCOM '08), 4th International Conference* (pp. 1-5).

da Silva, V. T., et al. (2004). A UML Based Approach for Modeling and Implementing MultiAgent Systems. In *Proceedings of 3rd International Joint Conference on Autonomous Agents and Multi Agent Systems*, New York (pp. 914-921).

Gorodetski, V., Karsaev, O., & Konushy, V. (2003). Mulit Agent System for Resource Allocation and Scheduling. In *Proceeding of 3rd International Workshop of Central and East European conference on Multi Agent System,* Prague, Czech Republic (pp. 236-246).

Janilma, A. R., Peres, D. V., & Bergmann, U. (2005). Experiencing AUML for MAS Modeling: A critical View. In *Proceedings of the First Workshop on Software Engineering for Agent Oriented System, Seas.*

Margus, O. J. A. (2001). Agent Based Software Design. In *Proceedings of Estonian Academy of Sciences and Engineering, 50,* 5–21.

Mohamad Noor, N. M., Abdul Samat, N. H., Yazid Saman, M., Suzuri Hitam, M., & Man, M. (2007). iWDSS-Tender: Intelligent Web-based Decision Support System for Tender Evaluation. In *Proceedings of the IEEE International Symposium on Signal Processing and Information Technology* (pp. 1011-1016).

Mumpower, J. L., & Darling, T. A. (1991). Modeling Resource Allocation Negotiations. In *Proceeding of the IEEE Twenty Fourth Annual Hawii International Conference* (Vol. 3, pp. 641-649).

Odell, J., Parunak, V., & Bernhard, D. (2000). Expending UML for Agents. In *Proceeding of The Agent Oriented Information Systems Workshop at 17th National Conference on Artificial Intelligence*, Austin, TX (pp. 3-17).

Project Monitoring System. (2006). *Department of Foreign Aid and Budgeting Monitoring, Ministry of Plan Implementation, Sri Lanka*. Retrieved from http://www.fabm.gov.lk

Suresh, S. (2004). AHP Based System for Formal R & D project Selection. *Journal of Scientific and Industrial Research, 63*, 888–896.

This work was previously published in International Journal of Agent Technologies and Systems, Volume 3, Issue 1, edited by Yu Zhang, pp. 1-10, copyright 2011 by IGI Publishing (an imprint of IGI Global).

Chapter 2
The Effects of Different Interaction Protocols in Agent–Based Simulation of Social Activities

Nicole Ronald
Eindhoven University of Technology, The Netherlands

Theo Arentze
Eindhoven University of Technology, The Netherlands

Harry Timmermans
Eindhoven University of Technology, The Netherlands

ABSTRACT

Decision making in models of activity and travel behaviour is usually individual-based and focuses on outcomes rather than the decision process. Using agent-based modelling techniques and incorporating interaction protocols into the model can assist in modelling decision-making in more detail. This paper describes an agent-based model of social activity generation and scheduling, in which utility-based agents interact with each other to schedule activities. Six different protocols are tested. The authors show that the model outcomes reflect minor changes in the protocol, while changing the order of the protocol leads to significantly different outcomes, hence the protocol plays a large role in the simulation results and should be studied in more detail.

1. INTRODUCTION

With occasional dissent (e.g., Mokhtarian & Salomon, 2001), travel demand is generally thought to be derived from the need to engage in activities. Most activities are undertaken individually,

DOI: 10.4018/978-1-4666-1565-6.ch002

and therefore decisions about where to go and how to get there can be taken (and modelled) in an individual manner. However, a proportion of activities are undertaken jointly, meaning some synchronisation is required.

While joint activities between household members have received interest (Timmermans & Zhang, 2009), these approaches have been statistical in nature and are generally limited to the few adults (and sometimes children) in the household. Adapting these two groups of larger sizes and variation is difficult.

In the context of agent-based systems, agents interact with each other using interaction protocols. These are mostly used for open systems and in simulations looking for an optimal strategy, such as auction strategies. For our context, we are seeking a method for modelling the decision processes of individuals in a realistic manner in order to see the effects on the overall environment, not to recommend strategies.

In this project, we are interested in the influence of the interaction protocol and decision making on the number, frequency and type of social activities generated and scheduled. As incorporating detailed interactions into agent-based models of activity-travel behaviour will add a lot of complexity and require more intensive data collections for validation, this is a necessary step in testing the sensitivity of the model and evaluating their usefulness.

The aim of this paper is to demonstrate the relevance of the interaction protocol by investigating the performance of a model with different protocols with respect to the number of activities generated and scheduled for individuals, pairs of individuals, and for the entire population. We begin with a review of activity modelling and interaction protocols. A model consisting of utility-based agents who are generating and scheduling two-person activities is described and the results are discussed. We conclude with recommendations for future work.

2. BACKGROUND

Agent-based modelling and multi-agent based systems are of interest to researchers in travel and transport modelling. A look at the latest proceedings of the AAMAS workshop on Agents in Traffic and Transportation (Klügl et al., 2010) shows that popular applications are travel simulations and freight handling and routing. Larger scale frameworks, such as MATSIM (http://matsim.org), can incorporate activity scheduling along with travel modelling and therefore have the ability to model activity choice in more detail.

2.1. Activity-Travel Modelling

Human activities are generated due to "physiological, psychological and economical needs" (Wen & Koppelman, 2000). A distinction is commonly made between subsistence (e.g., work-related), maintenance (e.g., keeping the household running), and leisure activities.

Non-discretionary activities such as work and school can be partly explained by the traveller's sociodemographic characteristics and generalised travel costs (Hackney & Marchal, 2007), as well as long-term decisions such as a decision to move to a particular town. Participation in and scheduling of, other activities is not as easily predicted. Social and leisure activities are the reported purpose for a large number of trips, ranging from 25 to 40% for various countries (Axhausen, 2006).

In current state-of-the-art activity-travel models, social activities, if at all scheduled, are assigned to random locations and times (Arentze & Timmermans, 2004) and do not take into account the constraints or preferences of friends. Being able to model these activities could lead to better prediction of activity schedules and forecasts of travel patterns and demand for urban facilities, in particular those relating to social and leisure activities.

A theory currently being explored for generating discretionary activities is based on needs. Activities both satisfy and generate needs and needs grow over time (Arentze & Timmermans, 2006). Maslow's hierarchy of needs has been proposed as a starting point (Miller, 2005), however it is difficult to collect data for model validation. A separate set of needs was proposed by Arentze and Timmermans (2006) which could be identified through empirical research.

2.2. Making Decisions in an Activity-Travel Context

Timmermans and Zhang (2009) note, in the context of household activities, that "models based on individual decision-making processes have dominated transportation research". The focus is more on the outcomes of the decision, rather than the process.

The nature of the activity-travel context leads us directly to considering a multi-issue context. There is the location of the activity, the participants, the time and day and duration, and the type of the activity to consider. As Mokhtarian et al. (2006, p. 268) pondered:

"Even within the leisure category itself, an activity may have multiple characteristics. When one goes to a ball game with friends, is the activity social, or entertainment? The answer probably affects the activity choice process, including the choice set of perceived alternatives: if the primary motivation is social, one may first decide to get together with friends, and then choose an activity around which to organize the gathering, whereas if the primary motivation is entertainment, one may first decide to attend the ball game and then see who else is able to join."

This shows that the order of decisions in an activity-travel context is rather complicated and could depend on many different things.

2.3. Interactions

One of the key ideas in agent theory is that agents should be social and/or interact with each other (e.g., Padgham & Winikoff, 2004). This has led to the development of agent languages. These languages provide a set of speech acts, that can be combined together to make formal protocols.

Most of the interest has been in representing repetitive tasks for e-commerce applications, such as forming contracts and auctions. The focus is therefore on competitive interactions, whereas our interactions are more cooperative.

The Contract Net Protocol (CNP) was proposed as a method for decentralised task allocation (Xu & Weigand, 2001). Following the initial proposal in the early 1980s, an extension was developed by Sandholm (1993) and applied to the distribution of delivery tasks to be undertaken by dispatch centres. The aim was to reduce transport costs. Each centre begins by calculating the routing for their current set of tasks. Following this step, centres can exchange tasks if it is more profitable to do so. This is done via a cycle of announcing the task, accepting bids, and awarding the task to the highest bidder.

Rindt et al. (2003) reports on the development of a simulation kernel for agent-based activity microsimulation based on the re-characterization of human activity as interaction between autonomous entities. They started from the idea that "human activity is the negotiated interaction of socially and physically situated individuals and settings" and as a result their kernel assumes that behaviour is adaptive. People, groups and resources (such as buildings) were represented as agents and used a variant of the contract net protocol to organise activities. The framework described was flexible and did not impose many restrictions on negotiations, but was not a complete model in itself.

While CNP makes sense for task allocation, it is not as suitable for activity generation and scheduling. Activities do not necessarily have to be carried out once proposed: they can be withdrawn or cancelled. Even when an activity has been generated, it is not a case of allocating it to one person: it might be that two or more people would be good companions for an activity. Unlike the dispatch centre example, there is no requirement for the global optimisation of travel costs. As a result, it does not appear to be a good starting point for developing our negotiation protocol.

As we are dealing with several issues or attributes, the literature on multi-issue negotiation is also useful. Wooldridge (2002) defines this as:

In *multiple-issue* negotiation scenarios, agents negotiate over not just the value of a single attribute, but over the values of multiple attributes which may be interrelated (p. 138).

They give the example of buying a car: as the buyer, you could be interested in the price, the length of the guarantee, and what extras can be included. The participants in our interactions need to agree on people, time and location, so this theory is relevant for us.

There are several ways of dealing with multi-issue problems (Fatima et al., 2006): discussing all issues together (package), discussing issues separately and independently (simultaneous), and discussing issues separately (sequential). Depending on the technique chosen, sometimes a discussion about the order of negotiation of the different issues is required. This order is called the agenda (Fatima et al., 2003) and can be defined before the negotiation begins (exogenously) or during the negotiation itself (endogenously).

However, as well as negotiating over prices of products, scheduling is another area that can be automated. Calendar agents are an area of interest, where meetings can be scheduled without human interference. Several different protocols are proposed by Wainer et al. (2007), including voting (where everyone sends their available times to the host, then preference the intersection of free time, and the host determines the best) and suggestion (where one time is suggested at a time until everyone has suggested the same time or is out). These protocols take into account the meeting time only.

3. MODEL DESCRIPTION AND DESIGN

Joint social activities are defined by the different people involved, their relationships and interactions with each other, and their activities in and possible movement around the environment. The topology of interactions is not homogeneous and clusters may form. Therefore agent-based modelling appears to be appropriate for our model, due to the complex relationships and interactions between individuals and the individuals' situatedness in an urban environment (Macal & North, 2006).

The model consists of agents located in a spatial environment, where they have a home location. This environment is represented by a network of locations. Each agent has a list of other agents he/she is friends with and a list of locations that he/she knows. They also have sociodemographic attributes (e.g., age, gender, car ownership, work status etc.) and a schedule with a certain number of open time periods. Each agent can undertake maximally one activity per time period.

Each pair of agents has a similarity measure, which follows from the notion of homophily. Pairs also keep track of when they last saw each other. Links are undirected, meaning that friendships are mutual.

The goals of the agents in the system are derived from the social needs of humans, which include interacting with, and gaining the respect and esteem of others. The agent goals are therefore:

- Making and maintaining (long-term) relationships with other people;
- Sharing experiences with other people, in the form of joint activity participation;
- Sharing (giving and gaining) information with other people; and
- Learning about their local environment.

In this paper we focus on the second goal of joint activity participation. Utility-based agents are used as this allows the agents to evaluate the outcomes of participating in different activities. This has advantages and disadvantages: utility functions are difficult to develop and, from the point of view of the agent community, tend to oversimplify the real-world processes (Wooldridge,

2002), however as the aim is to create a model of a sample population for a city, i.e., thousands of agents, the agent model needs to be simple in order to be scalable.

A utility function (Equation 1) has been developed to take into account the required issues -- the host of the activity (i), type (a) of the activity, location (l), day (d), time (y), the other person involved (j), duration (r), whether it is a work day or not (w_{id}), the work status of the host (w_i) --, essentially, what, where, when and who. On top of this, whether it is a work day or not (w_{id}) and the work status of the host (w_i) are also taken into account. This is based on the needs-based theory discussed in Section 2.1.

$$U_i(a,l,d,y,j) > r \times u^*(d, w_i, w_{id}) \qquad (1)$$

$$U_i(a,l,d,y,j) = V_i^{ady} + V_i^l + V_i^j - cost(l) + \varepsilon \qquad (2)$$

$$V_i^{ady} = f_t(\alpha_i^{ady}, d - t_a) \qquad (3)$$

$$V_i^l = f_t(\alpha_i^l, d - t_l) \qquad (4)$$

$$V_i^j = f_t(s_{ij}, d - t_j) \qquad (5)$$

$$f_t(x,t) = \left(\frac{2}{1 + e^{-xt}}\right) - 1 \qquad (6)$$

$$s_{ij} = Q_g + Q_a \qquad (7)$$

$$cost(l) = tt_i \qquad (8)$$

Activities can have a type (a), chosen from sharing experiences, sharing information, informal chatting, visiting each other, and other. The different types can be used to determine who is suitable for a given activity. Activities also have a location (l) with a type (home or out-of-home), which determine the duration of the activity (r).

The threshold for the function (u^*) is based on duration and whether the individual is working on the proposed day or not (Equation 1).

The components of the utility function U_i consider when an individual last undertook an activity (Equation 3), visited a location (Equation 4), or saw someone (Equation 5). These values (t_l, t_a, t_j) are combined with the date of the proposed activity d to find the last time the particular event happened. The utility increases over time (Equation 6), so that an activity/location/ person that an individual hasn't seen/visited for a while is more attractive than one seen/visited the previous day. The time of day (y) is used only as a constraint, e.g., if an activity has already been scheduled or if the inidividual is working.

The preferences for an activity with a particular type, day, and time (α_i^{ady}) and for a particular location (α_i^l) are also inputs to the model. In this instance of the model, we consider preferences to be unidimensional as a simplification. It could be that preferences are dependent on the composition of the group, for example, in terms of gender, cultural background, size of the group etc.

For each pair of individuals i and j, a similarity measure (s_{ij}) was calculated (Equation 7), taking into account age (Q_a) and gender (Q_g). The travel time to the location (tt_i) is also taken into account (Equation 8), based on the individual perception of the environment and distance, which contributes to a travel cost ($cost(l)$). All travel is assumed to start and end at the individuals' home location.

We further assume that interactions and activities are undertaken between two agents, who are connected to each other in the social network. This means that the social and location networks do not change (as new connections are not being made), therefore the centrality calculations do not change.

4. INTERACTIONS

In order to schedule activities, the agents need to negotiate with each other. As such, we use the package deal method (Fatima et al., 2006) that abstracts from negotiation issues (for example, the activity may determine the time and location or vice versa, or in which order they should be discussed). Two individuals are involved in each interaction: a host, who starts the interaction and makes the final decision, and a respondent.

Six different interaction protocols were tested for this paper. Protocols 1-5 begin as follows:

1. The host determines the best person to ask about an activity, based on an activity at the host's home.
2. Given this person (known as the respondent), the host determines the best activity to offer to that person.
3. Host proposes an activity.

In all cases, if the activity is accepted, the activity is added to both the host's and respondent's schedules.

4.1. Protocol 1: One-Shot

In this protocol, the respondent accepts or declines the host's suggested activity.

4.2. Protocol 2: Repeated

In this protocol, the respondent accepts or declines the host's suggested activity. If the respondent declines, the host repeatedly offers their next-best activity, until they have no options left or the respondent accepts a suggestion.

4.3. Protocol 3: All at Once

In this protocol, the host offers all their available activity options at once. The respondent evaluates them all and return their preference. A Borda vote

(i.e., where both individual's activity lists are numbered 1 to N and the activity with the lowest total is chosen) is used to find the best activity.

4.4. Protocol 4: Respondent Suggests Locations

This is identical to protocol 3, but includes an extra step where the respondent can suggest better locations for activities. These are added to the list and then included in the final vote.

4.5. Protocol 5: Respondent Suggests Durations

This is identical to protocol 3, but includes an extra step where the respondent can suggest shorter durations for activities. These are added to the list and then included in the final vote.

4.6. Protocol 6: Activity-Focused

Protocol 6 operates differently to the other protocols, in that the first step is to choose an activity, using a random person from the host's list of friends as a default. Once the activity is chosen, then the host offers it to their friend who gives them the best utility for the activity. If that friend declines, the host offers the activity to the next friend and so on, until someone accepts or everyone declines.

For this paper, only interactions and activities between two people were studied, however these protocols can be extended to larger groups using a one-to-many protocol structure.

The protocols satisfy a number of basic properties, such as termination, liveness, and safety. The protocols contain no loops and are completed in a bounded number of rounds. All messages are sent from one role to another (either from host to respondent or vice versa) and the messages are unambiguous regarding the next step. Both roles proceed towards termination states, either when an activity has been scheduled, when a respondent cannot suggest any suitable time slots or does not approve of the activities suggested, or all parties cannot agree on options to negotiate about.

5. ILLUSTRATION AND HYPOTHESES

The model was developed using Java, and analysed using R, a software environment for statistical computing. The results were analysed using ANOVA tests, t-tests and Kolmogorov-Smirnov tests.

The values of most of the parameters were set from a calibration process, using one protocol and data on social activities collected in Eindhoven (van den Berg et al., 2008). The environment contains nodes based on four-digit postcodes in Eindhoven. Each of the 102 individuals has a home location and knowledge of between 10 and 20 out-of-home locations, selected from 90 in the simulation.

The parameters for α_i^{ady} were set to 1.19 for all activity types, days and times. The values of α_i^{al} were set to 1.45 for all types and locations. The β values varied as shown in Table 1 and the threshold values are listed in Table 2.

The similarity value consists of two components, Q_g and Q_a. The former is equal to $\gamma_g(1-r_g)$, where r_g is 1 is both participants have different genders and 0 for the same gender. The latter is equal to $\gamma_a(4-r_a)$, where r_a is the difference between ages of the two participants, as their ages have been simplified to a 5 point scale. γ_a was set to 0.888 and γ_g was 0.713, following (Arentze et al., 2009).

A day is divided into four 6-hour parts: morning, afternoon, evening, and night. No activities are scheduled at night. Individuals working full time on a particular day are only available in the evening, and individual working part time are only available for either the morning or the afternoon and also the evening. This is a hard constraint.

The model was run for 28 days' warmup and then for 7 days of measurement. The results are averaged over 30 runs with different seeds.

The ideas behind our hypotheses are to explore whether the differences in the protocols do lead to differences in outcomes. This will allow us to see if making a specific rule in a protocol, such as compromising on duration in protocol 5, does affect the duration. Our hypotheses are:

1. There is a difference in the number of activities on a global scale.
2. There is a difference in the number of activities per pair.
3. There is a difference in the number of activities per person.
4. There is a difference in the number of negotiation failures and the type of failures.
5. Protocol 1 generates fewer activities than protocols 2 or 3.

Table 1. Parameter values for β_p, β_l, and β_a

β_p	β_l	β_a
0.05	home = 0.07	experience = 0.01
	out-of-home = 0.07	visiting = 0.04
		chatting = 0.07
		info = 0.03
		other = 0.07

Table 2. Threshold values, given an individual's work status and the type of day

Work status / Work day	None	Part day	Full day
None	1.688	1.757	4.050
Parttime	2.033	0.920	1.467
Fulltime	2.415	2.358	2.430

6. Protocol 4 leads to more variety in locations than protocol 3.
7. Protocol 5 leads to lower durations than protocol 3.
8. Protocol 6 leads to more variety in pairs than the other protocols.

6. RESULTS

6.1 Activities: Global

This can be tested using an ANOVA test. The result shows that there is a significant difference in the total number of generated actvities between protocols (df=5, F=3120.3, $p < 0.001$). As a result, hypothesis 1 can be accepted.

Figure 1 shows the difference between the different protocols. There is little difference between the first five protocols, however the protocol with a different issue order results in many more successfully organised activities.

6.2. Activities: Pair

This can be tested by looking at the distribution of activities and using a Kolmogorov-Smirnov test, or by using a t-test comparing the number of activities per pair.

Table 3 shows the results of Kolmogorov-Smirnov tests between all pairs of protocols. This shows that the distributions of activities for protocols 1-5 are not that different, whereas the distribution for protocol 6 is significantly different. Hypothesis 2 can be accepted.

Tables 4 show the results of t tests between all pairs of protocols. This also echoes the results of the previous table.

Figures 2, 3 and 4 show the distribution of activities for pairs using protocols 1, 4 and 6. While many pairs using protocols 1 and 4 do not interact at all, those using protocol 6 are a little more spread out.

6.3. Activities: Personal

This can be tested by looking at the distribution of activities and using a Kolmogorov-Smirnov test, or by using a t-test on the number of activities for each individual.

Table 5 shows the results of Kolmogorov-Smirnov tests between all pairs of protocols. This shows that the distributions of activities for protocols 2-5 are pretty much identical, whereas the distributions for protocols 1 and 6 significantly differ.

Tables 6 show the results of t-tests between all pairs of protocols. This echoes the previous results.

As a result, hypothesis 3 can be accepted. Figures 5, 6 and 7 show the distribution of activities for individuals using protocols 1, 4, and 6. In agreement with the first test, it is clear that protocol 6 is leading to a higher average of activities per person.

Figure 1. The number of activities for each protocol

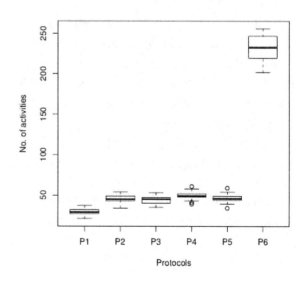

6.4. Failures

Comparing the number of failed interactions, i.e., those that do not result in an activity for some reason, shows that the protocols are significantly different (df=5, F=42153, $p < 0.001$). This is mostly due to protocol 6 though, which has a much better success rate than the others. Figure 8 shows how the protocols differ. Hypothesis 4 can be accepted.

6.5. Protocol 1: Fewer Activities

A t-test with the total activities for protocol 1 compared with each other protocol independently shows that protocol 1 is significantly different to all the other protocols ($p < 0.05$ in all cases) and has less activities in all cases. Hypothesis 5 can be accepted.

Table 3. p values comparing two protocols using a Kolmogorov-Smirnov test

Proto-col	1	2	3	4	5	6
1		0.78	0.93	0.65	0.87	0
2			1	1	1	0
3				1	1	0
4					1	0
5						0
6						

Table 4. p values comparing two protocols using a t-test

Proto-col	1	2	3	4	5	6
1		0	0.01	0	0.01	0
2			0.86	0.55	0.90	0
3				0.44	0.76	0
4					0.64	0
5						0
6						

Figure 2. Distribution of activities between pairs for protocol 1

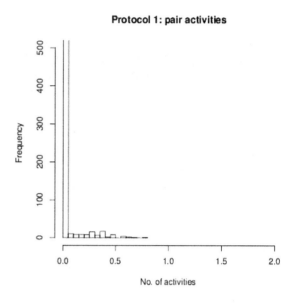

Figure 3. Distribution of activities between pairs for protocol 4

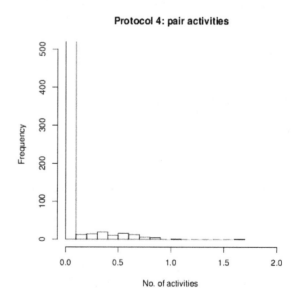

6.6. Protocol 4: More Locational Variety

One way of testing this hypothesis is to look at how far people travel. Compared to protocol 3, which is identical except for the respondent making suggestions about locations, protocol 4 causes people to travel further (t = 3.4075, df = 157.692, p < 0.001).

Another is to look at the difference in the number of out-of-home activities. Again, comparing to protocol 3, protocol 4 leads to people doing more out-of-home activities (t = 2.0755, df = 57.919, p < 0.05). As a results, hypothesis 6 can be accepted.

6.7. Protocol 5: Duration Variety

This can be tested by using a t-test.

A t-test with the duration of activities for protocol 5 compared to protocol 3 (identical except for the ability of the participant to change the activity duration) shows that they are significantly different (t = -5.2584, df = 57.083, p < 0.001). The difference in very small though, in the range of 1 to 3 minutes. Even so, hypothesis 7 can be accepted.

6.8 Protocol 6: Pair Variety

This was tested using correlation test (Pearson) on the relationship between similarity and the number of activities per pair and the home-to-home distance between pairs of individuals.

Table 7 shows the results for similarity and number of activities. Protocol 6 is the only protocol where there is a relationship.

Table 8 shows the results for home-to-home distance and number of activities. Protocol 6 is the only protocol where there is a small relationship.

Based on these results, hypothesis 8 can be accepted.

Figure 4. Distribution of activities between pairs for protocol 6

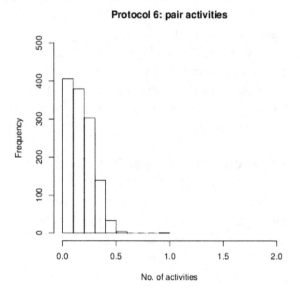

Figure 5. Distribution of activities for protocol 1

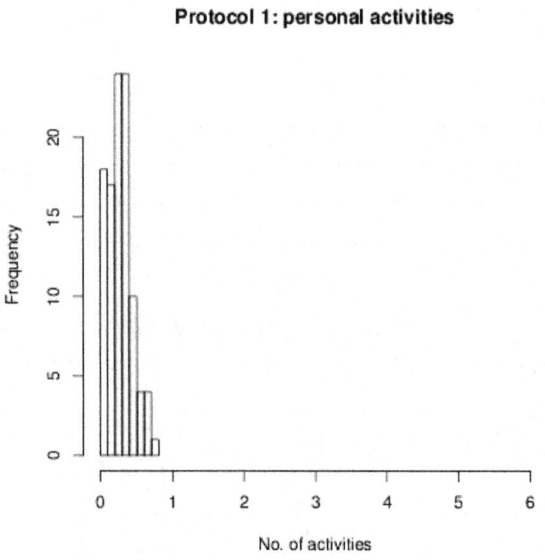

6.9. Discussion

In all cases, the outcome of the model corresponded to what was expected from the protocol. This is pleasing, as it means the protocol can be developed at the individual level based on data or theories about the real world. However, the most striking outcomes occur when the process order is altered. An explanation for the differences depending on whether the activity or person is chosen first could be that a person is chosen solely on similarity, and it could be that that person is not available at the same times as you. In the current model where only one request is permitted per day means that this fails quite often. Choosing the activity first, and then finding the best person to go with, pro-

vides a bit more flexibility. An alternative utility function could produce a different result.

7. CONCLUSION AND FURTHER WORK

Agent-based simulation is a method for experimenting with how people and the environment interact. For social/spatial decision making models, not only is the interaction with the environment important, but also with other agents.

In this paper, we evaluated a number of interaction protocols in the context of activity-travel behaviour. This is a cooperative multi-issue environment. It is shown that the actual process within the protocol can change the outcomes in expected ways, such as when the respondent has more input into location and duration, and can also change

Table 5. p values comparing two protocols using a Kolmogorov-Smirnov test

Proto-col	1	2	3	4	5	6
1		0	0	0	0	0
2			0.97	0.48	0.97	0
3				0.39	0.91	0
4					0.71	0
5						0
6						

Table 6. p values comparing two protocols using a t-test

Proto-col	1	2	3	4	5	6
1		0	0	0	0	0
2			0.71	0.19	0.74	0
3				0.10	0.49	0
4					0.34	0
5						0
6						

Table 7. Correlations between similarity and number of activities for all protocols

Protocol	p	cor
1	0.70	
2	0.57	
3	0.64	
4	0.74	
5	0.58	
6	0.00	0.389

Table 8. Correlations between distance and number of activities for all protocols

Protocol	p	cor
1	0.87	
2	0.46	
3	0.50	
4	0.45	
5	0.61	
6	0.00	-0.12

the outcomes quite radically when the process is reordered to select the activity first and the participants second. This means that it is important to study the real-life decision making process in detail in order to be confident that the simulation outcomes are applicable to the real world.

This version of the model is limited, in that the time of day has been aggregated and that no replanning or rescheduling occurs. Increasing the amount of detail in these dimensions could lead to alternative outcomes.

The model, in its current form, has not been fully validated -- only face validation has been presented. Given that different interactions do make a difference, it seems reasonable to proceed with collecting data and observations regarding how decisions are made. One method for this is to ask questions as part of an existing activity-travel survey on how the details of the final activity were determined. Another is to carry out face-to-face surveys to determine which issues or attributes are fixed first (not dissimilar to those in Clark & Doherty (2008) where survey participants were

Figure 7. Distribution of activities for protocol 6

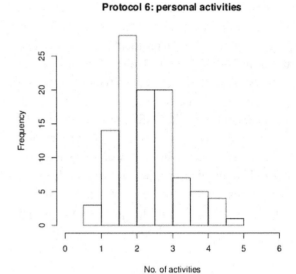

Figure 8. The number of failed interactions for each protocol

Figure 6. Distribution of activities for protocol 4

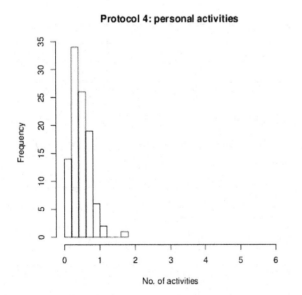

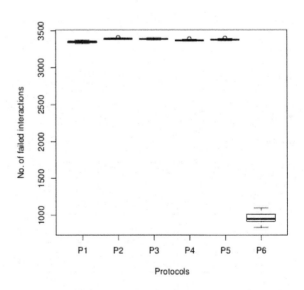

asked to recall whether the start time, end time, type, location, and people involved in an activity were fixed before the activity began). Another more intensive method is to ask people to roleplay organising an activity and observing the order in which issues are decided. All of these techniques can provide input into the protocol design. Enhanced activity-travel survey data (i.e., including "with whom" details) can be used for validation of the overall system.

Future work involves collecting data, in the form of stated preference surveys, on how people make activity-travel decisions and incorporating this into the model, possibly altering the issues and process. Further experimentation with heterogeneous protocols in the one simulation will also be undertaken, as well as varying activity group sizes.

REFERENCES

Arentze, T., van den Berg, P., & Timmermans, H. (2009). Modeling social networks in geographic space: Approach and empirical application. In *Proceedings of the Workshop on Frontiers in Transportation: Social Networks and Travel.*

Arentze, T. A., & Timmermans, H. (2006). Social networks, social interactions and activity-travel behavior: A framework for micro-simulation. *Environment and Planning. B, Planning & Design*, *35*(6), 1012–1027. doi:10.1068/b3319t

Arentze, T. A., & Timmermans, H. J. (2004). A learning-based transportation oriented simulation system. *Transportation Research Part B: Methodological*, *38*, 613–633. doi:10.1016/j.trb.2002.10.001

Axhausen, K. (2006). *Social networks, mobility biographies and travel: The survey challenges* (Tech. Rep. No. 343). Zurich, Switzerland: Institut für Verkehrsplanung und Transportsysteme.

Clark, A. F., & Doherty, S. T. (2008). Examining the nature and extent of the activity-travel preplanning decision process. *Transportation Research Record*, *2054*, 83–92. doi:10.3141/2054-10

Fatima, S. S., Wooldridge, M., & Jennings, N. R. (2003). Optimal agendas for multi-issue negotiation. In *Proceedings of the Second Annual Joint Conference on Autonomous Agents and Multiagent Systems* (pp. 129-136).

Fatima, S. S., Wooldridge, M., & Jennings, N. R. (2006). Multi-issue negotiation with deadlines. *Journal of Artificial Intelligence*, *27*, 381–417.

Hackney, J., & Marchal, F. (2007). Model for coupling multi-agent social interactions and traffic simulation. In *Proceedings of Annual Meeting on Frontiers in Transportation.*

Klügl, F., Bazzan, A. L. C., Ossowski, S., & Chaib-Draa, B. (Eds.). (2010, May 11). *Sixth Workshop on Agents in Traffic and Transportation*, Toronto, ON, Canada.

Macal, C. M., & North, M. J. (2006). Tutorial on agent-based modeling and simulation part 2: How to model with agents. In *Proceedings of the Winter Simulation Conference* (pp. 73-83).

Miller, E. (2005). An integrated framework for modelling short- and long-run household decision-making. In Timmermans, H. (Ed.), *Progress in activity-based analysis* (pp. 175–202). Oxford, UK: Elsevier. doi:10.1016/B978-008044581-6/50012-0

Mokhtarian, P. L., & Salomon, I. (2001). How derived is the demand for travel? Some conceptual and measurement considerations. *Transportation Research Part A, Policy and Practice*, *35*, 695–719. doi:10.1016/S0965-8564(00)00013-6

Mokhtarian, P. L., Salomon, I., & Handy, S. L. (2006). The impacts of ICT on leisure activities and travel: A conceptual exploration. *Transportation*, *33*, 263–289. doi:10.1007/s11116-005-2305-6

Padgham, L., & Winikoff, M. (2004). *Developing intelligent agent systems - A practical guide*. New York, NY: John Wiley & Sons. doi:10.1002/0470861223

Rindt, C. R., Marca, J. E., & McNally, M. G. (2003). An agent-based activity microsimulation kernel using a negotiation metaphor. In *Proceedings of the 82nd Annual Meeting of the Transportation Research Board*.

Sandholm, T. (1993). An implementation of the contract net protocol based on marginal cost calculations. In *Proceedings of the 11th National Conference on Artificial Intelligence* (pp. 256-262).

Timmermans, H. J., & Zhang, J. (2009). Modeling household activity travel behavior: Examples of state of the art modeling approaches and research agenda. *Transportation Research Part B: Methodological*, *43*, 187–190. doi:10.1016/j.trb.2008.06.004

van den Berg, P., Arentze, T., & Timmermans, H. (2008). Social networks, ICT use and activity-travel patterns: Data collection and first analyses. In *Proceedings of the 9th International Conference on Design and Decision Support Systems in Architecture and Urban Planning*.

Wainer, J., Ferreira, P. R. Jr, & Constantino, E. R. (2007). Scheduling meetings through multi-agent negotiations. *Decision Support Systems*, *44*, 285–297. doi:10.1016/j.dss.2007.03.015

Wen, C.-H., & Koppelman, F. S. (2000). A conceptual and methdological framework for the generation of activity-travel patterns. *Transportation*, *27*, 5–23. doi:10.1023/A:1005234603206

Wooldridge, M. J. (2002). *An introduction to multiagent systems*. Chichester, UK: John Wiley & Sons.

Xu, L., & Weigand, H. (2001). The evolution of the contract net protocol. In X. S. Wang, G. Yu, & H. Lu (Eds.), *Proceedings of the Second International Conference on Advances in Web-Age Information Management* (LNCS 2118, pp. 257-264).

This work was previously published in International Journal of Agent Technologies and Systems, Volume 3, Issue 2, edited by Yu Zhang, pp. 18-32, copyright 2011 by IGI Publishing (an imprint of IGI Global).

Section 2
Agent Collaboration

Chapter 3
A Collaborative Framework for Multiagent Systems

Moamin Ahmed
Universiti Tenaga Nasional, Malaysia

Mohd Sharifuddin Ahmad
Universiti Tenaga Nasional, Malaysia

Mohd Zaliman M. Yusoff
Universiti Tenaga Nasional, Malaysia

ABSTRACT

In this paper, the authors demonstrate the use of software agents to extend the role of humans in a collaborative work process. The extended roles to agents provide a convenient means for humans to delegate mundane tasks to software agents. The framework employs the FIPA ACL communication protocol which implements communication between agents. An interface for each agent implements the communication between humans and agents. Such interface and the subsequent communication performed by agents and between agents contribute to the achievement of shared goals.

1. INTRODUCTION

In human-centered collaboration, the problem of adhering to deadlines is a major issue. The diversity of tasks imposed on humans poses a major challenge in keeping time to implement scheduled tasks. One way of overcoming this problem is to use time management systems which track deadlines and provide reminders for time-critical tasks. However, such systems do not always provide the needed assistance to perform follow-up tasks in a collaborative process.

In this paper, we demonstrate the development and application of software agents to implement a collaborative work of Examination Paper Preparation and Moderation Process (EPMP) in

DOI: 10.4018/978-1-4666-1565-6.ch003

an academic faculty. We use the Foundation for Intelligent Physical Agents (FIPA) agent communication language (ACL) to implement message exchanges between agents to take over the communication tasks between humans. An interface for each agent implements the communication between a human and his/her corresponding agent. Such interface and the subsequent communication performed by agents and between agents contribute to the achievement of a shared goal, i.e., the completion of examination paper preparation and moderation.

We use the FIPA ACL to demonstrate the usefulness of the agents to take over the timing and execution of communication from humans to achieve the goal. However, the important tasks, i.e., preparation and moderation tasks are still performed by humans. The agents intelligently urge humans to complete the tasks by the deadline, execute communicative acts to other agents when the tasks are completed and upload and submit documents on behalf of their human counterparts.

This paper reports an extension to our previous work in the same project (Ahmed, Ahmad, & Mohd Yusoff, 2009). Section 2 of this paper briefly dwells on the related work of this research. In Section 3, we present the development of our framework that uses the software agent technology to solve the problems of EPMP. Section 4 discusses the development and simulation of the framework and Section 5 concludes the paper.

2. RELATED WORK

The development of our framework is inspired by the work of many researchers in agent, multi-agent, collaboration, and workflow systems (Chavez & Maes, 1996; Chen, Wolfe, & McLean, 2000; DeLoach, 1999; Ferber, 1999; Labrou & Finin, 1994; Muehlen & Rosemann, 2000; Steinfeld, Jang, & Pfaff, 1999; Tsvetovatyy et al., 1997; Wooldridge, 2002). Ferber (1999) and Wooldridge (2000) both presented a comprehensive introduc-

tion to the field of agent-based systems. Labrou and Finin (1994) proposed the Knowledge Query and Manipulation Language (KQML), an agent communication language for multi-agent coordination which has been developed further by the Foundation for Intelligent Physical Agents (FIPA) (FIPA, 2001, 2002a, 2002b).

A significant part of our work draws references from the work of Chavez and Maes (1996), and Tsvetovatyy et al. (1997). Both groups developed and demonstrated a multi-agent system (MAS) that carry out transactions and tasks on behalf of humans. Their applications focused on virtual markets based on MAS to address the need of autonomous agents to make automated purchasing for their owners. Kasbah (Chavez & Maes, 1996) and MAGMA (Tsvetovatyy et al., 1997) are MASs that provide a virtual market for buyer and seller agents to communicate, negotiate, and make a possible deal on their owners' behalf.

Other researchers attempt to resolve issues in collaboration involving individuals, groups and software agents (Steinfeld, Jang, & Pfaff, 1999; Chen, Wolfe, & McLean, 2000; Chen, Manikonda, & Durfee, 2008). For example, Steinfeld, Jang, and Pfaff (1999) developed TeamSCOPE, which is a collaborative system specifically designed to address problems faced by distributed teams. It is an integrative framework that focuses on facilitation of group members' awareness of group activities, communications, and resources. Chen, Wolfe, and McLean (2000) presented DIAMS, a system of distributed, collaborative agents to help users access, manage, share and exchange information. Chen, Manikonda, and Durfee (2008) proposed an innovative shared intelligence framework for flexible human-agent collaboration in which the level of collaboration is selected through a negotiated and iterative human-agent collaboration (HAC) process. This ensures that the needs of a system user are balanced with the availability of suitable experts to form and maintain an expert team that supports the user's decision-making

Many business processes use workflow systems to exploit their benefits such as automation, coordination, and collaboration between entities. A workflow describes the order of a set of tasks performed by various software and humans to complete a given procedure (Bramley, 2005). Repetitive workflows are often automated, particularly in organisations that handle high volumes of forms or documents according to fixed procedures. Fluerke, Ehrler, and Purvis (2003) described the advantages of their agent-based framework JBees, such as flexibility and ability to dynamically incorporate a new process model. Muehlen and Rosemann (2000) outlined the economic aspects of workflow-based process monitoring and controlling and the current state-of-the-art in monitoring facilities provided by current workflow management systems and existing standards. Savarimuthu, Purvis, and Fluerke (2004) described their system in which agents monitor and control the system based upon the data obtained through simulation.

3. DEVELOPMENT OF THE FRAMEWORK

The development of our framework is based on a five-phased cycle. The development process includes domain selection; domain analysis; domain modeling; tasks and message identification; and application.

3.1. Domain Selection: The EPMP Domain

The EPMP is operated by three groups of people: Examination Committee (EC), Lecturers, and Moderators. The goal of this collaborative process is to complete the examination paper preparation and moderation within a given duration.

The framework is concerned with the symbiotic relationship between an agent and its human counterpart. Consequently, we chose the EPMP as the domain for our framework in which both humans and agents work cooperatively.

3.2. Domain Analysis

The process starts when the Examination Committee sends out an instruction to lecturers to start prepare examination papers. A lecturer then prepares the examination paper, together with the solutions and the marking scheme (Set A). He/She then submits the set to be checked by an appointed moderator.

The moderator checks the set and returns it back with a moderation report (Set B) to the lecturer. If there are no corrections, the lecturer submits the set to the Examination Committee for further actions. Otherwise, the lecturer needs to correct the paper and resubmit the corrected paper to the moderator for inspection. If corrections have been made, the moderator returns the paper to the lecturer. Finally, the lecturer submits the paper to the Committee for further processing. Figure 2 shows the process flow of the EPMP.

If the moderated paper fulfills the required format, it is given to the EC Secretary for printing. Otherwise it is returned to the lecturer for corrections. The lecturers and moderators are given deadlines to complete the process in two preparation-correction-moderation cycles as shown in Table 1.

Lack of enforcement and the diverse tasks of lecturers and moderators cause the EPMP (Figure 1) to suffer from delays in actions by the academicians. Our investigation reveals that the lecturers and moderators do not observe the deadlines of the two 2-week moderation cycles. Some lecturers wait until the last few days of the second moderation cycle to submit their examination papers, which leaves insufficient time for the moderators to qualitatively scrutinise the papers.

Figure 1. The EPMP process flow

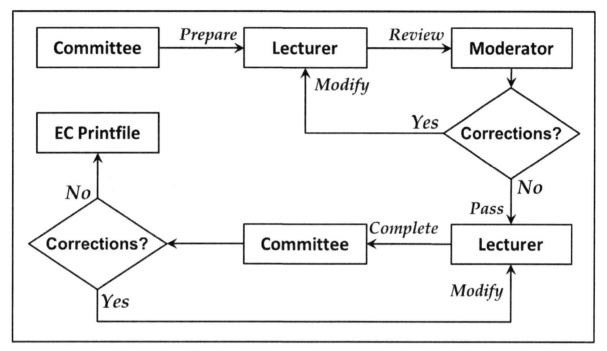

Due to the manual nature of the process, (e.g., lecturers personally deliver the documents to the moderators), there is no mechanism that records the adherence to deadlines and tracks the activities of defaulters. The absence of such mechanism makes it impossible for the Committee to identify the perpetrators who failed to submit their documents by the deadlines.

Notwithstanding, our observation reveals that all examination papers reached the committee by the last few days of the second moderation cycle albeit with numerous errors. In one instance, the percentage of papers returned for corrections (in content and format) was as high as 90%. Such high percentage has seriously burdened the Committee with keeping and maintaining the quality of examination papers.

The above analysis reveals two categories of problems in EPMP:

1. Human-related problems: The lack of coordination between the committee, moderators, and lecturers causes delays in document submission. There is also a lack of enforcement on the deadlines especially in the first moderation cycle.

Table 1. Examination preparation and moderation schedule

Tasks	Deadlines
Set A should be submitted to the respective moderators	Week 10
1st moderation cycle	Week 10 - 11
2nd moderation cycle (Set B)	Week 12 - 13
Set B should be submitted to EC	Week 14

Figure 2. Ontology and actions

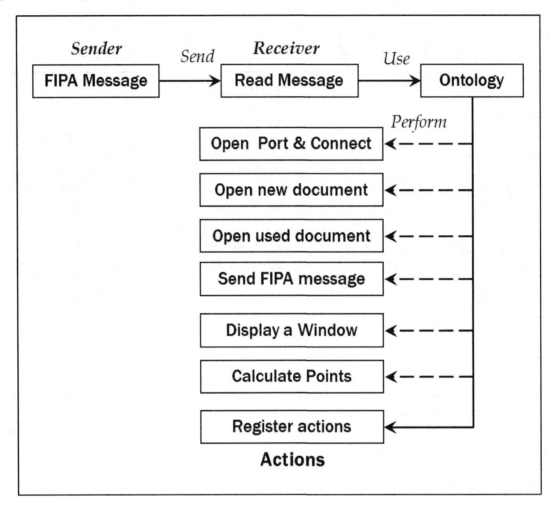

Due to the diversity of tasks imposed on lecturers and moderators, their need to remember and perform those other tasks is compelling. The EPMP's tasks and schedule add significant additional stress on their cognitive load, because they have to depend on themselves to follow through the process until the end.

2. System-related problems: The problems from the system's perspective are due to the manual nature of the system and its inability to provide:
    o   Consistent schedule for document submission, which could take two days depending on the circumstances affecting humans.
    o   Tracking of documents, in which case, the committee could not know the current location of the documents without querying the lecturers or moderators.
    o   Reminders, which are very important in urging humans to speed up the process.
    o   Recording of submission date, which could assist the committee in identifying defaulters.

- ◦ Evaluation of individual performance, to identify lecturers or moderators who are diligently fulfilling their obligations and those who are not.
- ◦ Enforcement on the two-cycle moderation schedule, which is not strictly implemented. Effectively, only one moderation cycle is implemented since the process takes the whole four weeks.

To resolve some of these problems, we resort to the use of software agents to take over the communication and document submission tasks by the agents and the reminding and alerting tasks directed to humans.

3.3. Domain Modeling

We develop the model by identifying the entities that are involved in the domain's dynamics. The entities of the EPMP which form the underlying theory of the model include humans, agents, environment, agent actions, schedule, documents used in the process, and a set of expressions, and terminologies used by humans and agents to advance the workflow. We first define each of these entities as follows:

Definition 1: An agent, $\alpha \in Ag$, where Ag is a set of agents, is defined as an entity which performs a set of actions, A, based on the states of the environment, E, to achieve its goal.

The agent performs a sequence of interleaving actions, $a_i \in A$, and environment states, $e_j \in E$, which is termed as a *run*, $r_k \in R$, where R is a set of runs of the agent (Wooldridge, 2009). Thus, an agent is a function that maps a run to actions, i.e.,

$\alpha: r_k \rightarrow a_i$, where $i, k \geq 1$.

We characterise only one of each of the Committee (C), Lecturer (L), and Moderator (M) agents in our model.

Definition 2: An agent action, a_i, is a discrete operation performed by the agent which contributes to the achievement of its goal. If A is a set of agent actions, then,

$A = \{ a_i \mid i \geq 1 \}$

We distinguish two types of action: *task* and *message exchange*. A task, $t_{m\alpha}$, is an action that an agent performs as a consequence of a message it receives from other agents whereas a message exchange, $x_{n\alpha}$, is a communicative action which the agent performs to advance the workflow, where m is the task number, n is the message exchange number and α refers to agents. Therefore,

$A = \{ t_{m\alpha}, x_{n\alpha} \mid m,n \geq 1 \}$

From Definition 1, $\alpha: r_k \rightarrow a_i$, but $a_i = \{t_{m\alpha}, x_{n\alpha}\}$, thus we redefine an agent as follows:

$\alpha: r_k \rightarrow \{ t_{m\alpha}, x_{n\alpha} \mid m,n \geq 1 \}$

Definition 3: An environment, E, influences and is influenced by the agent actions, i.e., if e_j is a state of an environment E, then the environment is the set of all the states.

$E = \{ e_j \mid j \geq 1 \}$

Definition 4: A schedule of a process is a time slot defined by the beginning and the end of the process. In our model, we define four schedules: the main EPMP schedule, the examination paper preparation, and the first and the second moderation cycles. For example, if δ_i is the beginning of a moderation cycle and δ_j is the end, then the schedule of a moderation cycle,

$\sigma = \delta_j - \delta_i$ where δ_j is the deadline, $\delta_i < \delta_j$, δ_i and δ_j has a date structure (dd-mm-yy) and σ is the number of days between two dates.

Definition 5: A document, $d_i \in D$, $i \geq 1$, and D is a set of documents used in a process, is an object which agents exchange on behalf of their human counterparts to advance the workflow.

In our model, the internal states of a document such as updates made by humans are opaque to the agents. However, agents monitor the spatial and temporal states of the document in folders to detect whether humans have indeed taken some actions on the document (e.g., submitted before the deadline).

Definition 6: An ontology term, $o_u \in O$, $u \geq 1$, and O is a set on ontology terms, is a keyword used by agents to communicate the semantics of their beliefs, desires, and intentions and other domain parameters.

In this model, we distinguish three types of ontology term: *task*, *performative*, and *object name*. We have defined a task, $t_{m\alpha}$, in Definition 2. A performative, p_i, is a keyword that defines a speech act (Labrou & Finin, 1999), which an agent may use e.g., PREPARE, while an object name, n_j, is an atom that identifies an object, which agents exchange and to be worked upon by humans, e.g., a moderation form. Therefore,

$$o_u = \{t_{m\alpha}, p_i, n_j\} \in O, \text{where } i, j, m, u \geq 1.$$

Definition 7: An ontology, Ω, is a structured construct of rules that defines the semantics of an ontology term and has the prolog clausal form,

$$\Omega \leftarrow T_1, ..., T_v.$$ where $v \geq 1$, Ω is the goal or head of the clause, and the conjuncts $T_1, ..., T_v$ are the sub-goals making up the body of the clause. Instantiations of these sub-goals are represented by o_u.

3.3.1. Tasks

As defined in Definition 2, a task is an action that an agent performs as a consequence of a message it receives from other agents. In modeling the EPMP, we analyse what tasks are required based on the model's logical and architectural requirements. Upon analysis of the domain, we formulate the following pre-compiled tasks, $t_{m\alpha}$, which an agent could select based on the state of the environment:

a. **Connect, $t_{1\alpha}$:** When an agent needs to send a message or when it senses a message, it makes a connection with a remote agent (peer-to-peer).

b. **Open document, $t_{2\alpha}$:** An agent opens a (new) document for the human Lecturer, Moderator, or Committee. The document could be a moderation form, committee form or examination paper. This task is required to automatically open the documents to encourage humans to update the documents.

c. **Disconnect, $t_{3\alpha}$:** When an agent has sent or received a message, this task disconnects the remote agent.

d. **Display a message window on the screen, $t_{4\alpha}$:** When an agent receives a message, it displays the message window on the screen. This message helps humans to know his/her task, the number of days left to submit or any other information about the state of examination paper.

e. **Log action, $t_{5\alpha}$:** An agent logs a message and its date with the details of the port number and IP address in a log file. The Head of Department is able to open the log file at any time.

f. **Remind action, $t_{6\alpha}$:** The Committee agent sends a remind message to an agent that currently holds the examination documents.

g. **Advertise, $t_{7\alpha}$:** When a deadline is breached and a human lecturer or moderator who holds the examination documents has not completed the required task, the corresponding agent informs this state of affair to all other agents that its human counterpart is delaying the process. This action motivates the human to submit before the deadline.

h. **Track documents, $t_{9\alpha}$:** The Committee agent tracks the documents to alert the agent which holds them. An agent which submits the documents writes a message in a track file. This track file belongs to the Committee agent and it has all the information about the documents' spatial and temporal states.

i. **Record action, $t_{10\alpha}$:** When an agent performs an action, it records the action in a subprogram to facilitate the monitoring of paper preparation and moderation even if the system is turned off.

j. **Calculate merit/demerit points, $t_{11\alpha}$:** An agent evaluates its human counterpart's compliance with deadlines by calculating merit/demerit points. This action could motivate humans to work much more diligently to avoid breaching the deadline. The merit/demerit points are recorded and updated in the log file (see (e)).

3.3.2. Message Exchanges

A message exchange is another type of action performed by agents to advance the workflow. We use the FIPA ACL (FIPA, 2002a) to implement message exchanges between agents. The message consists of a number of parameters, which include the mandatory performative, p_i, and other optional parameters, π_j, i.e.,

$$x_{n\alpha} \rightarrow (p_i,(\pi_j, f(\pi_j)), \ldots).$$ where i, j, n $\geq$ 1, and $f(\pi_j)$ is a function which evaluates and returns a value for π_j.

The use of performatives enables agents to recognise the intent of a requesting agent for a specific service. We use most of the parameters, π_j defined by FIPA and our own performatives. We define our own nine additional performatives from the analysis of the EPMP process which are Prepare, Check, Remind, Review, Complete, Modify, Advertise, Inform_all and Acknowledge. For example, in the Prepare, performative, the sender advises the receiver to start prepare examination paper by performing some actions to enable its human counterpart to do so. The content of the message is a description of the action

to be performed. The receiver understands the message and is capable of performing the action (FIPA, 2001).

3.3.3. Environment

Our analysis of the environment parameters required for the EPMP model reveals that the environment, E, consists of four parts:

a. **Status of uploaded files, e_1:** An agent checks its human counterpart if he/she has uploaded Set A or Set B to a specified folder. If he/she has done so, the agent checks the next step. This state assists the agent in monitoring the submission of documents.

b. **Status of deadlines, e_2:** An agent checks the system's date every day and compare it with the deadline. This state helps the agent to perform appropriate actions e.g., to send a remind message to an agent.

c. **Status of subprograms, e_3:** When an agent performs a task, it writes the action in a subprogram, e.g., when the Committee agent sends the PREPARE message, it writes this event in the subprogram, which it uses later for sending a remind message.

d. **Status of message signal, e_4:** An agent opens a port and makes a connection when it senses a message coming from a remote agent.

3.3.4. Ontology

In our model, the ontology defines the meaning of tasks, performatives and object names. The task ontology defines the meaning of tasks in agent actions. For example, in the task "Display a message window on the screen, $t_{4\alpha}$," an agent processes appropriate information and create a window to show the message on the screen for its human counterpart.

When an agent sends a message to a remote agent, the remote agent computes the meaning of the message by checking the semantics of the performative (FIPA, 2001). Similarly, object names like examination paper, lecturer form, moderation form, and committee form are ontology terms used in the EPMP. When an agent receives a message, it checks these object names and process the objects based on the performative. For example, when the Committee agent sends a PREPARE message to the Lecturer agent, it checks the Prepare ontology by which it opens the examination paper and the lecturer form.

The ontology describes the semantics of messages used in the model. This then triggers some action which consists of a number of tasks. The agent selects from these actions depending on the semantics of the message (Figure 2).

3.3.5. Schedules

We model the schedules, σ_i, as discrete timeslots. A schedule can be nested in another schedule. For example, the main schedule is the start of the EPMP until the final submission of examination documents. The second schedule is the examination paper preparation, the third is the first moderation cycle and the fourth is the second moderation cycle. The examination paper preparation, first moderation, and second moderation schedules are nested in the main EPMP schedule. We represent the structure as follows:

$\sigma_1 = \delta_{start}$ to $\delta_{end;}$ EPMP process duration,
$\sigma_2 = \delta_{start}$ to $\delta_{1start;}$ Examination paper preparation,
$\sigma_3 = \delta_{1start}$ to $\delta_{1end;}$ First moderation cycle,
$\sigma_4 = \delta_{2start}$ to $\delta_{2end;}$ Second moderation cycle,
where $\delta_{2start} = \delta_{1end}$, and $\delta_{2end} = \delta_{end}$.

Figure 3 shows the schedules' structure.

Two types of reasoning are performed on these schedules: reminding/alerting humans to complete the scheduled task before the deadlines, and calculating the merit/demerit points based on the deadlines and actual submission dates.

The Committee agent checks the dates δ_{1start} and δ_{2start} and inspects the documents' location from its track file. With this information it can decide to send a remind message to the appropriate agent.

An agent urges its human counterpart to submit the documents on time by its ability to evaluate him/her through awarding or penalising merit or demerit point depending on the date of submission. It registers all events and actions performed by its human counterpart and makes the information (events, actions, and points) available to the author-

Figure 3. The EPMP schedules

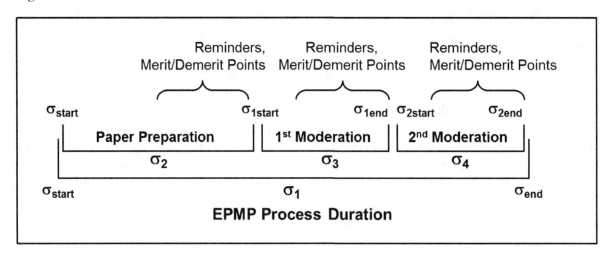

ity. With this system, we solved the problem of the humans' performance evaluation and provided a mechanism to motivate the humans to complete their tasks before the deadlines with consequential enforcement of the two moderation cycles.

An agent calculates the merit/demerit point depending on the deadline, actual submission date by human (moderator or lecturer), and the last submission date by the previous human (moderator or lecturer). For example, let us assume the following:

Lecturer deadline = L_D = 7th day
Actual submission date = Z = 4th day
Previous submission date = S_D = 0
Current agent points = P
Merit/Demerit Point formula:
$P = L_D - Z + S_D = 7 - 4 + 0 = 3$ pts.

3.3.6. Documents

Agents exchange documents by uploading the documents from the sender's to the receiver's folder. The agents always use updated documents and upon receiving them, the receiver agent opens the documents for its human counterpart. However, the human counterparts can always open the documents at any time through an interface.

While the internal states of the documents are opaque to the agents, agents reason on the spatial and the temporal states of the documents. They then perform the autonomous action of submitting the documents to the next recipient.

In reasoning the spatial state of the documents, agents check the status of the uploaded files in a specified folder. The state of the uploaded files becomes true when their human counterparts click a Submit button in their agent interface. The agents then check other states to make the right decision. For reasoning on the temporal state of the documents, agents refer to the schedules (i.e., deadlines, δ_{1end} and δ_{2end}). They use the deadlines to evaluate and perform appropriate actions. For example, if δ_{start} is true, the Committee agent sends the PREPARE message.

An overview of the complete EPMP model is shown in Figure 4. The diagram shows the entities and the proposed solutions to resolve some of the human- and system-related problems.

Figure 4. An overview of the EPMP model

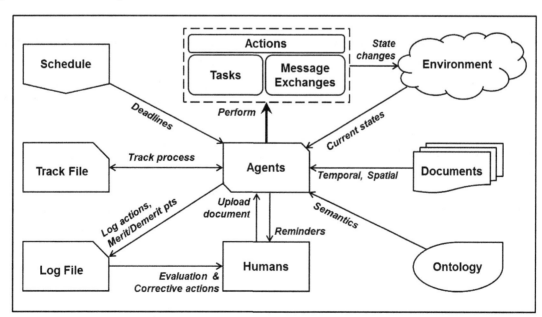

3.4. Task and Message Identification

We represent the tasks and message exchanges for each agent as $T_{\#X}$ and $E_{\#X}$ respectively, where # is the task or message exchange number and X refers to the agents C, M, or L. A message from an agent is represented by $\mu_{\#SR}$, where # is the message number, S is the sender of the message μ, and R is the receiver. S and R refer to the agents C, M, or L.

For system's tasks, $CN_{\#X}$ refers to the task an agent performs to enable a connection to a port and $DCN_{\#X}$ indicates a disconnection task. From the EPMP process flow, we identify the tasks and message exchanges that are required by each agent to complete the paper preparation and moderation process. For each agent, the following tasks and message exchanges are represented:

CN_{1X}: Agent X opens port and enables connection to initiate message exchange.

E_{1X}: Agent X sends a message μ_{1XL}, to L.

E_{2X}: Agent X sends an ACKNOWLEDGE message, e.g., μ_{1LX}, in response to a received message from L.

T_{1X}: X displays the message, e.g., μ_{1LX}, on the screen to alert its human counterpart.

T_{2X}: X opens and displays a new document on the screen.

E_{3X}: X sends a remind message to Agent L.

DCN_{1X}: Agent X disconnects and closes the port when it completes the tasks.

We develop an environment to include the system's parameters, agents' tasks and message exchanges, reminders and timers that enable agents to closely monitor the actions of their human counterparts. The side effect of this ability is improved autonomy for agents to make accurate decisions.

3.5. Application

In this phase, we apply the task and message representations to the EPMP domain. Based on the tasks and message exchanges identified in Section 3.4, we model the interaction sequences between the three agents.

The following interactions show the tasks and message exchanges between the three agents C, M, and L to complete the preparation and moderation process. These interactions do not include those activities for which human actions are required. Due to space limitation, we omit the tasks for paper corrections and second moderation.

a. Agent C
   ◦ **CN_{1C}:** Agent C opens port and enables connection when a start date is satisfied.
     ▪ C starts the process when the start date is true.
   ◦ **E_{1C}:** C sends a message μ_{1CL}, to L – PREPARE examination paper.
     ▪ L sends an ACKNOWLEDGE message, μ_{1LC}.
     ▪ C reads the ACKNOWLEDGE and checks the ontology.
     ▪ It then turns on a Timer to time the duration for sending reminder messages. It controls this timer by checking the date and file submission status every day and makes the decision to send reminder messages.
   ◦ **DCN_{1C}:** C disables connection and closes the port.

When Agent C decides to send a message autonomously it initiates the following actions:

- **CN$_{1C}$:** C connects to L.
  - ○ C makes this decision by checking its environment.
- **T$_{2C}$:** C sends a remind message to L.
  - ○ L receives the message and displays it on screen to alert its human counterpart.
- **DCN$_{3C}$:** C disconnects and closes the port when it completes the task.

b. Agent L

- **CN$_{1L}$:** Agent L opens port and enables connection when it receives the message from Agent C.
  - ○ L reads the performative PREPARE, checks the ontology.
- **E$_{1L}$:** L replies with a message μ_{1LC}, to C – ACKNOWLEDGE.
- **T$_{1L}$:** L displays the message μ_{1CL}, on the screen to alert its human counterpart.
- **T$_{2L}$:** L opens and displays a new document on the screen.
  - ○ L opens a new document to signal its human counterpart to begin preparing the examination paper.
- **T$_{3L}$:** L opens and displays the Lecturer form on the screen.
  - ○ Agent L opens the form which contains the policy to follow.
- **DCN$_{1L}$:** L disconnects and closes the port.

When the human Lecturer uploads a completed examination paper,

- **E$_{2L}$:** L sends a message μ_{2LM}, to M – REVIEW examination paper.
  - ○ M sends an ACKNOWLEDGE message, μ_{1ML}.
  - ○ L checks the states of the environment.
  - ○ When L receives the message μ_{1ML}, it turns on a Timer to time the duration for M to complete the moderation. It controls this timer by checking the date and file submission status every day and makes the decision to send reminder messages to M.

When L decides to send a reminder message autonomously, it performs the following actions:

- **CN$_{2L}$:** L connects with agent M.
- **T$_{1L}$:** L sends the remind message.
  - ○ M receives the message and displays the message to its human counterpart.
- **DCN$_{2L}$:** L disconnects when it completes its task.

c. Agent M

- **CN$_{1M}$:** M opens port and enables connection.
  - ○ M reads the REVIEW performative, checks the ontology and performs the next action.
- **E$_{1M}$:** M replies with a message μ_{1ML}, to L - ACKNOWLEDGE.
- **T$_{1M}$:** M displays the message μ_{2LM}, on the screen to alert its human counterpart.
- **T$_{2M}$:** M opens and displays the examination paper on the screen to alert the human moderator to start reviewing the paper.
- **T$_{3M}$:** M opens and displays the moderation form on the screen.
- **DCN$_{1M}$:** M disconnects from L when it completes its tasks.

If no corrections are required:

- **E$_{2M}$:** M sends a message μ_{2ML}, to L – PASS moderation.

d. Agent L

- **CN$_{3L}$:** L opens port and connects with M.
  - ○ Agent L reads the performative PASS and checks the ontology.
- **E$_{3L}$:** L replies with a message μ_{3LM}, to M – ACKNOWLEDGE.
  - ○ L turns off the Timer for message reminder because the deadline is satisfied and the documents have been submitted.
- **T$_{3L}$:** L displays the message μ_{2ML}, on the screen.
- **T$_{4L}$:** L opens and displays the moderated examination paper on the screen.

- T_{5L}: L opens and displays the completed moderation form on the screen.
- DCN_{3L}: L disconnects from Agent M and closes the port when it completes its task.
- CN_{4L}: L opens port and connects with C
- E_{4L}: L sends a message μ_{4LC}, to C – COMPLETE.
- DCN_{4L}: L disconnects from C and closes the port.
  e. Agent C
- CN_{2C}: C opens port and connects with L.
  ○ M reads the performative COMPLETE and checks the ontology.
- E_{2C}: C replies with a message μ_{2CL}, to L – ACKNOWLEDGE.
  ○ C turns off the Timer for message reminder because the deadline has been satisfied and the documents have been submitted.
- T_{1C}: C displays the message μ_{4LC}, on the screen to alert its human counterpart.
- T_{2C}: C opens and displays the moderated examination paper on the screen.
- T_{3C}: C opens and displays the Committee Form.
- DCN_{2C}: C closes the port and disconnect from M when it completes its task.

All these actions are executed if humans submit the documents before the deadlines. If the deadlines are exceeded (i.e., the Timers expired) and there are no submissions, then L advertises no submission and identifies the offending agent.

- CN_{5L}: L opens port and connects with M.
- E_{1L}: L sends advertise message to M and agent M displays the message to its human counterpart.
- DCN_{5L}: L disconnects from M and closes the port when it completes the task.
- CN_{6L}: L opens port and connects with C.
- E_{2L}: L send ADVERTISE message to C and agent C displays the message to its human counterpart.

- DCN_{6L}: L disconnects from C and closes the port when it completes the task.

Figure 5 shows the system's architecture and the ensuing interactions between agents.

4. SYSTEM DEVELOPMENT AND SIMULATION

We develop a prototype of the EPMP using Win-Prolog and its extended module Chimera, which has the ability to handle multi-agent systems (Win-Prolog, 2010). Chimera provides the module to implement peer-to-peer communication via the use of TCP/IP. Each agent is identified by a port number and an IP address. Agents send and receive messages through such configuration.

For the message structure, we use the parameters specified by the FIPA ACL Message Structure Specification (FIPA, 2002a). We include the performatives, the mandatory parameter, in all our ACL messages. We use our own performatives in the message structure, which are Prepare, Check, Remind, Review, Complete, Modify, ACK, Advertise, and Inform_all. To complete the structure, we include the message, content and conversational control parameters as stipulated by the FIPA Specification. The communication between agents is based on the BDI semantics as defined by FIPA (FIPA, 2001, 2002b). The BDI semantics gives the agents the ability to know how it arranges the steps to achieve the goal.

We reproduce below the sample codes that implement a communicative act of requesting the Lecturer agent to prepare the examination paper (see (a) in Section 3.5):

```
committee_dialog_
handler((committee,1003),msg_but-
ton,_,_):-
agent_link(committee, Link),
Prepare = prepare (
':sender', committee,
```

```
':receiver', lecturer,
':reply-with', achieve_the_mission,
':content', start_prepare_examina-
tion_paper,
':ontology', word_documents,
':language', prolog
),
agent_post(committee, Link, Prepare).
```

In ontology implementation, we implicitly encode the ontology terms within the software implementation of the agents themselves and thus are not formally published to an ontology service (FIPA, 2001). The sample codes show the ontology implementation after the Lecturer agent (L), receives the Prepare message from the Committee agent (C) (see (b) in Section 3.5):

Figure 5. The EPMP architecture

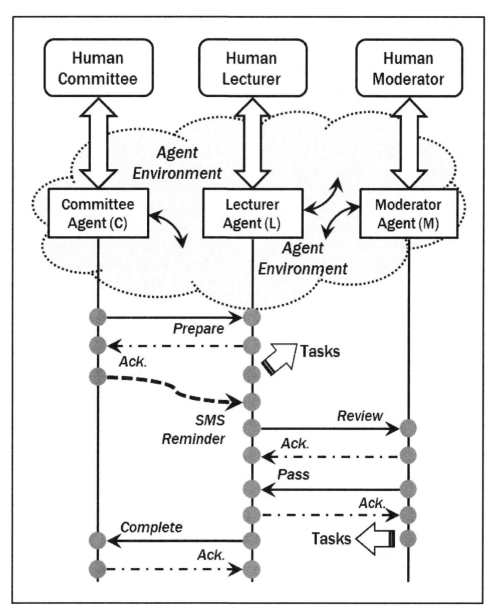

```
lecturer_handler(Name, Link,
prepare(Args)):-
start_prepare_examination_paper,
fipa_member(':sender', From, Args),
fipa_member(':reply-with', ReplyWith,
Args),
lecturer_reply(Name, From, ReplyWith,
done, Reply),
agent_post(Name, Link, Reply).
% Ontology calls
start_prepare_examination_paper:-
lecturer_reply_remote_agent,
new_word_documents,
lecturer_form,
lecturer_message.
```

4.1. Agent Interface

In this section, we show and explain a typical agent interface for human-agent communication. Figure 6 shows the interface for the Committee agent (C).

- **Upload to Lecturer File button:** The Committee uses this button to upload the Committee Form to Lecturer folder after filling in the details.

- **Upload to EC Print File button:** The Committee uses this button to upload the Examination Paper to print file.

- **Open Committee Form button:** The Committee uses this button to open Committee Form any time he/she likes to fill it.

- **Open Examination Paper button:** The Committee uses this button to open Examination Paper any time he/she likes to check it.

- **Agent Control Area:** This area is under the Committee agent control to communicate with other agents. It also contains the IP address and the port number for lecturer and moderator agents.

4.2. Simulation and Testing

We simulate and test the framework by deploying three human actors to play the roles of human Committee, Lecturer, and Moderator. These people communicate with their corresponding agents to advance the workflow. An interface for each agent provides the communication between the actors and their corresponding agents (Figure 6).

The test procedure described is based on the EPMP process flow. It is conducted to tease out the

Figure 6. Committee agent interface

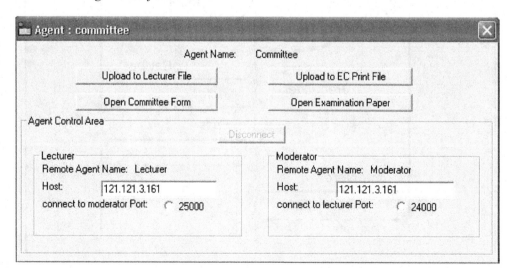

system's response to events that could happen in a real environment, e.g., a document submission. However, the preparation-moderation-correction tasks are significantly reduced by human actors merely writing a few lines of text, checking the text's structure, and correcting it.

1. Assume that the EPMP starts on the 1st of July. When the date is satisfied, the Committee agent sends the PREPARE message to announce the start of the process. The Lecturer agent shows the message to its human counterpart and opens the documents. It then sends an ACKNOWLEDGE message to the sender (Figures 7 and 8).

Figure 7. PREPARE message

Figure 8. ACKNOWLEDGE message

2. On the second day, if there is no submission, the Committee agent sends a remind message, which the Lecturer agent shows to its human counterpart and inform him/her the number of days left to submit (Figure 9).

Figure 9. REMIND message

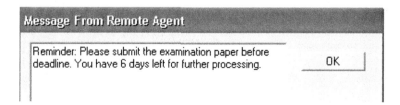

3. If, after three days, the human lecturer uploads the completed examination paper, his/her agent checks the date. If it is satisfied, it sends a REVIEW message to the Moderator agent. If the Moderator agent is offline, it will receive it as an offline message (Figure 10).

Figure 10. REVIEW message

4. If, after two days since receiving the message, the human moderator uploads the moderation form and the examination paper, his/her agent checks the date. If it is satisfied, it sends a CHECK message to the Lecturer agent (Figure 11).

Figure 11. CHECK message

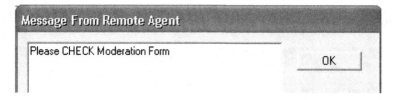

5. If there are no corrections, the human lecturer uploads the documents. His/her agent checks the date and if it is satisfied, it sends a COMPLETE message to the Committee agent. The Committee agent shows the message to its human counterpart and opens the documents for him/her to check the examination paper (Figure 12).

Figure 12. COMPLETE message

6. If the examination paper is satisfactory, the human committee uploads the examination paper to the EC print file. His/her agent sends an INFORM_ALL message to all agents to announce that the goal has been achieved,

i.e., the examination paper preparation and moderation process has been completed (Figure 13). All agents display this message on the screen for their human counterparts.

Figure 13. INFORM_ALL message

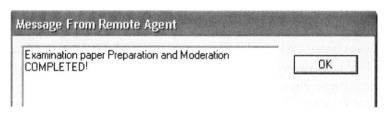

We reproduce below, records of the PREPARE and ACKNOWLEDGE actions of the Committee agent taken from the test results.

```
[fipa_message = prepare(':sender',
committee, ':receiver', lectur-
er, ':reply-with', task_completed,
':content', start_prepare_examina-
tion_paper, ':ontology', word_ docu-
ments, ':language', prolog), 'Link',
0, 'from host', '121.120.18.80',
'on port', 25000] Wed 01 Jul 2009
09:31:25.
 [fipa_message = ack(':sender', lec-
turer, ':receiver', remote_agent,
':in-reply-to', open_committee_form,
':content', start_prepare_examina-
tion_paper, report_ message, ':on-
tology', message, ':language',
prolog), 'Link', 1, 'from host',
'121.120.78.90', 'on port', 1135] Wed
01 Jul 2009 09:31:25.
```

4.3. Analysis of Results

Our framework helps reduce the problem of deadline breach and develops a relationship between humans and agents for agents to serve humans. Autonomous services from agents help reduce the cognitive strain in humans and improve the efficiency of work processes.

The results of the test indicate the correctness and completeness of the sequence of actions performed by the agents based on the states of the environment. With the features and autonomous actions performed by agents, the collaboration between human Committee, Lecturer and Moderator has been improved. The agents register dated actions, remind humans about the deadlines, advertise all agents if there is no submission upon expiry of the deadline, and award/penalise merit/demerit points to humans. While we cannot conclusively claim that the humans' cognitive load is somewhat reduced, i.e., the human actors can certainly ignore the deadlines of documents' submissions and their destinations. The alerting service provided by the agents ensures persistent reminders of the deadlines and agents submit the documents automatically to the intended recipients when a human has uploaded the documents to his/her folder.

All these actions and events are recorded in a log file as part of the agents' environment to track the process flow, which enables the agents to resolve any impending problems. The ease of uploading the files and the subsequent communicative acts performed by agents and between agents contribute to the achievement of the shared goal, i.e., the timely completion of examination paper preparation and moderation process.

Table 2 compares the features between the manual and the automated (agent-based) systems.

5. CONCLUSION

In this paper, we develop and implement a collaborative multi-agent framework using the FIPA agent communication language. We demonstrate the usefulness of the system to take over the timing and execution of scheduled tasks from humans to achieve a shared goal. While the important tasks are still performed by humans, the agents perform communicative acts when the tasks are completed. Such acts could help to reduce the cognitive strain on humans in performing scheduled tasks and improve the collaboration process.

The motivation in applying the technology for a collaborative process comes from the need to resolve problems arising from the dependence on human limited performance abilities. Currently, humans who have limited abilities to handle and coordinate events and their deadlines, play a major role in many collaborative processes. When faced with overwhelming workloads, some tasks are inevitably reduced in priority that could result in delays in task completion. A more adaptable and less stressful system, such as our agent-based system, could alleviate such problem.

We review the agent system as a feasible technology to explore and subsequently exploit the technology for our collaborative process that has three agents: Committee, Lecturer, and Moderator. The results of our simulation show that the agent-based system performs better than the manual system. Due to its communication and autonomous abilities, agents send messages depending on their environment and motivate humans to comply with scheduled deadlines. An interface for each agent provides a convenient means for humans to delegate mundane tasks to these agents. The use of such interface and the subsequent communication perform by agents and between agents contribute to the achievement of a shared goal.

This outcome of this research offers a useful tool for organised control in human-human collaboration using software agents to assist hu-

Table 2. Comparison between manual and automated systems

Features	Manual	Automated
Human cognitive load	High	Reduced
Process tracking	Not recorded (Human-dependent)	Recorded
Merit/demerit	No	Yes
Reminder/alerting	No	Yes
Offline messaging	Not applicable	Yes
Housekeeping	Inconsistent	Consistent
Document submission	Human-dependent	Immediate
Feedback	Human-dependent	Immediate

mans in keeping scheduled deadlines, document submission and communication. However, the decision to act before the deadlines solely rests on the humans themselves.

In our future work, we will analyse the technical issues involving one-to-many and many-to-many relationships between agents and implement the requirements for such phenomena.

REFERENCES

Ahmed, M., Ahmad, M. S., & Mohd Yusoff, M. Z. (2009). A review and development of agent communication language. *Electronic Journal of Computer Science and Information Technology, 1*(1), 7–12.

Bramley, I. (2005). *SOA takes off – New WebSphere SOA foundation extends IBM's lead with new system z9 mainframes as the hub of the enterprise* (2nd ed.). Armonk, NY: IBM.

Chavez, A., & Maes, P. (1996). Kasbah: An agent marketplace for buying and selling goods. In *Proceedings of the 1st International Conference on the Practical Application of Intelligent Agents and Multi-Agent Technology*, London, UK.

Chen, J. R., Wolfe, S. R., & McLean, S. D. W. (2000). A distributed multi-agent system for collaborative information management and sharing. In *Proceedings of the 9th International Conference on Information and Knowledge Management* (pp. 382-388).

Chen, W., Manikonda, V., & Durfee, E. (2008). A flexible human agent collaboration (HAC) framework for human-human activity coordination. In *Proceedings of the AAAI Fall Symposium*.

DeLoach, S. A. (1999). Multi-agent systems engineering - A methodology and language for designing agent systems. In *Proceedings of the Conference on Agent Oriented Information Systems* (pp. 45-57).

Ferber, J. (1999). *Multiagent systems*. Reading, MA: Addison-Wesley.

FIPA. (2001). *Ontology service specification: XC00086D*. Geneva, Switzerland: Author.

FIPA. (2002a). *ACL message structure specification: SC00061G*. Geneva, Switzerland: Author.

FIPA. (2002b). *Communicative act library specification: SC00037J*. Geneva, Switzerland: Author.

Fleurke, M., Ehrler, L., & Purvis, M. (2003). JBees – An adaptive and distributed framework for workflow systems. In *Proceedings of the IEEE/WIC International Conference on Intelligent Agent Technology*, Halifax, NS, Canada.

Labrou, Y., & Finin, T. (1994). *State of the art and challenges for agent communication languages*. Baltimore, MD: Department of Computer Science and Electrical Engineering, University of Maryland.

Local Programming Associates. (n. d.). *Chimera Agents for WIN-Prolog*. Retrieved from http://www.lpa.co.uk/chi.htm

Muehlen, M., & Rosemann, M. (2000). Workflow-based process monitoring & controlling – Technical & organizational issues. In *Proceedings of the 33rd Hawaii International Conference on Systems Sciences*, Wailea, HI.

Savarimuthu, B. T. R., Purvis, M., & Fleurke, M. (2004). Monitoring and controlling of a multi-agent-based workflow system. In *Proceedings of the Australasian Workshop on Data Mining and Web Intelligence*, Dunedin, New Zealand (pp. 127-132).

Steinfield, C., Jang, C., & Pfaff, B. (1999). Supporting virtual team collaboration: The TeamSCOPE system. In *Proceedings of the International ACM SIGGROUP Conference on Supporting Group Work*, Phoenix, AZ (pp. 81-90).

Tsvetovatyy, M., Gini, M., Mobasher, B., & Wieckowski, Z. (1997). MAGMA: An agent-based virtual marketplace for electronic commerce. *Applied Artificial Intelligence, 11*(6), 501–542. doi:10.1080/088395197118046

Wooldridge, M. (2009). *An introduction to multi-agent systems* (2nd ed.). New York, NY: John Wiley & Sons.

This work was previously published in International Journal of Agent Technologies and Systems, Volume 3, Issue 4, edited by Yu Zhang, pp. 1-18, copyright 2011 by IGI Publishing (an imprint of IGI Global).

Chapter 4
Initial Formulation of an Optimization Method Based on Stigmergic Construction

Aditya C. Velivelli
Ames Laboratory, USA

Kenneth M. Bryden
Ames Laboratory, USA

ABSTRACT

Sign-based stigmergic methods such as the ant colony optimization algorithm have been used to solve network optimization, scheduling problems, and other optimization problems that can be visualized as directed graphs. However, there has been little research focused on the use of optimization methods based on sematectonic stigmergy, such as coordination through collective construction. This paper develops a novel approach where the process of agent-directed stigmergic construction is introduced as a general optimization tool. The development of this new approach involves adopting previous work on stigmergic construction to a virtual space and applying statistical mechanics–based techniques to data produced during the stigmergic construction process. From this a unique procedure for solving optimization problems using a computational procedure that simulates sematectonic stigmergic processes such as stigmergic construction is proposed.

BACKGROUND AND MOTIVATION

Stigmergy is a form of implicit communication through the environment, used for instance by social insects, to perform collective tasks (Theraulaz & Bonabeau, 1999). Wilson (2000) identified two forms of stigmergy: 1) sematectonic

stigmergy and 2) sign- or marker-based stigmergy. Sematectonic stigmergy involves communication through modifications to a physical environment, whereas sign-based stigmergy involves communication via a signaling mechanism. Sematectonic stigmergy can be represented by examples such as the formation of trails (e.g., worn-down grass on frequently used routes), structure building by termites, and wasp nest construction. An example

DOI: 10.4018/978-1-4666-1565-6.ch004

for sign-based stigmergy is the phenomenon of ants laying down pheromones as they search for food. Ants follow pheromone-containing paths with greater probability, and the pheromones accumulate (even as earlier laid pheromones evaporate) as more ants travel on that path. Both forms of stigmergy consist of two classes of stigmergic mechanisms: quantitative and qualitative (Theraulaz & Bonabeau, 1999).

Consider an example of sematectonic stigmergy: termite arch building initially involves a group of termites that pick up mud pellets, inject a pheromone into them and deposit them at random locations. The next group of termites then deposit more mud pellets near and on the already existing pheromone concentrations. The mud heaps grow into columns and the columns tend to grow towards each other as the pheromones on the bottom evaporate. This process is quantitative or continuous stigmergy because the stimulus in the environment does not change; however, the amount of the stimulus can change and result in different responses (or probability of response) to the stimulus.

In contrast to termite arch building, during wasp nest construction the wasps deposit new nest elements on a lattice consisting of existing nest elements and available sites, depending on local observations of the existing nest arrangement. This process can be termed qualitative or discrete stigmergy because the wasps respond to a series of local rules or a discrete set of qualitatively different stimuli that result in different responses.

Several sources have used stigmergic optimization based on either the ant colony optimization algorithm (sign-based stigmergy) or particle swarm optimization techniques to solve control and optimization problems (Abraham, Grosan, & Ramos, 2006). Recent reviews of metaheuristic algorithms or nature-inspired methods have not mentioned optimization techniques based on qualitative sematectonic stigmergic methods (Blum, Aguilera, Roli, & Sampels, 2008; Bianchi, Dorigo, Gambardella, & Gutjahr, 2009).

MODELING STIGMERIC CONSTRUCTION

Assembled structures can emerge from numerous local interactions between the components or agents in a given environment. The motivation behind modeling stigmergy based collective construction is based on observations of paper wasps that build their nests by engaging in reactive, stimulus-response type behaviors. Although they may not have any explicit knowledge about the overall structure of the nest they are building, they can observe the local arrangements of existing nest elements. This observation leads to the insect behavior or response regarding depositing a new nest element. The local patterns that lead the insect to engage in a reactive behavior were termed stigmergic configurations by Theraulaz and Bonabeau (1995), who also performed a computational study of the nest construction of paper wasps. In their study the modeled wasps moved randomly in a three-dimensional lattice and reacted to stigmergic configurations when they were close enough to detect one. Theraulaz and Bonabeau designed the stigmergic configurations or rule sets manually. In a later study by Bonabeau, Guerin, Snyers, Kuntz, and Theraulaz (2000) the rule sets were evolved using a genetic algorithm.

Modeling of collective construction usually involves mobile agents carrying building blocks to the structure under construction and placing them at the appropriate sites. The collective construction process is also identical to self-assembly where the blocks being assembled are themselves the mobile agents (Jones & Matarić, 2003). To extend the construction of simple structures (such as built by paper wasps) to more complex and arbitrarily shaped pre-specified structures using mobile agents that assemble or carry blocks for assembly, the mobile agents are given a finite state machine and decentralized, local agent rules for shape formation. This extension of the functional capacity of the agents has been termed extended stigmergy by Werfel and Nagpal (2006).

Werfel and Nagpal (2006) modeled an environment where square-shaped building-blocks are moved by agents from their random initial positions in the workspace to the construction site (initially defined by a single seed block) whose shape is pre-specified. The square blocks in the incomplete structure form an implicit coordinate system that can be used by the agents for position reference. Werfel and Nagpal discussed four methods for specifying block attachment on a pre-assigned lattice (shape map). In all four methods, the agent moves around the perimeter of the structure under construction to locate a position for block attachment. Due to the use of a shape map, the agent's location is required for judging whether or not a block should be attached to a particular site on the shape map.

In the method called the communicating blocks method, each block can store a shape map of the entire target structure. Once the mobile agent carrying a block reaches the perimeter of the incomplete structure, the mobile agent queries the blocks surrounding a potential attachment site, and those blocks then determine according to their side states (and after possibly communicating with other blocks) whether attachment is possible. If a new block is attached, that block receives the shape map and its own location coordinates from its neighbors and sets its side states according to those of the neighbors. This method was found by Werfel and Nagpal to be the most efficient as it had the smallest total distance traveled by the agents, and it has the ability to fill the most number of locations.

The communicating blocks method was adapted by Koch (2008) to a virtual space with a continuous space environment (for movement of agents until they reach the construction site) where agent movement behavior is dictated by internal forces generated through behaviors corresponding to avoiding collisions, pursuing goals, and picking up blocks (similar to the forces described by Grushin and Reggia, 2006). The virtual engineering software VE-Suite (Huang &

Bryden, 2005; Xiao, Bryden, & McCorkle, 2005) provided the virtual space, as shown in Figures 1 and 2, for implementing the agent study. The construction problem framework is similar to the one set up by Werfel and Nagpal (2006). Building blocks are unit cubes that can be attached to each other on their sides adhering to the desired two-dimensional structure. In Figures 1 and 2, the unattached building blocks are white. One building block is initially positioned to indicate where construction should begin. Mobile agents (grey blocks in Figures 1 and 2) locate blocks, take them to the structure, and follow its perimeter until they find a valid attachment site. To prevent construction interference, unattached blocks are randomly placed a "safe" distance away from the structure. In this construction setting, the building blocks have the ability to store information, perform computations, and communicate with physically attached neighbors. The virtual space allows one to perform statistical mechanics studies on the parameters involved in collective construction.

Werfel and Nagpal's (2006) framework assumed the agents can perform the following tasks:

- Move in any direction and avoid collisions even while holding a block.
- Follow beacons to get to the building site and to block locations.
- Follow the perimeter of the building site and perceive turning a corner.
- Pick up blocks from caches and attach them to the structure.

These assumptions were addressed for the virtual framework by incorporating the integration of collision detection and rigid body dynamics, virtual sensors, and simplistic obstacle avoidance algorithms for the agents.

The boundaries of the construction world consist of a ground plane that the agents and building blocks rest upon and surrounding walls that are used to confine the dimensions of the construction environment. An obstacle avoidance

Figure 1. Construction problem framework implemented using VE-Suite. The virtual construction world consists of mobile agents (grey), building blocks (white), and a block-sized marker to designate the starting point for construction (black).

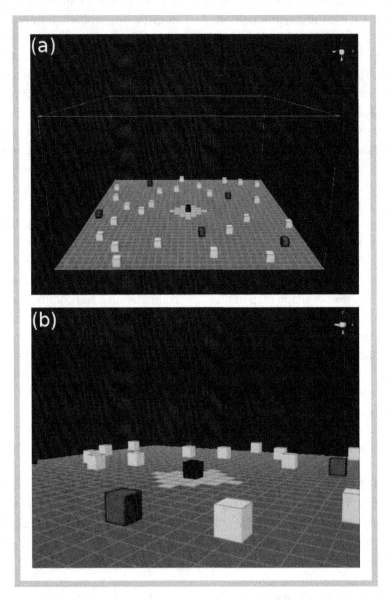

algorithm is implemented to avoid agents hitting the walls. This ensures that the components of the system will occupy a space that is relevant to the construction task at hand. The ground plane and walls represent static models because they are stationary in the environment. Static models are not affected physically by any of the other models in the scene. Therefore, forces are not calculated for these bodies. Building blocks are simple cube-shaped geometries. The building blocks are dynamic models because they are affected by the physical forces in the environment.

The agents are also simple cube-shaped geometries, but, unlike the building blocks, agents contain virtual sensors to gather information in the construction world. They use this information

Figure 2. A predefined structure under construction using the communicating blocks algorithm. Lightly shaded regions show the desired shape of the structure to be built.

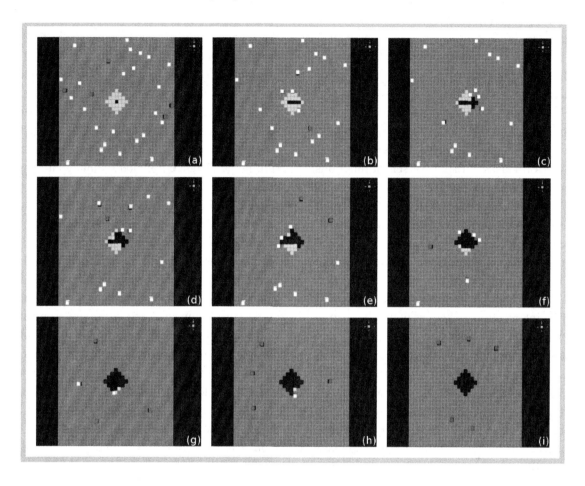

to decide upon their behavior for the construction task. The agents are dynamically represented and have the added ability to move across the ground plane. This movement is simulated in the virtual environment by applying small forces through a physics API.

Environmental information needed to direct mobile agents can be obtained from sensor devices such as cameras, and infrared and ultrasonic sensors. The agents need to find the blocks and the construction site, and simultaneously avoid obstacle collisions. To enable these behaviors,

different types of virtual sensors were created in VE-Suite to collect information. The virtual sensors in VE-Suite collect data for the agents. The virtual space initially incorporates three different types of sensors: ray proximity, sonar, and color detection. The ray proximity sensor returns the distance from the closest contact point of an object along the ray's path. This sensor is meant to emulate the large number of range finders available for robotic experiments. It is implemented in code using a basic ray intersection test with the remaining geometry in the environment. The color detection sensor collects color information in the construction world. To allow the agents to differentiate between blocks that are attached to the structure and blocks that are unattached, the blocks are colored differently depending on their current state of attachment. The color detection sensor can thereby be used to direct an agent towards building blocks and then to the construction site. The sonar sensor detects possible obstacles that the agents may encounter as they perform tasks. A real sonar sensor functions by emitting sounds and waiting for a return echo. By keeping track of the time it takes for a signal to return, a distance can be calculated for each targeted obstacle. A simplified concept of the sonar sensors is implemented in the virtual space by creating a circular pattern of ray intersection tests. If a ray contains multiple intersections, only the first intersection is used, as would be seen in a sonar reading. These readings are then fed into various real-time obstacle avoidance algorithms that calculate a total repulsive force in a direction away from the highest concentration of obstacles. Obstacle avoidance algorithms employ the idea of obstacles conceptually exerting forces on the mobile agents as they approach. This repulsive force is then combined with a target force, representing an agent's goal position, to produce a resultant vector of desired travel for the agent.

Readings are continuously taken from the sonar sensors while an agent is moving. As the agent comes in range of an obstacle, its sonar sensors register a detection event and record the distance information for the reading. In this way, a repulsive vector can be calculated with respect to the agent. This information is then sent to the obstacle avoidance algorithm to be merged with other readings and to process the resultant direction. This allows an agent to actively adjust its path to avoid collisions and does not require an agent to stop while it performs tasks.

SYSTEM STATES BASED ON DISTANCES

Werfel and Nagpal (2006) identified the sum of the distances traveled around the perimeter of an incomplete structure by all the agents throughout the construction process as a parameter that can be used in evaluating the time taken for construction. In this study this parameter (sum of distances) is denoted by D'. Each component of the sum is the distance traveled by an agent after it reaches the structure and travels around the perimeter before finding a valid attachment site for depositing the block. To compute this parameter, Werfel and Nagpal (2006) discretize their problem such that the construction is made to occur in a series of discrete steps, where at the beginning of each step the agents are randomly placed on a circle surrounding the structure site from afar. The agents then follow the original algorithm in moving toward the structure site to deposit blocks. In this re-arranged problem, the agents may already be holding the blocks while on the circle or may have to pick up the blocks before approaching the structure, and at the same time they need to avoid randomly placed obstacles. Once all the agents are done depositing their respective blocks, they instantaneously go back to the circle and position themselves randomly on the circle. This process repeats until the construction approaches completion. Because the construction now occurs in a series of steps, $D' = \sum_T D$ where D is the total distance traveled by all agents during a step in the construction cycle and is summed over all T steps taken to complete the construction in order to obtain the total distance D'.

In the present study, the authors extend the above discussion to the distribution of distance D among the N agents. At each step in the construction cycle, D will be equal to the sum of the individual distances d_i traveled (around the perimeter) by the agents, i.e., $D = \sum_N d_i$, where N

is the total number of agents. The d_i's can be grouped together when they are of the same value. The number of agents constituting each such group will be called the occupation number. All the occupation numbers taken together form a distribution of the total distance D for each step. This can also be interpreted as a sharing of the total distance D for a step among all N agents. The process of stigmeric construction creates an equilibrium distribution of distances as the structure nears completion. In this paper we seek to use this property of stigmeric construction as an optimization tool in state space rather than minimizing the construction time or total distance.

The state of the construction system at each step can be specified by indicating that agent No. 1 has distance d_x, agent No. 2 has distance d_y, agent No. N has distance d_z and so on. The d_i's can thus be used to define system states during the construction process. A certain class of states of the system for any given step in the construction cycle can be indicated by saying that $a_1, a_2, a_3, ..., a_m, ...$ of the N agents are in state 1, 2, 3, . . ., m, . . . respectively. This can be shown in Box 1.

This is meant to say that a_1 number of agents travel distance d_1, a_2 number of agents travel distance d_2 and so on. All system states can be taken into consideration through the classes that are described by all admissible possibilities of the sets of numbers a_m. The following constraints need to be satisfied:

$$\sum a_m = N \text{ and } \sum a_m d_m = D \qquad (1)$$

The number of system states possible from a given distribution of distance D can be given by the different permutations of that distribution:

$$W = \frac{N!}{a_1! \, a_2! \, a_3! \dots a_m! \dots} \qquad (2)$$

The total number of states that are possible (sum of W's from all possible distributions) represents the phase space of the system. The points in the phase space represent the complete spectrum of states through which the system will eventually flow when considered over a long time.

The most probable distribution can be said to be the one that gives W its maximum value. This is because the total number of states possible (sum of W's from all possible distributions) would be exhausted by the sum of those W's corresponding to distributions (number sets a_m) that do not deviate appreciably from the distribution that gives W its maximum value. Various sources for statistical mechanics (e.g., Sommerfeld, 1956) have computed the form of the number sets for which W takes its maximum value as follows:

$$a_m = a_0 \exp\left(-\mu \times d_m\right) \text{ given that } d_0 = 0 \qquad (3)$$

i.e., the population of agents at each distance level is inversely proportional to the exponential of that level's distance value. This would mean that the form of the distributions for the lower distance levels would look like the one shown in Figure 3. Figure 4 shows the two distributions of a total distance $20 \times L$ (where L is the length of a single block) among 20 agents. Increasing the number of agents and size of the structure (and thereby

Box 1.

State No.	1,	2,	3,	...,	m,	...
Distance Around Perimeter	d_1	d_2	d_3	...,	$d_{m'}$	...
Occupation Number	a_1	a_3	a_2	...,	$a_{m'}$	...

Figure 3. Population of distance levels

total distance traveled) would show a smoother exponential distribution as given by Eq. 3 and shown in Figure 3.

Since all agents are similar, the systems states that are specified by the permutations of the various distributions are all equally probable or likely to occur. Therefore, during any construction step, given the total number of possible system states Ω, the probability of a given state ν of the system is $P_\nu = 1/\Omega$. The assembly of all these states (for a given construction step) can be termed a microcanonical ensemble. A microcanonical ensemble is the assembly of all states with fixed total energy E, and a fixed size (Chandler, 1987). In this study, the total energy is analogous to the total distance D for a step, and the size is analogous to the number of agents and the size of the structure.

Boltzmann's principle interprets entropy as a measure of the number of possible microscopic states of a system in equilibrium (Sommerfeld, 1956). In the problem under discussion, this interpretation can be adapted to the number of system states possible for each step in the construction cycle, Ω (sum of all W's or just the maximum W) (Chandler, 1987).

$$S = k \log(\Omega) \tag{4}$$

Using thermodynamics relations, the temperature of the system at a given step in the construction cycle could be described through

$$(\partial S/\partial D)_{N,V} = 1/T \tag{5}$$

and inverse temperature as

$$\beta = (kT)^{-1} = (\partial \log \Omega/\partial D)_{N,V} \tag{6}$$

Here the total distance for a step, D, is analogous to energy E in the traditional definition (Chandler, 1987). N is the total number of agents, and V represents the size of the structure under construction.

Earlier, the microcanonical ensemble was mentioned. Here we consider a canonical ensemble, which is the assembly of all microstates with a fixed size, where energy (or distance in this study) can fluctuate (Chandler, 1987), and the system is kept at equilibrium by being in contact with a heat bath at given temperature T. A system that can be represented by a canonical ensemble is considered a subsystem of one for which the microcanonical is applicable. In the collective construction case, we can consider any agent from the N agents (microcanonical ensemble) to be a system (or subsystem) of its own in equilibrium with the rest of the systems (or agents), which can be termed a bath, denoted as B. Therefore, the canonical ensemble can be applied here. Each agent will have to choose from the same set of possible states or distances $d_1, d_2, d_3, \ldots$ available, and the distance d_ν of the agent (or system) under consideration will fluctuate among those states through contact with the bath. The combined distance of the agents populating the bath D_B is much larger than the distance d_ν of the agent under consideration. The sum $D_B + d_\nu$ is a constant for a given step because it is equal to the total distance D for that step. Considering any given system (agent) in one definite

Figure 4. Two distributions of a total distance 20 × L among 20 agents

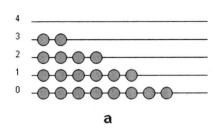

a

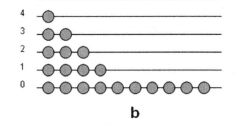

b

state ν, the number of states accessible to the system plus the bath is $\Omega(D_B) = \Omega(D - d_\nu)$. Therefore, the probability for observing the agent in state ν obeys

$$P_\nu \propto \Omega(D - d_\nu) = \exp\left[\log \Omega(D - d_\nu)\right] \qquad (7)$$

Because $d_\nu << D$, the logarithmic term in the above expression, $\log \Omega(D - d_\nu)$, can be expanded using the Taylor series:

$$\log \Omega(D - d_\nu) = \log \Omega(D) - d_\nu(d\log\Omega/dD) + \dots \qquad (8)$$

Noting Eq. 6, the following is obtained:

$$P_\nu \propto \exp(-\beta d_\nu) \qquad (9)$$

In essence, Eq. 6 is a relation showing that the probability of an agent traveling a given distance is proportional to the inverse exponential of that distance level over the system temperature for that particular step.

Each agent will have its own d_ν that exists independently of every other d_ν in D because all agents are moving simultaneously to find attachment sites. Therefore, the probabilities will also exist independently, which means the combined probability is a product of the individual probabilities.

$$P(D) \propto \exp(-\beta d_1) \times \exp(-\beta d_2) \times \dots \times \exp(-\beta d_N) \qquad (10)$$

Therefore,

$$P(D) \propto \exp(-\beta(d_1 + d_2 + \dots + d_N)) = \exp(-D/kT) \qquad (11)$$

Therefore, the probability of finding a given configuration, C_i, of agent distances at the end of a step is proportional to the inverse exponential relation of the total distance (of the configuration) divided by the system temperature for that step.

$$P(D(C_i)) \propto \exp(-D(C_i)/kT) \qquad (12)$$

Analogy to Simulated Annealing

A brief introduction to simulated annealing is given here before comparing it with stigmergic construction. The goal of simulated annealing (van Laarhoven, & Aerts, 1987) like most other optimization methods is to minimize a cost function, $F(\Phi)$, where the minimum of $F(\Phi)$ corresponds to the desired design outcome. The vector Φ specifies the design configuration, i.e., values of the design parameters in the problem.

The simulated annealing approach starts by selecting an initial guess Φ^0 and applying the Metropolis algorithm to it as follows:

- Generate a new Φ vector by randomly perturbing elements of Φ^k, k being the iteration number.

- If the difference in cost function $\Delta C^k = F\left(\Phi^{k'}\right) - F\left(\Phi^k\right)$ is negative, the cost function is lower for the new vector ($\Phi^{k'}$) and therefore is selected for the next iteration.

- If $\Delta C^k > 0$, then the new vector is accepted only when a random number $R \in (0,1) < \exp\left(-\Delta C^k / T\right)$, i.e., $\Phi^{k+1} = \Phi^{k'}$, otherwise the original solution is retained ($\Phi^{k+1} = \Phi^k$). T is the annealing temperature, which is a heuristic search parameter.

The above process is repeated for a specified number of iterations while keeping the same annealing temperature, until it results in configurations that have a Boltzmann probability distribution. That is, the probability of a given configuration is given by

$$P\{\text{configuration} = i\} = \frac{1}{Q(T)} \cdot \exp\left(-\frac{F\left(\Phi^i\right)}{T}\right) \tag{13}$$

where $Q(T)$ is a normalization constant.

The above process (Metropolis algorithm) is repeated at successively lower temperatures T; that is, the annealing temperature is lowered in steps, until successive cost function evaluations fall within a tolerance of the best solution found or until a specified total number of steps. This final 'frozen' configuration is taken as the solution at hand.

Implementing Stigmergic Construction as an Optimization Tool

Just as the probability distribution of the configurations in the simulated annealing method approaches the Boltzmann distribution after repeated iterations of the Metropolis algorithm at a given annealing temperature, the probability distributions of the configurations of agent distances at the end of a step in the stigmergic construction process also approaches the Boltzmann distribution (Eq. 12). (Recall that the construction occurs in a series of discrete steps.) The distance configuration (at the end of a construction step) is chosen through the random motion of agents involved in collective construction using basic sets of rules with no explicit communication among the agents. This distance configuration is chosen from a phase space of possible solutions; i.e., possible distance configurations that can complete that particular step. The agents can also avoid obstacles and pick up randomly placed blocks before heading to the construction site during each step. The chosen distance configuration (and thereby the total distance for the given step) can be viewed as optimal because it takes the system toward the final construction goal.

The simulated annealing approach involves reducing the temperature for each new step that consists of multiple iterations of the Metropolis algorithm. In contrast, as noted by Eq. 6, the temperature of the stigmergic construction system at each step decreases because the change in the total number of possible states (Ω) increases relative to the change in the total distance (D) traveled around the perimeter. Therefore, as the construction progresses, with each construction step the temperature decreases due to the inherent nature of the process and this does not require intra-step iterations unlike simulated annealing.

To implement stigmergic construction as an optimization tool, one can generate an initial vector (Φ) that specifies the initial guesses for all the design parameters, and randomly perturb it according to

$$\Phi^{k+1} = \Phi^k + R^k \delta \Phi^k \tag{14}$$

where the k iteration corresponds to the construction step k, $\delta \Phi$ is a vector of neighborhood size that controls the random disturbance of Φ, and R is a vector of random numbers of the same dimension as Φ. R is chosen through a correlation with the distance configuration vector (C_i). Although the distance configuration vector is made up of integer distance levels, it can be mapped into values between 0 and 1 to obtain R. The number of agents undertaking collective construction has to be equal or greater than the number of design parameters in the optimization problem. At the end of each construction step, the design configuration vector is updated according to Eq. 14, where R, the vector of random numbers corresponds to the distance configuration vector for that particular construction step. This drives the design configuration vector towards a Boltzmann distribution at the end of a given step (Eq. 14) because the distance configuration vector possesses a Boltzmann distribution at the end of each construction step. In contrast to this, within the simulated annealing algorithm a Boltzmann distribution of the design configuration vector is obtained after multiple iterations of the Metropolis algorithm. Consequently, if the shape undergoing stigmergic construction could be mapped to the desired optimization goal (such as locations of radiant heaters that bring about a desired temperature distribution in a radiant enclosure), this methodology could provide a more efficient tool for design optimization.

Towards the end of the construction process (i.e., completion of all construction steps), the design configuration vector will be optimal because it is obtained through a process that results in Boltzmann distributions after each step while advancing toward the goal of construction of the given shape. (This can be correlated with the minimum of the cost function of the optimization problem.) The temperature (Eq. 6) of the construction system decreases with each construction step, and the entropy (Eq. 4) of the system increases with each construction step until maximum entropy is reached toward the end of the construction, thus implying a state of equilibrium is reached.

The convergence toward an optimal solution for the design configuration vector also depends on the total number of construction steps taken for completing the shape. The total number of construction steps is equal to the total number of blocks (size of the shape) divided by the total number of agents (size of the design configuration vector). Because the design configuration vector size is fixed by the optimization problem, increasing the number of blocks or the size of the shape results in a greater number of iterations or construction steps to gradually evolve the design configuration vector toward the optimal solution.

Experiments and Results

Experiments were run in a virtual space to obtain the distance configuration vectors for three different cases featuring different numbers of agents constructing a given structure whose size corresponded to the total number of blocks. The experimental results in Tables 1, 2, and 3 record the evolution of the distribution of distances among the agents as the construction proceeded toward completion in a series of discrete steps. The purpose of the experiments was to validate the theory described earlier in the section titled "System States Based on Distances." The virtual space consisted of a ground plane measuring 191 × 191 with surrounding walls that were the same dimension in height. The walls were detectable by the agents' ray proximity and sonar sensors as would be the case in a real environment. Agents and blocks were both unit cubes measuring 1 × 1 × 1.

The desired shape being built was stored as an occupancy matrix—a Boolean map—and can be seen in Figures 1 and 2. The occupancy matrix can be any shape, but the shape in this study was chosen for its symmetry with respect to the environment. In this way, the space around the structure was consistent, and the effects on an agent's obstacle avoidance system were minimized. To complete the structure, 264 spaces needed to be occupied. An initial block was placed at 0, 0, the center of the ground plane, as a marker to designate the starting point for construction. The start block was given the occupancy matrix, and its location and side states were updated accordingly. The 263 blocks left to complete the structure and the agents were randomly placed in the environment a "safe" distance away from the structure so as to not interfere with construction. Finally, the range was set for the agents' sensors to limit what they could perceive in the environment.

During the building phase, the blocks were scattered randomly throughout the grid and therefore acted as obstacles. Tables 1, 2, and 3 show the results for simulations where the number of agents was 66, 44, and 33, with the total number of blocks at 264 and a total grid size of 191×191. The distance level d is the distance traveled by an agent around the perimeter (represented by d_m in Eq. 1). It is zero when the agent is able to deposit a block (according to the rules) at the structure as soon as it approaches it. The occupation number O.N. (represented by a_m in Eq. 1) for each distance level d represents the number of agents that traveled the distance d for the given construction step (represented by Step in the tables).

The results show that during the earlier construction steps (steps 1 and 2) the lower distance levels were heavily populated (high occupation numbers). This observation is in agreement with the earlier discussion in the section "System States Based on Distances" and with Figures 3 and 4. For instance, as shown in Table 1, which includes a total of 66 agents, the first construction step featured a distance configuration vector where 40 agents shared the distance level of zero, and 14 agents shared the distance level of one (for traveling a distance equal to the length of one block). With the later construction steps, as equilibrium

was approached (increasing entropy according to Eq. 6), the agents were evenly distributed among all distance levels, this being a consequence of increasing entropy or decreasing temperature of the construction system (Eq. 12). For instance, as shown in Table 3, towards the completion of construction (steps 7 and 8) most agents possessed unique distance levels, or in other words there was only one agent in most of the distance levels. A few of the distance levels contain 2 or 3 agents, which as a consequence of the construction algorithm, were stochastically assigned those distance levels for sharing.

For implementing Eq. 14, each component of the design configuration vector Φ (Eq. 14) was randomly assigned one of the construction agents at the beginning of the simulation. The vector R in Eq. 14 was computed through a mapping with the distances d traveled by the agents during the construction step k.

CONCLUSION

The agents involved in the process of collective construction interact with each other through the structure under construction and make decisions based on local conditions, thereby giving the process a stigmergic character. This paper describes an initial formulation of a method that uses the process of qualitative sematectonic stigmergy (stigmergic construction) to solve a general optimization problem. Experimental results validate the theory that the lower distance levels are heavily populated with agents during earlier construction steps and as the construction approaches completion (equilibrium), the distance levels are more evenly populated with agents. The stigmeric construction procedure involves computing the optimal design configuration vector (optimization problem parameters) by evolving the distribution of distances towards the maximum entropy or equilibrium condition. The next challenge is to

Table 1. 66 agents, d is the distance level. O.N. is the occupation number, and STEP is the construction step

STEP 1		STEP 2		STEP 3		STEP 4	
d	O.N.	d	O.N.	d	O.N.	d	O.N.
0	40	0	9	0	1	7	1
1	14	1	8	2	4	8	2
2	7	2	8	3	1	9	1
3	4	3	9	4	1	10	1
4	1	4	5	5	2	12	1
		5	4	6	1	14	2
		6	3	7	6	19	1
		7	4	8	4	20	1
		8	1	9	1	21	1
		9	2	10	2	24	2
		10	3	11	2	25	1
		11	2	12	3	26	1
		12	1	13	1	27	3
		13	1	14	2	28	1
		15	1	15	2	31	3
		17	1	16	3	33	3
		18	1	17	1	34	2
		19	1	19	3	35	1
		20	1	20	1	37	1
		25	1	21	1	38	2
				22	3	39	2
				24	3	40	1
				25	4	41	1
				26	2	42	1
				27	3	44	1
				28	1	46	1
				29	1	48	2
				30	1	49	2
				31	1	50	2
				32	2	51	2
				34	1	52	2
				37	1	53	1
				39	1	57	1
						58	1
						59	1
						60	1
						67	1
						70	1

continued on following page

Table 1. continued

						78	1
						85	1
						87	1
						90	1
						98	1
						111	1
						113	1
						115	2
						117	1
						120	1

map a practical optimization problem into the space of the stigmergic construction problem.

The advantages of an optimization method based on stigmergic construction are as follows:

- Unlike simulated annealing, which involves repeated iterations (applying the Metropolis algorithm) at every step to arrive at the desired Boltzmann configuration, the stigmergic construction method arrives at the desired Boltzmann configuration in a stepwise manner without intra-step iterations.
- Stigmergic construction is highly parallel when compared to other stigmergic optimization methods including simulated annealing. This is because there is no requirement for communication between the agents and because the agents make their decisions based on the local character of the structure they are constructing.

One drawback of the current method is the storage of the shape map or occupancy matrix, which requires a shared memory parallel computer because the blocks in the structure communicate information among their neighbors to update their states as the structure is constructed. However, the stigmergic construction algorithm can be updated to allow implementation on a distributed memory machine.

Future work includes applying the stigmergic construction based optimization algorithm to practical optimization problems and optimal control problems. Formulating theory for mapping optimization problem cost functions to geometrical shapes will be the next research step to be undertaken. As methodologies for these mappings are created and understood, it is hoped that it will be possible to optimize complex systems such as power plants through qualitative sematectonic stigmergic methods.

ACKNOWLEDGMENT

This research was supported by the US Department of Energy – Fossil Energy Program under Contract No. DE-AC02-07CH11358 through the Ames Laboratory.

Table 2. 44 agents, d is the distance level. O.N. is the occupation number, and STEP is the construction step

STEP 1		STEP 2		STEP 3	
d	O.N.	*d*	O.N.	*d*	O.N.
0	24	0	7	1	2
1	6	1	2	2	3
2	6	2	3	3	4
3	5	3	10	4	5
4	2	4	6	5	5
5	1	5	9	6	3
		6	2	7	2
		7	2	8	2
		8	1	9	6
		9	1	10	3
		11	1	11	3
				12	2
				13	1
				14	1
				15	1
				16	1
STEP 4		STEP 5		STEP 6	
d	O.N.	*d*	O.N.	*d*	O.N.
4	1	10	2	11	1
6	1	12	2	13	1
7	1	13	1	18	1
8	2	14	1	19	1
9	5	15	1	22	1
10	1	16	3	23	2
11	2	17	1	24	1
12	4	18	3	25	1
13	2	19	1	26	1
15	2	20	1	27	3
16	3	21	3	28	1
17	4	22	2	32	2
18	1	23	1	33	1
19	2	24	3	35	1
21	1	26	2	36	1
22	1	27	1	38	1
23	1	29	3	39	1
24	1	30	1	40	3
25	3	31	2	41	2

continued on following page

Table 2. continued

26	2	32	2	42	1
30	1	36	2	46	1
31	1	43	1	48	1
32	1	44	1	49	2
41	1	46	1	50	3
		54	1	52	1
		62	1	54	1
		68	1	57	2
				63	3
				83	1
				84	1
				142	1

Table 3. 33 agents, d is the distance level. O.N. is the occupation number, and STEP is the construction step

STEP 1		STEP 2		STEP 3		STEP 4	
d	O.N.	d	O.N.	d	O.N.	d	O.N.
0	17	0	3	4	1	6	2
1	3	1	2	5	8	7	1
2	3	2	2	6	3	8	1
3	2	3	5	7	1	10	1
4	5	4	6	8	1	11	5
5	1	5	3	9	3	12	2
8	2	6	2	10	1	13	2
		7	1	11	3	14	1
		8	1	12	3	15	2
		9	1	14	1	16	1
		10	2	15	3	17	3
		11	1	18	1	18	2
		12	1	19	1	19	1
		14	1	22	2	21	1
		16	1	25	1	22	2
		17	1			23	2
						27	2
						29	1
						36	1

continued on following page

Table 3. continued

STEP 5		STEP 6		STEP 7		STEP 8	
d	O.N.	d	O.N.	d	O.N.	d	O.N.
7	1	18	1	24	1	40	1
11	1	20	1	29	2	49	1
12	2	22	1	34	1	53	1
16	1	23	2	35	1	55	1
17	4	24	1	40	3	61	1
18	2	25	1	42	1	64	1
20	3	26	2	43	1	70	1
21	3	27	1	44	1	74	1
24	2	29	2	48	1	75	1
26	1	30	3	50	2	76	1
30	1	32	1	51	2	78	1
31	4	34	1	53	2	88	1
32	1	35	2	56	2	89	1
33	2	39	1	59	1	90	1
34	1	40	2	63	1	92	1
38	1	41	2	64	1	94	1
39	1	42	2	67	1	96	1
42	1	43	1	68	1	100	1
45	1	46	1	70	1	102	2
		48	1	77	1	104	2
		50	1	79	1	110	1
		52	1	82	2	111	1
		57	1	83	1	112	1
		78	1	97	1	113	1
				118	1	119	2
						121	1
						132	1
						136	1
						138	1
						141	1

REFERENCES

Abraham, A., Grosan, C., & Ramos, V. (Eds.). (2006). *Stigmergic optimization. Studies in computational intelligence* (*Vol. 31*). Heidelberg, Germany: Springer-Verlag.

Bianchi, L., Dorigo, M., Gambardella, L. M., & Gutjahr, W. J. (2009). A survey on metaheuristics for stochastic combinatorial optimization. *Natural Computing, 8*, 239–287. doi:10.1007/s11047-008-9098-4

Blum, C., Aguilera, M. J. B., Roli, A., & Sampels, M. (Eds.). (2008). *Hybrid metaheuristics: An emerging approach to optimization. Studies in computational intelligence* (*Vol. 114*). Heidelberg, Germany: Springer-Verlag.

Bonabeau, E., Guérin, S., Snyers, D., Kuntz, P., & Theraulaz, G. (2000). Three-dimensional architectures grown by simple 'stigmergic' agents. *Bio Systems, 56*, 13–32. doi:10.1016/S0303-2647(00)00067-8

Chandler, D. (1987). *Introduction to modern statistical mechanics*. New York, NY: Oxford University Press.

Grushin, A., & Reggia, J. A. (2006). Stigmergic self-assembly of prespecified artificial structures in a constrained and continuous environment. *Integrated Computer-Aided Engineering, 13*, 289–312.

Huang, G., & Bryden, K. M. (2005). Introducing virtual engineering technology into interactive design process with high-fidelity models. In *Proceedings of the Winter Simulation Conference*, Orlando, FL (pp. 1958-1967).

Jones, C., & Matarić, M. (2003). From local to global behavior in intelligent self-assembly. In *Proceedings of the IEEE International Conference on Robotics and Automation*, Taipei, Taiwan (pp. 721-726).

Koch, J. B. (2008). *Autonomous construction agents: An investigation framework for large sensor network self-management* (Master's thesis). Available from ProQuest Dissertations and Theses database (UMI No. 1461866)

Sommerfeld, A. (1956). *Thermodynamics and statistical mechanics*. New York, NY: Academic Press.

Theraulaz, G., & Bonabeau, E. (1995). Coordination in distributed building. *Science, 269*, 686–689. doi:10.1126/science.269.5224.686

Theraulaz, G., & Bonabeau, E. (1999). A brief history of stigmergy. *Artificial Life, 5*, 97–116. doi:10.1162/106454699568700

van Laarhoven, P. J. M., & Aarts, E. H. L. (1987). *Simulated annealing: Theory and applications*. Dordrecht, The Netherlands: Reidel.

Werfel, J., & Nagpal, R. (2006). Extended stigmergy in collective construction. *IEEE Intelligent Systems, 21*, 20–28. doi:10.1109/MIS.2006.25

Wilson, E. O. (2000). *Sociobiology: The new synthesis*. Cambridge, MA: Harvard University Press.

Xiao, A., Bryden, K. M., & McCorkle, D. S. (2005). VE-suite: A software framework for design-analysis integration during product realization. In *Proceedings of the ASME International Design Engineering Technical Conferences and Computers and Information in Engineering Conference: Vol. 3. 25th Computers and Information in Engineering Conference, Parts A and B*, Long Beach, CA (pp. 859-867).

This work was previously published in International Journal of Agent Technologies and Systems, Volume 3, Issue 4, edited by Yu Zhang, pp. 19-36, copyright 2011 by IGI Publishing (an imprint of IGI Global).

Section 3
Social Simulation

Chapter 5
Meta-Monitoring Using an Adaptive Agent-Based System to Support Dependent People in Place

Nicolas Singer
University of Toulouse, France

Sylvie Trouilhet
University of Toulouse, France

Ali Rammal
University of Toulouse, France

ABSTRACT

In this paper, the authors propose software architecture to monitor elderly or dependent people in their own house. Many studies have been done on hardware aspects resulting in operational products, but there is a lack of adaptive algorithms to handle all the data generated by these products due to data being distributed and heterogeneous in a large scale environment. The authors propose a multi-agent classification method to collect and to aggregate data about activity, movements, and physiological information of the monitored people. Data generated at this local level are communicated and adjusted between agents to obtain a set of patterns. This data is dynamic; the system has to store the built patterns and has to create new patterns when new data is available. Therefore, the system is adaptive and can be spread on a large scale. Generated data is used at a local level, for example to raise an alert, but also to evaluate global risks. This paper presents specification choices and the massively multi-agent architecture that was developed; an example with a sample of ten dependant people gives an illustration.

DOI: 10.4018/978-1-4666-1565-6.ch005

INTRODUCTION

In the year 2020, more than 20% of the industrial countries population will be over 65 (Mc Morrow, 2004) (Figure 1). This leads to organizational and financial problems for the healthcare systems. To reduce costs, and to improve their welfare, home-monitoring systems can bring solutions to help elderly people staying at home.

Our project takes place in this context. It aims to help healthcare professionals by increasing the number of elderly people looked after in their home with an adaptive and non-intrusive remote assistance. Our approach tackles the home monitoring issue in a collective and cooperative way. It is based on a study of several state-of-the-art home care systems, and differs from them in that it is centred on groups instead on individuals.

We collect individual monitoring with the aim of detecting global behaviour patterns. In this article, we focus on how communities emerge from a multi-agent classification process. In such context, a multi-agent architecture is suitable because of the distribution of input data and the need for scalability: adding or removing sensors, without impacting the system's functioning.

Patterns collected at a micro level are used to estimate the state of elderly people, to link them to their community at a macro level, to try to forecast the evolution of their activity and also to evaluate global risks (Figure 2).

This paper is divided into three sections. First, we present many home-monitoring systems and show how our system is different. Secondly, the multi-agent classification method used in our system is described. We tested this method with a small group of elderly. This experimentation is described in the last section. We also give the first results and we highlight the future developments.

HOME-MONITORING SYSTEMS AND MULTI-AGENT APPROACH

Classical Systems

According to Mark Weiser (1991), "the most profound technologies are those that disappear. They weave themselves into the fabric of everyday life until they are indistinguishable from it". Home monitoring systems apply this concept of ubiquitous computing for making correct decision based on obtaining the right information at the

Figure 1. Population ages 65 and over (% of the total population)

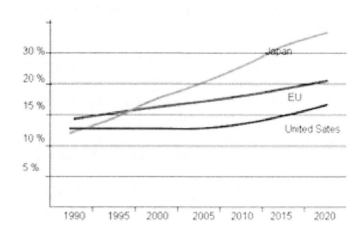

Figure 2. Risk detection and alert generation

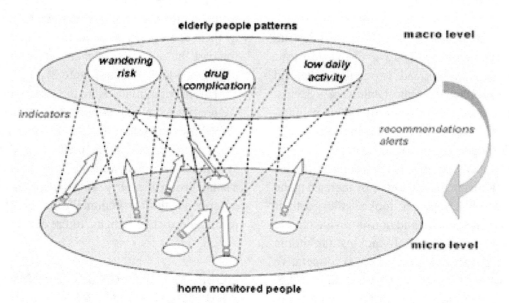

right time. These systems aim to monitor the status of patients allowing pervasive care. They use a collection of sensors to analyze sensor's signals in order to recognise problems and to generate appropriate alarms.

One of the first is the PROSAFE project which attempts to automatically identify the daily activities of a monitored person (Chan, Campo, & Estève, 2003). The processing of collected data is carried out on doctor's request with an adapted interface. The final operational objective is to detect any abnormal behaviour such as a fall, a runaway or an accident. The research objective is to gather characteristic data about the nightly or daily activities of the patient. More precisely, the system can describe events that take place during monitoring time (time spent in bed or in the toilets, entering or leaving the bedroom, moving inside the home), build a database with all abnormal situations detected, and finally build statistics about past activities. At the hardware level, the system configuration uses a ground network (a mobile version is also usable). Currently acquisition and data processing are local and monitoring is both local and distant. One of the main features of this project is to be based on real time analysis of data.

This work has inspired more recent projects. This is the case of the GERHOME project (2005), led by two French research centres. This project intends to create a smart home for weak people. It combines data provided by video cameras with data provided by environmental sensors attached to house furnishings (Zouba, Bremond, & Thonnat, 2010). This objective can also be found in the European project SOPRANO (2010) for service-oriented programmable environment for older Europeans (Virone & Sixsmith, 2008). Let's also talk of the European OLDES project (2010), which tackles the problem of the elderly people access to the new technologies. It tries to create low cost hardware with very easy-to-use interfaces. An international selection of smart home projects is given in Chan, Estève, Escriba, and Campo (2008).

Multi-Agent Systems

Because of the strong distribution of the data and the dynamicity of the environment, some systems have chosen a multi-agent architecture. Each agent can tackle a given task; then agents communicate each other to build a global response.

Let's talk about the e-Vital project (Sakka, Prentza, Lamprinos, Leondaridis, & Koutsouris, 2004) (Cost-Effective Health Services for Interactive Continuous Monitoring of Vital Signs Parameters). It is a modular and ambulatory telemedicine platform. Its objective is to increase patient's feeling of safety concerning their health. Patients and care-givers feed a central database with some measuring equipment. The developed device allows staff to take measurements and data collected to be sent to the resident doctor. This doctor can remotely diagnose whether there is a problem that needs them to visit or that requires the resident to receive hospital treatment. By way of a personal digital assistant (PDA), the e-Vital server connects monitoring devices produced by several manufacturers. The server is a multi agent system where each agent focuses on a specific task related to the medical stored data. For example, an alert manager is specialized for the raising of alert messages, a profile manager for access management and a schedule manager for healthcare scheduling. The e-Vital project is mainly hardware and tries to solve the interoperability problems between non compatible devices. It focuses on communication protocols and on the central database format. These objectives (care protocol, devices interoperability) are different from ours but the approach is similar: e-Vital is an open system with several interconnected modules, one of which being a multi-agent system.

The AILISA project (Intelligent Apartments for effective longevity) is an experimental platform to evaluate remote care and assistive technologies in gerontology (Noury, 2005). This ambitious project regroups specialists of smart homes, networks and computing, electronics, and signal processing. More precisely, the project sets up a monitoring platform composed of a home equipped with a set of sensors and health devices. This equipment is completed by a smart shirt with several sensors and electronics embedded in the textile to detect falls and by a smart assistant robot for ambulation to secure the displacements and assist the person during transfers.

Geriatric Ambient Intelligence (GerAmI) is an intelligent supervision system that provides up-to-date patient data (Corchado, Bajo, & Ajith, 2008). Its main aim is to support elderly and Alzheimer's patients in all aspects of daily life, predicting potential hazardous situations and delivering physical and cognitive support. The system combines simple tasks like the verification of the location of patients with complex tasks like the creation and supervision of a daily planning for a nurse.

Others multi-agent monitoring systems are also relevant. Aingeru, by using semantic web and agent technologies implemented with JADE, provides an active monitoring: it can monitor vital signs and generates an alarm when necessary. It is technically based on the use of PDAs and wireless communication (Tablado, Illarramendi, Bagüés, Bermúdez, & Goñi, 2004).

The K4care and SAPHIRE systems are more recent projects in the field of Multi-Agent systems for e-health. In the home care system K4care (2006), intelligent agents are implemented to edit, adapt, and merge ontologies, and build formal intervention plans. These agents constitute a multi-agent system that provides e-services to care-givers, patients and citizens. Those services are delivered through the Internet and the mobile telephony. The SAPHIRE project provides a Multi-Agent system for the monitoring of chronic diseases both at hospital and in home environments based on a semantic infrastructure. The system is based clinical guidelines and the case of disparate care providers with heterogeneous information systems (Laleci, Dogac, Olduz, Tasyurt, Yuksel, & Okcan, 2008).

The main difference between these systems and ours resides in the application level: when our system is a group-centred system, the others are patient-centred systems; they survey only one person; thus, there is a duplication for each individual looked after. None of these systems collects individual monitoring for merging global behaviour patterns (Rammal, Trouilhet, Singer, & Pécatte, 2008). Nevertheless, patterns of monitored people could be used to estimate the status of someone in relation to their community or to integrate new comings.

To collect numerous individual patterns and build collective one, our system must be able to handle complex data. We can't rely on a centralized algorithm because data is heavily distributed, not always available and often partial. First, we can't imagine a single system to monitor every person in his home. Second, each person will be equipped with his own set of apparatus, leading to heterogeneous data. Classical algorithms are inadequate in such a context and only approximate, fault tolerant and flexible solutions can be proposed.

We propose a multi-agent system able to generalize, which builds a classification of monitored people. An agent watches over one or more indicators of a group of people. An indicator is data about daily activities, positions and physiological information. In a first step, the agent applies a local classification method and obtains an incomplete patterns' partition. Next, the partial partitions are compared each other in order to build a complete classification. We conceived an open system: new people or/and new indicators bring in new agents or/and new patterns.

ARCHITECTURE AND COOPERATION PROTOCOL

Multi-Agent Classification

Figure 3 presents our agent-based architecture for distributed classification. This architecture requires a pre-treatment of input data before starting the classification. Indeed, this phase depends on the application domain. It is achieved in using a "distributor" agent and involves several steps:

- each classification agent selects the subset of data to classify among the data available;
- each classification agent chooses the most suitable classification algorithm;
- each classification agent computes the most adequate settings to handle its data set (normalization and weight of attributes).

Let $O_1, \ldots, O_n$ be objects to classify, each object is described by p numerical attributes $X_1, \ldots, X_p$, so each object O_i is represented by a vector $(x_1^i, \ldots, x_j^i, \ldots, x_p^i)$ where x_j^i is the value of attribute number j of O_i.

x_j^i can be normalized by two ways:

Normalization between [0;1]:

$$\overline{x}_j^i = \frac{x_j^i - x_j^{min}}{x_j^{max} - x_j^{min}}$$

where x_j^{min} (resp. x_j^{max}) is the minimum value (resp. maximum value) of attribute O_x.

Linear normalization:

$$\overline{x}_j^{\,i} = \frac{x_j^i - x_j}{\sigma_j}$$

where x_j^i is the average value of attribute X_j, and σ_j is the standard deviation of attribute X_j:

$$\sigma_j = \sqrt{\frac{1}{n} \sum_{i=1}^{n} (x_j^i - x_j)^2}$$

The attribute weighting phase consists in finding the adequate weight vector such as:

$$W = \left(w_1, \ldots, w_p \right) and \sum_{j=1}^{p} w_j = 1.$$

Let A_1, …, A_k be classification agents of the system. After the phase of pre-treatment each agent has its own subset of normalized and weighted data to classify. In the first step of the classification process (called the local classification) each agent builds its clusters by applying the classification algorithm chosen during the pre-treatment phase (ISODATA algorithm for example). Each cluster is characterized by a mid-vector that will be used to calculate the distance between classes in the generalization phase of the classification. After the local classification phase, agents look for other suitable agents to form groups and consolidate their results. Indeed, this phase is important because agents cannot work all together. For example if two agents work on a totally distinct set of attributes, they cannot combine their results.

To form groups, agents used the weights of their attributes, because they represent the importance of these attributes according to the application domain. If two agents A_i and A_j have the sum of the weights of their common attributes (S_c^{ij}) greater than the sum of the weights of their non-common attributes (S_{nc}^{ij}), then these two agents should be in the same group. The algorithm of acquaintances group constitution is as seen Algorithm 1.

Each group of agents tries to match the different classes obtained during the local classification phase. This correspondence is made by calculating the distances between different classes. We chose the weighted Euclidean distance to make this calculation based on common attributes.

Let A and A' be two agents in the same group, $\{X^{AA'}\}$ the set of common attributes, C a resulting class from A, with mid-vector $\{x^1,...,x^q\}$, C' a resulting class from A', with mid-vector $\{x^1,...,x^r\}$, and w_j the weight of attribute X_j.

The weighted Euclidean distance between C and C' is given by:

$$d_w\left(C, C'\right) = \sqrt{\sum_{X_j \in X^{AA'}} w_j (x^j - x^{'j})^2}$$

Each agent A_i calculates the distance between its own classes and those of other agents of its group; then each class of A_i knows its corresponding classes in other agents.

The correspondence between classes can be used for two purposes as requested by the user: to merge the closest classes or to infer the affiliation class of an object, already classified by A_i, among the classes of A_j without the need to re-applying the classification algorithm of the agent A_j.

Therefore each group of agents forms its own classification. The advantage of this method is that it offers several classifications that can be interpreted by several ways, depending on the attributes used by each agent.

Algorithm 1.

```
For each agent A_i {A_1, …, A_k} Do
        Create a new group G_i
        Add A_i to G_i
        For each agent A_j {A_1, …, A_k} with i ≠ j Do
                If  Then
                        Add A_j to G_i
                EndIf
        EndFor
        Add G_i to the set of groups
EndFor
```

Figure 3. Agent-based architecture

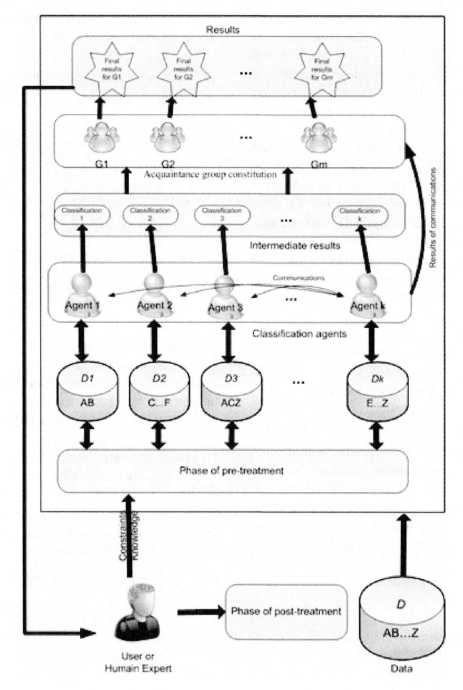

This system is adaptive because it solves:

- The problem of distributed data: There is a horizontal distribution of people between agents. Agents monitor a subset of people, and interactions between agents allow the construction of a global acceptable solution.
- The problem of heterogeneous data: There is also a vertical distribution of attributes between agents. It is not necessary to have the same set of attributes for each agent.
- The problem of fault tolerance: Missing data will not impact the global functioning. For example if a captor fails, the weight of the missing indicator will become zero without preventing the final calculation of distances.
- The problem of dynamicity in an open environment: new people can be allocated to an existing agent according to their attributes or monitored by a new created agent.

Step-by-Step Example

Thereafter we apply our proposal on an example with 4 agents, 10 objects and 6 attributes. We consider that after the phase of pre-treatment, agent A1 knows the values of attributes X1, X2 and X3 for objects O1, O2, O3, O4, and O5. Agent A2 knows the values of attributes X4, X5, and X6 for objects O6, O7, O8, O9, and O10. Agent A3 knows the values of attributes X1, X3, and X5 for objects O1, O3, O5, O7, and O9. Finally agent A4 knows the values of attributes X2, X4, and X6 for objects O2, O4, O6, O8, and O10. Weights of attributes X1 to X6 are respectively 6, 1, 4, 3, 2, and 5. The weight of an attribute represents its importance related to a given classification problem. So objects do not have the same attributes (it will often happen in real situations). For example, O1 has only four attributes. Each object has attributes suited to its case.

By applying a local classification method (in our case ISODATA) each agent builds its partition. Each class is characterized by a mid-vector calculated by ISODATA. The result of the local classification is:

Agent A1:
C1 = {O1,O4,O5} with mid-vector
{X1 = 7;X2 = 8;X3 = 5}
C2 = {O2,O3} with mid-vector
{X1 = 5;X2 = 4;X3 = 10}
Agent A2:
C3 = {O6,O7,O9} with mid-vector
{X4 = 9;X5 = 1;X6 = 2}
C4 = {O8,O10} with mid-vector
{X4 = 3;X5 = 10;X6 = 6}
Agent A3:
C5 = {O1,O5} with mid-vector
{X1 = 6;X3 = 6;X5 = 5}
C6 = {O7,O9} with mid-vector
{X1 = 9;X3 = 8;X5 = 1}
C7 = {O3} with mid-vector
{X1 = 5;X3 = 9;X5 = 10}
Agent A4:
C8 = {O2,O6} with mid-vector
{X2 = 5;X4 = 8;X6 = 3}
C9 = {O4,O8,O10} with mid-vector
{X2 = 7;X4 = 4;X6 = 5}

According to the call for participation algorithm, we compute that there are two groups of agents. The first group contains A1 and A3, and the second group contains A2 and A4. By applying the weighted Euclidean distance, we calculate distances between classes of each group.

dw(C1,C5) = 3.16
dw(C1,C6) = 7.74
dw(C1,C7) = 9.38
dw(C2,C5) = 8.36
dw(C2,C6) = 10.58
dw(C2,C7) = 2
dw(C3,C8) = 2.82

dw(C3,C9) = 10.95
dw(C4,C8) = 10.95
dw(C4,C9) = 2.82

After the calculation of distances, we find that some classes have to be merged (these distances are bolded above). This is the case of the three classes C1, C5, and C6, the two classes C2 and C7, C3 and C8, and finally C4 and C9.

Therefore the result of the generalized classification is:

First agents group A1, A3:
C1 = {O1,O4,O5,O7,O9} with mid-vector {X1 = 7.28;X2 = 8;X3 = 6.14;X5 = 3}
C2 = {O2,O3} with mid-vector {X1 = 5;X2 = 4;X3 = 9.66;X5 = 10}
Second agents group A2, A4:
C3 = {O2,O6,O7,O9} with mid-vector {X2 = 5;X4 = 7.4;X5 = 1;X6 = 2.4}
C4 = {O4,O8,O10} with mid-vector {X2 = 7;X4 = 3.6;X5 = 10;X6 = 5.4}

The new classes thus obtained have new mid-vectors. These vectors are the average of the attributes values of objects belonging to the same class.

To avoid inappropriate merging, we set a minimum threshold for the distance between classes. This threshold is based on the weights of the attributes. If the distance between two classes is greater than this threshold, they do not merge, even if they are close in the sense described above.

IMPLEMENTATION AND FIRST RESULTS

Meta Monitoring Application

The system is based on a variety of sensors carried by monitored people or installed in their homes. Those sensors are presence and movement sensors or medical measuring apparatus. The data com-

ing from sensors are transformed into indicators. Indicators are information on which the system will generate its classification. They are data about daily activities, positions and physiological information. Their abstraction from raw data requires a software layer. The work presented here doesn't deal with the details of the set of sensors involved, or with this extra software layer.

Indicators are collected by data-processing agents constituting the system. Because the system is strongly distributed (several people living in different houses must be surveyed), indicators of two people will not be inevitably collected by the same agent. The various indicators of an individual could be collected by several agents too. It means that for example an agent collects the blood pressure of someone while another collects the sleeping time. There can also be some overlaps in this vertical and horizontal distribution. For example two agents can collect the number of times the same person goes to the toilet.

In our e-health implementation, three agents Ai collect eleven indicators Ii concerning ten people Pi (see Table 1 for the meaning of the attributes and Table 2 for their values for each people. Let's note that values will be normalized between zero and one).

Data is horizontally distributed with people overlaps. Agent A1 collects data about people from number one to six. Agent A2 is affected to people number six to ten, and agent A3 takes care of people number five to eight.

For the clarity of the example, we state that the weight of each attribute is 1 (each attribute is equally important).

The local, partial classification of each agent gives the results of Table 3. Agent A1 finds five classes, A2 two classes and A3 three classes.

Agents use the restricted cooperation protocol (call for participation / acquaintances group constitution / multi-agent classification). A consequence of our distribution is that the second step of our algorithm gives a single group with all agents.

Table 1. Indicators

I_1 Corporal Temperature
I_2 Systolic blood pressure (in mmHg)
I_3 Diastolic blood pressure (in mmHg)
I_4 Sleeping time
I_5 Number of times the person gets out of bed in the night
I_6 Number of times the person goes to the toilet in day
I_7 Time spent in the kitchen
I_8 Time spent in the living room
I_9 Number of times the person gets outdoor
I_{10} Longest immobility daytime
I_{11} Eating disorder (true or false)

The computing of distances between classes and the merging of the closest give the final five classes of Table 4.

ANALYSIS OF RESULTS AND DISCUSSIONS

The results of our method are satisfactory. The class of normal people (P6, P7, P9, and P10) clearly emerges. The algorithm is accurate to separate normal people from others. Ill people are classified in four groups: P1, P3, and P8 are aggregated, probably because they are very mobile (nightly overactive or wandering), P2 and P5 are isolated (both are fevered), same as P4.

We can compare the multi-agent classification to the one made by ISODATA shown in Table 5.

Both results are close. The number of clusters obtained by ISODATA is three against five for our method. The main difference is that ISO-DATA has included P4 and P5 in the same class of normal people. So in this example, it seems that the centralized approach is less discriminant than the multi-agent one. Of course, it should be confirm on a larger population sample.

To conclude, the example shows that multi-agent classification can be a good replacement when a centralized approach is not possible.

The medical aspect of the classification has to be confirmed by organizations of assistance to elderly people. These organizations often use an evaluation grid of the dependence degree to determine the service needed by people. The matching of the two evaluation ways should validate our

Table 2. Indicators values of ten people

	P_1	P_2	P_3	P_4	P_5	P_6	P_7	P_8	P_9	P_{10}
	Nocturnally overactive			Daytime underactive		Normal people		Wandering	Normal people	
I_1	37.5 C	40C	37C	37.5C	39C	37.5C	37C	37.5C	37C	37C
I_2	190	180	170	110	100	150	140	190	145	138
I_3	120	110	120	60	50	90	80	120	90	70
I_4	6h	4h	6h	13h	12h	6h	7h	7h	8h	7h
I_5	10	11	7	2	3	0	1	2	1	3
I_6	7	14	7	6	5	8	7	8	6	7
I_7	1h30	45mn	2h	30mm	15mm	1h30	2h	3h	1h30	2h
I_8	3h	2h	1h	4h	3h20	2h	3h	3h	2h	2h
I_9	2	1	2	0	1	2	3	6	3	2
I_{10}	2h	1h30	2h	4h	3h	1h30	2h	15mn	1h30	2h
I_{11}	true	false	true	true	false	false	false	true	false	false

Table 3. Local clustering of agents A1, A2 and A3 with mid-vectors for each cluster

	A_1										
	I_1	I_2	I_3	I_4	I_5	I_6	I_7	I_8	I_9	I_{10}	I_{11}
$C_1(P_4)$	0.17	1	1	0.33	0.18	0.33	1	0.5	1	0	1
$C_2(P_2)$	1	0.89	0.85	0	1	1	0.18	0.25	0.17	0.33	0
	0.17	0.56	0.57	0.22	0	0.33	0.45	0.25	0.33	0.33	0
$C_3(P_6)$	0.67	0	0	0.89	0.27	0	0	1	0.17	0.73	0
$C_4(P_5)$	0.08	0.89	1	0.22	0.77	0.22	0.54	0.25	0.33	0.46	1
$C_5(P_1, P_3)$											
	A_2										
	I_1	I_2	I_3	I_4	I_5	I_6	I_7	I_8	I_9	I_{10}	I_{11}
	0.17	1	1	0.33	0.18	0.33	1	0.5	1	0	1
$C_1(P_8)$	0.04	0.48	0.46	0.33	0.11	0.22	0.54	0.31	0.41	0.4	0
$C_2(P_6, P_7, P_8, P_9, P_{10})$	A_3										
	I_1	I_2	I_3	I_4	I_5	I_6	I_7	I_8	I_9	I_{10}	I_{11}
$C_1(P_5)$	0.67	0	0	0.89	0.27	0	0	1	0.17	0.73	0
$C_2(P_8)$	0.17	1	1	0.33	0.18	0.33	1	0.5	1	0	1
$C_3(P_6, P_7)$	0.08	0.5	0.5	0.28	0.04	0.28	0.54	0.37	0.42	0.4	0

Table 4. Final results of the multi-agent classification

Cluster	Cluster Members	Mid-Vector										
C_1	P_4	0.17	0.11	0.14	1	0.18	0.11	0.09	0.75	0	1	1
C_2	P_2	1	0.89	0.86	0	1	1	0.18	0.25	0.17	0.33	0
C_3	P_6, P_7, P_9, P_{10}	0.09	0.51	0.51	0.28	0.05	0.28	0.51	0.31	0.39	0.38	0
C_4	P_5	0.67	0	0	0.89	0.27	0	0	1	0.17	0.73	0
C_5	P_1, P_3, P_8	0.14	0.96	1	0.29	0.38	0.29	0.84	0.41	0.78	0.15	1

Table 5. Isodata global clustering result

	I_1	I_2	I_3	I_4	I_5	I_6	I_7	I_8	I_9	I_{10}	I_{11}
$C_1(P_1, P_3, P_8)$	0.11	0.92	1	0.26	0.57	0.26	0.	0.33	0.55	0.31	1
$C_2(P_4, P_5, P_6, P_7, P_9, P_{10})$	0.17	0.34	0.33	0.54	0.15	0.17	0.38	0.5	0.3	0.55	0.17
$C_3(P_2)$	1	0.89	0.86	0	1	1	0.18	0.25	0.17	0.33	0

approach and also could consolidate the relevance of the grid criteria.

Later, medical organizations can use the system to follow the evolution of the dependence degree of people. Thus, somebody leaving his original class to enter a new one could be re-evaluated by the organization, and the assistance could be adapted to his new behaviours.

Finally, this classification could have other main uses like:

- Having global and anonymous statistical data about old people looked after in their own homes.
- Allowing generating specialized alarms depending on the detected event. Once the classification is set up and people status is known, decisions can be taken to personalize the monitoring of someone - activated sensors, generated alarms and danger zone.
- Remote monitoring of people suffering from chronic problems of health. This help is for already detected people, suffering of cardiac and pulmonary insufficiencies, asthma or Alzheimer disease. The possibility of having a global vision of several monitored people can bring richer and more relevant information on the follow-up. The distribution in classes and the historic of the patterns evolution (system training) should allow new people entering the system to get a better service; in particular, it should make it possible to generate more appropriate alerts according to the incurred risk.

CONCLUSION

We proposed a multi-agent architecture for people home monitoring. This architecture is adaptive and robust: it allows adapting the monitoring to people

profiles, gaining experience during operation and also handling and coordinating a big number of people geographically distributed.

The algorithm described above builds dynamic classifications according to indicators. It can be applied in many applications especially if they are in an open environment. This adaptability is the result of two essential characteristics. The first is the dynamic evolution of classifications – if needed, new data and new indicators can be added at any moment, and the system is able to reconfigure its classes and generate new classification patterns. The second is that the system is generic with respect to indicators and thus is able to function on any type of applications having strongly distributed entries.

Traditional classification methods are not adapted to this context and it has been necessary to propose new distributed classification methods like the multi-agent classification of our system.

To evaluate its performances, we have selected significant numerical vectors of values and we have observed the formation of classes with a sample of elderly people. To validate the system in a real scale, we have to test in an environment composed of the whole elderly people, members of the C-Vital association.

REFERENCES

K4CARE project. (2006). Retrieved August 20, 2010, from www.k4care.ne

Chan, M., Campo, E., & Estève, D. (2003). PROSAFE: a multisensory remote monitoring system for the elderly or the handicapped. In *Proceedings of the 1st International Conference on Smart homes and health Telematics (ICOST 2003)*, Paris (pp. 89-95).

Chan, M., Estève, D., Escriba, C., & Campo, E. (2008). A review of smart homes—Present state and future challenges. *Computer Methods and Programs in Biomedicine, 91*(1), 55–81. doi:10.1016/j.cmpb.2008.02.001

Corchado, J. M., Bajo, J., & Abraham, A. (2008). GerAmi: Improving Healthcare Delivery in Geriatric Residences. *IEEE Intelligent Systems*, 19-25. *GERHOME project*. (2005). Retrieved August 20, 2010, from gerhome.cstb.fr

Laleci, G. B., Dogac, A., Olduz, M., Tasyurt, I., Yuksel, M., & Okcan, A. (2008). SAPHIRE: A Multi-Agent System for Remote Healthcare Monitoring through Computerized Clinical Guidelines. In Annicchiarico, R., Cortés, U., & Urdiales, C. (Eds.), *Agent Technology and e-Health* (pp. 25–44). Berlin: Birkhäuser Verlag. doi:10.1007/978-3-7643-8547-7_3

Mc Morrow, K. (2004). *The Economic and Financial Market consequences of Global Ageing*. New York: Springer.

Noury, N. (2005). AILISA: Experimental platforms to evaluate remote care and assistive technologies in gerontology. In *Proceedings of 7th international workshop on enterprise networking and computing in healthcare industry (HEALTHCOM 2005)*, South Korea (pp. 67-72).

OLDES project. (2010). Retrieved August 20, 2010, from www.oldes.eu

Rammal, A., Trouilhet, S., Singer, N., & Pécatte, J. M. (2008). An Adaptive System for Home Monitoring Using a Multiagent Classification of Patterns. *International Journal of Telemedicine and Applications*.

Sakka, E., Prentza, A., Lamprinos, I. E., Leondaridis, L., & Koutsouris, D. (2004). Integration of monitoring devices in the e-Vital service. In *Proceedings of the 26th Annual International Conference of the Engineering in Medicine and Biology Society (EMBC 2004)* (Vol. 4, pp. 3097-3100).

SOPRANO project. (2010). Retrieved August 20, 2010, from www.soprano-ip.org

Tablado, A., Illarramendi, A., Bagüés, M. I., Bermúdez, J., & Goñi, A. (2004). Aingeru: an Innovating System for Tele Assistance of Elderly People. In *Proceedings of the 1st International Workshop on Tele-Care and Collaborative Virtual Communities in Elderly Care (TELECARE)* (pp. 27-36).

Virone, G., & Sixsmith, A. (2008). Monitoring Activity Patterns and Trends of Older Adults. In *Proceedings of the 30th IEEE-EMBS (Engineering in Medicine and Biology)*, Vancouver, Canada (pp. 20-24).

Weiser, M. (1991). The Computer for the Twenty-First Century. *Scientific American, 265*(3).

Zouba, N., Bremond, F., & Thonnat, M. (2010). An Activity Monitoring System for Real Elderly at Home: Validation Study. In *Proceedings of the 7th IEEE International Conference on Advanced Video and Signal-Based Surveillance (AVSS 2010)*, Boston.

This work was previously published in International Journal of Agent Technologies and Systems, Volume 3, Issue 1, edited by Yu Zhang, pp. 40-51, copyright 2011 by IGI Publishing (an imprint of IGI Global).

Chapter 6
Simulating Tolerance in Dynamic Social Networks

Kristen Lund
Trinity University, USA

Yu Zhang
Trinity University, USA

ABSTRACT

This paper studies the concept of tolerance in dynamic social networks where agents are able to make and break connections with neighbors to improve their payoffs. This problem was initially introduced to the authors by observing resistance (or tolerance) in experiments run in dynamic networks under the two rules that they have developed: the Highest Rewarding Neighborhood rule and the Highest Weighted Reward rule. These rules help agents evaluate their neighbors and decide whether to break a connection or not. They introduce the idea of tolerance in dynamic networks by allowing an agent to maintain a relationship with a bad neighbor for some time. In this research, the authors investigate and define the phenomenon of tolerance in dynamic social networks, particularly with the two rules. The paper defines a mathematical model to predict an agent's tolerance of a bad neighbor and determine the factors that affect it. After defining a general version of tolerance, the idea of optimal tolerance is explored, providing situations in which tolerance can be used as a tool to affect network efficiency and network structure.

INTRODUCTION

In multi-agent systems, different agents aim to achieve different goals, yet must develop some system of cooperation within the system (Axelrod, 1997; Davidsson, 2002). In this research, the systems of social networks (Epstein, 1999; Watts, 1999; Newman, 2003) are of particular interest to

us. In such systems, all agents are self-interested and try to maximize their own utility. This can be done by adjusting their strategy or by adjusting their environment and disconnecting from agents while making connections with others. These systems can be governed by pre-determined rules to control individual decision making and social interactions. The existence of a basic network model, such as random network, small-world net-

DOI: 10.4018/978-1-4666-1565-6.ch006

work (Watts, 1999), and scale free network (Newman, 2003), couple with some economic game, provides a network of self-interested agents with specific goals, and the application of individual decision making rules and social interaction rules make the network dynamic, resulting in questions about the final network structure, such as stability, efficiency, and tolerance.

The current research in this direction occurs on two different levels: a low-level decision that an agent must make to determine its game strategy, and a higher-level decision to change the links in the network, and, ultimately, the overall network structure. Most of the current research uses the static network so only the low-level decision is achieved, i.e. the agents can only change their own actions but not other agents that they are connected to. Here a network will be called *static* if edges are never created or removed after the generation of the graph. Static networks may well model social behaviors in a relative stable environment such as a community where people barely move around and always keep the same relationships to others.

Our research focuses on *dynamic networks* that the edges are created and removed as the network evolves. Therefore in our system, both the low-level decision on agent's individual actions and higher-level decision on agent's social interactions are considered to help agents maximize their utility. The dynamic network approach can model many dynamic systems such as behaviors in social network service (SNS) where agents frequently change their relationships to others. Examples include the friendship networks of high school students (Fararo & Sunshine, 1964), the network of citations between scientific papers (Redner, 1998), links between web pages on the World Wide Web (Albert & Barb'asi, 2002) and network of human sexual contact (Liljeros, Edling, Amaral, Stanely, & Aberg, 2001).

In dynamic social networks, several social interaction rules have been developed to improve agents' decision-making processes so that they break off connections with agents that are not

beneficial. One of these social interaction rules is called the Highest Weighted Reward (HWR) in order to give agents the ability to update their neighborhood in a social network (Wu & Zhang, 2009). The HWR rule weighted recent rewards from a relation more than that of the long-time-ago rewards. Agents' decision about whether to keep a relationship or not is based on if the weighted rewards is greater than the weighted average reward earned from every relationship. Adopting the HWR rule, one can easily transform a classic static network into a dynamic network with few restrictions on how agents observe their neighbors and how agents make the decision about when to keep an existing connection or disconnect it so they can connect to a new neighbor. A special case of the HWR rule is when the weight is 1 so all previous interactions are weighted as the same in agent's current decision. We call this special case another rule – the HRN rule (Highest Rewarding Neighborhood) (Zhang & Leezer, 2009).

In the HWR rule, some degree of tolerance between agents has been noticed. That is, an agent may not break off a connection with a harmful neighbor. We call this phenomenon *tolerance*. The primary goal of this study is to develop a full understanding of tolerance in social networks and its effects. We will first provide models to predict tolerance in the social networks that use the HWR rule. Once these have been established and confirmed, our goal will be to develop further conclusions about tolerance in social networks: we will compare the developed models and study the effects of tolerance in social networks to develop an understanding of how control of tolerance in a dynamic network can be used.

Tolerance is one of the newest problems being discussed in dynamic social networks. By studying the causes and effects of tolerance in social network models, it can be consciously used in the development of new social interaction rules, rather than simply being a side effect of many rules with no determined cause. This paper studies tolerance in networks in two main areas:

1. Identification of the cause of tolerance in the social network model.
2. The development of a mathematical model to describe tolerance and apply results to a network simulation.

The paper is structured as the following. We first give a literature review of tolerance in fields of social psychology and provide other backgrounds of dynamic networks, individual decision rules, and social interaction rules. Then we introduce both the HRN rule and the HWR rule that lead to the phenomenon of tolerance in a social network. After that, we define the model of tolerance based on the two rules. Next, we describe the environment of our model. Finally we present our experiments showing the causes and effects of tolerance in a dynamic social network.

RELATED WORK

Tolerance in Social Psychology

The main problem with tolerance in scholarly work is that it is used by many groups to mean many different things. In this review, there are three main definitions of "tolerance," and only one of these completely corresponds to the tolerance which we wish to investigate. The first of these definitions of tolerance was described by sociologists as an individual's acceptance of others that differ from the given individual's norm or culture. This definition was implied in the use of a tag which defined tolerance in a multi-agent system designed to study the emergence and maintenance of cooperation in evolving populations (Riolo, Cohen, & Axelrod, 2001). Each agent had a tag with two traits: a trait τ in [0,1] and a tolerance threshold $T \geq 0$. The more tolerant an agent was, the more willing it would be to cooperate with agents with different traits. This was calculated by having an agent A cooperate with another agent B if and only if $|\tau_A - \tau_B| \leq T_A$. This idea of tolerance is evident

in real life, and certainly interesting, but it is not what we first seek to define. However, this idea is still interesting and may be considered later in the project.

The next definition of tolerance is found in articles by psychologists and primate behaviorists that discuss the level of "tolerance" in primates (Gilby & Wrangham, 2008; Melis, Hare, & Tomasello, 2006; Wobber, Wrangham, & Hare, 2010). Unfortunately, none of these papers seemed to provide an explicit definition of tolerance, perhaps accepting that it is part of the psychological/behavioral vocabulary that its readers should know. It is pretty clear, though, to ascertain that tolerance is referred to as willingness to cooperate (measured, typically, in willingness to share food) (Hare, Melis, Woods, Hastingsn, & Wrangham, 2007). This definition is surprisingly un-intuitive, but the majority of papers found on tolerance have been in this field, using this definition. They generally center around the comparison of chimpanzees and bonobos, the closest phylogenetic neighbors to chimpanzees (Anderson, 2007). Bonobos differ in that they show more relaxed social relationships and maintain trusting behavior that is generally referred to as youthful. Most papers refer to the "emotional-reactivity hypothesis," which predicts that bonobos will cooperate with each other more successfully because of the bonobos' more relaxed social relationships (including higher tolerance of sharing food). In experiments, this has shown to win over the "hunting hypothesis," which emphasizes the fact that chimpanzees have been observed hunting cooperatively for longer (Anderson, 2007).

One experiment, however, does discuss 'social reversal learning,' which matches to our definition of tolerance (Wobber, Wrangham, & Hare, 2010). This experiment included two people, one which would have food and another that wouldn't. One person would consistently have food every time, and the chimpanzees and bonobos would learn to go to that person for food. Then, when the opposite person had food instead, the number of 'turns' that the monkeys spent going to the original person for food was recorded. Just as bonobos were more tolerant of sharing food (attributed to juvenile behavior that was retained into adulthood), bonobos were also slower to switch people -- much like an agent choosing to maintain a connection with an uncooperative neighbor. The study speculated that this 'social reversal learning' and the food tolerance which they discussed had the same source in the bonobos. This would suggest that the tolerance modeled in this study is much related to the tolerance studied in bonobos.

The definition of tolerance we provide does exist in scholarly literature: psychologists have defined tolerance as "acceptance of the inevitable stresses and strains of relationships" in studying tolerance in humans at college institutions (Benenson, Markovits, Fitzgerald, Georoy, Flemming, & Kahlenberg, 2009). By studying the demographics of roommate reassignments in several universities, surveys of perceptions of roommates, and running experiments involving the manipulation of friendship beliefs, this study suggests that males are more tolerant than females. This paper is mostly interesting for its similar use of the term 'tolerance,' as an explicitly male-vs-female model is most likely not going to exist in this project.

The existence of academic literature on tolerance shows an interest present in fields of social psychology. We hope to apply these social-psychological ideas to a multi-agent system approach toward the study of dynamic social networks.

Dynamic Networks

Although a significant amount of research has been devoted to network structure, the subject of Dynamic Network models is still relatively new, and (probably) central to the problems addressed in this REU. In the structures previously mentioned, it is assumed that once two nodes in a network are linked, there is no change to the connection. In a dynamic network environment, links between nodes in a network may be added

or removed. This process may be either random or determined by social interaction rules. In one study of social networks, dynamic network models are organized into two main categories: network evolution models and nodal attribute models (Toivonen, Kovanen, Kivela, Onnela, Saramaki, & Kaski, 2009). Network evolution models are defined as those in which the addition of new links in dependent on the local network structure, and nodal attribute models are those in which the probability of each link existing depends only on nodal attributes. The study further subdivides network evolution models into growing models and dynamical models, and the study includes exponential random graph models, which are more traditional models, for completeness. The paper suggests that the models that most accurately produced degree distributions and clustering spectra that agreed with data were those which fell under the category of network evolution models, or models which incorporated structural dependencies. However, some nodal attribute models also successfully dealt with assortative networks and community structures.

Dynamic network structures have been handled a number of different ways, several of which are listed here.

Random Networks

It is worthwhile to mention randomly dynamic networks as trivial case; no major papers are referenced here about them, but it is worth noticing that using some random distribution, one can remove or add links in a network to create a randomly dynamic network, though the lack of structure makes this largely inapplicable to social networks.

Growing Networks: Evolution Rules

One way to approach Dynamic Networks is to view them as growing networks. Jin, Girvan, and Newman propose a model of the growth of social networks from an empty network with few general principles (Jin, Girvan, & Newman, 2001). The three major elements used to determine their network growth model are:

1. Meetings take place between players at a high rate if the players have one or more mutual friends, and at a low rate otherwise.
2. Links between players who rarely meet will decay over time.
3. There is an upper level of friendships an individual in the network can maintain.

For simplicity, the network was also restricted to a closed population of fixed size. The parameters chosen to determine network growth are clearly intuitive, and are intended merely as a "reasonable stab at realism." The model relies heavily on the concepts of time and links which have intensities associated with them. It also requires some sort of "meeting" to be simulated with varying regularity. A model with such parameters quickly becomes cumbersome, and the article also presents a simplified, more stylized version of the initial requirements presented to develop a more efficient system. Revisions included removing the idea of connection strength − nodes were either connected or not connected. Then, rather than having the connection decay over time, there would be an increased probability per unit of time that the connection would disappear. The rate at which two individuals met was simplified to a linear equation based on their number m of mutual friends. This provides a model that is both conceptually simpler and easier to simulate, as there is no continuous time simulation method required (an algorithm using time-steps is implemented instead). The models generated with these basic social rules resulted in clustering, one of the core elements of community structures.

Genetic Algorithms

Genetic algorithms provide another approach to an evolving network. Genetic algorithms are interesting in that they provide an opportunity for an agent to mutate, adding an interesting aspect of randomness. This is generally achieved through a system of genetic tags. Tags are a socially distinguishable mark that allows agents to classify other agents (Edmonds, Norling, & Hales, 2009). One common algorithm used to manipulate genetic models is the SLAC algorithm.

The SLAC (Selfish Link-based Adaptation for Cooperation) is an evolutionary algorithm typically applied to tag models. In this algorithm, nodes attempt to improve their situation by mimicking better-performing nodes. For some node i, the SLAC algorithm compares it to a randomly selected node j. If the utility of j is greater than or equal to the utility of i, then $N(i):= N(j) \cap j$. Furthermore, in the context of tag models, there is occasionally a low probability that i will then mutate. This algorithm has been shown to allow a network to evolve gradually to higher social optima (Rossi, Arteconi, & Hales, 2009).

INDIVIDUAL BEHAVIOR RULES

Definition 1: An *individual decision rule* is a rule which determines how an agent evaluates its reward and selects its next action, if changes in an agent's strategy are allowed in the social network used.

As social networks contain a group of self-interested agents, these agents must have some type of agenda and method for achieving this agenda. There are typically two behavior rules to develop a social convention. We introduce them in the following.

Simple Majority Rule

By Jordi Delgado (2002), the Simple Majority Rule states that an agent will conform to the actions of agents around it. For a network of N agents, the initial state of a system can be initialized to be randomly S or $\bar{S}$ for every agent (a good example would be from the Pure Coordination Game, in which an agent may cooperate, S, or defect, $\bar{S}$). For a randomly chosen j^{th} agent of this network, agent j has k neighbors. Of these neighbors, there are k_s neighbors in state S and $k - k_s$ neighbors in state $\bar{S}$. If agent j is in state S, the Simple Majority Rule states that j will move to state $\bar{S}$ with probability

$$f_\beta \left(k_s \right) = \frac{1}{1 + e^{2\beta(\frac{2k_s}{k}-1)}} \tag{1}$$

This Simple Majority Rule has been generated by Delgado with the addition of β, since as β→∞ there is a change of state only when more than half of j's neighbors are in state $\bar{S}$. This rule provides a simple and intuitive way of dealing with an agent's choice in game strategy.

Highest Cumulative Reward Rule

Shoham and Tennenholtz (1997) define the Highest Cumulative Reward Rule as an update rule such that an agent switches to a new action if and only if the total payoff obtained from that action in the latest m iterations is greater than the payoff obtained from the currently-chosen action in the same time period. This rule guarantees eventual emergence of coordination and of cooperation in games. Notice that neither this rule nor the Simple Majority Rule was developed in dynamic networks, but instead ones in which links did not change. In fact, the concept of dynamic networks is not entirely relevant to the problem of individual behavior rules as used by this paper, as the Simple

Majority Rule and Highest Cumulative Reward Rule can both be applied in either type of network.

SOCIAL INTERACTION RULES

Definition 2: A *Social Interaction Rule* is a rule for dynamic social networks which provide some function for evaluating the relationship between agents i and j, R_{ij}. This function is developed with a given threshold τin mind such that, for R < τ, the connection is dropped. These social interaction rules also provide some rubric for making new connections.

Based on this definition, we previously developed two social interaction rules, as described in the following.

Highest Rewarding Neighborhood (the HRN Rule)

Definition 3: (HRN) According to the Highest Rewarding Neighborhood rule for social interaction, an agent maintains a relation with another agent if and only if the average reward earned from that relationship is no less than a specified percentage (called the threshold, τ) of the average reward earned from all of the agent's relationships.

Leezer and Zhang (2009) define the HRN rule with the idea that an agent would only wish to maintain beneficial relationships. For an agent i, allocation rule u, and action a from the set of all available actions, we define the total reward for agent i to be $r_i = \sum ju(a_i, a_j)$, where $\in N(i)$, the neighborhood of agent i. Then the average reward with each neighboring agent is computed as:

$$\bar{r}_{ij} = \frac{\sum r_{ij}}{t} \tag{2}$$

where t is the number of time steps. This value is then compared to the average reward received from all neighboring nodes, given by:

$$r_{total} = \frac{\sum_{j N(i)} \bar{r}_{ij}}{N(i)} \qquad (3)$$

Finally, if $\bar{r}_{ij}$ is lower than r_{total} by a predetermined threshold τ, then the link between i and j is broken and the agent that chose to end the relationship then links to a new agent, which is determined by the structure of the network.

$$\frac{\bar{r}_{ij}}{r_{total}} < \qquad (4)$$

The HRN rule creates a "high rewarding neighborhood", and the ability of an agent to add and drop connections results in cooperating neighborhoods in which all agents play Pareto-optimal strategies.

However, Wu and Zhang (2009) notice that the HRN rule allows distant results to affect an agent's decision-making ability just as much as more recent decisions, an unrealistic detail. This flaw prompted a modified version of the HRN, called the Highest Weighted Reward rule (or HWR rule):

Highest Weighted Reward Rule (the HWR Rule)

Definition 4: (HWR) According to the *Highest Weighted Reward* rule, an agent will maintain a relationship if and only if the weighted average reward earned from that relationship is no less than a specified percentage (called the threshold, τ) of the weighted average reward earned from every relationship.

Wu and Zhang extend the HRN rule by adding a weight which weighs recent rewards more than previous rewards (Wu & Zhang, 2009). In this algorithm, the agents continue to evaluate relationships based on the average reward for its neighborhood, but time begins to play a factor as well, making the agents in this situation more forgiving" (this also brings up the issue of tolerance, seen in 7.3). To calculate the average reward for every agent, they use the following formula:

$$AvgReward = \frac{TotalReward}{1 + w + w^2 + w^3 + \ldots + w^{n-1}} = \frac{TotalReward}{\frac{1 - w^{n-1}}{1 - w}} \qquad (5)$$

This is then compared to the average total reward for the neighborhood of an agent:

$$AvgTotalReward = \frac{GeneralTotalReward}{1 + w + w^2 + w^3 + \ldots + w^{n-1}} = \frac{GeneralTotalReward}{\frac{1 - w^{n-1}}{1 - w}} \qquad (6)$$

Finally to decide if a neighbor is bad so the agent will disconnect with it, we compare the ratio of *Average Reward* vs *Average Total Reward* with the threshold τ. The rule is as the following.

$$\begin{cases} if\ \dfrac{AR_t}{ATR_t} >, & keep\,the\,neighbor \\ Otherewise,\ disconnect\,bad\,neighbor \end{cases} \qquad (7)$$

This algorithm results in a stable network with fully cooperative communities under the pure coordination game.

The above definitions are given under the assumption that the agent has infinite memory, which means the agent can remember all past interactions and their relative payoffs. However, this may not always be the case in real world. Therefore, sometimes we set a memory limit L. In that case, the agent will only remember the interactions in the last L turns. But the decision is made in a similar way.

MODELS OF TOLERANCE

Definition 5: We define a *stable* connection as a connection which, given that nothing changes, will never be broken.

Definition 6: *Tolerance* is the description of an agent's willingness to maintain an unstable connection with some other agent.

Definition 7: We call an agent that chooses to maintain an unstable connection for n turns *n-tolerant*.

Here we describe the models that have been developed for the HRN and HWR rules.

Highest Rewarding Neighborhood

Consider the case where a connection between some agents i and j has been intact for k turns, and then on turn n agent j switches actions. We can calculate r_{ij} for c time steps after this switch by the sequence R_c:

$$R_c = \begin{cases} r_{ij}(k) & if\, c = 0 \\ \dfrac{(k + c - 1) R_{c-1} + G(a_i, a_j)}{k + c} & if\, c > 0 \end{cases}$$
(8)

where $G(a_i, a_j)$ is the payout that agent i receives for playing a game G with agent j. For the rest of the context, we abbreviate $G(a_i, a_j)$ as G.

In order to develop a continuous approximation of this sequence, we consider a very small time period $\Delta c \in [0,1]$. Then we rewrite formula (8) in continuous form as:

$$R_c = \frac{(k + c - \Delta c) R_{c-\Delta c} + \Delta c G}{k + c}$$
(9)

Distributing and subtracting all of the R_c terms on the left side, we then get that

$$(k + c)R_c - (k+c)\, R_{c\text{-}\Delta c} + \Delta c R_{c\text{-}\Delta c} = \Delta c G$$
(10)

We then isolate

$$\frac{R_c - R_{c-\Delta c}}{\Delta c}$$
(11)

and by taking the limit as $\Delta c \to 0$, we get the differential equation

$$\frac{dR}{dc} = \frac{G - R}{k + c}$$
(12)

Through integration, we come to the continuous equation

$$R(c) = \frac{Gc + kr_{ij}}{k + c}$$
(13)

Notice that in the evaluation of agents in the HRN model, a connection is broken between agents i and j if and only if by the formula (4):

$$\frac{\overline{r}_{ij}}{r_{total}} < \tau$$

where τ is the predetermined threshold value. This is equivalent to saying that

$$\frac{R(c)}{\overline{r}_{total}} < \tau, or\, R(c) < \overline{r}_{total}\, \tau$$
(14)

We can then solve the inequality for c:

$$c < \frac{k(r_{ij}(k) - \overline{r}_{total}\, \tau)}{\overline{r}_{total}\, \tau - G}$$
(15)

Thus, the *n*-tolerance for some agent *i* toward *j* in *N(i)* can be defined as

$$n = \frac{k(r_{ij}(k) - \overline{r}_{total}\tau)}{\overline{r}_{total}\tau - G} \tag{16}$$

Highest Weighted Reward

The Highest Weighted Reward model serves as a generalization of the Highest Rewarding Neighborhood rule in which a weight is added to past rewards so that the current rewards are most important.

For two agents *i,j*, that have been good neighbors for *k* turns and have changed to an unfair strategy for *c* turns, we define a sequence

$$R_c = \begin{cases} r_{ij}(k) & c = 0 \\ \dfrac{R_{c-1}\sum_{i=1}^{k+c-1} w^i + G}{\sum_{i=1}^{k+c} w^{i-1}} & c > 0 \end{cases} \tag{17}$$

This is incredibly messy; fortunately, however, a continuous definition is intuitively:

$$R(c) = \frac{\sum_{i=1}^{k} r_i w^{k+c-i} + \sum_{i=1}^{c} Gw^{c-i}}{\sum_{i=1}^{k+c} w^{i-1}} \tag{18}$$

The series involved in these equations are geometric series, and are easily simplified. We choose to first define them in series form in order to give an idea of the origins of the formula and to provide a version that, when $\omega = 1$, produces the HRN model. Since, for a geometric series, if $r \neq 1$,

$$\sum_{i=1}^{n} r^i = \frac{1 - r^{i+1}}{1 - r} \tag{19}$$

we can apply this to our definition of *R(c)* to get

$$R(c) = w^c \left[w^k \sum_{i=1}^{k} \frac{r^i}{w^i} + \frac{G\left(1 - \frac{1}{w^c}\right)}{w - 1} \right] \left(\frac{1 - w}{1 - w^{k+c}}\right) \tag{20}$$

Like in the HRN rule, a connection is dropped between agents i and j if and only if

$$\frac{\overline{r}_{ij}}{\overline{r}_{total}} < \tau \tag{21}$$

where τ is the predetermined threshold value. If we solve for *c* in

$$R(c) < \overline{r}_{total}\tau \tag{22}$$

we get that

$$c < \frac{\ln\left(\overline{r}_{total}\tau - G\right) - \ln[w^k(1-w)\sum_{i=1}^{k}\frac{r^i}{w^i} + w^k\overline{r}_{total}\tau - G]}{\ln w} \tag{23}$$

Furthermore, we can verify this model by setting $\omega = 1$. Clearly this does not work immediately, since we simplified most of the geometric series using the assumption that $\omega \neq 1$. However, through the application of L'Hôpital's rule, we get that

$$\lim_{w \to 1} \frac{\ln(\overline{r}_{total}\tau - G) - \ln[w^k(1-w)\sum_{i=1}^{k}\frac{r^i}{w^i} + w^k\overline{r}_{total}\tau - G]}{\ln w} \tag{24}$$

$$= \frac{\sum_{i=1}^{k} r_i - k\overline{r}_{total}\tau}{\overline{r}_{total}\tau - G} \tag{25}$$

$$= \frac{kr_{ij}(k) - k\overline{r}_{total}\tau}{\overline{r}_{total}\tau - G} \tag{26}$$

which is exactly what we would expect!

So for the HWR rule, the n-tolerance for some agent *i* toward *j* in *N(i)* can be defined as

$$n = \frac{\ln(\bar{r}_{total}\,\tau - G) - \ln[w^k(1-w)\sum_{i=1}^{k}\frac{r^i}{w^i} + w^k\bar{r}_{total}\,\tau - G]}{\ln w}$$

(27)

Stability of Connections

One of the main interests of study in social networks is the idea of stability. Here, we define a given connection between two agents as *stable* if, assuming all agents' actions remain the same, the connection will not be broken. As stated before, for a connection to not be broken, it must be that

$$R(c) \geq \bar{r}_{total}\,\tau$$

(28)

We now must modify this so that, for stability,

$$\lim_{c \to \infty} R(c) \geq \bar{r}_{total}\,\tau$$

(29)

This condition is the same for both the HRN model and the HWR model (for simplicity, we can call R(c) the reward for the HRN model, and $R_\omega(c)$ the reward for the HWR model). Our problem then becomes

$$\lim_{c \to \infty} \frac{Gc + kr_{ij}(k)}{k + c} \geq \bar{r}_{total}\,\tau$$

(30)

and

$$\lim_{c \to \infty} w^c \left(w^k \sum_{i=1}^{k}\frac{r^i}{w^i} + \frac{G(1 - \frac{1}{w^c})}{w - 1}\right)\left(\frac{1-w}{1-w^{k+c}}\right) \geq \bar{r}_{total}\,\tau$$

(31)

The limit of both *R(c)* and $R_\omega(c)$ is *G*, so we can then say that as long as

$$G \geq \bar{r}_{total}\,\tau$$

(32)

for either the HWR or HRN model, the connection between two agents as stable.

ENVIRONMENT

The environment of our model has the following properties. These are what our experiments (see Section EXPERIMENTS) are based on.

- All trials run in a random network.
- The number of connections in the network remains the same throughout the trial.
- Every time when a connection is broken, both agents have a 50% chance to gain the right to connect to a new neighbor. But only one of them will eventually make a new neighbor. This restriction guarantees the number of connections remains the same.
- All agents have a limit memory size of k.
- All agents adopt the ideal learning rule, which means the agent will always choose the action that the majority of its neighbors used in the last turn. If there is same number of neighbors adopting different actions, the agent will not change its current action.
- The agents can only see local information. They do not know the payoff matrix and the identities of their neighbors.
- Our domain is the two-action Pure Coordination Game. It is a simple game in which agents receive a reward in the event they choose the same strategy and a penalty in the event they choose different strategies. Table 1 shows the payoff matrix for the Pure Coordination Game we use.

Notice that there are two equal Nash Equilibrium in the game: (Cooperate, Cooperate) and (Defect Defect). Notice that the optimal strategy depends on the strategy of an agent's neighbor. However, when this game is played with multiple neighbors, the optimal strategy is the strategy adopted by the majority of an agent's neighbors.

EXPERIMENTS

To demonstrate the theorems, we have run several preliminary experiments and watch for the causes and effects of tolerance. Agents are connected by a random network and play the two-action pure coordination game defined in Table 1. The time discount $w=0.95$. The memory limit $L=10$. The experiments are run in a relative small scale with only 300 agents. Each result is the average of 30 trials. The system is initialized with 50% "cooperate" agents and 50% "defect" agents. Throughout the trial, we keep track of four attributes:

- **Total Neighbor Lost:** this is the number of the connections broken in each turn.
- **Number of Cooperation:** this is the number representing the size of cooperation camps.
- **Number of Defect:** this is the number representing the size of defect camps.
- **Number of Perfect Agents:** here we call an agent a perfect agent when all of its neighbors play the same actions as it does. An agent with no neighbor can also be viewed as a perfect agent.

Effect of Threshold τ on Tolerance

As shown in Figure 1, when the threshold increases, the average n-tolerance in a social simulation

Table 1. Payoff matrix for the pure coordination game

	Cooperate	Defect
Cooperate	1, 1	0,0
Defect	0,0	1,1

decreases. This relationship makes sense when considering that the condition for breaking a connection follows formula (4):

$$\frac{\overline{r}_{ij}}{\overline{r}_{total}} < \tau$$

Effect of Weight W on Tolerance

As the weight on past rewards increases in this experiment, agents begin to value their neighbors' past actions more strongly (shown in Figure 2). This means that n-tolerance increases as the weight increases. The effect of weight on tolerance, however, is much weaker than the effect of the threshold on tolerance. This makes sense, as the weight has a smaller effect on the condition for breaking a connection.

TOLERANCE IN DIFFERENT GAMES

So far, tolerance has only been mentioned with respect to the Pure Coordination Game. While this has been helpful in identifying the problem with a simple payoff method, it severely restricts the usefulness of the tolerance model. Thus, we introduce a few extra 2x2 payoff matrices from game theory to demonstrate the flexibility of our tolerance model.

Brief Introduction to Games

Note that we use games from game theory to quickly and efficiently produce reasonable payoff matrices. This is unnecessary, however: any utility function would suffice.

Pure Coordination Game

In the Pure Coordination Game, two agents are rewarded when choose the same strategy, but not when they disagree. There is no "better" choice

Figure 1. Average N-Tolerance with respect to Threshold (τ)

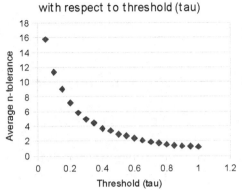

Table 2. Payoff matrix of Stag Hunt

	Cooperate (Stag)	Defect (Rabbit)
Cooperate (Stag)	(2,2)	(0,1)
Defect (Rabbit)	(1,0)	(1,1)

to get one by working together. Alternatively, a hunter could also choose to hunt a rabbit for a smaller but also definite payoff. If one hunts for a stag and another for a rabbit, the one hunting for a stag will have no payoff while the one hunting for a rabbit will have a small, but better, payoff.

This game is particularly interesting because there are two Nash equilibria: either cooperate-cooperate or defect-defect. Cooperate-cooperate is the payoff-dominant strategy, while defect-defect is the risk-dominant strategy (meaning that it seeks to avoid risk). Table 2 is the payoff matrix of Stag Hunt.

Figure 2. Average N-Tolerance with respect to Weight (ω)

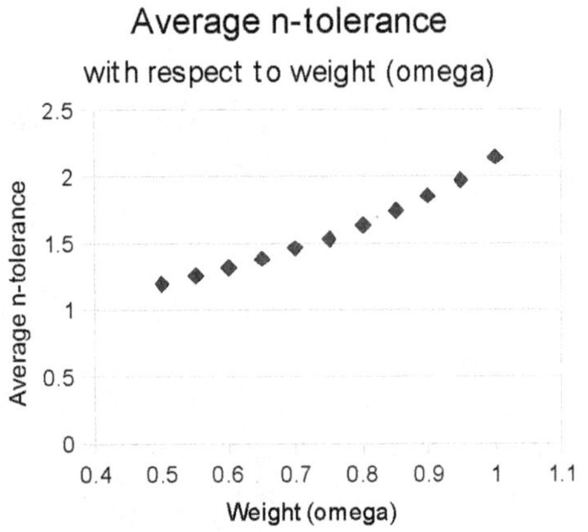

Prisoner's Dilemma

In the Prisoner's Dilemma, two (guilty) suspects are arrested by the police. However, the police don't have enough evidence to convict them of the crime, but have enough information to put them in jail for a short period of time on minor charges. Each suspect is questioned separately. If one testifies and one stays silent, then the betrayer goes free and the other goes to jail for five years. If both testify, both go to jail for four years. Finally, if the accomplices stay silent, each will have only two years in jail. Since the agents in our model seek to maximize payoff, the payoff matrix is written in terms of years free in the five-year period. The Nash equilibrium in this situation is (defect, defect), but it is not the Pareto optimal solution: (cooperate, cooperate) yields the highest overall reward. Table 3 is the payoff matrix of Prisoner's Dilemma.

between cooperating and defecting: the strategies an agent can choose are basically the same. The Highest Weighted Reward rule was designed with this game in mind, but it can be used for more games. The payoff matrix of the Pure Coordination Game is sown in Table 1.

Stag Hunt

Suppose two people were hunting together. If they were to both hunt for a stag, they would be able

Table 3. Payoff matrix of prisoner's dilemma

	Cooperate (Silence)	Defect (Testify)
Cooperate (Silence)	(3,3)	(0,5)
Defect (Testify)	(5,0)	(1,1)

Modifications to the Model

The model of tolerance becomes slightly more complicated when using games other than the Pure Coordination game. Previously, G represented the game played while not cooperating, and G is assumed to be a constant throughout the time period c. However, in more complex games, G is not constant, as there are different payoffs that can be received while still having an unstable connection. Therefore, instead of using the constant G, we use the allocation function γ: action x action $\rightarrow$ **Z** that gives the appropriate reward from the payoff matrix based off of the agents' actions a_i and b_i at time step $k+i$:

$$R\left(c\right)=w^{c}\left[w^{k}\sum_{i=1}^{k}\frac{r_{i}}{w^{i}}+\frac{\sum_{i=1}^{c}\gamma\left(a_{i},b_{i}\right)\left(1-\frac{1}{w^{c}}\right)}{w-1}\right]\left(\frac{1-w}{1-w^{k+c}}\right)$$

(33)

With this modification made, the model works about as well as it did for the pure coordination game, with a marginally larger percent error.

Tolerance and Strategy

Figure 3 compares the level of tolerance to the decision made when playing a game. Many agents of different threshold levels were placed in the same simulation while interacting with each other and playing the same game. Of course, one drawback to this experiment was the use of the Simple Majority Rule, as connections to several high-tolerance agents would change the action of a low-tolerance agent, despite a decrease in payoff.

However, in the cases that there would be two clusters of decisions, there were general trends in the strategy picked based on tolerance level. In Prisoner's Dilemma, agents with the lowest tolerance were most likely to defect, though the entire network became more likely to defect. The clearest and most striking trend, however, was in Stag Hunt. This game is more interesting than Pure Coordination and Prisoner's Dilemma because, like Pure Coordination, there are two Nash equilibra, but like Prisoner's Dilemma, there is a striking difference between these strategies. Agents with a high n-tolerance, seeking to avoid risk (as they were more likely to get a 'bad' partner and not break the connection), were more likely to defect to select the risk-dominant strategy. Agents with a very low n-tolerance, on the other hand, sought to maximize payoff and therefore cooperated in order to choose the payoff-dominant strategy.

The Use of Tolerance to Induce Community Structure

Tolerance was manipulated in order to induce a more realistic form of community structure from a random graph in two experiments.

Use of Tags

By implementing a tag system, we are able to generate a network similar to the karate club network observed by W.W. Zachary. He tracked the relationships in a karate club which split into two factions over a few years, and the resulting network has been used widely in social network research (Newman, 2004). In order to obtain this type of structure where there is a mixture of two groups, we include a tag for each of the agents that categorizes it as one of two 'types'. An agent's connections remain random, but it is considerably more tolerant of those that share its tag type than those that don't. In this manner, we can develop an idea of prejudice or preference in a network and divide a graph into two intermingled groups.

Figure 3. The level of tolerance to the decision made in Stag Hunt

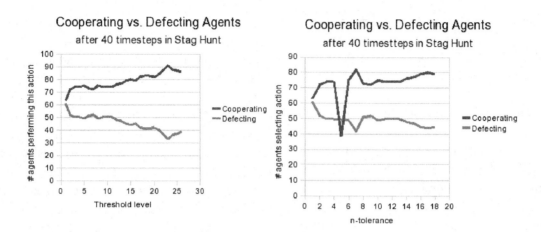

Optimal Tolerance for Network Stability

One way to characterize community structure in a social network is to examine the number of triangles that exist (notice that many triangles can be easily identified in Zachary's karate club network). Therefore, another experiment written uses tolerance to encourage the existence of triangles in network structure. If two agents share at least one mutual friend, they will be much more tolerant of each other than otherwise. This way, once triangles occur, there is more incentive to keep them. The result is in Figure 4.

Optimal Tolerance for Network Stability

Since we can control the average n-tolerance in a network by changing the threshold, the problem of setting that threshold to achieve an "optimal" tolerance, if one exists, arises. We must first define what we are looking for in an optimal tolerance. We initially considered the idea of selecting the level of n-tolerance that would yield the highest reward. However, n-tolerance is partially based on the average total reward, and the feedback loop caused by the relationship complicated our results. Instead, we focus on the amount of time it takes a network to reach a stable state.

Definition 8: We call an n-tolerance *optimal* if there is no n-tolerance that generates a stable network in fewer time steps.

Notice that a level of tolerance greater than 1 will never yield a stable network, as all average or below-average agents will be dropped each time. Therefore we can restrict the threshold to [0,1]. In empirical results shown in Figure 5, an n-tolerance of 1.25 to 1.75 tends to be best. This range, strangely enough, is the same for all games played, though different patterns arise. None of the current results on optimal tolerance, however, have a mathematical base. Development of a model for optimal tolerance is therefore left as future work.

CONCLUSION

We have presented a mathematical model of tolerance to predict the *n*-tolerance of an agent. In the experiments, we adjust the parameters of the model to control the level of tolerance within a given social interaction rule. Although the work here was done only with the Highest Rewarding Neighborhood rule and the Highest Weighted

Figure 4. The level of tolerance measured by the number of triangles in Stag Hunt

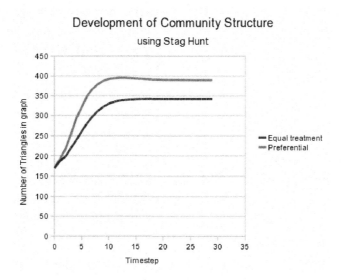

Figure 5. N-Tolerance in Prisoner's Dilemma (left), Pure Coordination (middle), and Stag Hunt (right)

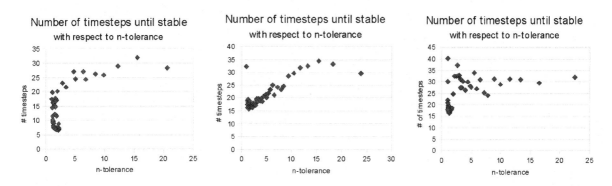

Reward rule, this idea could be extended toward any social interaction rule in a dynamic network. Such extensions could be made in the future, and comparisons between the tolerance models of different rules would be very interesting to see. Along those lines, it would be good to do some psychological research to test whether the factors of our model of tolerance match the factors of tolerance in people. A comprehensive list of the factors of tolerance in people could then be compared with the models of tolerance to test the veracity of the social interaction rules used.

Further research could also be done on the idea of an optimal tolerance, though current research has not suggested that there is a clear solution. Another interesting possibility for a future problem is to study a combination of network phenomena such as stability and network structure. For example, one could examine the effect of different levels of tolerance in agents on the structure of the network or the efficiency of the network.

ACKNOWLEDGMENT

This work was supported in part by the U.S. National Science Foundation under Grants IIS 0755405 and CNS 0821585.

REFERENCES

Albert, R., & Barb'asi, A. L. (2002). Statistical Mechanics of Complex Networks. *Modern Physics*, 47-97.

Anderson, J. R. (2007). Animal Behavior: Tolerant Primates Cooperate Best. *Current Biology, 17*(7). doi:10.1016/j.cub.2007.02.005

Axelrod, R. M. (1997). *The Complexity of Cooperation: Agent-Based Models of Competition and Collaboration*. Princeton, NJ: Princeton University Press.

Benenson, J. F., Markovits, H., Fitzgerald, C., Georoy, D., Flemming, J., Kahlenberg, S. K., & Wrangham, R. W. (2009). Males' Greater Tolerance of Same-Sex Peers. *Psychological Science, 20*(2). doi:10.1111/j.1467-9280.2009.02269.x

Borenstein, E., & Ruppin, E. (2003). Enhancing Autonomous Agents Evolution with Learning by Imitation. *Journal of Artificial Intelligence and Simulation of Behavior, 1*(4), 335–348.

Davidsson, P. (2002). Agent-Based Social Simulation: A Computer Science View. *Journal of Artificial Societies and Social Simulation, 5*(1).

Delgado, J. (2002). Emergence of Social Convenetions in Complex Networks. *Artificial Intelligence*, 171–185. doi:10.1016/S0004-3702(02)00262-X

Edmonds, B., Norling, E., & Hales, D. (2009). Towards the Evolution of Social Structure. *Computational & Mathematical Organization Theory*, 15.

Epstein, J. (1999). Agent-Based Computational Models and Generative Scoail Science. *Complexity, 4*(5). doi:10.1002/(SICI)1099-0526(199905/06)4:5<41::AID-CPLX9>3.0.CO;2-F

Fararo, T. J., & Sunshine, M. H. (1964). *A Study of a Biased Friendship Net*. Syracuse, NY: Syracuse University Press.

Gilby, I. C., & Wrangham, R. W. (2008). Association patterns among wild chimpanzees (Pan troglodytesschweinfurthii) reflect sex differences in cooperation. *Behav Eloc Sociobiol, 62*(11).

Hare, B., Melis, A. P., Woods, V., Hastingsn, S., & Wrangham, R. (2007). Tolerance Allows Bonobos to Outperform Chimpanzees on a Cooperative Task. *Current Biology, 17*(7). doi:10.1016/j.cub.2007.02.040

Jin, E. M., Girvan, M., & Newman, M. E. J. (2001). The Structure of Growing Social Networks. *Physical Review E: Statistical, Nonlinear, and Soft Matter Physics, 64*(4). doi:10.1103/PhysRevE.64.046132

Liljeros, F., Edling, C. R., Amaral, L. A. N., Stanely, H. E., & Aberg, Y. (2001). The Web of Human Sexual Contacts. *Nature*, 907–908. doi:10.1038/35082140

Melis, A. P., Hare, B., & Tomasello, M. (2006). Engineering cooperation in chimpanzees: tolerance constraints on cooperation. *Animal Behaviour, 72*(2). doi:10.1016/j.anbehav.2005.09.018

Newman, M. E. J. (2003). *The Structure and Function of Complex Networks*. Society for Industrial and Applied Mathematics.

Newman, M. E. J. (2004). Detecting Community Structure in Networks. *The European Physical Journal B, 38*(2). doi:10.1140/epjb/e2004-00124-y

Redner, S. (1998). How Popular is Your Paper? An Emprical Study of the Citation Distribution. *Eur. Phys.*, 131-134.

Riolo, R. L., Cohen, M. D., & Axelrod, R. (2001). Evolution of cooperation without reciprocity. *Nature*, *414*, 6862. doi:10.1038/35106555

Rossi, G., Stefano, A., & Hales, D. (2009). Evolving Networks for Social Optima in the Weakest Link Game. *Computational & Mathematical Organization Theory*, *15*(2). doi:10.1007/s10588-008-9051-1

Shoham, Y., & Tennenholtz, M. (1997). On the Emergence of Social Conventions: Modeling, Analysis and Simulations. *AI*, 139-166.

Toivonen, L., Kovanen, L., Kivela, M., Onnela, J.-P., Saramaki, J., & Kaski, K. (2009). A Comparative Study of Social Network Models: Network Evolution Models and Nodal Attribute Models. *Social Networks*, 31.

Watts, D. J. (1999). *Small Worlds*. Princeton, NJ: Princeton University Press.

Wobber, V., Wrangham, R., & Hare, B. (2010). Bonobas Exhibit Delayed Development of Social Behavior and Cognition Relative to Chimpanzees. *Current Biology*, *20*(3). doi:10.1016/j.cub.2009.11.070

Wu, Y., & Zhang, Y. (2009). Stability Analysis in Dynamic Social Networks. In *Proceedings of the Symposium on Agent-Directed Simulation (ADS'09), the 2010 Spring Simulation Multiconference (SpringSim'10)*, Orlando, FL.

Zhang, Y., & Leezer, J. (2009). Emergence of Social Norms in Complex Networks. In *Proceedings of the Symposium on Social Computing Applications (SCA09), The 2009 IEEE International Conference on Social Computing (SocialCom-09)*, Vancouver, Canada (pp. 549-555).

Zimmermann, M., & Eguiluz, v. (2005). Cooperation, Social Networks and the Emergence of Leadership in a Prisoners Dilemma with Adaptive Local Interactions. *Physical Review*.

This work was previously published in International Journal of Agent Technologies and Systems, Volume 3, Issue 1, edited by Yu Zhang, pp. 52-68, copyright 2011 by IGI Publishing (an imprint of IGI Global).

Chapter 7
Modeling Virtual Footprints

Rajiv Kadaba
The University of Texas at Austin, USA

Suratna Budalakoti
The University of Texas at Austin, USA

David DeAngelis
The University of Texas at Austin, USA

K. Suzanne Barber
The University of Texas at Austin, USA

ABSTRACT

Entities interacting on the web establish their identity by creating virtual personas. These entities, or agents, can be human users or software-based. This research models identity using the Entity-Persona Model, a semantically annotated social network inferred from the persistent traces of interaction between personas on the web. A Persona Mapping Algorithm is proposed which compares the local views of personas in their social network referred to as their Virtual Signatures, for structural and semantic similarity. The semantics of the Entity-Persona Model are modeled by a vector space model of the text associated with the personas in the network, which allows comparison of their Virtual Signatures. This enables all the publicly accessible personas of an entity to be identified on the scale of the web. This research enables an agent to identify a single entity using multiple personas on different networks, provided that multiple personas exhibit characteristic behavior. The agent is able to increase the trustworthiness of on-line interactions by establishing the identity of entities operating under multiple personas. Consequently, reputation measures based on on-line interactions with multiple personas can be aggregated and resolved to the true singular identity.

1. INTRODUCTION

The way that an individual's identity is created and experienced is fundamentally different in the

DOI: 10.4018/978-1-4666-1565-6.ch007

virtual world. The basic cues used to uniquely identify individuals in the real world are missing, making the association between an entity and its identity ambiguous (Turkle, 1997). This research creates a model of the virtual world which dispels this ambiguity, allowing the virtual personas created by an entity to be linked together. Informally, a virtual persona is a name and its associated attributes, which an entity uses to communicate with other personas.

The virtual world in the context of this research refers collectively to various explicit or inferred social networks. Examples of explicit social networks are websites such as Facebook, Orkut, MySpace, and LinkedIn. Social networks can be inferred from the digital traces of interaction between entities, or individuals, on the Internet, such as in the blogosphere (Kumar et al., 2004), online discussion forums, knowledge sharing sites, IRC logs and the co-occurrence of names in the large amount of textual data on the Internet (Jin et al., 2007). In an explicit social network there exists a framework by which entities can specify to whom they are related and the context of this relationship.

Access to explicit networks is generally controlled (Grimmelmann, 2008) because of the privacy concerns of its participants (Acquisti & Gross, 2006). Inferred social networks lack the privacy mechanisms of explicit networks as its users assume they are as anonymous as they wish to be. The work in this paper counters this assumption since users must engage in consistent and information rich interactions in order to provide value to the framework. The establishment of the reputation of an entity's virtual persona within the framework is an important motivating factor for its consistent use, as others use reputation to assess the reliability of information associated with the persona (Donath, 1999). Every new persona created will need to establish its reputation within its social network, which requires time and effort. This penalty associated with creating a persona which is capable of meaningful interaction makes a persona valuable. Virtual personas with erratic interactions are not worth detecting as they have little value.

In a more general sense; an entity is an agent interacting within a multi agent framework. An agent could be a software program that acts according to an internally specified set of goals, or objectives. An agent can also be a dedicated piece of hardware designed to accomplish a particular task in the virtual world. An agent can even be a team of humans operating under a common goal. This research explores the canonical example of matching multiple virtual personas to a single human entity.

Search engines treat personal names and pseudonyms as keywords, giving virtual personas the same status as ordinary text. Queries for people's names only find occurrences with verbatim matches to the query text while they may have interacted extensively, using various personas. The model proposed in this paper can be used to find more accurate results for the information associated with an individual available publicly on the web. Augmenting web search with the ability to link entities and their personas can be perceived as an attack on an individual's privacy, as information which may have been exchanged with the expectation of anonymity granted by a virtual persona is now linked back to its progenitor. Conversely this research can also contribute to an individual's ability to safeguard their privacy and protect their identity from theft. As the concept of identity in the virtual world is formalized and an upper bound on the ability of a determined adversarial agent is found, techniques to remain anonymous in spite of sophisticated statistical tools can be developed. Further, software agents who are capable of warning users of the unintended inferences which can be made with the data they publish may also be possible.

The proposed technique for resolving multiple personas requires that an entity exhibit characteristic behavior across multiple personas. Measurable entity behaviors can be both content-based and link-based. Content-based behaviors include the creation of text content as well as any metadata created by the entity such as endorsements of other content. Link-based behaviors include any action which defines the structure of a network, such as message passing or "befriending". One application of this research is in the task of anti-aliasing in social networks. Anti-aliasing (Novak et al., 2004) is the task of identifying when a single user has multiple aliases in a social network. This is important in trust networks, as a distrusted user or set of users, after being removed from a network (by a moderator, for example), can insert themselves into a network at a later point in time with a pseudonym. Agents capable of continuously associating personas with the singular identity of an entity will offer increased assurance of entity reputations based on interactions of associated personas.

The proposed technique is not designed to resolve multiple personas into a single entity when that entity exhibits completely different behavior in different networks. One example is the task of resolving a person with two social networks: a professional network, and a personal network. The person may not speak (create content) about similar topics, and he or she may not even interact with any of the same people across the two different networks. Resolving each persona to a single entity is extraordinarily difficult in this situation without trustworthy metadata such as an IP address or name. The technique presented here requires characteristic behavior across personas. Section 4 shows that the technique is successful at matching two different sets of anonymized data in which the same people are likely to be talking to the same other people about the same topics. Consequently, agents can assess trustworthiness of individual personas and relate those trustworthiness assessments to the singular identity associated with those personas. This research offers the groundwork for establishing the connection between the multiple personas and a singular entity identity.

2. RELATED WORK

The privacy of individuals, referenced in social network data released to researchers, application developers, and marketing organizations is ostensibly protected by anonymizing the social graph, as their goal is to make inferences about the aggregated data not specific individuals. Privacy preserving data mining is a research area in which data sets are modified and algorithms developed which do not compromise privacy (Verykios et al., 2004). Based on the background information available to an attacker and the definition of private information, vertex, edge and graph properties can be used to compromise privacy. Therfore, anonymization algorithms are designed with a specific model of an attacker and the intended use of the anonymized network. Zhou et al. (2008) classify anonymization methods into two categories. Methods which cluster vertices and edges, and replace the graph elements in each cluster by the cluster mean. This effectively hides information of individual users. Graph modification by randomly adding and/or removing vertices and edges such that the overall properties of the graph are maintained.

Individual users however are unable to protect their virtual personas with these methods as they require knowledge of the entire graph. Furthermore, the utility of their persona will be limited if most of their interactions are used to safeguard their privacy. The only way a user can attempt to safeguard the anonymity of his personas without altering the information he wishes to communicate is to ensure the personas have different names.

Approaches to the reverse task of de-anonymization are usually based on unique subgraphs in the anonymized social network, and can be classified into active and passive attacks (Backstrom et al., 2007). Active attacks are attacks in which nodes that form a unique subgraph are inserted into the graph before it is anonymized (for example, before being released to the public for research of other purposes). As this subgraph is known a priori it can be used to identify other nodes in the released graph. Passive attacks (Narayanan & Shmatikov, 2009) are similar, however no nodes are inserted, instead a small group of nodes collude to generate a subgraph which is later used to re-identify adjacent nodes.

De-anonymization of individuals in an anonymized data set is equivalent to linking personas in two different social networks as the attackers background information is also a social network. These techniques de-anonymize nodes using structural properties of graphs and are not designed to target specific nodes. They also rely on the fact that both networks have many nodes in common. Purely structural equivalence techniques break down if the neighborhood of an individual node changes drastically. The work presented here uses structural information in addition to persona content for de-anonymization.

In contrast to graph-based approaches, Novak et al. (2004) use a content-based approach where they reconcile online personas to unique users by clustering the content associated with the personas, such that each cluster represents a unique user. The data is derived from an online discussion board by only considering text associated with a persona independent of relation information. Similar to the approach used in this paper, two sets of personas are synthetically created, although by random division. Random division allows words from specific topics to appear in every division which will not occur in real data as topics discussed will change. Text originating from specific threads of discussion available in every division makes the disambiguation task easier than if the topics were continuously evolving. Temporal division as used here addresses this problem by correctly capturing topic evolution.

Bhattacharya and Getoor (2006) were the first to use a Latent Dirichlet Model for entity resolution. Their approach focuses on processing database queries on systems with uncertain and imprecise references (Bhattacharya & Getoor,

2007). Their work is designed to resolve unintentional ambiguities that are caused by mismatched records, whereas the work presented here focuses on resolving personas acting on a network.

Jin et al. (2007) extract social networks from the web using hypertext data retrieved from search engine queries. The nodes in the network are named entities which are known a priori. Edges are inferred using heuristics from co-occurrence of names, and the type of relationship the edge represents is determined from the query text. Queries consist of the entity names and the type of relationship. Staddon et al. (2007) have leveraged web search to determine unintended inferences which can be drawn from data published on the web. Keywords are extracted from data intended to be published using TF-IDF (Term Frequency - Inverse Document Frequency) and are used to construct queries to search engines. New keywords in the results of these queries not present in the original keyword set represent inferences which can be drawn from the web. Both these techniques only find information associated with a specific name i.e. they assume an individual has only one persona on the Internet. Although the results are interesting they bring little insight to the true nature of identity on the web.

3. MODELING ENTITIES AND PERSONAS

Entities communicate on the web using identifiers unique within a framework making the identifier - framework combination also unique. At Internet scope the identifier can be an IP or email address depending on the protocol, or a username in the scope of a Web 2.0 application. The identity of an entity possessing an identifier is characterized by the set of other identifiers it has communicated with and the content of this communication, collectively referred to as its virtual signature.

3.1. Model and Definitions

Definition 3.3.1: An entity ξ is something capable of independent interaction, which can be uniquely identified in the real world.

An entity can be an individual or software agent. Individuals by default are unique as they can have only one instance in the real world. A software agent may not be unique as it is very easy to create many instances of the same agent. Therefore, all instances of the same software agent which exhibit the same behavior are considered collectively a single entity regardless of their physical location. Entities interact on the web through a framework using a persona, which is an instantiation of an entity within the framework. An entity can possess more than one persona within a given framework.

Definition 3.1.2: A framework is an implementation of software and associated protocols which enable entities to interact.

Definition 3.1.3: A persona π is a tuple *(i,d)*, where *i* is an identifier unique within a framework and *d* is a *n*-tuple of associated information and attributes which an entity uses to establish its identity and interact within a social network. For every persona there exists exactly one entity.

A social network (Definition 3.1.4) is used to model the virtual signatures of entities or personas which are nodes in the network such that two nodes are connected if they have communicated. Again, the criteria for considering whether that communication has occurred depends on the framework.

Definition 3.1.4: A social network S is a vertex and edge labeled undirected graph $G = (V,E)$, where *V* is a set of either exclusively entities or personas and *E* is a subset of the Cartesian product $V \times V$ such that $(v, v) \notin E$. No self

loops are allowed since they are meaningless in a communication graph. Every edge (u,v), $u,v \in V$ has a label γ and every vertex has a label χ, which is arbitrary information associated with the edge or vertex.

The *Entity-Persona Model* (Figure 1) consists of a social network of entities S_Ξ and at least one social network of personas S_Π. S_Ξ is a real world social network of entities whose personas need to be linked. S_Π is a social network of personas inferred from the records of the framework in which the entities in S_Ξ communicate. The label of vertex u_π, χ_π in the graph G_Π of S_Π is $\pi(i,T(d))$ and the label $\gamma_{\pi_1\pi_2}$ of edge $\left(u_{\pi_1}, v_{\pi_1}\right)$ between vertex $u_{\pi 1}$ labeled by π_1 and vertex v_{π_1} labeled by π_2 is $T\left(d_{\pi_1} \bigcup d_{\pi_2}\right)$. T is an operation which reduces d to its semantics which is outlined in section 3.3. Hence, the social network of personas is vertex labeled by the semantics of information generated by the personas and edge labeled by the semantics of all the information exchanged by the personas it connects.

Definition 3.1.5: The virtual signature of a persona π in the context of the *Entity-Persona Model* is the social network S_Π rooted at the node of the persona.

The identity of a persona is defined by the structure of S_Π and the semantics of the graph labels. S_Π is not unique to a persona as it is a social network of personas, however its local view can be unique making its virtual signature also unique.

3.2. Problem Specification

Linking entities and their corresponding personas can be formally expressed as finding a mapping between a set of *n* entities $\Xi = \{\xi_1, \xi_2, ..., \xi_n\}$ which are nodes in a social network S_Ξ and a set of *m* personas $\Pi = \{\pi_1, \pi_2, ..., \pi_m\}$. Π may be partitioned into $P = \{\Pi_1, \Pi_2, ..., \Pi_l\}$ a collection of *l* subsets of

Figure 1. The entity-persona model as it is initialized

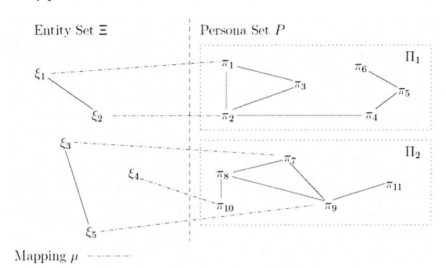

Π if the personas exist in l different frameworks. Each framework is expressed as a separate social network in the model.

Definition 3.2.1: A mapping μ is a binary relation on $\cup_{i=1}^{l} S_E \times S_{\pi_i}$, where $(\xi, \pi) \in \mu, \xi \in S_E, \pi \in S_{\pi_i} \Leftrightarrow$ entity ξ has created persona π.

From the information exchanged within each framework, P can be inferred. A query on the model is a set of entities Ξ and a mapping μ which maps every entity in Ξ to at least one persona in P. If no mapping between an entity and a persona is known, the query algorithm will not have an example to train on making mapping the personas of the entity impossible. The social network S_Ξ and the mapping μ are only partially known. From this information the complete social network S_Ξ and μ must be inferred. This can be accomplished by,

1. Selecting a entity $\xi \in \Xi$.
2. For (ξ, π_ξ) in mapping μ, find a set Π_{new}, which contains all $\pi \in P$, that best match π_ξ by some objective criteria.

3. Update mapping μ such that $\mu = \mu \cup_{q \in \Pi_{new}} (\xi, q)$.
4. Update S_Ξ such that if two mapped personas have an edge between each other, their corresponding entities have an edge in S_Ξ.
5. Repeat.

3.3. Semantic Similarity

If the virtual signatures (Definition 3.1.5) of personas are to be compared, it follows that there must be a way to compare their local views of their social network. Graphs can be compared structurally using combinatorial algorithms (Cordella et al., 2004) or by comparing their spectra (Umeyama, 1988). In a social network however the nodes and edges are labeled requiring the development of the means to compare these labels.

The edge labels of a social network are the inferred semantics of the relation- ship the edges represent. The vertex labels are the inferred semantics of all the information generated by an entity through the persona associated with the vertex. These semantics must be short descriptions of the information they are inferred from, while maintaining as much discriminative information as possible.

For a persona π_1 which is a tuple *(i, d)*, the vertex labels are the semantics of the textual information in d_{π_1} and the edge labels are the semantics of the information in $d_{\pi_1} \bigcup d_{\pi_2}$ which will be referred to as textual information associated with a graph label *D*. *D* is treated as a collection of terms without any ordering known as the "bag of words" model. An entity using one persona may use different terms in another, but both are likely to have a large number of common terms giving rise to personas that have similar labels at their vertices and incident edges. Three transform functions to infer the semantics of *D* and metrics to compare them are presented.

3.3.1. Vocabulary Approach

The simplest technique to infer the semantics of text associated with a persona is to construct a vector of unique terms in the text and assign it to a graph element label. This can result in a very high dimensional vector if the number of unique terms is very large but it is very simple to compute, as the time complexity is linear in the number of terms. Labels can be compared by using the Jaccard index, which measures the similarity between two sets $\chi1$ and $\chi2$.

$$J\left(\chi_1, \chi_2\right) = \frac{\left|\chi_1 \cap \chi_2\right|}{\left|\chi_1 \cup \chi_2\right|}$$

This produces a score between 0 and 1, with 1 being exactly the same. This technique captures stylometric information such as consistent misspellings to discriminate between personas but cannot capture information such as favorite words. It is particularly weak at discriminating when the number of terms in the original text is very small.

3.3.2. TF-IDF Approach

Term Frequency - Inverse Document frequency is a popular technique in information retrieval to infer which terms best represent a document in a corpus. In the case of the Entity-Persona Model, the document is the textual information associated with a persona and the corpus is the collection of all persona.

First a vocabulary of all the terms used by every persona in the model is constructed. A term frequency vector is then constructed for each label χ_j and is normalized by the total number of terms used in D_{χ_j}. It has the same dimensionality as the vocabulary vector. Term frequency tf_{t_i} of the term t_i is given by,

$$tf_{\chi_j, t_i} = \frac{\text{number of times ti occurs in } D_{\chi_j}}{\text{total number of terms in } D_{\chi_j}}$$

Next an inverse document frequency vector of t_i, the ith term in the vocabulary is constructed which measures the number of occurrences of the term across all the personas. It is also normalized by the number of personas in the model and used on a log scale.

$$idf_{t_i} = \log \frac{\text{number of nodes in } S_{\Pi}}{\text{number of occurrences of } t_i}$$

Finally, a vector to be assigned to each label χ_j is constructed by finding the $tf - idf$ of every term.

$$tf - idf_{\chi_j, t_i} = tf_{\chi_j, t_i} \times idf_{t_i}$$

Terms which are distinctive of a document but not of the corpus get a higher $tf - idf$. This technique can reduce the dimensionality of the feature space to a greater extent than the previous approach as only the most important terms can

Figure 2. Graphical model of the Latent Dirichlet Allocation

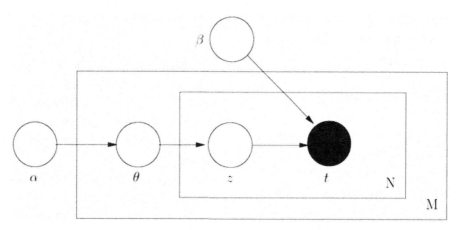

be considered i.e. terms with the highest $tf - idf$. To compare labels χ_j and χ_k the cosine similarity between their vectors is computed,

$$\text{Cosine Similarity}_{\chi_j, \chi_k} = \frac{\sum_{\forall i} tf - idf_{\chi_j, t_i} \times tf - idf_{\chi_k, t_i}}{\left\| tf - idf_{\chi_j} \right\| \times \left\| tf - idf_{\chi_k} \right\|}$$

Cosine similarity results in a score between −1 and 1 with 1 being exactly the same.

Therefore a higher score implies that the labels being compared are similar.

3.3.3. Multinomial Topic Distribution Approach

The previous techniques are not robust, as an entity may not have interacted sufficiently using a particular persona to use enough of the terms characteristic of it. When a persona has just begun to interact, the vector constructed based on words associated with him/her will be very sparse, when projected on the high-dimensional space consisting of the entire dataset vocabulary. This sparseness means that the cosine similarity score might be zero or close to zero, even when comparing two edges with high semantic similarity.

Instead of a collection of raw terms, a label can be a probability distribution over topics. Topics capture the high level semantics of the terms and are not inferred from the textual information associated with a single persona, rather from all the personas in the Entity-Persona Model. Each graph label has a topic assigned to it with higher probability if it is likely that the terms in the text have come from that topic. If a persona has used very few terms, a complete set of topics can still be inferred by leveraging the statistical term use of all the other personas. A multinomial distribution is a convenient way of representing the topic distribution. As the probability of all the topics in a multinomial distribution must sum to unity, a sparse vocabulary vector can be transformed into a non sparse vector of topic probabilities.

Latent Dirichlet Allocation (Figure 2) proposed by Blei et al. (2003), is a generative model which can capture the inter document statistical structure of a corpus. It posits that the words in a document are generated from a set of topics. Each topic is a probability distribution over words. Therefore a document is generated by first picking a topic and then picking a word from that topic, for every word in the document.

The generative process to generate terms from k topics can be outlined as follows:

1. Choose length of textual information associated with a graph element, $N \sim Poisson(\eta)$.
2. Choose a topic distribution $\theta \sim Dirchlet(\alpha)$.
3. For each of the N terms t_n
   a. For each of the N terms t_n
   b. Choose a term t_n from $p(t_n \mid z_n, \beta)$

β is a $k \times V$ matrix, where V is the number of unique terms used by all the personas. Every row of β is a vector of $p(t_n \mid z)$, i.e. the probability of a term given a topic. α and β are the prior probabilities which are initialized to be non informative. This can be changed if external knowledge about the frameworks being modeled is available. The joint probability distribution of D is given by,

$$p(t \mid \alpha, \beta) = \int_\theta P(\theta \mid \alpha) \left(\prod_{n=1}^{N} \sum_{z_n} p(Z_n \mid \theta) p(t_n, \mid z_n, \beta) \right) d\theta$$

Using the point probability estimate $p(t_n/D)$ obtained from term frequencies, the maximum likelihood estimates of the hyper parameters α and β can be obtained by employing a variational Bayes Expectation-Maximization algorithm as detailed in Blei et al. (2003). The parameters of the multinomial distribution over topics for the graph labels are contained in a k dimensional vector of $p(z_n|D)$ for n from 1 to k where N_{unique} is the number of unique terms in D.

$$p(Z_n \mid D) = \frac{\Gamma(\sum_i freq(t_i))}{\prod_i \Gamma(freq(t_i))} \prod_{i=1}^{N_{unique}} P(t_i \mid z_n)^{freq(t_i)}$$

Kullback-Leibler divergence is a non symmetric measure of the difference between two probability distributions. This can be used to compare two homogeneous graph labels. If p_{ξ_1} and p_{ξ_2} are two vectors of the parameters of the distributions associated with labels χ_1 and χ_2, then the similarity between them is given by,

$$D_{KL}(p_{\xi_1} \mid\mid p_{\xi_2}) = \sum_{i=1}^{k} p_{\xi_1}(i) \log_2 \frac{p_{\xi_1}(i)}{p_{\xi_2}(i)}$$

Although KL divergence is not a true distance measure, its scores can be compared meaningfully. The score is the difference in bits required to encode the two distributions with a score of 0 bits indicating that the distributions are exactly the same.

McCallum et al. (2007) proposed an Author-Recipient-Topic (ART) generative model of a social network, which is an extension of LDA. The topic distribution θ is conditioned on the distributions of authors and recipients of messages. The pairwise topic distribution between two authors can be inferred using such a model. The Entity-Persona Model achieves this by actually constructing the social graph. The ART model however, will not be able to use the social structure of the graph if its actors exchange information about very different topics which can be handled by the Entity-Persona Model.

3.4. The Persona Mapping Algorithm

The problem the Persona Mapping algorithm addresses is as follows: a single entity has created two different personas s and t in two separate social networks. Provided with graphs G_S and G_T corresponding to the two social networks, and the vertex corresponding to persona s in G_S, the algorithm attempts to identify correctly the vertex corresponding to t in G_T. The attempt is based on a semantic comparison of the information associated with s in G_S with the information available for the personas in G_T: the algorithm returns a vertex in the target graph which has the maximum overlap between its virtual signature and the signature of s. G_S and G_T can be identical, in this case the target is an entity with multiple personas within the same social network.

The Persona Mapping algorithm can be divided into three steps.

3.4.1. Candidate Vertices Identification

During this step, a similarity score is calculated between the source vertex s and every vertex in the target graph G_T. The score is computed by comparing the vertex labels using one of the semantic similarly measures described in section 3.3. The similarity scores are inserted into a max priority queue. The priority queue enables the prioritization of the most likely matches according to semantic similarity, allowing the more computationally expensive structural similarity measure to stop if a satisfactory score is found.

3.4.2. Vertices Neighborhood Comparison

This step of the algorithm consists of a modified simultaneous Breadth First Search of the two graphs G_S and G_T. The candidate vertices are popped from the max priority queue constructed in Step 1 one by one. For each candidate vertex c, a pairwise score between the incident edges on c, and the edges incident on source vertex s, is computed. The pair of edges with the highest score are said to be mapped, and the respective neighbors to s and c that are part of the mapped edges, are called mapped neighbors. That is, let ss' and cc' be such a pair of mapped edges: then the s' and c' as a pair are called mapped neighbors.

These mapped neighbors are added to the ends of FIFO queues (one for each graph) maintained for the purpose of breadth first search. This means that, eventually, the neighborhoods of s' and c' will be compared using edge-based similarity, as part of the simultaneous breadth first search. The final similarity score of a vertex with the source vertex is a weighted mean of the similarity between all pairs of mapped neighbors. The weighing approach is discussed in section 3.4.3.

The data structures this step maintains are as follows:

1. Two FIFO queues, Q_S and Q_T, which are initially seeded with the starting vertices.

2. An auxiliary graph G_A, which is initialized with a single node labeled by the mapping *(s,c)*. Its purpose is to maintain the best effort match between the structure of G_S and G_T. The vertex mappings of newly mapped edges are added to the auxiliary graph and the vertices in the vertex pairs mapped are queued on their respective FIFO's.

3. A third auxiliary data structure that keeps track of the 'color' of each vertex is maintained to make sure that an already explored vertex is not explored again. All vertices are initially colored white; when a vertex is queued it is colored black. Next time a vertex is a candidate to be queued as part of a mapped edge, its color is examined. If the color is black, the edge mapping is ignored. This is to insure that all vertices are unambiguously mapped.

Vertex pairs are popped out from the two FIFO's until they are empty or a limit Δ of the depth of the Breadth First Search is reached. The mapping thus achieved between the graph G_T rooted at c and G_S rooted at s is a best effort match, because the maximum number of neighbors mapped is the smaller of the number of neighbors of each vertex, and the mappings are assigned in a greedy fashion.

3.4.3. Auxiliary Graph Score Calculation

After the auxiliary graph is created its score is computed by averaging the vertex scores of vertices at equal path lengths from the starting vertex and combining them in a linear combination weighted by a Gaussian with standard deviation σ. This score is compared with the score of the previous candidate vertex. If the previous score is greater by ε the previous candidate vertex is returned and the

Algorithm 1. Persona mapping algorithm

```
MAP-NODE(G_S, G_T, s, ε, σ, Δ)
 1  Q ← ∅
 2  for each vertex v ∈ V[G_T]
 3       do Q ← GET-VERTEX-SCORE(G_S, G_T, s, v)
 4  while Q ≠ ∅
 5       do VertexScore ← MAXIMUM(Q)
 6          c ← EXTRACT-MAX(Q)
 7          Q_S, Q_T ← INITIALIZE-QUEUES(s, c)
 8          G_A ← INITIALIZE-GRAPH(s, c, VertexScore)
 9          while Q_S ≠ ∅ and CHECK-DEPTH(Δ)
10               do node_1 ← DEQUEUE(Q_S)
11                  node_2 ← DEQUEUE(Q_T)
12                  AssignedEdges ← MAP-EDGES(node_1, node_2)
13                  UPDATE-GRAPH(G_A, AssignedEdges)
14                  Q_S, Q_T ← UPDATE-QUEUES(Q_S, Q_T, AssignedEdges)
15          Score ← GET-COMBINED-SCORE(G_A, σ)
16          if LastScore − Score ≥ ε
17              then return LastC
18              else LastScore ← Score
19                   LastC ← c
```

algorithm terminates, otherwise it continues until all candidate vertices are examined for structural congruence. A gaussian of high kurtosis can be chosen to give the vertex score of the source to candidate mapping vertex higher weight and a flat curve gives equal weight to the scores of the all the vertices in the auxiliary graph. The parameter ε is chosen as a balance between runtime and the need for the algorithm to attempt to discriminate between very similar personas.

As the personas of an entity may not have the same neighbors in their social graphs, the structure of the local view of their social network can vary. Depending on the framework the personas are

Algorithm 2. Best effort edge mapping

```
MAP-EDGES(G_Z, G_T, u, v)
 1  for each vertex v ∈ Adj[u]
 2       do Consumed[v] ← NIL
 3          for each vertex u ∈ Adj[s]
 4               do Assigned[u] ← NIL
 5                  P ← GET-EDGE-SCORE(G_s, G_T, u, v)
 6  while P ≠ ∅
 7       do r ← MAXIMUM(P)
 8          s, t ← EXTRACT-MAX(P)
 9          if ¬ Consumed[s] and Assigned[t] = 0
10              then Consumed[s] ← true
11                   Assigned[t] ← r, s
12  return Assigned
```

inferred from they may exchange information on very different topics making semantic information unreliable. If both semantic and structural information change drastically a persona may not be able to be mapped correctly, but if only one of them change the algorithm can take this into account by decide on the weight of the scores of vertices in the auxiliary graph. The larger the path length between the vertex which maps the source vertex to the candidate vertex and a vertex in the auxiliary graph, the less that vertex contributes to the score. If $s_{i,d}$ is the score of the ith vertex at path length d then the score of the similarity of the candidate vertex to the source vertex is given by:

$$score = \sum_{d=0}^{\Delta} \frac{\sum_{\forall i} s_{i,d}}{|s_{i,d}|} \left(\frac{1}{\sqrt{2\pi}} \right) e^{-\frac{d^2}{2}}$$

3.5. Discussion: Time Complexity

Subgraph isomorphism is a NP-complete problem; the Persona Mapping Algorithm avoids this pitfall. It builds an intersection graph between two subgraphs greedily to check for similarity making the problem tractable. The time complexity of the algorithm is $O(n^4 + n \log n)$. However, large real world social networks have node degrees which generally follow a power law distribution (Adamic et al., 2001; Amaral et al., 2000). Therefore the edge mapping routine will take on average $O(d^2)$, where d is the average node degree of the network resulting in an overall time complexity of $O(n^2)$. The use of Δ to limit the depth of the breadth first search results in a further decrease in running time to build the auxiliary graph. Empirically a depth of 2 or 3 is sufficient to achieve a correct mapping as larger depths will include the entire graph due to the small world phenomenon (Kleinberg, 2000), which in most cases is unnecessary.

Percentage of personas mapped correctly is a good measure of performance on a given data set. It is argued by Narayanan and Shmatikov

(2009) that this metric is flawed because nodes which are impossible to map will bias the results. However, this does not matter while measuring relative performance on a given data set. Finding a mapping between one entity and its personas is as important as the other, using measures such as node degree or centrality to give more weight to the successful mapping of more important nodes is meaningless here. For the same reason doing well on personas with relatively less information associated with them is also not considered.

4. EXPERIMENTS

4.1. Outline of Experiments

This section presents experiments which validate the Entity-Persona Model and the Persona Mapping Algorithm against the Enron data set. The experiments test the robustness of the algorithm and the semantic similarity measures it uses by artificially partitioning the data set. At least 50% of the entities in the data set had their personas correctly mapped in every case.

The Enron data set (Figure 3) was initially released by the Federal Energy Regulatory Commission as part of its Western Energy Markets investigation. The particular version used by this work has been prepared by Shetty and Adibi (2004). This data set is an appropriate test bed for this research as it is only composed of text and the link structure is easy to infer. As it is a very mature data set, it required minimal preprocessing to make it usable. Its size also makes it appropriate for this research while still exhibiting many of the properties of large social networks such as average path length, node degree distribution and clustering coefficient which the persona mapping algorithm exploits.

The Enron data set consists of 517,431 emails from the mail accounts of 151 Enron employees between January 1998 to December 2002 with

Figure 3. Distribution of Enron email volume over a 2 year period

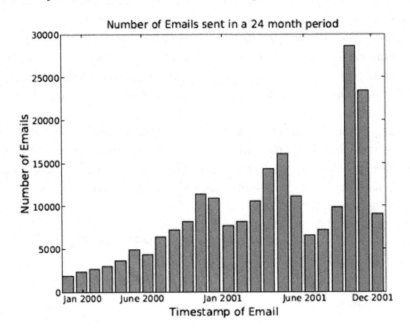

most of the email volume occurring between January 2000 and December 2001. It contains emails that originate or are sent to addresses outside those of the employees in the dataset, these have not been considered in these experiments. The Entity-Persona Model is populated by considering every email address as a node and an edge between two nodes is added if they have exchanged at least one email. The vertex labels of the social network are inferred from an unordered collection of terms in the text of all the emails sent or received by a node. The edge labels are inferred from the common emails exchanged. Only the subject and body of the emails are considered. To simulate anonymous interaction personal names and email addresses are filtered out. No stop words or stemming is used as this will not allow the stylometric features of the text to be captured. The goal of the persona mapping algorithm is to map personas unknown to it. A true test of its capabilities is its ability to map personas attempting to be anonymous. Although the web is full of this kind of data, it will be im-

possible to verify if the algorithm has made a correct mapping as this would require entities to volunteer this information. The next best approach is to synthetically create data sets to run the algorithm on, allowing the mappings to be easily verified. This research uses temporal partitioning on the Enron data set.

The data set is partitioned into eight sets based on when an email is sent as shown in Table 1. The effect of the change in topics of the emails and change in graph structure can be explored. From Table 2 it can be seen that each of the partitions has a different graph structure. At the local view of a node the graph changes significantly with some nodes communicating with completely new neighbors. The partition with the largest email volume is chosen to derive the source graph, this is the graph which the mapping between an entity and a persona is known. The seven other partitions are used to derive the target graphs whose personas need to be mapped.

Table 1. Partitioning the Enron data set

Graph Type	Graph Name	Partition by Email Date	
		Start Date	End Date
Source Graph	G_S	1st October 2001	31st December 2001
	G_{T1}	1st July 2001	31st August 2001
	G_{T2}	1st April 2001	30th June 2001
	G_{T3}	1st January 2001	31st March 2001
Target Graph	G_{T4}	1st October 2000	31st December 2000
	G_{T5}	1st July 2000	31st August 2000
	G_{T6}	1st April 2000	30th June 2000
	G_{T7}	1st January 2000	31st March 2000

4.1. Comparison of Semantic Similarity Techniques

The semantic similarity techniques presented in section 3.3 which are used by the Persona Mapping Algorithm are compared here. The experiment measures the percentage of personas successfully mapped between the source and seven target data sets. The success of these techniques depends on term usage by the entities in the data sets. An analysis of the dataset showed that the number of unique words used by an entity is weakly correlated with the volume of communication. This is the basis of the success of using textual information to find mappings as an entity does not have to have communicated extensively for there to be enough information to uniquely identify it.

The algorithm was run with σ set as 0.6, Δ as 1 and ε as 0.002. These settings give more weight to the score of the mapping of the candidate vertex to the source and less to the scores of their common neighbors. This can interpreted as the algorithm has less confidence in that entities use their personas to communicate with the same people and more confidence in that exchanging similar information across all their personas. A smaller Δ implies the algorithm only looks at the immediate neighbors of the personas for structural congruence.

The Jaccard index to compare persona vocabulary was the more successful se- mantic similarity measure. It was also the least consistent in producing successful mappings as the time between which an entity used its persona increased. This implies it is the least robust to changes in specific topics of communication. It is also the least computationally intensive technique to transform raw text into a representation which can be compared.

Table 2. Graph statistics

Statistic	G_S	G_{T1}	G_{T2}	G_{T3}	G_{T4}	G_{T5}	G_{T6}	G_{T7}
Nodes	139	137	140	109	107	93	79	58
Node Degree (Max)	63	54	63	24	22	18	11	14
Node Degree (Avg)	11	8	7	6	5	4	3	2
Edges	825	616	531	345	328	234	127	88
Email Volume (Avg)	531	466	418	457	448	432	306	338
Email Volume (Med)	257	192	116	66	58	24	2	0

Table 3. Comparison of time required to map

Semantic Similarity Technique	Average Mapping Time
Jaccard Index	$2.18s$
TF-IDF	$25.25s$
LDA	$0.1s$

Only one pass was required to populate the vocabulary vectors which label the graph.

TF-IDF performs more consistently although with a lower correct mapping rate. As term frequency is taken into account, it is less sensitive to rarely used terms. It correctly mapped the same subset of entities through all the data sets. It requires at least two passes over the email text to form the TF-IDF vector and is very slow at finding a mapping because the length of its vector is the size of the vocabulary of all the personas.

The topic distribution was learned using LDA with 500 topics, this was converted to a vector of probabilities of each topic given the text. The vector was then compared using KL Divergence when the algorithm required a label to be compared. The performance of this technique was not consistent through all the data sets, it was however the fastest in actually converging to a mapping. Since a goal of this research is to produce scalable and correct mappings, it is has the best performance-accuracy trade-off of all the semantic similarity measures. The preprocessing to learn the topic distributions was very computationally expensive as the Expectation-Maximization (EM) algorithm required a large number of iterations to converge (Table 3). This could be corrected in the future by using Gibbs sampling to learn the parameters of the generative model.

An experiment was also conducted to find the optimum number of topics for the Enron data set using the GT 1 partition (Figure 4). The maximum number of topics was set at 2000 as EM took over 12 hours to converge for a 2000×89259 probability of word given topic matrix. A decrease in the dimensionality of the topic distribution had very little effect the mapping success rate.

5. CONCLUSION

This research formally defines the problem of identifying the personas of entities on the web and proposes a solution to identify the two personas of an entity which exist in two separate social networks. The solution can be easily extended to the more general problem of multiple social networks and multiple personas. It also provides a generalized model of personas virtual footprint, enabling models derived from heterogeneous sources to be compared meaningfully while capturing as much discriminative information as possible.

The Entity-Persona Model is a formal model of the social graph and the Persona Mapping Algorithm operates on this model to produce mappings between entities and their personas. The Entity-Persona Model was populated by synthetically partitioning the Enron data set and the algorithms performance was studied in terms of correctness and runtime. It correctly mapped over 90% of personas when the partitions were contiguous in time and this decreased to 50% when the partitions were two years apart. This models a typical scenario where cliques of entities have migrated across frameworks, losing and gaining links in the process as Enron's employees have started working on different projects in different roles. It does not capture the scenario in which a

Figure 4. Comparison of semantic similarity techniques

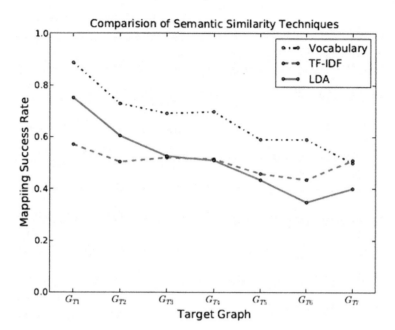

single entity participates in different frameworks and exchanges information on unrelated topics. This however does not mean the algorithm cannot work in such a scenario, as long as the similarity distance metric between an entities personas is less than the distance between every other persona pair the correct mapping will be found.

Discovering bounds on what information generated by an entity is necessary and sufficient to uniquely identify its persona, remains an open question. It is apparent that the relative information entropy between the digital signatures of personas to be compared must differ by at least one bit in order to discriminate between them, which gives a definite lower bound for necessary information and can occur in a fully connected social network. This lower bound however is not very useful in a real world situation as every virtual persona will have a unique signature. An empirical bound on the sufficiency of information can be found if all personas in the data set have been mapped correctly. However, it will be impossible to know this a priori as the purpose of the algorithm is to find unknown mappings. It may be possible to provide a confidence measure of a new mapping by using user feedback to establish certain known mappings and measuring the algorithms success rate on these mappings weighted by their similarity.

The Persona Mapping Algorithm has a worst case time complexity of n^2, with a runtime of 0.1s per mapping using Latent Dirchlet Allocation to measure semantic similarity on 300 personas. It is also easily parallelizable as the score of each potential mapping can be calculated independently, making it easily adaptable to distributed computing frameworks such as MapReduce (Dean & Ghemawat, 2008). This allows the algorithm to scale to web scale data sets while allowing the user to perform queries interactively.

REFERENCES

Acquisti, R., & Gross, R. (2006). Imagined communities: Awareness, information sharing, and privacy on the facebook. In *Proceedings of the 6th Workshop on Privacy Enhancing Technologies* (pp. 36-58).

Adamic, L. A., Lukose, R. M., Puniyani, A. R., & Huberman, B. A. (2001). Search in power law networks. *Physics Review Letters E, 64*(4), 046135.

Amaral, L. A. N., Scala, A., Barthelemy, M., & Stanley, H. E. (2000). Classes of small-world networks. *Proceedings of the National Academy of Sciences of the United States of America, 97*(21), 11149–11152. doi:10.1073/pnas.200327197

Backstrom, L., Dwork, C., & Kleinberg, J. (2007). Wherefore art thou? Anonymized social networks, hidden patterns, and structural steganography. In *Proceedings of the 16th International Conference on World Wide Web* (pp. 181-190).

Bhattacharya, I., & Getoor, L. (2006). A latent dirichlet model for unsupervised entity resolution. In *Proceedings of the SIAM Conference on Data Mining.*

Bhattacharya, I., & Getoor, L. (2007). Collective entity resolution in relational data. *ACM Transactions on Knowledge Discovery from Data, 1*(1), 1–36. doi:10.1145/1217299.1217304

Blei, D. M., Ng, A. Y., & Jordan, M. I. (2003). Latent dirichlet allocation. *Journal of Machine Learning Research, 3*, 993–1022. doi:10.1162/jmlr.2003.3.4-5.993

Cordella, L., Foggia, P., Sansone, C., & Vento, M. (2004). A (sub)graph isomorphism algorithm for matching large graphs. *IEEE Transactions on Pattern Analysis and Machine Intelligence, 26*(10), 1367–1372. doi:10.1109/TPAMI.2004.75

Dean, J., & Ghemawat, S. (2008). MapReduce: Simplified data processing on large clusters. *Communications of the ACM, 51*(1), 107–113. doi:10.1145/1327452.1327492

Donath, J. (1999). *Identity and deception in the virtual community*. London, UK: Routledge.

Grimmelmann, J. (2008). *Facebook and the social dynamics of privacy*. Retrieved from http://www.scribd.com/doc/9377908/Facebook-and-the-Social-Dynamics-of-Privacy

Jin, Y., Matsuo, Y., & Ishizuka, M. (2007). Extracting social networks among various entities on the web. In *Proceedings of the 4th European Conference on the Semantic Web* (pp. 251-266).

Kleinberg, J. (2000). The small-world phenomenon: An algorithmic perspective. In *Proceedings of the 32nd ACM Symposium on Theory of Computing* (pp. 163-170).

Kumar, R., Novak, J., Raghavan, P., & Tomkins, A. (2004). Structure and evolution of blogspace. *Communications of the ACM, 47*(12), 35–39. doi:10.1145/1035134.1035162

Mccallum, A., Wang, X., & Corrada-Emmanuel, A. (2007). Topic and role discovery in social networks with experiments on enron and academic email. *Journal of Artificial Intelligence Research, 30*, 249–272.

Narayanan, A., & Shmatikov, V. (2009). *De-anonymizing social networks*. Retrieved from http://www.cs.utexas.edu/~shmat/shmat_oak09.pdf

Novak, J., Raghavan, P., & Tomkins, A. (2004). Anti-aliasing on the web. In *Proceedings of the 13th International Conference on World Wide Web* (pp. 30-39).

Shetty, J., & Adibi, J. (2004). *The Enron email dataset database schema and brief statistical report*. Marina del Rey, CA: Information Sciences Institute.

Staddon, J., Golle, P., & Zimny, B. (2007). Web-based inference detection. In *Proceedings of 16th USENIX Security Symposium* (pp. 1-16).

Turkle, S. (1997). *Life on the screen: Identity in the age of the Internet*. New York, NY: Simon & Schuster.

Umeyama, S. (1988). An eigendecomposition approach to weighted graph matching problems. *IEEE Transactions on Pattern Analysis and Machine Intelligence*, *10*(5), 695–703. doi:10.1109/34.6778

Verykios, V. S., Bertino, E., Fovino, I. N., Provenza, L. P., Saygin, Y., & Theodoridis, Y. (2004). State-of-the-art in privacy preserving data mining. *SIGMOD Record*, 33.

Zhou, B., Pei, J., & Luk, W. (2008). A brief survey on anonymization techniques for privacy preserving publishing of social network data. *ACM SIGKDD Explorations Newsletter*, *10*(2), 12–22. doi:10.1145/1540276.1540279

This work was previously published in International Journal of Agent Technologies and Systems, Volume 3, Issue 2, edited by Yu Zhang, pp. 1-17, copyright 2011 by IGI Publishing (an imprint of IGI Global).

Chapter 8
History Sensitive Cascade Model

Yu Zhang
Trinity University, USA

Maksim Tsikhanovich
Bard College, USA

Georgi Smilyanov
Bard College, USA

ABSTRACT

Diffusion is a process by which information, viruses, ideas, or new behavior spread over social networks. Traditional diffusion models are history insensitive, i.e. only giving activated nodes a one-time chance to activate each of its neighboring nodes with some probability. But history dependent interactions between people are often observed in the real world. This paper proposes the History Sensitive Cascade Model (HSCM), a model of information cascade through a network over time. The authors consider the "activation" problem of finding the probability of that a particular node receives information given that some nodes are initially informed. In this paper it is also proven that selecting a set of k nodes with greatest expected influence is NP-hard, and results from submodular functions are used to provide a greedy approximation algorithm with a 1–1/e–ε lower bound, where ε depends polynomially on the precision of the solution to the "activation" problem. Finally, experiments are performed comparing the greedy algorithm to three other approximation algorithms.

INTRODUCTION

Network diffusion is the process by which some nodes in a network influence their neighboring nodes. Depending on different diffusion models (introduced in Related Work and Background), the nodes that are already active can influence their neighbors to become active as well.

Many real-world phenomena can be seen as network diffusion. Examples include the spread of infectious diseases (Gladwell, 2000), the spread of new ideas and technologies (Surowiecki, 2004), marketing (Domingos & Richardson, 2001; Wortman, 2008), technology transfers (Bass, 1969; Brow & Reinegen, 1987), computer virus transmission (Albert, Jeong, & Barabasi, 2000), and power systems (Watts, 2002). Classic instance of diffusion is found in marketing and experimental

DOI: 10.4018/978-1-4666-1565-6.ch008

economics (Wortman, 2008; Kempe, Kleinberg, & Tardos, 2003, 2005). Consider a company that introduces a new product to the market. It might try to identify the consumers with the largest willingness to pay and sell it to them. But this might not guarantee profit maximization in the long run. Suppose instead that the company finds the people with most influence over some group (e.g. friends, family) and offers the product to them. Building on this plausible scenario, Domingos and Richardson (2001) introduce the notion of "network value" of a consumer and define it as the influence the consumer has on others in her social network:

"A customer whose intrinsic value is lower than the cost of marketing may in fact be worth marketing to when her network value is considered. Conversely, marketing to a profitable customer may be redundant if network effects already make her very likely to buy."

A diffusion model is commonly used to answer the *influence maximization problem*: What is the best set of nodes to activate initially so that the number of active nodes in the end of the diffusion process is maximized? It is NP-Hard in all models we mention in Related Work and Background. However, approximation algorithms for obtaining reasonably good solutions exist.

As described by Kempe et al. (2003), there are two basic diffusion models: 1) the *linear threshold model* (Granovetter, 1978), in which a node becomes active if a predetermined fraction, called a threshold, of the node's neighbors are active, and 2) the *independent cascade model* (Culotta, 2003), whenever a node becomes active, it gets a one-time chance to activate each of its neighboring nodes with some probability. There is a rich literature in both models; especially the independent cascade model has gained much attention in present day. Goldenberg et al. (2001) simulate Word-of-Mouth information diffusion through strong ties among members of the same

network and weak ties among individuals belonging to different network. They found the influence of weak ties on the information diffusion is almost as strong as the influence of strong ties. Cowan and Jonard (2004) study diffusion of knowledge in different network structures. They find that the performance of the system exhibits clear "small world" properties, in that the steady-state level of average knowledge is maximal when the structure is a small world (that is, when most connections are local, but roughly 10 percent of them are long distance). In viral marketing, Leskovec et al (2007) simulate information cascade in a real person-to-person recommendation network. They discover that the distribution of cascade sizes is approximately heavy-tailed; cascades tend to be shallow, but occasional large bursts of propagation can occur.

The model that we propose is called the *History Sensitive Cascade Model* (HSCM) (Zhang, 2009). Traditional diffusion models are all history "insensitive", i.e. only giving activated nodes a one-time chance to activate each of its neighboring nodes with some probability. But history dependent interactions between people are often observed in real world. For example, in viral marketing and advertising, a customer may not decide to buy a product at their first time receiving the recommendation or watching the advertisement, but they may gradually accept the product and decide to buy it after several rounds of such interactions. To simulate this kind of the interactions, HSCM allows that activated nodes receive more than a one-time chance to activate their neighbors. This is a better assumption as in the reality people interact with each other multiple times over some time period. We provide an in depth comparison between HSCM and several of the common diffusion models in Related Work and Motivation.

The HSCM model can be understood as a modified Independent Cascade Model, but is different from the generalized framework (proposed by Kempe) designed to unify the Independent

Cascade Model and the Linear Threshold Model underneath a single mathematical threshold. For one major difference, our model allows that activated nodes receive more than a one-time chance to activate their neighbors. A node can switch from being uninformed to being informed, but not the reverse. The rationale of this model is the classical threshold mechanism of collective action: a consumer does not feel social pressure if just a few people around her behave in a particular way but once these people reach a certain number then she suddenly decide to change her mind and she behaves differently (Granovetter, 1978).

In this paper we give a formal description of the HSCM model. We present algorithms for inference in HSCM. We consider the "activation" problem of finding the probability of a particular node receiving information given that some nodes are initially informed. We also prove that the *influence maximization problem* in HSCM is NP-hard, and use results from submodular functions (Goundan & Schulz, 2007; Nemhauser & Wolsey, 1978) to provide a greedy approximation algorithm with a *1–1/e–ε* lower bound, where ε depends polynomially on the precision of the solution to the "activation" problem. Finally, we perform experiments to compare the greedy algorithm to three other approximation algorithms.

RELATED WORK AND BACKGROUND

We will use an example to introduce the related work on diffusion models as well as to show the difference between HSCM and these existing models. Figure 1 is our graph.

Suppose Alice, in high school, is dating Bob. Also, Alice is best friends with Cathy who is barely acquainted with a college boy named Donald. Suppose Donald has two college friends named Ethan and Francine and that these two friends are also dating. The connecting lines represent avenues of contact: Alice routinely communicates with Cathy (her best friend) and Bobby (her boyfriend); but she doesn't know Donald, Francine, or Ethan. Now suppose that Cathy recently bought an iPod and likes it very much. The question we are interested in is what is the probability that other people in the network will be influenced by Cathy and buy an iPod at any given time in the future.

In literature, there are two common diffusion models that have been used to solve the above question that we are interested in. The first is the *Linear Threshold Model*, which says that a node becomes active if a predetermined faction of the node's neighbors is active. Figure 2 illustrates this rule. Here the predefined threshold is 60%; red (dark) nodes mean the nodes that have already being activated via the link pointing to them, and we are determined if the centre bold node will be activated in the given situation. Since the centre node has five neighbors and three of them (i.e. 60%) have been active, so the centre node will be active too. The second model is the *Independent Cascade Model*. Under this model, an active node gets a one-time chance to activate each of its neighboring nodes with some probability. Figure 3 illustrates this rule. Here the probability is 50%, as a consequence, the already active central bold node makes two of its neighbors active too.

The HSCM model that we propose shares the progressiveness feature of the existing models but it is *history sensitive*. We can find many examples in really world that people influence each

Figure 1. An example Diffusion Network

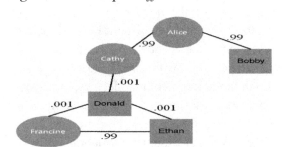

Figure 2. An Example of LTM

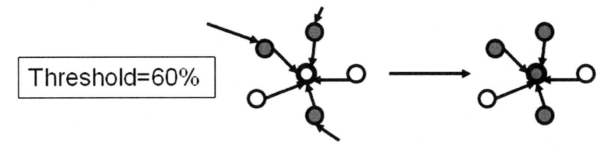

Figure 3. An Example of the CM

other by more than one time and the previous influence enhances the current influence. Let's refer to Figure 1 again for an example scenario. The probability attached to each link is called the "spreading probability", representing the chance that the influence of the iPod ideology will spread across that line during a fixed length of time. In this example, let's suppose this length of time equals one week. It is reasonable to think that Alice has a higher chance of being influenced by Cathy not only because the spreading probability between them is higher but also this probability will be increased if they spend more time together, under the assumption that Alice's has no bias to iPod as others, i.e. nobody in this system has a strong attitude in favoring or disfavoring iPod originally.

It should be noted that we are not suggesting real world situations are always like this. Certainly one could argue that Alice after many weeks of being pestered by Cathy would decide out of annoyance never to buy an iPod. Or she may simply become "immune" to Cathy's sug-

gestions, becoming less and less likely to buy an iPod with each passing exposure to Cathy's iPod ideology. These concerns are valid. But that doesn't mean historical data should be entirely disregarded as is the case in all diffusion models we have encountered.

PROBLEM DEFINITIONS

There are several interrelated problems we are trying to solve; all of them are related to the History Sensitive Cascade Model, which we now introduce formally.

Definition 1 History Sensitive Cascade Model: The HSCM model is represented by a directed and weighted graph $G = (V, E)$; V represents the finite set of vertices in the graph, and E represents the finite set of edges in the graph. Furthermore, there exists a function $A: V \rightarrow \{0, 1\}$, where for each vertex $v \in V$, $A(v) = \{1$ if v is active, 0 if v is inactive$\}$. The

HSCM model takes on states, where each state is defined as the set of vertices that are active, and inactive, as a result there are $2^{|V|}$ distinct states. The HSCM model transitions between states over time steps. We say the model is on the tth time step if t time steps have passed. Over any given time step, any active vertex v_1 can activate any inactive vertex v_2 with probability $w(e_{v1,v2})$ if $e_{v1,v2} \in E$, where $w: E \rightarrow [0; 1]$ is the function that returns the weight of a given edge, and $e_{v1,v2}$ denotes the edge from v_1 to v_2. Furthermore, an active vertex can't be deactivated, and therefore HSCM is *progressive*.

Vertex Activation Problem

The first problem we are trying to solve is called the Vertex Activation Problem (*VAP*), which is defined below.

Definition 2 Vertex Activation Problem: Given an instance of an HSCM, and a time step t, what is the probability that a vertex v is active on the tth time step?

Kempe, et al declared that *VAP* is an open problem that can be bound by its approximation problem (Kempe, Kleinberg, and Tardos 2003, 2005). Next we state the *VAP* approximation problem.

Definition 3 *VAP* Approximation Problem: Let $VAP: G \times v \times V \times N \rightarrow [0, 1]$ be $VAP(G, v, A, t)$ is the probability of vertex v being active in the HSCM instance represented by graph G, with initially active vertices A and time step t. Find a function $Z: G \times v \times V \times N \rightarrow [0, 1]$ such that Z runs in time polynomial to all its inputs, and either a) $\alpha Z(G, v, A, t) \geq VAP(G, v, A, t)$ for some lower bound $\alpha \in (0, 1]$, or b) $P[Z(G, v, A, t) = VAP(G, v, A, t)] \geq \beta$ where P is the probability function, and $\beta \in (0, 1]$.

Influence Maximization Problem

Once we have the solution to the Vertex Activation Problem, or an approximation, we use the solution to solve a problem about a set V of vertices, particularly, we ask what is the expected amount of the vertices in V activated by the tth time step, if some set of vertices A will be chosen to be active initially. We call this amount of vertices the *influence* of the initially active set A for t time steps.

Definition 4 Influence Function: We define the influence function $\sigma: V \times N \rightarrow R$ for a particular instance of the HSCM model represented by graph G and for a time step t as $\sigma(A, t) = \sum VAP(G, v, A, t)$.

This use of the solution to the Vertex Activation Problem lends itself to be integrated as part of a solution for an optimization problem. The optimization problem is the Influence Maximization Problem, which is stated as follows.

Definition 5 Influence Maximization Problem: Given a HSCM, whose graph is $G = (V, E)$, and a time step t, which subset U, $U \subseteq V$, should be selected such that $\sigma(U, t)$ is maximum?

In the next section we show why this is NP-hard; so as with the Vertex Activation Problem, we focus on solving an approximation problem. The approximation problem related with the Influence Maximization Problem is stated as follows,

Definition 6 Influence Maximization Approximation Problem: Given a HSCM represented by the graph $G = (V, E)$, which subset U, $U \subseteq V$, should be selected such that $\sigma(U, t) \geq \alpha\sigma(U^*, t)$, where U^* denotes the optimal solution for some $\alpha \in (0, 1]$?

Once again the goal is to find a polynomial-time approximation algorithm. α represents a lower bound to the performance algorithm, and the goal is to reach the largest possible α. Alternatively as with the Vertex Activation Approximation problem (see Definition 3) we may ask what is the probability of our algorithm returning the optimal solution, or even more likely we will end up saying what is the probability that α takes on a particular value.

SOLUTIONS

Vertex Activation Problem

We use a state-transition matrix, which we use as part of a Markov chain in order to solve *VAP* exactly. Entry i, j in the state transition matrix is the probability of the system transitioning from state i to state j, where each state is determined by which vertices are active in it. Therefore there are $2^{2|V|}$ total entries in the matrix. Each can be calculated in polynomial time: by examining which vertices is possible to activate from state i and determining the possibility that only those in j are activated, and no others. Once this matrix is calculated, we use a result from Markov chains: we multiply it t times to simulate the system for t steps, and multiply it by a vector which determines the initial state. Last, we sum the probability of the matrix in a state where the vertex we're interested in is active, and return this sum as the answer to *VAP*.

Since the matrix is of dimension $O(2^{|V|})$ and we can multiply matrices of size n in $O(3^n)$, it follows that we can solve *VAP* exactly in $O(2^{3|V|})$ time. This result is open to two different interpretations. First, since this algorithm runs in exponential time, and no time is spent doing useless work, one may intuitively believe that the Vertex Activation Problem is NP-hard. On the other hand it is not surprising that this algorithm runs in exponential time, because a model with a transition matrix

is reducible to 3SAT, so maybe the exponential runtime is caused by the particular algorithm we use, and is not an inherent property of the problem.

Vertex Activation Approximation Problem

We approximate vertex activation by sampling. We define the experiment we are working with as follows,

Definition 7 Vertex Activation Approximation Problem: Given a HSCM instance represented by the graph G, a set of initially active nodes A, and a number of time steps, t, execute the history sensitive cascade, described in Algorithm 1.

The possible outcomes of the experiment define the sample space, in our case this is $\{T: T \in \wp(V)\}$, where each element refers to the set of vertices that are active. We define the random variable X_i as

$$X_i = \begin{cases} 1 & if \ v_i \in T_c \\ 0 & otherwise \end{cases} \qquad (1)$$

where T_c refers to the current outcome of the experiment. Let $VAP(G, v_i, A, k)$ be the function that solves the Vertex Activation Problem (see Definition 2), and thus it returns the probability that for an HSCM instance represented by the graph G, a initially active set A and a time step k, that the vertex v_i is active. This is the function we are interested in approximating. Notice that $VAP(G, v_i, A, k) = P(X_i = 1)$ for the experiment performed over G, A, k. Also notice that the expectation of X_i,

$$E[X_i] = \mu = 1 \times P(X_i=1) + 0 \times P(X_i=0) \qquad (2)$$

is equivalent to *VAP*.

Phrasing *VAP* in terms of determining the mean of a distribution based on samples lets us use standard statistical results to bind how well or poorly our sampling will approximate *VAP*. We follow the methods suggested by Law (2007) Suppose we have a confidence level, $1-\alpha$, and a interval half length of β, and we want to know how many samples are needed in order for

$$1 - \alpha \approx P(\overline{X_i} - \beta \le \mu \le \overline{X_i} + \beta) \quad (3)$$

to be true, where $\overline{X_i}$ is defined as the sample mean as the following

$$\overline{X_i} = \frac{\sum j = 1^n X_{ij}}{n} \quad (4)$$

where X_{ij} refers to the value of X_i on the jth of n experiments. The number of samples necessary to achieve this bound is given by

$$N(\alpha, \beta) = \min\left\{k : tk - 1, 1 - \alpha / 2\sqrt{\frac{\overline{s}^2}{k}} \le \beta\right\} \quad (5)$$

where $tk - 1, 1 - \alpha/2$ is the upper $1 - \alpha/2$ critical point for the t distribution with $k - 1$ degrees of freedom. $\overline{s}^2$ denotes the sample variance,

$$\overline{S}^2 = \frac{\sum j = 1^n (X_{ij} - \overline{X_i})^2}{n - 1} \quad (6)$$

This result follows from the Central Limit Theorem (Chung, 1974), and it is the case that as $n\to\infty$, then a) the distribution of the X_i's becomes normal and b) $\overline{S}^2 \to Var(X)$. Then Equation 5 also provides an exact $100(1-\alpha)$ percent bound, instead of an approximate one.

We use an algorithm that computes I samples of X_i in $O(It|V||E|)$ time, where t is the number of steps the model should be able to go through. We present the algorithm to compute one sample.

Algorithm 1. HSCM Sampling Algorithm for Cascade of Length t

```
Require: t > 1, HSCM instance represented by G
for i = 1 to t do
    for all v ∈ V do
        if A(v) = 1 then
            for all u ∈ V: e_{v,u} ∈ E do
                r ← a random number in [0; 1]
                if r < w(e_{v,u}) then
                    A(u) ← 1
```

This algorithm simply simulates the HSCM process. In order to achieve a some bound related to β with $100(1-\alpha)$ percent certainty, we keep executing the sampling algorithm while the number of iterations we have done is less than $N(\alpha, \beta)$. We use the mean and standard deviation of the sample we have so far for evaluating $N(\alpha, \beta)$.

Influence Maximization Approximation Problem

First we prove that the exact version of the problem (see Definition 5) is NP-hard. Then we provide an algorithm that solves the approximation problem (Definition 6).

Influence Maximization is NP-Hard

Theorem 1: The Influence Maximization Problem is NP-hard.

Proof. We follow the method of Jennifer Wortman, and prove this problem is NP-hard by reducing it to the set cover problem. In the set cover problem we are given a set $U = \{u_1, u_2, ..., u_n\}$ and a collection of subsets $S_1, ..., S_m$ and a integer k. We wish to determine whether there exist k subsets such that their union is the whole set U.

Given an instance of the set cover problem, we construct an instance of the activation maximization problem (which is an HSCM) as follows. First, create an empty graph $G = (V, E)$. Then construct $V = (\cup i = 1^m S_i) \cup (\cup j = 1^n u_j)$. For each $i \in \{1, 2, \ldots, m\}$ and each $j \in \{1, 2, \ldots, n\}$ add $e_{vi,vj}$ to E if and only if $u_j \in S_i$; we let $w(e_{vi,vj}) = 1$ for all i, j.

Suppose now that we have an algorithm, which can solve the activation maximization problem. Thus, we can assume that we have the subset of V, T, where $|T| = k$, such that the expected size of the set of vertices activated is maximized after the 1st time step. Since the weight of each edge in E is 1, an edge between $v_1, v_2 \in V$ lets us conclude that v_1 activates v_2 given that v_1 is active. This lets us determine the expected size of set activated by T, denoted $\sigma(T)$, where $\sigma: V \rightarrow R$ is the influence function. We do this by performing breadth-first searches[1] starting from each element in T, while maintaining a record of the nodes encountered by the search, adding to it new vertices when they are discovered, and finally returning the size of this record.

Finally, we consider whether $\sigma(T) \geq n+k$. Suppose that indeed $\sigma(T, 1) \geq n+k$. Since the nodes corresponding to the subsets S_i have no incoming edges, we expect all k of them will be active since they were selected to be members of T. In order to get n more nodes to be active, because the nodes corresponding to the subsets S_i do not have edges between one-another, all n nodes corresponding to each $u_i \in U$ must be active. Thus there exist some k subsets $S_1, S_2, \ldots, S_k$ that cover U. Conversely, if $\sigma(W,1) < n + k$ then even though k subsets are active, even the activation maximizing solution W is not able to choose k subsets that cover U. □

General Lower Bound on Approximation

Since the exact maximization problem is NP-hard, our goal is to come up with an approximation algorithm, to which we can assign a lower bound.

Kempe, Kleinberg, and Tardos (2005) introduce the following theorem (Mossel & Roch, 2007).

Theorem 2: Let f be a non-negative, monotone, submodular function on sets.
1. The greedy algorithm, which always picks the element v with largest marginal gain $f(S \cup \{v\}) - f(S)$, is a $1 - 1/e$-approximation algorithm for maximizing f on k-element set S.
2. A greedy algorithm which always picks an element v within $1 - \varepsilon$ of the largest marginal gain results in a $1 - 1/e - \varepsilon`$ approximation, for some $\varepsilon`$ depending polynomially on ε.

We apply this theorem to σ. We know σ is monotone increasing from (Zhang, 2009), who proved it with the notion of absorbing processes in Markov chains, and because we will prove it is submodular below, we know that the following greedy algorithm provides solution that is at least $1 - 1/e - \varepsilon$ of the optimal solution, where ε is polynomially related to the precision of our approximation to *VAP*. Algorithm 2 is the greedy algorithm. Recall that Algorithm 1 is an $O(It|V||E|)$ algorithm for approximating σ. Thus the greedy algorithm runs in $O(kIt|V|^2|E|)$.

Algorithm 2. Maximum Influencing Set of Size k for Cascade of t Steps

```
Require: int k ≥ 1, int t ≥ 1, Graph G
  res ← {}
  for i = 1 to k do
    maxVal ← 0
    v* ← null
    for all v ∈ V − res do
      if σ(res ∪ v) ≥ maxVal then
        maxVal ← σapprox(res ∪ v, t)
        v* ← v
  res ← res ∪ v*
  return res
```

Submodularity of Influence

Theorem 3: The influence function, $\sigma(A, t)$, is submodular for all instances of the HSCM.
Proof. Consider the case when we wish to find the influence of a set A for an HSCM represented by the graph G for t time steps. Next, consider an edge from a node in A, v to an inactive node u that has weight $w(e_{v,u})$. Since we are determining the influence of A, we let all nodes it contains be initially active. Then the probability that v activates u after t time steps is $1-(1-w(e_{v,u}))^t$. Notice that this is the same as if there were t edges from v to u, where each could only try to activate u once. Using this idea, $\sigma(A, t)$ can be expressed in terms of the Independent Cascade Model's influence function introduced by Kempe, Kleinberg, and Tardos (2003).

Consider an arbitrary node v. If the shortest path from a node in A to v contains d edges, then the first time step t_j for which $P(G, v, A, t_j) > 0$ is $t_j = d$. Consider a node u for which v lies on the shortest path to a node in A. It follows that $P(G, v, A, t_u) > 0$ for $t_u = t_j + 1$. Now, consider a particular execution of the HSCM, if v is activated on the t_j^{th} time step, then it will have $t - t_j$ chances to activate u. However, unless $v \in A$, it could happen that v gets activated at a later time step, and in that case it will have less chance to activate u.

We introduce the random variable X, which encodes a particular execution of the HSCM as an Independent Cascade Model. The possible executions can be enumerated by first considering all the cases of when nodes with $d = 1$ get activated, and for each of those all the cases when nodes with $d = 2$ get activated, and so on until $d = t - 1$. In each execution X_i, if a node v gets activated at t_v, we add all of v's edges to the graph represented by X_i $t - t_v$ times; thus we simulate the execution of the HSCM where v gets $t - t_v$ opportunities to active its descendants.

If we let $\sigma I(A)$ denote the influence function for the Independent Cascade Model, then we can express

$$\sigma(A, t) = \sum X_i P(X_i) \sigma I(A) . \qquad (7)$$

Since $\sigma I(A)$ is proven to be submodular and since a linear combination of submodular functions is also submodular, it follows that $\sigma(A, t)$ is submodular.$\square$

A Lower Bound on the Accuracy of the Greedy Approximation Algorithm

In this section we look at how our approximation algorithm for *VAP* affects the lower bound to the greedy approximation algorithm.

Definition 8 Bonferroni Inequality: If for some mean μs and some interval Is, $P(\mu s \in Is) = 1 - \alpha s$, then for n means $P(\mu 1 \in I1 \wedge \mu 2 \in I2 \wedge \ldots \wedge \mu n \in In) = 1 - \sum i = 1^n \alpha i$. See Law (2007).

Suppose we have a graph with 10,000 nodes, and we wish to achieve a confidence level of 90 percent ($\alpha = 0.1$) that the lower bound of the greedy algorithm is $1 - 1/e$. By the Bonferroni Inequality we need αs such that $0.9 = 1 - 10000\alpha s$, and we get $\alpha s = 1/100000$. Then let $\beta = 100$, or some other value, and perform $N(\alpha s, \beta)$ samples. Then continue taking samples such that the highest sample lies in an interval that does not overlap with any other interval anything less than completely (we assume round-o_ error is negligible). At this point we are 90 percent certain that each mean lies in the intervals we have derived from sampling, and thus we are 90 percent certain that at any stage of selecting vertex 1, …, k as a member of the optimal set, we select the vertex with actually the highest marginal influence. Thus overall we are 0.9^k percent certain that we have a $1 - 1/e$ approximation, and for example if $k =$

30, $\alpha = 0.9965$ and $\alpha s = 3.5/10000000$. With such low αs, in most graphs $N(\alpha, \beta)$ will be enormous, and not polynomial in the accuracy of the greedy approximation.

EXPERIMENTS

Testing the VAP Approximation Algorithm (Algorithm 1)

Experiment Definition and Hypothesis

Definition 9: Given a sample mean $\overline{X}_i$, and a interval half length β, if we compute $N(\alpha, \beta)$ samples, how many percent of 500 tries will satisfy the condition $\overline{X}_i - \beta \leq \mu i \leq \overline{X}_i + \beta$?

We hope this percentage will be greater than $(1 - \alpha)100$ percent. Failure will suggest that our model is skewed from the normal distribution, and more than $N(\alpha, \beta)$ samples are necessary to achieve a specific confidence interval. In this case we will refer back to Law (2007). Furthermore, we can only perform this experiment on small graphs (up to 11-12 nodes), because calculating μi means solving *VAP* exactly, which we do in exponential time.

Procedure and Results

Since we needed to know μi, we worked with a graph consisting of 11 nodes, and added edges from all nodes i to nodes j iff $i < j$, in total we had 55 edges. We let the weight of each edge be 0.23. We let the set of initially active nodes be A = {0}. We then asked, given this graph, what is the probability of node 10 being activated after 4 time steps. The exact *VAP* solver returned the value 0.979016.

We then turned to the bounding problem, and let $\alpha = 0.05$ and $\beta = 0.005$. This means we were looking at the number of runs necessary in order

to produce results that were in the interval $I = (0.974, 0.984) \times 95$ percent of the time. For each try ('try' as in Definition 9) we first took 1000 samples, and then kept taking samples until Equation 4 was satisfied. The number of samples that ended up being taken per try was in the range from 2500 to 4000.

The main result is that out of 500 tests, 479 were in the interval I. Thus, experimentally, P($\overline{X}_i \in I$) = 0.958, which is better than the 0.95 we hoped for. This suggests that the distribution of the sample means is skewed towards normal, and $N(\alpha, \beta)$ should be sufficient to achieve a $\pm \beta$ interval with $(1-\alpha)100$ percent certainty.

Maximization Approximation Problem

In this section we compare the greedy algorithm against other commonly used heuristics.

The *sum of weights* heuristic computes the sum of the weights of all outgoing edges for all nodes and chooses the node with the highest sum. The *highest degree* heuristic chooses the node with the highest number of outgoing edges. The *central distance* heuristic first determines the average distance from each node to all other nodes and then ranks the nodes by increasing distance. The idea is that nodes with short distance to all other nodes are "central" to the network and thus are more influential. Since the graph is not fully connected, we just assign some very big number for the distance when there is no path between two nodes. *Random* refers to an algorithm that picks nodes uniformly at random. In this case, the representative result is given by the average of 30 runs of the algorithm.

Each evaluation of the gain from some node involves determining the value of the influence function applied to the set containing this node. Since computing this is difficult by itself, we determine it using a simulation. The simulation is run certain number of times and the average is taken as the representative value when evaluating candidate nodes. The time it takes for the simulation to complete depends on the density of the network, so we decided to run it for 1000 times for the first experiment and 100 times for the rest. Now, we should stress that in the worst case the decreased accuracy of the simulation can result in unstable node selections (e.g. picking different nodes for each run if they have sufficiently close expected gains), but the expected number of active nodes (size of active set) is preserved. This makes sense because in all experiments we are interested in the size of the target set, not in which nodes it particularly contains.

Small Network, Random Weights

In this experiment we use a graph of 1000 nodes and 5000 edges randomly connecting them. Each edge is also assigned a random weight. The time step is set to 3.

Results are shown on Figure 1 and we can clearly see that the greedy algorithm beats all other heuristics by a wide margin. We can also observe that the sum of weights heuristic outperforms highest degree. This is because it is essentially an improved version of highest degree – taking into

consideration not only the number of edges, but also the specific property (weight) of each one. Finally, we observe that the algorithm, which selects nodes randomly, performs worse than all other heuristics for all experiments; this is because the random algorithm does not consider any properties of the network.

Figure 4 also intuitively confirms the submodularity of the influence function. As we can see the performance of the greedy algorithm and all heuristics is increasing at decreasing rate. This is always the case, but is especially easy to see here – because of the relatively small network the "capacity" for increase is limited and gets smaller after each activated node. Observe that it takes around 40 nodes to activate more than 85% of the network in three steps.

Large Network, Random Weights

Figure 5 shows an essentially the same experiment, but for a much bigger network – 10000 nodes and 50000 links. Time step is still 3. Here we can clearly see that the highest degree heuristic outperforms the centrality heuristic. In a bigger network, the number of outgoing edges

Figure 4. 1000 Nodes, 5000 Links Network with Random Weights

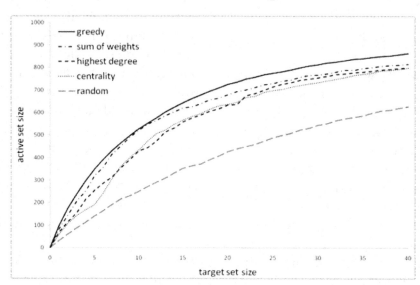

Figure 5. 10000 Nodes, 50000 Links Network with Random Weights

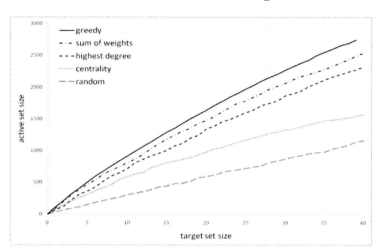

Figure 6. 10000 nodes, 50000 links network with constant weights of 0.2

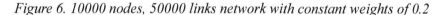

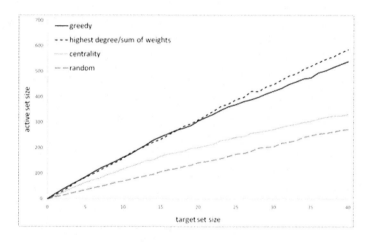

for a node is a much more reliable indicator than the distance from the node to other nodes. Note that the general order of the performance for all algorithms is preserved in this experiment. We also see that the graphs are increasing but at a much lower rate. This is because the *capacity* of each newly activated node to activate others is not limited early on as it is in the smaller network. It takes many more nodes before the effect of adding a new node starts to vanish.

Large Network, Constant Weights (0.2)

We also performed an experiment on a random 10000 nodes, 50000 links network with constant weights set to (0.2). In this case (Figure 6) it turned out that the greedy algorithm performs slightly worse than the highest degree heuristic. We think that the advantage of the greedy algorithm is that it can actually \look ahead" a few nodes when selecting a node. But while this context proves

Figure 7. 10000 nodes, 50000 links network with constant weights of 0.2, size of target set is 25

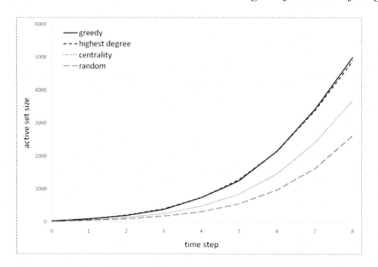

helpful in the previous experiments, here it is almost useless in comparison to just looking at the degree: in this case you cannot learn much more by simulating the process that by merely looking at the outgoing degree of the nodes.

Figure 7 shows how the number of active nodes is related to the time step. The network we used is the same as in the previous experiment (Figure 6) and the size of the target set is fixed to 25. We can see that the greedy algorithm and the highest degree heuristic have almost indistinguishable performance. We speculate that in the long run this will stay the same or greedy will slightly outperform highest degree.

CONCLUSION

We have formalized the HSCM model. There are several interesting problems/lessons related to the HSCM model in-and-out of itself. One interesting future work is to come up with better results than we were able to come up with. The goal is to provide a lower bound, where the accuracy

of the greedy influence maximization solver is polynomially related to the number of samples taken when finding the vertex with the greatest marginal gain. We recommend referring either to the original proof of the lower bound to the greedy algorithm in [19] or a more general version in [12], we also recommend [16]. Another further work is that, we have chosen to work with *VAP* as defined, and the influence maximization problem. However, we can also look at this problem in terms of time minimization. The optimization problem then becomes to determine the set of *k* nodes such that the time *t* is minimized for which the expected number of nodes activated is some value c. The corresponding version of *VAP* would be to ask what is the time step *t* such that $P(G, v, A, t) \geq \theta$ for some $\theta \in (0, 1)$.

ACKNOWLEDGMENT

This work was supported in part by the U.S. National Science Foundation under Grants IIS 0755405 and CNS 0821585.

REFERENCES

Albert, R., Jeong, H., & Barabasi, A. (2000). Error and attack tolerance of complex networks. *Nature, 406*, 378–382. doi:10.1038/35019019

Bass, F. (1969). A new product growth model for consumer durables. *Management Science, 15*, 215–227. doi:10.1287/mnsc.15.5.215

Brown, J., & Reinegen, P. (1987). Social ties and word-of-mouth referral behavior. *The Journal of Consumer Research, 14*(3), 350–362. doi:10.1086/209118

Chung, K. L. (1974). *A course on probability theory*. New York, NY: Academic Press.

Cowan, R., & Jonard, N. (2004). Network structure and the diffusion of knowledge. *Journal of Economic Dynamics & Control, 28*(8), 1557–1575. doi:10.1016/j.jedc.2003.04.002

Culotta, A. (2003). *Maximizing cascades in social networks*. Amherst, MA: University of Massachusetts.

Domingos, P., & Richardson, M. (2001). Mining the network value of customers. In *Proceedings of the 7th ACM SIGKDD International Conference on Knowledge Discovery and Data Mining* (pp. 57-66).

Gladwell, M. (2000). *The tipping point*. Boston, MA: Little Brown.

Goldenberg, J., Libai, B., & Muller, E. (2001). Talk of the network: A complex systems look at the underlying process of word-of-mouth. *Marketing Letters, 3*(12), 211–223. doi:10.1023/A:1011122126881

Goundan, P. R., & Schulz, A. S. (2007). *Revisiting the greedy approach to submodular set function maximization*. Retrieved from http://www.optimization-online.org/DB_FILE/2007/08/1740.pdf

Granovetter, M. (1978). Threshold models of collective behavior. *American Journal of Sociology, 83*(6), 1420–1443. doi:10.1086/226707

Kempe, D., Kleinberg, J., & Tardos, E. (2003). Maximizing the spread of influence through a social network. In *Proceedings of the 9th ACM SIGKDD International Conference on Knowledge Discovery and Data Mining* (pp. 137-146).

Kempe, D., Kleinberg, J., & Tardos, E. (2005). Influential nodes in a diffusion model for social networks. In L. Caires, G. F. Italiano, L. Monteiro, C. Palamidessi, & M. Yung (Eds.), *Proceedings of the 32nd International Colloquium on Automata, Languages and Programming* (LNCS 3580, pp. 1127-1138).

Law, A. M. (2007). *Simulation & modeling analysis*. New York, NY: McGraw Hill.

Leskovec, J., Krause, A., & Guestrin, C. (2007). Cost-effective outbreak detection in networks. In *Proceedings of the 13th ACM SIGKDD International Conference on Knowledge Discovery and Data Mining* (pp. 420-429).

Mossel, E., & Roch, S. (2007). On the submodularity of influence in social networks. In *Proceedings of the Thirty-Ninth Annual ACM Symposium on Theory of Computing* (pp. 128-134).

Nemhauser, G. L., & Wolsey, L. A. (1978). Best algorithms for approximating the maximum of a submodular set function. *Mathematics of Operations Research, 3*(3), 177–188. doi:10.1287/moor.3.3.177

Surowiecki, J. (2004). *The wisdom of crowds*. New York, NY: Random House.

Watts, D. J. (2002). A simple model of global cascades in random networks. *Proceedings of the National Academy of Sciences of the United States of America, 99*(9), 5766–5771. doi:10.1073/pnas.082090499

Wortman, J. (2008). *Viral marketing and the diffusion of trends on social networks*. Philadelphia, PA: University of Pennsylvania.

Zhang, Y. (2009). A deterministic model for history sensitive cascade in diffusion networks. In *Proceedings of the IEEE International Conference on Systems, Man and Cybernetics* (pp. 1977-1982).

ENDNOTE

[1] We terminate each breadth-first search upon reach a node with no outgoing edges, and we are guaranteed that there are no cycles in the graph G we constructed.

This work was previously published in International Journal of Agent Technologies and Systems, Volume 3, Issue 2, edited by Yu Zhang, pp. 53-66, copyright 2011 by IGI Publishing (an imprint of IGI Global).

Chapter 9
Norms of Behaviour and Their Identification and Verification in Open Multi-Agent Societies

Wagdi Alrawagfeh
Memorial University of Newfoundland, Canada

Edward Brown
Memorial University of Newfoundland, Canada

Manrique Mata-Montero
Memorial University of Newfoundland, Canada

ABSTRACT

Norms have an obvious role in the coordinating and predicting behaviours in societies of software agents. Most researchers assume that agents already know the norms of their societies beforehand at design time. Others assume that norms are assigned by a leader or a legislator. Some researchers take into account the acquisition of societies' norms through inference. Their works apply to closed multi-agent societies in which the agents have identical (or similar) internal architecture for representing norms. This paper addresses three things: 1) the idea of a Verification Component that was previously used to verify candidate norms in multi-agent societies, 2) a known modification of the Verification Component that makes it applicable in open multi-agent societies, and 3) a modification of the Verification Component, so that agents can dynamically infer the new emerged and abrogated norms in open multi-agent societies. Using the JADE software framework, we build a restaurant interaction scenario as an example (where restaurants usually host heterogeneous agents), and demonstrate how permission and prohibition of behavior can be identified by agents using dynamic norms.

DOI: 10.4018/978-1-4666-1565-6.ch009

INTRODUCTION

Research in the multi-agent systems has adopted several concepts from different disciplines. From philosophy, for example, human behaviours are captured based on a model of human Beliefs, Desires and Intentions (Bratman, 1987). Explicitly representing these mental states in agent architectures produces agents whose behaviours are affected by the adopted Belief, Desire and Intentions. Another example is the concept of norms from social science, which govern the behaviours of the society's individuals. Accordingly, researchers in multi-agent systems have adopted the concept of norms to imitate the collective behaviours of human society. Creating software agents that are aware of norms helps to regulate or predict the behavior of the agents, and also to make the development and coordination of multi-agent systems easier to manage (Dastani et al., 2008; Dignum, 1999). A system of autonomous agents regulated by norms is called a *normative multi-agent system* (Lopez, 2003). In (Boella et al., 2008), researchers provide a more elaborate definition of a normative multi-agent systems as "a multi-agent system organized by means of mechanisms to represent, communicate, distribute, detect, create, modify, and enforce norms, and mechanisms to deliberate about norms and detect norm violation and fulfillment". Normative systems models (including the concepts of permission, obligation and prohibition), combined with multi-agent systems, suggest a promising model for human and artificial agent societies (Boella et al., 2010).

Some researchers have concentrated on how to use norms to regulate and predict agents' behaviours and how to enforce agents compliance with the norms without limiting agents' autonomy. For this purpose, two approaches have been used, *regimentation* and *enforcement* (Grossi et al., 2007). In case of regimentation, agents have no ability to violate norms; the norms are considered to be a hard constraint. Obviously, the regimentation approach decreases agents' autonomy drastically. In the enforcement approach, agents decide to comply with or violate a norm, which has consequences determined by the enforcement regime. This decision might be based on the agents' beliefs, intentions, obligations, desires or something else. This choice is related to the concept of autonomy in artificial agents. When an agent violates a norm, a sanction might be applied to the violator agent as a means of enforcement, and this sanction (or punishment) plays a role in encouraging agents to comply with norms. Similarly, a reward might be granted to an agent that respects a norm. The objective for such enforcement is commonly to produce stable and predictable behavior of the overall system (Castelfranchi, 2004).

Mechanisms by which agents can adopt norms have been studied, which differentiate between rational and irrational norm adoption (Elster, 1989). Some researchers proposed several rational strategies for norm adoption (Lopez, 2003; Conte et al., 1999). Others deal with resolving norms conflicts and inconsistency at the time of adopting norms (Kollingbaum & Norman, 2003). This may happen when an agent joins a society and needs to adopt new norms to function within that society. For example, an agent may adopt an obligation that it previously considered prohibited. Norms might be established in several ways: they might be assigned by a legislator (Boman, 1999), might emerge or be negotiated among agents (Boella & van der Torre, 2007), or be acquired by machine learning techniques that are based on previous experience (Koeppen & Lopez-Sanchez, 2010).

Taking into consideration that the norms in a society are subject to change or even disappear, agents need a mechanism to identify/infer these changes. Also, when an agent joins a new society, it may use a similar mechanism to identify/infer the norms of this society for adoption. Norms have a significant role in regulating, controlling and predicting agents' behaviours. From the perspective of the individual agent, it is important to know which behaviour is acceptable or not acceptable in a particular society. Identifying changing norms helps agents to adapt their plans for achieving their goals (Savarimuthu et al., 2010).

Two groups of researchers address the problem of identifying norms in multi-agent systems. Researchers (Andrighetto et al., 2008; Campenni et al., 2008) have presented EMIL, a simulation of complex social systems. One issue currently being investigated in EMIL involves the mechanisms for new norm identification. They are working on a cognitive architecture based on mental representations which would allow norms to affect the behaviour of autonomous agents. Their agents are not subjected to punishment in case of norm violation. Researchers (Savarimuthu et al., 2009, 2010a, 2010b, 2010c) have proposed and demonstrated their framework of identifying and inferring norms (prohibitions and obligations) based on observing agents' interactions and observing special events that include punishment (*sanctions* and *rewards*). In Savarimuthu et al. (2009) they proposed an internal agent architecture for identifying prohibited norms. In Savarimuthu et al. (2010a), they applied data mining approaches to infer obligation norms in a multi-agent society. In Savarimuthu et al. (2010b) they have investigated how to infer the conditions behind conditional norms. They send inferred candidate norms to a norm verification component (V.C) to decide whether this candidate norm is actually a norm for the society or not.

Their verification component works as follows.

The recognizer agent asks its neighbor agents whether the candidate norm is an actual social norm or not. An example might be the symbolic equivalent of the question "Am I obliged to tip a waiter that serves me in this society?". This question would be represented in terms of the formal representation of a sequence of events that obliges a tip. Based on the reply the recognizer agent adopts the candidate norm as a verified actual norm, or rejects it. To avoid incorrect or deceptive responses, three agents are randomly selected and asked to verify the norm. The decision to adopt the norm is based on the majority answer. If the majority answer was affirmative the recognizer agent adopts the candidate norm as identified verified norm.

In this paper, we argue that the V.C used in Alrawagfeh et al. (2011a) and Savarimuthu et al. (2009, 2010a, 2010b, 2010b) is not designed to work in open multi-agent societies. We revisit the Modified Verification Component (M.V.C) presented in Alrawagfeh et al. (2011b) that is applicable in open multi-agent systems. We also present a further modification on Alrawagfeh et al. (2011a), the Modified Dynamic Verification Component (M.D.V.C) which allows an agent to dynamically infer new adopted and abrogated norms in open multi-agent societies. We show that (M.D.V.C) preserves the consistency among norms before adopting an identified norm.

This paper is structured as follows: we state our view of norms. We argue that the unmodified V.C does not work well in open multi-agent societies. A brief review of our previously proposed norm identification architecture is presented. We describe the component M.V.C and explain how it works in an open multi-agent system. Next, we present the M.D.V.C. and describe the experiments that we have performed and the results obtained. The discussion of our work is presented and concluding comments are presented. Finally, we outline future work.

WHAT IS A NORM?

Due to the differing concepts of norms in different disciplines, there is no universal definition of norm. Various definitions have been proposed for norm (Boella et al., 2006, 2009; Lopez, 2003; Lopez et al., 2002; Savarimuthu et al., 2009; Shoham & Tennenholtz, 1995; Verhagen, 2000). These definitions suggest the following characteristics related to norms:

- They are a soft-constraint on actions.
- They are shared among the individuals in a society.
- Violation of a norm may be subject to punishment while compliance with a norm may prompt a reward.
- They emerge as a result of complex interactions among individuals over a period of time.
- They are subject to change or may disappear altogether.

We attempt to incorporate these characteristics by developing two types of norms, namely the *permission norm* and the *prohibition norm*, which we define as follows:

a. **Permission norm:** a sequence of event(s) that do not result in a punishment. Therefore, agents anticipate no punishment from a sequence adopted as a permission norm.
b. **Prohibition norm:** a sequence of event(s) that may result in a punishment. Therefore, agents should not act out this sequence of events if they want to avoid a punishment.

THE V.C IN OPEN MULTI-AGENT SOCIETY

The norm identification mechanism in Alrawagfeh et al. (2011a) and Savarimuthu et al. (2009, 2010a, 2010b, 2010c) is composed of two components: the Candidate Norm Identification (C.N.I) and Verification Component (V.C). The C.N.I identifies the candidate norms from observed agents interactions or *events*. The V.C is applied to each candidate norm. In an agent performing norm identification, the V.C selects other agents and asks them whether the candidate norm is a norm or not (Figure 1).

This V.C mechanism causes problems if we want to use it in *open* multi-agent societies; those societies that are heterogeneous in the sense that agents may have different internal architecture, possibly created by different designers (Grossi, 2007; Koeppen & Lopez-Sanchez, 2010). Generally, the problems fall into two categories:

a. Agents in an open society/system may not know or understand the concept of norm or be aware of norms. We do not want to assume they have particular internal states, the

Figure 1. The verification component (V.C.), the recognizer agent picks a candidate norm (CN) from the candidate norms base and asks three agents whether CN is a norm or not. If the majority answer is affirmative, then CN is stored as an identified norm

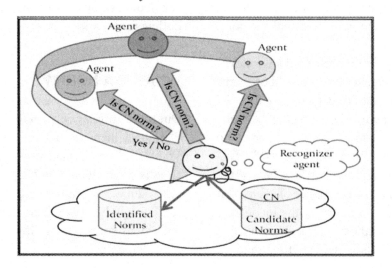

ability to represent mental states or to reason about norms or events. The V.C inquiry by a recognizer agent as to the existence of a norm would not be understood by agents in an open systems that do not represent or deal with the concept of norm. As a result, V.C is not suitable for an open multi-agent society.

b. Open multi-agent societies contain agents that may be owned by different stakeholders (Huynh et al., 2004). Consequently, each agent or a group of agents may have its own objectives, possibly in conflict with other agents. Accordingly, we should allow for the possibility of a competitive atmosphere appearing in such systems. Competitive agents could deliberately give misleading or false information. Even if an agent wants to be honest and give true response, the V.C mechanism may encourage the selected agent to give a perfidious or dishonest response. Consider the following example:

Suppose that a recognizer agent called *Fan* asks an agent called *Thermo* the following question: "Am I allowed to open the window?" or "Is the opening-window sequence of events prohibited?" From this kind of question, the asked agent Thermo could deduce that the agent Fan wants to open the window. Consequently, if this event sequence (opening-window) complies with the objectives of the agent Thermo, then it may respond that this act is not prohibited even though the act was a prohibited norm. As a result, Thermo may accomplish its objective while deflecting the punishment to Fan. In other words, Thermo's response will be in conformity with its objectives instead of being in conformity with the society's norms.

REVISION OF THE NORM IDENTIFICATION ARCHITECTURE

This section briefly presents a revision of the norm identification components of the internal architecture of the recognizer agent first proposed in Alrawagfeh et al. (2011a).

The architecture includes algorithms to recognize and dynamically infer permission and prohibition norms in open multi-agent system. A norm is represented as an event or a sequence of events. A permission norm is a sequence of event(s) that do not trigger punishment if agents execute them. A prohibition norm is a sequence of event(s) that may trigger punishment if agents execute them. Punishment is represented in the system as a special event which sanctions an agent. Regular events represent the acts that agents can perform; special events such as a sanction are created in response to norm violation. Figure 2, reproduced from Alrawagfeh et al. (2011a), shows the norm identification architecture composed of storage components and processing components.

Storage Components

a. **Prohibition Norm Base.** The prohibition norms of a system/society. Generally, its contents could be initialized at the time the system or society is engaged, and/or by the prohibition norms identification process.

In our experiments, its contents are created entirely by the norm identification mechanism.

b. **Permission Norm Base.** The permission norms of a system/society. As with the prohibition norms base, contents are assigned by the permission norms identification process.

Figure 2. Internal agent architecture of permission and prohibition norm identification

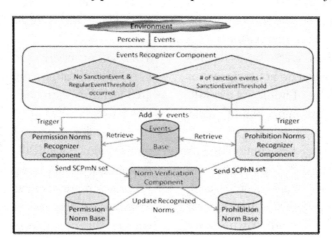

c. **Events-Base**. A record (a circular buffer) for each agent that is observable by the recognizer agent in the system/society. Any observable acts of an agent are saved as events in the corresponding agents' record in the *Events-Base* in the recognizer agent. In our experiments, the recognizer agent has access to a record of acts of all observable agents.

1. Processing Components:

a. **Events recognizer component.** This is the recognizer agent's "eyes" on the environment. This component observes the events in the agent environment, distinguishing between regular and special events. The perceived events are saved in the Events-Base, which is used for norm identification. The norm recognizer components (b and c below) are triggered by this component, based on the pattern of the observed events. For more details see the main algorithm in Alrawagfeh et al. (2011a).

b. **Prohibition norm recognizer component.** This identifies the Selected Candidate Prohibition Norms (*SCPhN*), based on observed events. Selections are based on event frequency preceding sanction events. More frequent events, that precede a sanction/special event, are inferred to be more likely to cause the sanction (prohibition norm). This component is triggered every time the events recognizer component counts a sanction event. For more details see algorithm-2 in Alrawagfeh et al. (2011a).

c. **Permission norm recognizer component.** This finds the Selected Candidate Permission Norms (*SCPmN*) based on regular events observation. The selection of candidate permission norms is based on the repetition of regular events without intervening sanction/special events. Frequency of event patterns is used to infer the likelihood of a candidate permission norm. This component is triggered when the number of regular events, during a time period, crosses a particular Regular Event Threshold (RET) value, and no sanction event occurred during that period. For more details see algorithm-3 in Alrawagfeh et al. (2011a).

d. **Norm verification component** (V.C) (Alrawagfeh et al., 2011a; Savarimuthu et al., 2009, 2010a, 2010b, 2010c). Chosen agents are asked whether the Selected Candidate Norm exists in the society as a norm or not. Three agents are asked in the existing implementations.

THE MODIFIED VERIFICATION COMPONENT (M.V.C)

The norm identification architectures that have been presented in Alrawagfeh et al. (2011a) and Savarimuthu et al. (2009, 2010a, 2010b, 2010c) are not designed to work in open multi-agent systems. The idea of a more general verification component comes from the fact that all agents, regardless of their internal architectures, designers, owner or types, must exhibit some standard behaviour(s) (including basic communication capabilities) in order to participate in a society, even though their internal architecture may be unknown. In this work, we assume that agents can communicate using the Foundation for Intelligent Physical Agents (FIPA)'s Agent Communication Language (ACL) (Foundation for Intelligent Physical Agents, 2002). We also assume that agents have the capability to perform acts that are relevant to a particular system/society. However, agents do not have to be able to provide information about their internal states, such as what norms they believe.

The idea of M.V.C is that instead of asking agents whether a candidate norm (sequence of event/s) is a norm or not, the recognizer agent asks other agents whether they can execute the sequence of event/s or not. This type of question avoids a proposal explicitly framed using the norm concept. Our M.V.C implementation is modeled on the standard FIPA's Contract Net Interaction Protocol (Foundation for Intelligent Physical Agents, 2002). The recognizer agent represents the initiator who sends CFPs. In our approach the recognizer agent does not need to accept any proposals, since it does not need the action to be performed.

The M.V.C has two steps (Figure 3):

1. Selecting agents to be asked

Particular agents are selected and a CFP is sent to them. The CFP requests proposals for performing a sequence of event/s (which is effectively the candidate norm). Asking more than one agent about the same sequence of events mimics the approach from the original V.C of attempting to mitigate misleading information. There are alternative strategies for the selection process, such as selecting the agent based on some measure of

Figure 3. The modified verification component (M.V.C.), the recognizer agent picks a candidate norm (CN) from the candidate norms. It sends CFP (to perform CN) to a particular number of agents. If the majority response is affirmative, then CN is stored as an identified norm

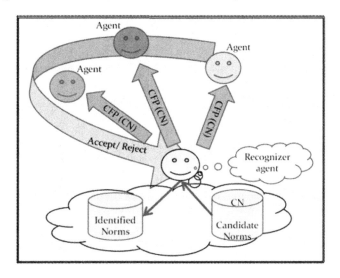

trust or reputation or preferentially selecting those "native agents" that have been participating in this society for a long time and may therefore be more acclimated to norms. In our extant experiments, the agents are selected randomly.

2. Asking the selected agents

The recognizer agent sends a CFP to the selected agents. The decision to accept the selected candidate norm is based on the majority response to the CFP (see Algorithm 1, taken from Alrawagfeh et al. (2011b). In case of candidate prohibition norms verification, if the recognizer agent receives negative proposals "refuse" from the majority of the selected agents then the candidate prohibition norm will be identified as a prohibition norm. Otherwise no norm is identified. The use of refuse messages (negative proposals) to infer prohibition of certain actions is a strong inference regarding the intent of the responding agents. There are other possible reasons agents might not make a proposal, which should be considered designs. In case of candidate permission norm verification, if the recognizer agent receives affirmative proposals from the majority of the selected agents then the candidate permission norm will be identified as permission norm. Otherwise no norm is identified.

Example: consider a book-trading-system that is composed of sellers, buyers and shippers agents. Assume some books are concerned. Suppose that the recognizer agent wants to verify that buying the "*Anarchist CookBook*" is permitted. The recognizer agent will send a CFP to buyer agents asking them to submit their proposals to buy the book.

Using semantic language SL, one possible FIPA's communication language, the CFP read as follows:

```
(cfp
:sender (agent-identifier:name Re-
coginzerAgent)
:receiver (set (agent-identifier:name
Buyer))
:content
"((action (set (agent-identifier:name
Buyer)
(Buy Book Big-River-Big-Sea-Untold-
stories-of-1949))
)"
:ontology Book-Trading
:language fipa-sl)
```

Algorithm 1. Modified NormVerification() pseudocode

Input: Selected-Candidate-Prohibition-Norms (SCPhN) set / or Selected-Candidate-Permission-Norms (SCPmN) set.
Output: prohibition norm(s) / or permission norm(s).
Parameter: **NumberofWiseAgents** the number of selected agents.
  Select **NumberofWiseAgents** agents from the society's agents
  If the input is SCPhN
    For each ϕ SCPhN
      Send CFP to the selected agents. // *the content of the CFP is the sequence of events ϕ.*
      If the majority of proposals were negative then add ϕ to Prohibition norm base.
  If the input is SCPmN
    For each ψ SCPmN
      Send CFP to the selected agents. // *the content of the CFP is the sequence of events ψ.*
      If the majority of proposals were affirmative then add ψ to permission norm base.

THE MODIFIED DYNAMIC VERIFICATION COMPONENT (M.D.V.C)

Since Agents could adopt a new norm or abrogate an existing one, we modified the V.C in order to be able to dynamically infer and recognize the evolution of society's norms. We called it Dynamic Verification Component (D.V.C). The D.V.C preserves consistency in identifying the prohibition and permission norms. For more details see algorithm-5 in Alrawagfeh et al. (2011a).

Here we apply to (D.V.C) the same modification that we applied to (V.C) – call it (M.D.V.C). In the M.D.V.C, instead of asking whether a candidate norm is norm or not, the recognizer agent sends to a particular number of agents a CFP to perform the candidate norm (see Algorithm 2).

In the case of verifying a candidate prohibition norm:

If the majority of the received proposals are negative then the candidate prohibition norm is matched against the permission norms. If it does not match any of them then the candidate prohibition norm is stored in the prohibition norms-base. However, if the candidate prohibition norm matches a permission norm then the matched permission norm is deleted from the permission norms-base and the candidate prohibition norm is added to the prohibition norms-base.

In the case of verifying a candidate permission norm:

If the majority of the received proposals are affirmative then the candidate permission norm is matched against the prohibition norms. If it does not match any of them then it is stored in the permission norms-base. If it matches a prohibition norm then the matched prohibition norm is deleted from the prohibition norms-base and the candidate permission norm is added to the permission norms-base. Consequently, the recognizer agent maintains the consistency among the permission and prohibition norms. Therefore, the recognizer agent will not have an action defined as prohibition norm and permission norm at the same time.

EXPERIMENTS

In this section we describe a restaurant scenario and discuss the results obtained by applying our proposed architecture and algorithms in Alrawagfeh et al. (2011a.).

Algorithm 2. ModifiedDynamicNormVerification() pseudocode. It provide the ability of dynamically infer norms.

Input: Selected-Candidate-Prohibition-Norms (SCPhN) set / or Selected-Candidate-Permission-Norms (SCPmN) set.
Output: prohibition norm(s) / or permission norm(s).
Parameter: **NumberofWiseAgents** the number of selected agents.
  Select **NumberofWiseAgents** agents from society's agents
  If the input is SCPhN
    For each ϕ SCPhN
      Send CFP to the selected agents. // *the content of the CFP is the sequence of events ϕ.*
      If the majority proposals were negative then
        Add ϕ to Prohibition norm base.
        Remove all permission norms (ψ) from permission-norm base where $\phi = \psi$ or ϕ is a part of ψ.
  If the input is SCPmN
    For each ψ SCPmN
      Send CFP to the selected agents. // *the content of the CFP is the sequence of events ψ.*
      If the majority proposals were affirmative then
        Add ψ to permission norm base.
        Remove all prohibition norms (ϕ) from prohibition-norm base where $\phi = \psi$ or ϕ is a part of ψ.

Firstly, the experiments use the verification component (V.C) as described in Alrawagfeh et al. (2011a) and Savarimuthu et al. (2009, 2010a, 2010b, 2010c). Secondly, the experiments use our proposed modified verification component (M.V.C). Finally, in the case that norms change, the experiment uses (M.D.V.C). We use the JADE-3.7 software framework to build the restaurant multi-agent society. As reported in Alrawagfeh et al. (2011b), the experiments are tested on a society of 22 agents.

Restaurant Scenarios

Our restaurant society consists of customer agents and a restaurant supervisor agent. The customer agents form a heterogeneous society. We assume that they are owned by different owners and have their own goals and objectives. Based on this heterogeneity in the system, some agents may have no concept of a norm. The dynamics of the society includes the following events: *{Reserving, Eating, Dropping, Paying, Smoking, Tipping, Yelling, Leaving}*. The supervisor agent monitors and punishes customer agents. Any customer that violates any of the norms of the restaurant is sanctioned by the supervisor agent. We assume that the supervisor already knows the prohibition norms of the society. A prohibition norm is a sequence of events. In our experiments, *Dropping, Smoking* and *Yelling* are separate prohibition norms. Customer agents are able to execute any event in the restaurant as many times as they want, and they are sanctioned if they violate the restaurant society norms. We ignore the semantic problems in the events that a customer agent may perform, for example, in our scenarios the customer may Eat, Reserve, Leave, Eat and then Pay, in an order that is not semantically rational.

Newcomer Agent Scenario

In this scenario, before a newcomer participates in the society, he will try to infer the norms that govern this society. We make the following assumptions in this scenario:

1. Agents in our restaurant society use the FIPA's Agent Communication Language (ACL).
2. The restaurant society has some disobedient customer agents who sometimes violate the norms.

The restaurant society in this experiment consists of two groups of customer agents and one supervisor agent: The first group consists of ten agents, who understand the concept of norm. The second group of ten agents has a different internal architecture and do not have the concept of norm.

In this experiment we compare the verification component (V.C) and the modified verification component (M.V.C) relative to the efficiency of inferring prohibition norms. The component that infers norms using the smaller number of observed events is considered to be more efficient.

In this scenario, 50% of agents do not understand the concept of norm. In case of applying the Verification Component (V.C) the possibility of selecting agents that do not understand the concept of norm equals 50%, consequently, 50% of agents are capable of replying. In the case of applying the Modified Verification Component (M.V.C) 100% of agents are capable of replying, since the inquiry that is used in this component asks about behaviours instead of norms. So, all polled agents may reply no matter whether they understand the concept of norm or not.

The experiment was repeated ten times. The number of observed events, in each execution, required to identify norms was recorded. The average number of observed events was then calculated for the ten executions.

The experiment results, Figure 4, shows that using the architecture and algorithms from Alrawagfeh et al. (2011b) with the verification component (V.C) described in Alrawagfeh et al. (2011a) and Savarimuthu et al. (2009, 2010a, 2010b, 2010c), newcomer agent infers all restaurant prohibition norms (Dropping, Smoking, Yelling) by event 165.5 (on average), while the Figure 5 shows that the modified verification component (M.V.C) achieves the same thing by event 43.4 (on average). Figure 6 shows that the modified verification component (M.V.C) needs fewer events to infer the prohibition norms than the verification component (V.C).

Obviously, the V.C needs more events to infer norms, since it asks about the norms, and in our society only half of the agents are aware of the concept of norm. The recognizer agent selects three agents randomly and asks them about the norms. The probability of selecting agents who are aware of norms equals 0.5. Consequently the probability of getting a reply from the selected agent equals 0.5. But in case of M.V.C the probability of getting reply equals 1.0. In other words, in case of V.C, as the probability of existing agents that are not aware of norms increases, the probability of failure of identifying norms also increases. Since M.V.C does not ask about norms

Figure 4. When around 46 events were perceived by the observer agent, it inferred one prohibition norm. At event 95 it inferred 2 and at 165 it inferred all prohibition norms in the society

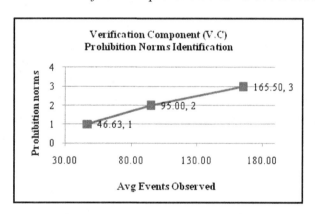

Figure 5. When around 17 events were perceived by the observer agent, it inferred one prohibition norm. At event 31 it inferred 2 and at 43 it inferred all prohibition norms in the society

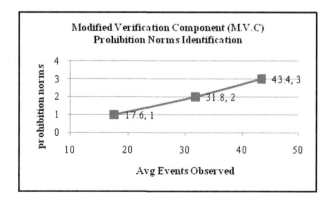

Figure 6. The verification component (V.C) needs more events than the modified verification component (M.V.C) in order to infer the society norms

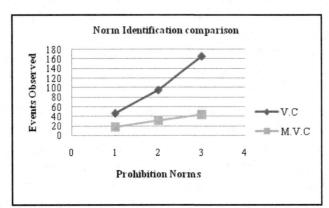

it is not affected by the heterogeneity of our restaurant society. Normally, as Figure 4 and Figure 5 show, the norm identification success increased as the events executed in the society increase.

Norms Changing Scenario

This scenario tests the M.D.V.C and it is a complement to the previous scenario. It starts after the newcomer agent identified all prohibition norms in the restaurant society. After event 44, the restaurant supervisor changes the society's norms, by adopting a new prohibition norm (Tipping), and abrogating another (Smoking). The experiments in Figure 7 and Figure 8 show how customer agents, who apply our architecture, proposed in Alrawagfeh et al. (2011a), and use our proposed M.D.V.C, can identify the changed norms.

As we see in Figure 7, at event 62 the new adopted norm (Tipping) is identified before the abrogation of (Smoking) is identified. At event 82 and event 92 the agent identifies more permission norms.

As we see in Figure 7, at event 92 the recognizer agent identifies the abrogation of the prohibition norm (Smoking) and loses the prohibition norm (Dropping). Losing the identified prohibition

norm (Dropping) could result from the following situation: when this norm (Dropping) is violated or executed by agents and before the sanction for this violation is issued, the permission norm inference component is triggered. Then it may be identified as permission norm and consequently removed from the prohibition norm base. But, as we see at event 110 in Figure 7 when the sanctions are issued and the prohibition norm inference component is triggered, the mistaken abrogated prohibition norm is identified again.

Indeed, this point shows how the M.V.D.C preserves the consistency among norms: in Figure 7, after event 92 and before event 110 (Dropping) is identified as a permission norm. At event 110 the sanction for violating the (Dropping) has been issued, then the (Dropping) is identified as a prohibition norm; but before adopting it as a prohibition norm (M.D.V.C) takes it out from the permission norms base. Therefore the consistency is preserved among permission and prohibition norms.

Also, we read from Figures 7 and 8 at event 92 and 110, that the number of identified prohibition norms decreased, the identified permission norms increased, and vice versa.

Figure 7. When 44 events were perceived, there is no change of prohibition norm base. D, S, Y and T represent (Dropping, Smoking, Yelling and Tipping, respectively). After event 44 the restaurant norms are changed by abrogating S and adopting T. At event 62 the agent infer extra norm T, this means the agent adopts the new norm T before abrogating the old one S. At event 92 the agent infers the abrogated prohibition norm S and loses a prohibition norm D. At event 110 it identifies the losing norm

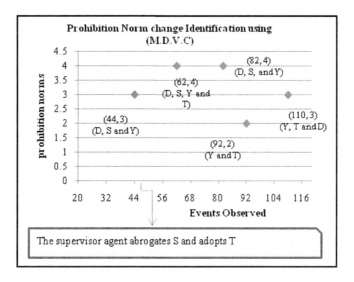

Figure 8. The number of permission norms is decreased by the increasing of prohibition norms, as seen at event 92 and 110. Also the figure shows that number of identified permission norms is increased by the increasing of executed events.

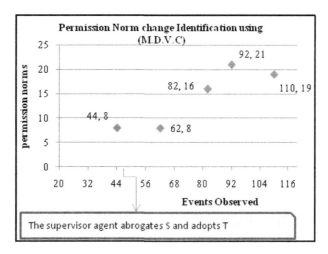

DISCUSSION

Norms have been used as a way to regulate and predict agent's behaviour in multi-agent societies. Each agent has its goals and objectives and has its plans for achieving them, so its behaviour will be affected by its goals and objectives. So, if there are agents belonging to different owners in the same society then their goals may be different and so would be their behaviour. But, if there are norms governing this society, then agents have a means of predicting the behaviour of other agents.

Another advantage for establishing norms in a society is to limit agents' chaotic behaviour by encouraging agents to comply with norms, and at the same time preserving the agent's autonomy by permitting them to violate the norms, if they want. In other words, norms prevent agents degenerating from autonomy to chaos.

Identifying society's norms in general helps agents in predicting and regulating behaviour, in addition to their role in goal formation and plan adoption. Some researchers that work in norm identification imitate human-nature's behaviours in identifying societies' norms. Human nature, in case of joining a new society and wanting to know its norms, is to ask other human agents about them. The verification component that has been proposed in Savarimuthu et al. (2009, 2010a, 2010b, 2010c) uses this idea of asking other agents about the norms. The strong assumption behind this idea is that agents in the society have the concept of norm in their internal architecture. But, this is not the case in open multi-agent societies.

Usually, open multi-agent societies imply heterogeneity. Therefore, asking other agents about norms in an open multi-agent society is not useful. The modified verification component has less restrictive assumptions, such as: the agents in the society can communicate by a particular agent communication language. All agents, regardless of their internal architectures, have behaviour and they can communicate with each other in different ways, such as, passing messages. Based on these assumptions, the modified verification component asks other agents about their behaviour ability, using the FIPA's ACL's CFP communication act and it is modeled on the FIPA's Contract Net Interaction Protocol. Experimentally, we have shown that the modified verification component can work to identify norms in an open multi-agent society. Also, we have shown that our modified

dynamic verification component can be used to dynamically infer and identify adoption or abrogation of norms while preserving the consistency between permission norms and prohibition norms.

CONCLUSION

In this work we show how the verification component that has been used in Alrawagfeh et al. (2011a) and Savarimuthu et al. (2009, 2010a, 2010b, 2010c) does not work well in open multi-agent societies, and its probability of failure in identifying norms increases as the number of agents who do not understand the concept of norm increases. The proposed modified verification component can identify norms in open multi-agent societies, even if all agents in the society have no norm concept in their internal architecture. We have also shown how our proposed modified dynamic verification component can identify and dynamically infer the changes that may occur on the norms of an open society. We created a restaurant society scenario, using the JADE software framework, and applied it to our proposed architecture and algorithms in Alrawagfeh et al. (2011a) along with our proposed modified verification component on the restaurant society.

Based on the results in the second scenario (when the agent loses an identified norm), we conclude that, the success of our proposed component in inferring the correct norms depends on the ability and efficiency of the punisher agent (the supervisor agent) in recognizing the norms violation and issuing a sanction event. Therefore, we need to investigate the role of the punisher agent (who applies punishments) in the norms identification process.

FUTURE WORK

As future work, we plan to modify our way of selecting agents for norm verification; currently we are working on taking into account the agents' trustworthiness, reputation and experience.

Because of agents' unreliability and self-interest in open multi-agent systems, agents may not participate and reply to the recognizer agent's verification question. Hence, we plan to encourage agents to participate and hopefully give correct information. To this end, we plan to associate a reward with the CFP posed to them. We attempt to provide a reward appropriate to an agent's goals. Hence, in this case, there is greater chance of agents' participation.

In the near future, we plan to integrate our approach to norm identification and our modified verification component with the BDI architecture and analyze the interaction of norms with respect to mental states.

REFERENCES

Alrawagfeh, W., Brown, E., & Mata-Montero, M. (2011, April 3-7). Identifying norms of behaviour in open multi-agent societies. In *Proceedings of the Agent-Directed Simulation Symposium as part of the Spring Simulation Multi-conference*, Boston, MA.

Alrawagfeh, W., Brown, E., & Mata-Montero, M. (in press). Identifying norms of behaviour in multi-agent societies. In *Proceedings of the Seventh Conference of the European Social Simulation Association*, Montpellier- France.

Andrighetto, G., Campenni, M., Cecconi, F., & Conte, R. (2008). The complex loop of norm emergence: A simulation model. In *Proceedings of the Second World Congress on Simulating Interacting Agents and Social Phenomena* (pp. 17-33).

Boella, G. Pigozzi, & van der Torre, L. (2009). Five guidelines for normative multi-agent systems. In *Proceedings of the Symposium on Normative Multi-agent Systems*.

Boella, G., Gabriella, P., Munindar, P., & Harko, V. (2010). Normative multiagent systems: Guest editors' introduction. *Logic Journal of IGPL*, *18*(1), 1–3. doi:10.1093/jigpal/jzp079

Boella, G., & van der Torre, L. (2007). Norm negotiation in multiagent systems. *International Journal of Cooperative Information Systems*, *16*(1), 97–122. doi:10.1142/S0218843007001585

Boella, G., van der Torre, L., & Verhagen, H. (2006). Introduction to normative multiagent systems. *Computational & Mathematical Organization Theory*, *12*(2-3), 71–79. doi:10.1007/s10588-006-9537-7

Boella, G., van der Torre, L., & Verhagen, H. (2008). Introduction to the special issue on normative multiagent systems. *Journal of Autonomous Agents and Multi-Agent Systems*, *17*, 1–10. doi:10.1007/s10458-008-9047-8

Boman, M. (1999). Norms in artificial decision making. *Artificial Intelligence and Law*, *7*(1), 17–35. doi:10.1023/A:1008311429414

Bratman, M. E. (1987). *Intention, plans and practical reason*. Cambridge, MA: Harvard University Press.

Campenni, M., Andrighetto, G., Cecconi, F., & Conte, R. (2008, September 1-5). Normal = normative? The role of intelligent agents in norm innovation. In *Proceedings of the Fifth Conference of the European Social Simulation Association*.

Castelfranchi, C. (2004). Formalizing the informal? Dynamic social order, bottom-up social control, and spontaneous normative relations. *Journal of Applied Logic*, *1*(1-2), 47–92. doi:10.1016/S1570-8683(03)00004-1

Conte, R., Castelfranchi, C., & Dignum, F. (1999). Autonomous norm acceptance. In J. P. Müller, A. S. Rao, & M. P. Singh (Eds.), *Proceedings of the 5th International Workshop on Intelligent Agents: Agents, Theories, Architectures, and Languages* (LNCS, 1555, pp. 99-112).

Dastani, M., Grossi, D., Meyer, J.-J. C., & Tinnemeier, N. (2008). Normative multi-agent programs and their logics. In *Proceedings of the Workshop on Knowledge Representation for Agents and Multi-Agent Systems* (pp. 236-243).

Dignum, F. (1999). Autonomous agents with norms. *AI and Law*, *7*, 69–79.

Elster, J. (1989). Social norms and economic theory. *The Journal of Economic Perspectives*, *3*(4), 9–117.

Foundation for Intelligent Physical Agents. (2002). *FIPA ACL message structure specification* (Tech. Rep. No. SC00061G). Geneva, Switzerland: Foundation for Intelligent Physical Agents.

Foundation for Intelligent Physical Agents. (2002). *FIPA contract net interaction protocol specification* (Tech. Rep. No. SC00029H). Geneva, Switzerland: Foundation for Intelligent Physical Agents.

Grossi, D. (2007). *Designing invisible handcuffs: Formal investigations in institutions and organizations for MAS.* Unpublished doctoral dissertation, Utrecht University, Utrecht, The Netherlands.

Grossi, D., Aldewereld, H., & Dignum, F. (2007). Designing norm enforcement in e-institutions. In P. Noriega, J. Vázquez-Salceda, G. Boella, O. Boissier, V. Dignum, N. Fornara, & E. Matson (Eds.), *Proceedings of the International Workshop on Coordination, Organizations, Institutions, and Norms in Agent Systems II* (LNCS 4386, pp. 101-114).

Huynh, T. D., Jennings, N. R., & Shadbolt, N. R. (2004). Fire: An integrated trust and reputation model for open multi-agent systems. In *Proceedings of the 16th European Conference on Artificial Intelligence* (pp. 18-20).

Koeppen, J., & Lopez-Sanchez, M. (2010). Generating new regulations by learning from experience. In P. Noriega, J. Vázquez-Salceda, G. Boella, O. Boissier, V. Dignum, N. Fornara, & E. Matson (Eds.), *Proceedings of the International Workshop on Coordination, Organizations, Institutions, and Norms in Agent Systems II* (LNCS 4386, pp. 72-79).

Kollingbaum, M. J., & Norman, T. J. (2003). Norm adoption and consistency in the NoA agent architecture. In M. M. Dastani, J. Dix, & A. El Fallah-Seghrouchni (Eds.), *Proceedings of the First International Workshop on Programming Multi-Agent Systems* (LNCS 3067, pp. 169-186).

Lopez, F. (2003). *Social powers and norms: Impact on agent behaviour.* Unpublished doctoral dissertation, University of Southampton, Southampton, UK.

Lopez, F., Luck, M., & d'Inverno, M. (2002). Constraining autonomy through norms. In *Proceedings of the First International Joint Conference on Autonomous Agents and Multi Agent Systems* (pp. 674-681).

Ostrom, E. (2000). Collective action and the evolution of social norms. *The Journal of Economic Perspectives*, *14*, 137–158. doi:10.1257/jep.14.3.137

Savarimuthu, B. T. R., Cranfield, S., Purvis, M., & Purvis, M. (2009). Internal agent architecture for norm identification. In J. Padget, A. Artikis, W. Vasconcelos, K. Stathis, V. T. da Silva, E. Matson, & A. Polleres (Eds.), *Proceeding of the 5th International Workshop on Coordination, Organization, Institutions and Norms in Agent Systems* (LNCS 6069, pp. 241-256).

Savarimuthu, B. T. R., Cranfield, S., Purvis, M., & Purvis, M. (2010). A data mining approach to identify obligation norms in agent societies. In L. Cao, A. L. C. Bazzan, V. Gorodetsky, P. A. Mitkas, G. Weiss, & P. S. Yu (Eds.), *Proceedings of the 6ᵗʰ International Workshop on Agents and Data Mining Interaction* (LNCS 5980, pp. 43-58).

Savarimuthu, B. T. R., Cranfield, S., Purvis, M., & Purvis, M. (2010). Identifying conditional norms in multi-agent societies. In M. De Vos, N. Fornara, J. V. Pitt, & G. Vouros (Eds.), *Proceeding of the 6th International Workshop on Coordination, Organization, Institutions and Norms in Agent Systems* (LNCS 6541, pp. 19-24).

Savarimuthu, B. T. R., Cranfield, S., Purvis, M., & Purvis, M. (2010). *Norm identification in multi-agent societies.* Retrieved from http://otago.ourarchive.ac.nz/handle/10523/1031

Shoham, Y., & Tennenholtz, M. (1995). On social laws for artificial agent societies: Off-line design. *Artificial Intelligence, 73*(1-2), 231–252. doi:10.1016/0004-3702(94)00007-N

Verhagen, H. (2000). *Norm autonomous agents.* Unpublished doctoral dissertation, Royal Institute of Technology and Stockholm University, Stockholm, Sweden.

This work was previously published in International Journal of Agent Technologies and Systems, Volume 3, Issue 3, edited by Yu Zhang, pp. 1-16, copyright 2011 by IGI Publishing (an imprint of IGI Global).

Section 4
E-Business Simulation

Chapter 10
Enhanced Reputation Model with Forgiveness for E-Business Agents

Radu Burete
University of Craiova, Romania

Amelia Bădică
University of Craiova, Romania

Costin Bădică
University of Craiova, Romania

Florin Moraru
University of Craiova, Romania

ABSTRACT

Trust is a very important quality attribute of an e-service. In particular, the increasing complexity of the e-business environment requires the development of new computational models of trust and reputation for e-business agents. In this paper, the authors introduce a new reputation model for agents engaged in e-business transactions. The model enhances classic reputation models by the addition of forgiveness factor and the use of new sources of reputation information based on agents groups. The paper proposes an improvement of this model by employing the recent con-resistance concept. Finally, the authors show how the model can be used in an agent-based market environment where trusted buyer and seller agents meet, negotiate, and transact multi-issue e-business contracts. The system was implemented using JADE multi-agent platform and initially evaluated on a sample set of scenarios. The paper introduces the design and implementation of the agent-based system together with the experimental scenarios and results.

DOI: 10.4018/978-1-4666-1565-6.ch010

INTRODUCTION

Reputation is one of the important concepts that help to make more informed and intelligent decisions for selection of partners in e-business transactions (Chang, Hussain, & Dillon, 2006). In a digital economy populated with a multitude of electronic services, participants to the global electronic market, usually buyers and sellers are represented using software agents (Fasli, 2007). Similarly to human society, an agent will agree to engage in a new business relation governed by a set of contractual terms and conditions, only with reputable business partners. This means that, if an agent has a good reputation in a society of agents, other agents will decide to select him for engaging together in future business transactions.

Closely related to reputation is the concept of trust. Successful e-businesses are usually based on creation and maintenance of a solid trust relationship with their potential customers over a period of time (Srinivasan, 2004). Trust is a complex concept that has a multitude of facets. Although there is no full agreement on its definitions, *trust* can be understood as a subjective measure of an agent's belief in another agent's capabilities, honesty and reliability based on its own direct experiences (one-to-one relationship), while *reputation* can be understood as an objective measure of an agent's belief in another agent's capabilities, honesty and reliability based on recommendations received from other agents (one-to-many relationship) (Badica et al., 2006).

So, in order to clarify the terminology, given two agents a and b, we shall talk about reputation of agent a for agent b as the measure of the degree of b's belief in the capability, honesty and reliability of agent a. We shall denote this value with $R_{b,a}$. Usually in such a relation, agent a is said to have *trusted* role, while agent b is said to have *trusting* role (Jøsang, Ismail, & Boyd, 2007). Note that, according to this view of the reputation, parameters a and b can represent singleton agents, as well as groups of agents.

Distinction between trusting and trusted roles in a business relation points out to the two facets of the trust-reputation dichotomy. According to the reputation facet, we can talk about the reputation of agent a as seen by agent b, while according to the trust facet we can talk about the trust developed by agent b in agent a. In this paper we only consider the concept of reputation, as we believe that this concept is more appropriate to e-business domain. Intuitively, reputation can be used to qualitatively characterize a given business, as well as reputation is closer to frequently encountered marketing concepts like brand and image (Jøsang, Keser, & Dimitrakos, 2005).

Traditionally, reputation is evaluated by collecting feedback during history of previous interactions between business partners (Badica et al., 2006; Ganzha et al., 2006). There are many approaches for modeling and evaluation of reputation in agent systems, ranging from simple rating methods to more complex mathematical models based on graphs or sophisticated uncertainty or logic models (see the following survey papers (Sabater & Sierra, 2005; Wang & Lin, 2008; Jøsang, Ismail, & Boyd, 2007).

In our proposal we model e-business as a semi-competitive environment where agents will have to decide if to engage or not in e-business transactions with a given partner (Foued et al., 2009). Their decision is taken based on reputation of the potential partners, i.e., the higher partner's reputation is then the higher is considered the agent's utility (i.e., the agent will benefit more) by engaging with that partner.

In our model we consider that agents are grouped into "societies". We consider two societies: buyer society and seller society. With respect to these two societies, following the initial proposal of (Foued et al., 2009), depending on the sources of information that we can use for computing reputation, we define four types of reputation: (i) direct reputation of a given seller for a given buyer; (ii) direct reputation of a given buyer for a given seller; (iii) reputation of given seller for buyers' society; (iv) reputation of sellers' society for a given buyer.

Direct reputations (i.e., first two types) are then augmented with forgiveness factor model (Henderson, 1996) that basically proposes the application of "philosophy of reconciliation". This means that, as time is passing, each agent should forget the mistakes made by his or her partner in former e-business transactions. Additionally, our forgiveness factor model introduces an optimistic view of the reality. This means that an agent should always give credit to his partner, i.e. initially or equivalently after a sufficiently large time passed without any interaction, reputation of the partner should have or increase to the highest possible value.

The paper is structured as follows. Following the overview of related works, we start by introducing our computational reputation model and we show how this model can be enhanced with forgiveness factor and con-resistance. We follow with a design outline of the multi-agent system that we used in our experiments and with a discussion of our experimental results. Finally we present our conclusions and we point to future works.

RELATED WORKS

With the advent of Internet-based open global environments, like e-business, social networks, and online communities, the concepts of trust and reputation became very important. This tendency is also reflected by the increasing number of research publications that address the problem of developing new computational models of online trust and reputation. In this context, agent-based computational approaches are an important trend for implementation and experimentation with computational trust and reputation models.

An early reputation system that improves the simple averaging scheme used by eBay and Amazon with the notion of reliability of the reputation value is SPORAS (Zacharia & Maes, 1999). Dif-

ferently from our approach, two agents may rate each other only once. So, if two agents interact more times, only the most recently submitted ratings are kept by the system.

The paper (Sabater & Sierra, 2001) introduces the REGRET model that defines subjective reputation as direct reputation calculated from an agent's set of impressions. An impression is the subjective evaluation of an agent on a certain aspect of a certain outcome. Relating REGRET with our approach, we can map a contract to an outcome and a contract term to a certain aspect of this outcome. Now it can be easily seen that our model is closely related to REGRET, while being more specifically tailored to model reputation of agents that transact e-business contracts.

A trust model for evaluation of buyer and seller agents that operate in an open market environment, together with the design and implementation of a supporting system were described in the papers Badica et al. (2006) and Ganzha et al. (2006). The proposed model was specifically tailored to address the needs of a particular agent-based e-commerce environment. The model is using results of trust-significant one-to-one interactions between sellers and buyers to adjust trust values and also adopts an "amnesia" approach – i.e. as the time is passing without any transactions going on, agents become neutral to trust. While "amnesia" model resembles our "forgiveness" model, the difference is that we use an optimistic rather than neutral view of reality that stimulates better further agents' interaction on the market.

A new trust management framework for distributed e-business environments was proposed in the paper Sathiyamoorthy, Iyenger, and Ramachandran (2010). This framework is inspired by trusted third parties, policy-based and reputation-based models. The proposed trust metric combines trust based on direct experience and feedback from peers and it uses an averaging scheme, quite similar to our approach. However, this approach does not include neither forgiveness nor amnesia models.

A new trust and reputation model called FIRE – coming from "**fi**des" (which means "trust" in Latin) and "**re**putation" was introduced in the paper Huynh, Jennings, and Shadbolt (2006). FIRE integrates interaction trust, role-based trust, witness reputation, and certified reputation to provide trust metrics. FIRE was shown to provide agents with better utility and to effectively respond to changes occurred in agents' environment.

A new mathematical model of reputation for semi-competitive agent environments was presented in the paper Foued et al. (2009). This model improves existing models by adding information about (i) agent reputation for different groups and (ii) agent's group reputation. This model was an initial source of inspiration for our approach. We have applied this model by considering two agent groups: seller group and buyer group and we enhanced it with forgiveness factor model as suggested by Henderson (1996).

A new and very different computational model of trust for cognitive e-business agents was proposed in the paper Scarlat and Maries (2009) with the goal of enhancing collective intelligence within organizations. This model was studied experimentally using the preferential attachment hypothesis on evolving social interaction networks.

Finally note that there are also papers that survey problems and approaches of computational trust and reputation management for online environments.

A systematic classification of computational trust and reputation models according to 7 dimensions was proposed in the paper Sabater and Sierra (2005): (i) conceptual model, (ii) information sources, (iii) visibility types, (iv) model's granularity, (v) agent behavior assumptions, (vi) type of exchanged information, and (vii) trust/reputation reliability measure. According to this classification, our approach can be described as follows: (i) game-theoretical (i.e. reputation represents utility obtained by numerical aggregation of results of past interactions); (ii) it combines direct experiences with sociological information

– as in our model agents are grouped into agent societies; (iii) it combines subjective view (direct reputation) with objective view (at the level of an agent society); (iv) it is single-context, as it only applies to the pre-defined context of an e-business transaction for buying and selling a goods; (v) seller agents can fail to provide all terms of a signed contract, and this can be detected by buyer agents; (vi) this dimension does not apply to our model, as we do not use witness reputation; (vii) we do not provide a reliability measure of the reputation value.

A two dimension classification of trust and reputation measures according to (i) specificity-generality and (ii) subjectivity-objectivity criteria was proposed in the paper Jøsang, Ismail, and Boyd (2007). According to this classification, our model can be described as follows: (i) general, as opinion of a participant about the result of a contract is evaluated by averaging its individual opinions about how each term of the contract was achieved and (ii) combining the private subjective view (direct reputation) with the public objective view at the level of a group of agents.

Paper Wang and Lin (2008) contains a light overview and classification of the most important problems and their proposed solutions of reputation-based trust management in e-commerce environments. With respect to the trust management categories introduced there, our approach can be simply described as "trust evaluation method for multi-agent environments". With respect to the type of the management architecture, our approach can be classified as semi-centralized (or semi-distributed equally well, i.e., between distributed and centralized). More specifically, our approach is partly distributed, as each buyer agent evaluates directly each seller agent, as well as centralized at the level of a society, as both direct and society reputation can be taken into consideration for trust-based decision making regarding the involvement into future e-business transactions.

REPUTATION MODEL WITH FORGIVENESS

Reputation Types

E-business transactions are modeled as "signed contracts". A contract is signed between a buyer and a seller agent following a negotiation process. The buyer sends a call for proposals to each member of the seller society. Some sellers are able to satisfy the terms and conditions of the call and decide to cooperate by submitting a proposal. The buyer will select the mostly preferred seller (that maximizes his own utility) and his selection will trigger the definition of a "signed contract" between the buyer and selected seller. In what follows we generalize this view to a generic "signed contract" that describes the terms and conditions for the provision of a certain service by a provider agent to a requester agent.

A contract between two agents that decided to cooperate specifies the set of terms of the service that the provider agent agrees to offer to the requester agent. So in fact we have a "multi-issue signed contract" that governs the transaction between those two agents. For example, if the provider agent is a seller and the requester agent is a buyer then the contract will specify the terms of the sell, possibly including things like: on time delivery, delivery of the right product, warranties, etc. If S is the set of terms and each term k has a given weight w_k that measures the importance of the term for the requester agent then the requester can evaluate the utility of the contract as: $C = \Sigma_{k \in S} w_k t_k$ where $t_k = 1$ if the requester agent is happy with the term k of delivered service, otherwise $t_k = 0$. Note that, as the weights of service terms satisfy $w_k \geq 0$ and $\Sigma_{k \in S} w_k = 1$, it easily follows that $0 \leq C \leq 1$.

In our model we focus on an e-commerce environment, so we found naturally to consider two agent societies: buyer society $B = \{b_1, b_2, \ldots, b_m\}$ and seller society $S = \{s_1, s_2, \ldots, s_n\}$, where m is the number of buyers and n is the number of

sellers. Buyer agents are looking for engagement in e-business transactions with seller agents. A transaction involves signing and carrying out a contract between two agents. Based on the agent grouping into societies and following the proposal of (Foued et al., 2009), we defined four types of reputation measures.

Direct reputation is defined between a buyer agent and a seller agent based on the results of past contracts made between them. If $|B| = m$ and $|S| = n$ then we can define $2mn$ reputations between buyers b_i and sellers s_j (note that the reputation relation is not symmetric). Value of direct reputation is updated after carrying out each contract with formula $R' = \lambda C + (1 - \lambda)R$ where R' and R are new and previous values of direct reputation, while C is the value of last contract carried out between the agents. Parameter $0 < \lambda < 1$ controls the relative importance of the value of the current contract in the updated value of direct reputation. It is easy to observe that if $R > 0$ then $R' > 0$, so if initial value of direct reputation is not zero then direct reputation will always be strictly positive. But according to the optimistic view of the world, initial values for all direct reputations are set to 1, and so it easily follows that in our model direct reputation values are always strictly positive.

Note that we have both *direct reputation of a given seller for a given buyer*, as well as *direct reputation of a given buyer for a given seller*. This is not difficult to understand as one can easily note that a contract signed between a buyer and a seller defines a set of commitments for seller, as well as a set of commitments for buyer. For example, the seller commits to deliver a product with a given set of features, at a given price and before a given deadline, while the buyer commits to accept and pay for a delivered product with the given set of features that was received on time.

Reputation of a given seller for the buyers' society is defined between buyer society and each member of the seller society and defines the image of the seller for the entire buyer society. This reputation is influenced by the direct reputation of that given seller for each buyer. If $|S| = n$ then we can define n reputations between the set of buyers B and seller s_j. Reputation of a given seller for buyers' society is computed as average of direct reputations of that given seller s_j for each member b_i of buyer society, i.e., $R_{B,j} = (\Sigma_{i \in B} R_{i,j}) / m$, where $R_{i,j}$ is the direct reputation of seller s_j for buyer b_i.

Reputation of the sellers' society for a given buyer is defined between each member of buyer society and seller society. This reputation is influenced by the direct reputation of each seller for that given buyer. If $|B| = m$ then we can define m reputations between and b_i and S. Reputation of sellers' society for a given buyer is computed as average of each seller s_j for that given buyer b_i, i.e., $R_{i,S} = (\Sigma_{j \in S} R_{i,j}) / n$, where $R_{i,j}$ is direct reputation of seller s_j for buyer b_i.

Forgiveness Factor

Reputation is cumulative and dynamic, so its value depends on time. As time is passing, reputation can be updated in the following two ways: (i) whenever a new contract is signed and carried out between a seller agent and a buyer agent, reputation is updated to incorporate also the status of contract results; (ii) whenever a sufficiently large quiescence time Δt without any signed contracts has passed, reputation is updated by being slightly increased.

Forgiveness factor acts by triggering the update of direct reputation according to the following equation: $R(t+\Delta t) = \min\{(1+\alpha)R(t), 1\}$. Here Δt and $\alpha > 0$ are the parameters of forgiveness factor model. Parameter α controls the proportion by which reputation is increased, while Δt controls the speed at which reputation is increased. Note that according to this equation, the reputation value will always be at most 1. If there are no contracts signed for a sufficiently long time then the value of reputation will converge to 1, thus reflecting our optimistic assumption about the reality.

The pair of parameters $(\Delta t, \alpha)$ characterizes a given trusting agent and thus can be considered as defining the *trusting agent forgiveness profile*.

For example, the larger the value of α is and the smaller the value of Δt is then the higher is the trusting agent capacity to forgive, i.e. that trusting agent is able to forgive faster. For the case when the trusting party has role of buyer, we can define the *buyer forgiveness profile*.

Note also that basically forgiving means that the trusting agent will increase the trusted agent's reputation with a given increment $\alpha R(t)$. The reputation increment is proportional with the current value of the reputation $R(t)$. This can be interpreted as follows: if an agent is trusting more a partner (i.e., the partner has a higher reputation $R(t)$) then he is also capable to forgive faster the partner's mistakes (because the value of the reputation increment $\alpha R(t)$ is higher). Moreover, as $R(t) > 0$, it follows that the reputation increment $\alpha R(t)$ is strictly positive, so it determines the trusted agent's reputation to strictly increase.

Adding Con-Resistance

Similarly to the human society, an agent will decide to transact a new contract with another agent if and only if the agent that provides the required service has a good reputation that was acquired by successful interactions that were carried out over a significant period of time. Following Salehi-Abari and White (2009), a *confidence man*, the long term for *con-man*, is someone who takes advantage of others after gaining their confidence by building a good reputation and then exploiting it for his own private purposes. This behavioral pattern is known as *confidence trick*. Here we briefly outline how our reputation model based on forgiveness factor could be enhanced with the con-resistant feature inspired by the recent work reported in Salehi-Abari and White (2009).

There are two key points in dealing with confidence tricks to build con-resistant reputation models. Firstly, whenever a confidence trick is detected, the reputation of the con-man agent must be more severely reduced than before. Basically this can be achieved by increasing the value of the parameter λ that controls the relative importance of the value of the current contract in the updated value of the direct reputation to a new value $\lambda' > \lambda$. Assuming that a confidence trick was detected, this means that the value of the current contract C is low, while the agent has a high reputation $R > C$. So updating the direct reputation with the formula $R' = \lambda'C + (1 - \lambda')R$ will produce a value strictly lower than $\lambda C + (1 - \lambda)R$ (i.e., than the value that would have been obtained by ignoring the confidence trick detection).

Moreover, after each subsequent successful interaction or quiescence period following the detection of a confidence trick, the reputation of the con-man agent must be more cautiously increased. So, whenever a successful interaction follows the detection of a confidence trick, the reputation must be increased with a lower increment. In this case the con-man has a low reputation but the value of the current contract C is high, i.e., $C > R$. The effect can be easily achieved by decreasing the value of the parameter λ that controls the relative importance of the value of the current contract C in the updated value of the direct reputation to a new value $\lambda' < \lambda$. Finally, whenever a quiescence period follows the detection of a confidence trick, forgiveness should be slower. This effect can be easily achieved by updating the trusting agent forgiveness profile $(\Delta t, \alpha)$ to $(\Delta t', \alpha')$ such that $\alpha' \leq \alpha$ and $\Delta t' \geq \Delta t$ and at least one inequality is strict.

Note that punishments should be larger after each defection, in order to discourage the con-man agent to play the confidence trick game. Also, punishments can be weakened according to the forgiveness factor model. These extensions of our reputation model are left as future work.

DESIGN AND IMPLEMENTATION

We designed and implemented a multi-agent system incorporating our reputation model, using the JADE multi-agent platform (Bellifemine, Caire, & Greenwood, 2007). The system represents a distributed marketplace where software agents associated to buyers and sellers can meet, negotiate and transact using multi-issue e-business contracts.

The system architecture is shown in Figure 1. According to our model, in the system we can find two agent groups: *SellerSociety* group and *BuyerSociety* group.

Note that in our operational model we have experimentally evaluated only three types of reputations, as follows: (i) direct reputation of a given seller for a given buyer, (ii) reputation of given seller for buyers' society, and (iii) reputation of sellers' society for given buyer. Basically this means that in our model we have only recorded how buyers evaluate sellers based on contracts signed between them. Also note that the system can be extended by adding a new functionality to allow sellers to evaluate buyers' reputation using the same modeling principles and without affecting the current architecture of the system shown in Figure 1.

BuyerSociety agent group contains the following types of software agents: *Buyer*, *BuyerManager*, and *InterpreterB*:

- **Buyer** agent is basically the agent that represents a buyer in an e-business application. More than one agent of this type may be started in the system, and each of them represents a different buyer that can select sellers to interact with. At least one *Buyer* is required for running the system.
- **BuyerManager** agent acts as the manager of the buyer society. Each *Buyer* agent that joins the system will have to report his results to the *BuyerManager* agent. Only one *BuyerManager* agent is currently allowed in the system. According to Figure 1, each *Buyer* agent sends to the *BuyerManager* agent the result of each contract that was carried out with a *Seller* agent. The results are stored by *BuyerAgent* onto a database. Note that the system execution is driven by the *BuyerSociety* agent group and therefore

Figure 1. System architecture

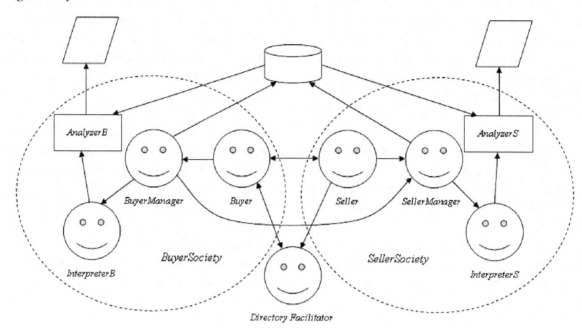

the *BuyerManager* agent is responsible with the detection of the end of the execution, i.e., when a predetermined number of contracts were finalized.

- **InterpreterB** agent acts as interpreter of the information that is captured during the system execution on the buyers' side. Its main purpose is to interpret and analyze this information in order to dynamically generate a form that displays the execution results regarding reputations that were computed on the buyers' side. For that purpose, the *InterpreterB* agent utilizes a non-agent software component called *AnalyzerB*.

SellerSociety agent group contains the following types of software agents: *Seller, SellerManager*, and *InterpreterS*:

- **Seller** agent is basically the agent that acts as seller in an e-business application. More than one agent of this type may be started in the system, and each of them represents

a different seller that the buyers may select for signing contracts together. At least one *Seller* is required for running the system.

- **SellerManager** agent acts as the manager of the seller society. Each *Seller* agent that joins the system will have to report its results to the *SellerManager* agent. A single *SellerManager* agent is allowed in the system. According to Figure 1, each *Seller* agent sends to *SellerManager* the result of each contract that was carried out with a *Buyer* agent. The set of final results is stored by the *SellerManager* agent onto a database.

- **InterpreterS** agent acts as interpreter of the information that is captured during the system execution on the sellers side. Its main purpose is to interpret and analyze this information in order to dynamically generate a set of forms that displays execution statistics regarding results of contracts signed and components sold. For that purpose *InterpreterS* utilizes a non-agent software component called *AnalyzerS*. Note that the system execution is driven by the buyer agents. The end of the execution is initially recognized by the *BuyerManager* agent, and consequently the other agents are notified accordingly (see Figure 1).

The system execution is organized into execution sessions. During a session, each buyer agent b_i has a specific number of contracts c_i to sign before it goes offline. Let θ be the time unit between two consecutive signings of contracts. It represents the time required for carrying out a given contract. Each buyer issues a new call for proposals for signing a new contract after each θ time units. It follows that the execution time of each buyer agent b_i during a session is equal to $c_i\theta$. If each buyer b_i starts its activity at time T_i then the total execution time of a session will be $\max_{1 \leq i \leq m}\{T_i + c_i\theta\} - \min_{1 \leq i \leq m}\{T_i\}$, where m is the total number of buyers that participate in the system.

We assume that we have a finite set C of commodities that are transacted during an execution session. For each commodity $c \in C$, seller s_j is able to provide a quantity $q_{c,j}$. Note that if $q_{c,j} = 0$ then commodity c is not available for sell at seller s_j during the current execution session.

An execution session is composed of three main phases that are performed sequentially: (i) initialization phase, (ii) transactions phase, and (iii) post-processing phase. In what follows we shall describe each phase in detail.

During the initialization phase, agents are created and initialized. First step is creation of agents of the *SellerSociety* agent group. When a *Seller* agent goes online, he first registers to JADE's *Directory Facilitator* known also as *DF* agent (Bellifemine, Caire, & Greenwood, 2007), and then he initializes the commodities that he is able to sell, i.e., his own product catalogue and their corresponding quantities. Then the agents of the *BuyerSociety* agent group are created. When a new *Buyer* agent goes online, he first gets the list of *Seller* agents that are currently available in the system by querying the *DF* agent. He sends the list

of available *Seller* agents to the *BuyerManager* agent during the next step and then he informs the *BuyerManager* agent that he will start the execution session – i.e., the process of transacting contracts with the *Seller* agents.

InterpreterB and *InterpreterS* agents perform the analysis and the interpretations of the data acquired during the execution and then display the results, during the post-processing phase. Note that *SellerManager* and *BuyerManager* agents are also used for storing all the information acquired during the execution onto a central database. In order to achieve their purpose, these agents are continuously updated by *Seller* and *Buyer* agents, whenever new information is generated during execution, until the end of the execution session is reached.

In what follows we present the details of the interactions between agents during the transactions phase of an execution session (see Figure 2). Those interactions comprise both interaction protocols and messages exchanged between the agents. Execution is driven by the *Buyer* agents that continuously contact *Seller* agents in order to sign new contracts.

According to the interaction diagram shown in Figure 2, whenever a *Buyer* agent is starting the execution, he first notifies the *BuyerManager* agent using message *start_sim* also passing the total number of contracts *maxContr* he will have to transact during the current session. Then the *Buyer* agent randomly generates a commodity *comType* that will be transacted in the current contract and asks *Seller* agents if they can provide that commodity using message *do-have(comType)*. *Seller* agents respond either with the message *do-have-yes(comType)* or with the message *do-have-no(comType)* if they can provide or not the commodity *comType*.

In the next step the *Buyer* agent selects a *Seller* agent with the highest reputation among those that responded positively to his request, using message *buy(comType)* – this is the moment when we consider that a contract for selling commodity

Figure 2. Agent interactions during an execution session

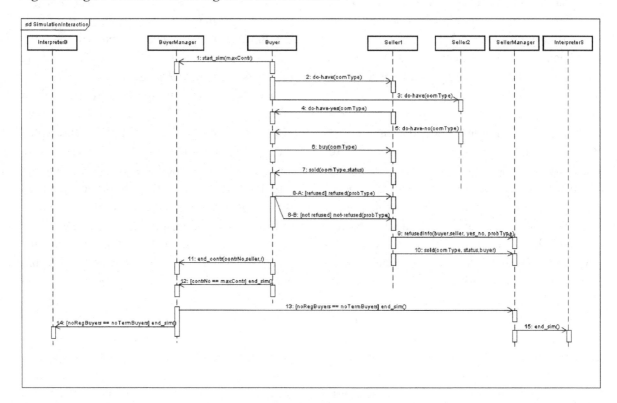

comType by selected *Seller* to the current *Buyer* is signed. Carrying out this contract is modeled by the exchange of messages *sold(comType, status)* and respectively *refused(probType)* or *not-refused(probType)*. Here the *status* parameter represents the problems that can occur in a contract on the selling side, i.e things like delivery problems or poor quality of sold product. In our model we consider that each of these problems can independently occur with a given probability. Additionally, the parameter *probType* represents the problems that can occur on the buying side, like for example delayed payment by the buyer for the bought product.

Then the *Seller* agent sends the results of the current transaction to the *SellerManager* agent using messages *refusedInfo(buyer, seller, yes_no, probType)* and *sold(comType, status, buyer)*, while the *Buyer* agent informs the *BuyerManager* agent that a new contract was finalized, using the

message *end-contr(contrNo, seller, r)*. Note that parameter *contrNo* represents the number of the contract, parameter *seller* represents the *Seller* partner of the contract and parameter *r* represents the updated direct reputation of *Seller*. When the latest contract is finalized, i.e., the *contrNo = maxContr* condition becomes true, the *Buyer* notifies the *BuyerManager* using message *end-sim* that he reached the end of the execution session. When the *BuyerManager* agent detects the end of the execution session for all *Buyer* agents, i.e., the condition *noRegBuyers = noTermBuyers* evaluates to true (number of registered buyers equals number of terminated buyers), he notifies both agents *InterpreterB* and *SellerManager*. Finally, *SellerManager* notifies *InterpreterS*, and both agents *InterpreterB* and *InterpreterS* can start the interpretation and analysis of the data acquired during the execution, during the post-processing phase.

EXPERIMENTAL RESULTS

Experimental Scenario

We have performed a series of experiments with our multi-agent system that implements the reputation model with forgiveness factor. In this section we discuss the results obtained with a simple e-commerce scenario consisting of 8 buyer agents: *dan, sorin, ana, radu, alex, george, john, mike* and 9 seller agents: *cel, emag, magic, mcomp1, ..., mcomp6*. This scenario is about trading PCs and PC components. In particular, we considered the following set of commodities: $C = \{laptop, printer, keyboard, cpu, monitor\}$. Commodities that are available at each seller are shown in Table 1.

In this scenario a buyer evaluates the result of a contract according to a set S of 4 criteria: delivery problems, quality problems, pricing problems, and other problems. The weights of these criteria were set as follows: $w_1 = 0.2$, $w_2 = 0.4$, $w_3 = 0.3$, and $w_4 = 0.1$. The parameter that controls the importance of the current contract for updating the direct reputation was set to $\lambda = 0.5$. The number of contracts signed by each buyer was set to $c_i = 10$.

In order to capture the "goodness" of a seller agent behavior, we introduce the seller profile as a tuple of values $(p_k)_{k \in S}$ such that $0 \le p_k \le 1$ for all $k \in S$, where S is the set of terms that the seller agrees to provide to a given buyer after signing a contract. p_k represents the probability of the seller in failing to provide the promised quality of term k of the service. This means that the lower is the value of the probability p_k, the better is the quality of term k of the service. In our scenario we considered only two seller profiles: *normal* profile and *bad* profile, each characterized by its own set of probabilities, as shown in Table 2. Note that assignment of profiles to seller agents was shown in Table 1.

We also defined two buyer profiles: *normal* profile and *forgiving* profile as shown in Table 3. The buyer profile is characterized by the values of the two parameters of the forgiveness factor model $(\Delta t, \alpha)$. Note that the quiescence time for increasing reputation was set $\Delta t = 3\theta$ for both buyer profiles, where θ represents the time unit of the execution. Note that in our experiments the time unit was set to 1 second.

Comparing Direct Reputations Without and with Forgiveness Factor

On Figure 3 we show a comparison of direct reputation without forgiveness factor (Figure 3a) with direct reputation with forgiveness factor (Figure 3b) of seller *cel* for buyer *radu*. On Figure 3b, note that for 3 time units (contracts with numbers 2, 3, and 4) buyer *radu* does not sign any contract

Table 1. Commodities sold and profiles of seller agents in the experimental scenario

Seller agent	Commodities	Profile
Cel	*{laptop, cpu}*	*bad*
Emag	*{laptop, keyboard, printer, cpu}*	*bad*
Magic	*{laptop, monitor, cpu}*	*bad*
mcomp1	*{laptop}*	*normal*
mcomp2	*{laptop}*	*normal*
mcomp3	*{cpu}*	*normal*
mcomp4	*{laptop}*	*normal*
mcomp5	*{keyboard}*	*normal*
mcomp6	*{printer}*	*normal*

Table 2. Seller profiles for the experimental scenario

Seller profile	Delivery problems	Quality problems	Pricing problems	Other problems
normal	0.30	0.20	0.20	0.30
bad	0.45	0.35	0.35	0.45

Table 3. Buyer profiles for the experimental scenario

Buyer profile	Δt	α	Assigned buyer agents
normal	3θ	0.1	*{dan, radu, alex, george, john, mike}*
forgiving	3θ	0.2	*{ana, sorin}*

with seller *cel*. Therefore, according to the rule of forgiveness factor, reputation is slightly increased. On the other hand, note that reputation remains constant on Figure 3a, while no new contracts are signed.

Comparing Direct Reputations of Same Seller for Buyers with Normal and Forgiving Profiles

Figure 4 shows a comparison of direct reputations of same seller (*emag* in this particular case) for buyer agents with different profiles (*mike* buyer with *normal* profile and *ana* buyer with *forgiving* profile).

According to Figure 4a, the 6-th contract signed by buyer *mike* was realized with seller *emag*. As *emag* has a bad profile, after a single contract his reputation for buyer *mike* decreases drastically from 1 to 0.8. This is because result of contract 6 has been evaluated as 0.6 by *mike*, with the meaning that some of the terms of contract 6 were not fulfilled during this transaction. Moreover, as buyer *mike* has a *normal* profile, applying forgiveness factor, he will increase reputation of *emag* with 0.1 in each subsequent step, as during steps 7, 8, 9, and 10 there are no more contracts signed between *mike* and *emag*.

Analyzing Figure 4b we can observe that the contract realized by buyer *ana* with seller *emag* decreases *emag*'s reputation for *ana* from 1 to 0.8.

Figure 3

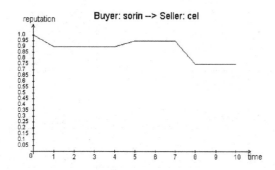

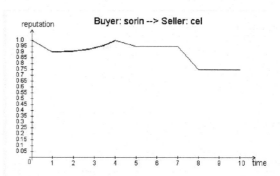

a. Direct reputation without forgiveness factor *b. Direct reputation with forgiveness factor*

However, as *ana* has a *forgiving* profile, during steps 8, 9, and 10 she will increase *emag*'s reputation with 0.2 (not with 0.1, as for the *normal* profile), so reputation will be restored to 1.

Comparing Direct Reputations of Sellers with Normal and Bad Profile for Same Buyer

Figure 5 shows a comparison of direct reputations of seller *mcomp6* with *normal* profile and seller *magic* with *bad* profile for the same buyer (*sorin* in this particular case).

Figure 4. Comparison of direct reputations of emag seller for mike buyer (normal profile) and ana buyer (forgiving profile)

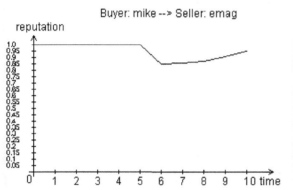

a. Direct reputation of emag *seller for* mike *buyer with* normal *profile*

b. Direct reputation of emag *seller for* ana *buyer with* forgiving *profile*

Figure 5. Comparison of direct reputations of mcomp6 (normal profile) and magic (bad profile) sellers for sorin buyer

a. Direct reputation of mcomp6 *seller (normal profile) for buyer* sorin

b. Direct reputation of magic *seller (bad profile) for buyer* sorin

As can be seen on Figure 5b, seller *magic* fails to meet contract terms in more situations – contracts signed in steps 2, 3, 8, and 10. The most obvious situation is that of contract 3 where reputation significantly decreases from 0.9 to 0.55. However, buyer *sorin* having a forgiving profile will partly restore *emag*'s reputation during steps 4, 5, 6, and 7 reaching at this step a reputation of 0.75.

However, on Figure 5a we can see the result of transactions carried out between seller *mcomp6* with *normal* profile and *forgiving* buyer *sorin*. *mcomp6* only fails once and hence its reputation decreases to 0.9.

Comparing Reputations of Sellers with Normal and Bad Profile for Buyer Society

Figure 6 presents a comparison of reputations of seller *mcomp6* with *normal* profile and seller *emag* with *bad* profile for the entire buyer society. Note that these values were obtained by averaging the direct reputations of *mcomp6* and *emag* sellers for each of the 8 members of the buyer society.

Figure 6b clearly highlights the *bad* profile of *emag* seller. Its reputation has a decreasing tendency. There are only two points (2 and 4) when the reputation is slightly increasing because of the forgiveness factor. Also note the strong decrease of the reputation in the first step, thus confirming the *bad* profile of *emag*.

Figure 6a clearly shows the *normal* (i.e., better than *bad*) profile of *mcomp6* seller, as compared with the *bad* profile of *emag* seller. On this figure we can see only a single decrease of the reputation, as compared with 4 decreases as it is shown on Figure 6b.

Reputation of Seller Society for Buyer

Figure 7 displays the reputation of seller society for *radu* buyer agent. Note that this value of reputation was obtained by averaging direct reputations of each seller agent for *radu* buyer agent. The decreasing tendency of this reputation for a given

Figure 6. Comparison of direct reputations of mcomp6 (normal profile) and emag (bad profile) sellers for buyer society

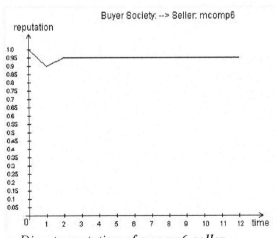

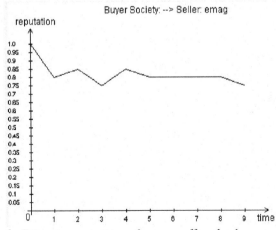

a. Direct reputation of mcomp6 *seller (*normal *profile) for buyer society*

b. Direct reputation of emag *seller (*bad *profile) for buyer society*

Figure 7. Reputation of seller society for radu buyer agent

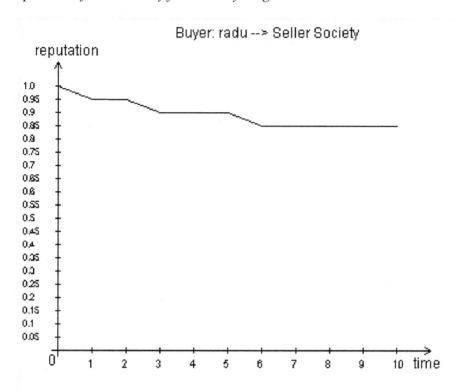

buyer (*radu* in this special case) can be explained taking into account the composition of the seller society – 6 sellers with *normal* profile and 3 sellers with *bad* profile. Note that both *normal* and *bad* seller profiles have non-zero failure probabilities for contractual terms.

CONCLUSION

In this article we proposed a simple reputation model for agent societies that is appropriate for agent-based e-business applications. The model is enhanced with addition of forgiveness factor parameters, according to the philosophy of reconciliation and considering an optimistic view of reality. We also outlined a solution for adding con-resistance to this model, although this feature needs further investigation and experimentation and consequently were planned as future work.

The model was experimentally implemented and initially evaluated with the help of JADE multi-agent system in a sample scenario involving two agent societies: buyer society and seller society. We plan to extend our multi-agent system to be able to model other forms of reputation (for example to capture how sellers evaluate buyers), and also to incorporate the con-resistance aspect. Moreover, we plan to perform more experiments involving a significantly larger number of buyer and seller agents with different profiles, and also to evaluate the resistance of our enhanced model to confidence tricks.

ACKNOWLEDGMENT

The work reported in this paper was supported by the national research project "SCIPA: Servicii software semantice de Colaborare si Interoperabilitate pentru realizarea Proceselor Adaptive de business" between Software Engineering Department, University of Craiova, Romania. This article is a revised an updated version of the paper: Burete, R., Bădică, A., & Bădică, C. (2010). Reputation Model with Forgiveness Factor for Semi-competitive E-Business Agent Societies. In *Networked Digital Technologies* Part II (pp. 402-416). *Communications in Computer and Information Science, 88.* Springer. National Authority for Scientific Research, Romania.

REFERENCES

Bădică, C., Ganzha, M., Gawinecki, M., Kobzdej, P., & Paprzycki, M. (2006). Towards trust management in an agent-based e-commerce system – initial considerations. In A. Zgrzywa (Ed.), *Proceedings of the MISSI 2006 Conference* (pp. 225-236). Wroclaw, Poland: Wroclaw University of Technology Press.

Bellifemine, F. L., Caire, G., & Greenwood, D. (2007). *Developing Multi-Agent Systems with JADE.* New York: John Wiley & Sons Ltd. doi:10.1002/9780470058411

Chang, E., Hussain, F., & Dillon, T. (2006). *Trust and Reputation for Service-Oriented Environments: Technologies for Building Business Intelligence and Consumer Confidence.* New York: John Wiley & Sons, Ltd. doi:10.1002/9780470028261

Fasli, M. (2007). *Agent Technology for E-Commerce.* New York: John Wiley & Sons.

Foued, B., Ait-Kadi, D., Mellouli, S., & Ruiz, A. (2009). A reputation-based model for semicompetitive multi-agent systems. *International Journal of Intelligent Information and Database Systems, 3,* 146–162. doi:10.1504/IJIIDS.2009.025160

Ganzha, M., Gawinecki, M., Kobzdej, P., Paprzycki, M., & Bădică, C. (2006). Functionalizing trust in a model agent based e-commerce system. In M. Bohanec et al. (Eds.), *Proceedings of the 2006 Information Society Multiconference* (pp. 22-26). Ljubljana, Slovenia: Josef Stefan Institute Press.

Henderson, M. (1996). *The Forgiveness Factor – Stories of Hope in a World of Conflict.* Saint Paul, MN: Grosvenor Books USA.

Huynh, T. D., Jennings, N. R., & Shadbolt, N. R. (2006). An integrated trust and reputation model for open multi-agent systems. *Autonomous Agents and Multi-Agent Systems, 13*(2), 119–154. doi:10.1007/s10458-005-6825-4

Jøsang, A., Ismail, R., & Boyd, C. (2007). A survey of trust and reputation systems for online service provision. *Decision Support Systems, 43,* 618–644. doi:10.1016/j.dss.2005.05.019

Jøsang, A., Keser, C., & Dimitrakos, T. (2005). Can we manage trust? In P. Herrmann, V. Issarny, & S. Shiu (Eds.), *Trust Management, Third International Conference, iTrust'2005* (LNCS 3477, pp. 93-107). New York: Springer.

Sabater, J., & Sierra, C. (2001). A reputation model for gregarious societies. In *Regret: A reputation model for gregarious societies* (pp. 61–69). Montreal, Canada: Regret.

Sabater, J., & Sierra, C. (2005). Review on computational trust and reputation models. *Artificial Intelligence Review, 24,* 33–60. doi:10.1007/s10462-004-0041-5

Salehi-Abari, A., & White, T. (2009). Towards con-resistant trust models for distributed agent systems. In *Proceedings of the 21st International Joint Conference on Artifical Intelligence (IJCAI 2009)* (pp. 272-277). San Francisco: Morgan Kaufmann Publishers Inc.

Sathiyamoorthy, E., Iyenger, N., & Ramachandran, V. (2010). Agent based trust management framework in distributed e-business environment. *International Journal of Computer Science & Information Technology*, 2, 14–28.

Scarlat, E., & Maries, I. (2009). Towards an increase of collective intelligence within organizations using trust and reputation models. In N. T. Nguyen, R. Kowalczyk, & S. M. Chen (Eds.), *First International Conference on Computational Collective Intelligence. Semantic Web, Social Networks and Multiagent Systems (ICCCI 2009)* (LNCS 5796, pp. 140-151). New York: Springer.

Srinivasan, S. (2004). Role of trust in e-business success. *Information Management & Computer Security*, 12(1), 66–72. doi:10.1108/09685220410518838

Wang, Y., & Lin, K. J. (2008). Reputation-oriented trustworthy computing in e-commerce environments. *IEEE Internet Computing*, 12, 55–59. doi:10.1109/MIC.2008.84

Yu, B., & Singh, M. P. (2000). A social mechanism of reputation management in electronic communities. In *Cooperative Information Agents IV - The Future of Information Agents in Cyberspace (CIA 2000)* (LNCS 1860, pp. 154-165). New York: Springer.

Zacharia, G., & Maes, P. (2000). Trust management through reputation mechanisms. *Applied Artificial Intelligence*, 14(9), 881–908. doi:10.1080/08839510050144868

This work was previously published in International Journal of Agent Technologies and Systems, Volume 3, Issue 1, edited by Yu Zhang, pp. 11-26, copyright 2011 by IGI Publishing (an imprint of IGI Global).

Chapter 11
Multi–Agent Negotiation Paradigm for Agent Selection in B2C E–Commerce

Bireshwar Dass Mazumdar
Banaras Hindu University, India

Swati Basak
Banaras Hindu University, India

Neelam Modanwal
Banaras Hindu University, India

ABSTRACT

Multi agent system (MAS) model has been extensively used in the different tasks of E-Commerce such as customer relation management (CRM), negotiation and brokering. The objective of this paper is to evaluate a seller agent's various cognitive parameters like capability, trust, and desire. After selecting a best seller agent from ordering queue, it applies negotiation strategies to find the most profitable proposal for both buyer and seller. This mechanism belongs to a semi cooperative negotiation type, and selecting a seller and buyer agent pair using mental and cognitive parameters. This work provides a logical cognitive model, logical negotiation model between buyer agent and selected seller agent.

INTRODUCTION

E-Commerce is the movement of business onto the World Wide Web (WWW). This movement has been broken up into two main sectors: business-to-business (B2B) and business-to-customer (B2C).

An agent is a software program that acts flexibly on behalf of its owner to achieve particular

objectives. Buyer agent gives instructions to its agent to fulfill his all needs. An agent must be a good listener, analyzer and cooperative in nature; as well as has the quality of good coordination, good communication and negotiation with other agents (Jennings et al., 2003).

Hence the software agent should be autonomous, reactive and proactive.

Multi agent system (MAS) model has been extensively used in the different tasks of E-Com-

DOI: 10.4018/978-1-4666-1565-6.ch011

merce such as CRM, negotiation and brokering. A survey report provided by international data group (IDG) by its subsidiary IDC (http://www. idc.com), estimates that the global market for software agents grew from $7.2 million in 1997 to $51.5 million in 1999, and that it will reach $873.2 million in 2008. IDC also assumes that the dramatic growth in B2B e-commerce will accelerate the demand for agents. BargainFinder (Krulwich, 1996) was the first system of this kind to employ agents and it operated in the following way: If a customer wants to buy a music CD, BargainFinder will launch its agent to collect the prices from a predefined set of CD shops, and then it will select the CD with the lowest price for the customer. Another similar example is Priceline (http://www.priceline.com), which carries out the same set of tasks for airline tickets, hotel rooms, and cars. Agent-based E-Commerce solutions are also available such as the Lost Wax E-Commerce Platform (http://www.lostwax.com) supports buyers and sellers in both public and private trading environments and the agent-based modules can represent differing trading mechanisms (such as auctions, contracting, and negotiation). Lost Wax has worked with a number of leading companies operating trading systems in a variety of sectors. The living markets platform (http://www. living-systems.com) is an agent-based product for real-time optimization of processes in business networks. Various Multi-agent models have been developed e.g. Chan, Cheng, and Hsu (2007) introduced an autonomous agent that represents the owner of an online store to bargain with customers. They consider that customers' behaviors are different, and the store should identify a customer's characteristics and apply different tactics to make profits from customers. Various customer orientation based models (Lee & Park, 2005; Bae, Ha, & Park, 2002) have proposed a survey based profitable customer segmentation system that conducts the customer satisfaction survey

and deploy mining processes for the profitable customer segmentation.

Our approach focuses on the problem description and the basic definition of different types of agents. In this part, we define "Agent Model" in 3-stages: (1) need identification, (2) brokering (product brokering and merchant brokering), (3) negotiation. In the remainder of the paper, we present our work on agent selection and negotiation. We first describe our models. The major parts of the flow charts that implement the models are described also. Empirical validation and Evaluation is described in next part. Results of various experimentations are shown in later. Finally conclusions of the work are described.

PROBLEM DESCRIPTION

The process of brokering as often occurs in E-Commerce involves a number of agents. A buyer agent looking for products may be supported by a broker agent that takes its buyer agent's queries and contacts other agents or looks at the web directly to find information on products within the buyer agent's scope of interest.

The proposed model consists of three stages of CBB (Consumer Buying Behavior) model of B2C E-Commerce (Jennings et al., 2005). These stages are: need identification, seller selection and negotiation. In the first stage need identification tells the buyer agent recognizes a need for some product through a profile. This profile may be appearing to broker agent in many different ways. Secondly the seller selection involves the "broker agent" to determine what product is to be bought to satisfy this need and finding the seller that offered item at desired price. The main techniques used by the brokers in this stage are (1) feature-based filtering i.e. item based on brand and quality (2) constraint-based filtering i.e., the agent specifying price range and date limit. In agent mediated

E-Commerce context it is common for seller agents to have capabilities, commitment and trust for processing the new business. Third stage "negotiation" requires negotiating the terms and conditions under which the desired items will be delivered. Automated negotiation capabilities are essential for the automated B2C E-Commerce. The buyer agent contacts with broker agent, the broker agent determines the desire (wishes) of the buyer agent. Then the broker matches products and sellers and selects one of the best proposals. The broker agent negotiates with seller agent on behalf of buyer agent to obtain best deal which satisfies both parties.

In this model there are four types of agents with their different functionalities. Buyer Agent (Buyer) is the agent who needs to buy some items from another agent. Seller Agent (Seller) is the agent who sells items to the buyer. Broker Agent (Broker) is the agent who acts as a mediator between buyer and seller. He identifies the need of the buyer agent and then selects the best seller agent by evaluating the profile of the various seller agents and finally negotiates between buyer and seller agent. Feedback Agent is the agent, who keeps all responses of sellers and buyers which are itself given by buyers and sellers and gives feedback information to broker if buyer is not satisfied the service of seller, as well as it also warns to seller and buyer if any problem occurred in between their relationships.

PROPOSED APPROACH

Our proposed approach consists of two logical models and an interaction model. The logical models are Cognitive model and negotiation model. The interaction model is shown by UML diagram which depicts the various modes of interaction among different types of agents.

Cognitive Model

The performance, desire, intention, capability, commitment, trusts seller agent has been computed on the basis of cognitive computational method. Performance, capability, intention, desire, preference, commitment are multiple attribute functions of the items that was sold or purchased in best, fair or defective categories. The level of trust is determined by the degree of initial success of the agent experience. Cognitive parameters of seller agents help to select best seller agent.

The preference, capability, desire, intention, commitment, trust of agent has been computed as follows:

Performance: An agent's performance plays an important role in social practical reasoning where an action is to be selected in order for given intention to be fulfilled (Panzarasa, Jennings, & Norman, 2002).

Capability: Capability totally depends upon the preferences and performance of items (selected items) given by seller's agents.

Desire: An agent's desires are conceived of as the states of the world that the agent wishes to bring about (Frances, Barbara, Treur, & Verbrugge, 1997).

Intention: It is actually the goal that an agent wants to achieve; an agent intention will give a guideline of what to do (Panzarasa, Jennings, & Norman, 2002).

Commitment: An agent individual intention towards a state of affairs entails the agent's commitment to acting towards the achievement of that state (Panzarasa, Jennings, & Norman, 2002).

Trust: Trust is developed by seller agent by which broker agent can select (choose) the best seller who fulfills the requirements of buyer (Castelfranchi & Falcone, 1998).

The above points are expressed in terms of logical parameters as follows: (Mazumdar & Mishra, 2009)

The performance is calculated on the basis of number of items that are sold in best category, numbers of items that are sold in fair best category, number of items that are sold in defective category by the seller agent. Hence, the performance of ith agent for jth items is

$$P_i^j \equiv \left\langle I_i^{j,bs}, I_i^{j,fs}, \sim I_i^{j,ds} \right\rangle$$

Where, P_i^j is the performance of ith seller for jth item, $I_i^{j,bs}$ is the jth type best items that was sold by ith agent, $I_i^{j,fs}$ is jth type fair items that was sold by ith agent, $I_i^{j,ds}$ is the defective items that was sold by i th agent.

b.   The capability is computed on the basis of performance and total number of items sold.

Where, $(Capability)_i$ is the capability of the ith agent; the capability shows the how much items can be sold handled by a particular seller agent. Hence, the capability of ith agent is:

$$(Capability)_i \equiv \left\langle \sum_{j=1}^{n} P_i^j \right\rangle$$

Where, $(Capability)_i$ is the capability of ith agent for performance of jth items, P_j^i is the performance of ith seller for selection of jth item.

Desires denote states that agent wish to do the task which is based upon the performance of ith agent for jth items. Hence, desire of ith agent is:

$$(Desire)_i \equiv \left\langle \sum_{jp=1} I_i^{jp,bs}, \sum_{jp=1} I_i^{jp,fs}, \sum_{jp=1} I_i^{jp,ds} \right\rangle$$

Where, $(Desire)_i$ is the desire of the ith seller, $I_i^{jp,bs}$ is the number of selected items types best sold items by ith agent, $I_i^{jp,fs}$ is number of selected items types fair sold items by ith agent, $I_i^{jp,ds}$ is the number of selected items types defective sold items by ith agent.

The intention computed on the basis of choice (desire) and preference and performance of ith agent. Hence, intention of ith agent is:

$$(Intention)_i \equiv \left\langle (Desire)_i, \sum_{j=1} P_i^j \right\rangle$$

e.   Commitment is computed on the basis of intention and capability of ith seller agent. Hence,

Commitment of ith agent is:

$$(Commitment)_i \equiv \left\langle (Intention)_i, (Capability)_i \right\rangle$$

f.   The Trust is computed on the basis of commitment and capability of an agent. Hence,

Trust of ith agent for buyer agent is:

$$(Trust)_i \equiv \left\langle (Commitment)_i, (Capability)_i \right\rangle$$

Qualitative Composition Rules

The composition of qualitative variables L, M, H is based upon the following rules:

*   **Rule 1:** If two variables are equal then the composition amounts to the same either variable level such as L $\oplus$ L=L, M $\oplus$ M=M, H $\oplus$ H=H

- **Rule 2:** If two qualitative variables are unequal then the composition amounts to the greater level of the variable: $L \oplus M = M, L \oplus H = H, M \oplus H = H$
- **Rule 3:** If the two qualitative variables differ by two levels then the composition level is the average level between the two levels. Such as $H \oplus L = M$
- **Rule 4:** If any negation value of qualitative variables comes then it converts into:

$\sim H = L, \sim L = H, \sim M = M$

Two types of rules are generated: **Finding to Hypothesis (FH)** and **Hypothesis to Finding (HF)** rules

FH Rules: It correlates the numerical values or range of numerical values of parameters to appropriate or imprecise values. The imprecise or qualitative values are Low (L), Medium (M), and High (H).

In the case of performance:

- IF parameter is within this range (0-4) THEN parameter is low.
- IF parameter is within this range (4-7) THEN parameter is medium.
- IF parameter is within this range (7 and above) THEN parameter is high.

In the case of desire:

- IF parameter is within this range (0-4) THEN parameter is low.
- IF parameter is within this range (4-5) THEN parameter is medium.
- IF parameter is within this range (5 and above) THEN parameter is high.

In the case of intention:

- IF parameter is within this range (0-0.2) THEN parameter is low.
- IF parameter is within this range (0.2-0.4) THEN parameter is medium.
- IF parameter is within this range (0.4 and above) THEN parameter is high.

In the case of capability:

- IF parameter is within this range (0-4) THEN parameter is low.
- IF parameter is within this range (4-5) THEN parameter is medium.
- IF parameter is within this range (5 and above) THEN parameter is high.

In the case of commitment:

- IF parameter is within this range (0-0.4) THEN parameter is low.
- IF parameter is within this range (0.4-0.8) THEN parameter is medium.
- IF parameter is within this range (0.8 and above) THEN parameter is high.

In the case of trust:

- IF parameter is within this range (0-2) THEN parameter is low.
- IF parameter is within this range (2-5) THEN parameter is medium.
- IF parameter is within this range (5 and above) THEN parameter is high.

In the case of desired price:

- IF parameter is within this range (0-27) THEN parameter is low.
- IF parameter is within this range (27-35) THEN parameter is medium.
- IF parameter is within this range (35 and above) THEN parameter is high.

In the case of offered price:

- IF parameter is within this range (0-27) THEN parameter is low.
- IF parameter is within this range (27-35) THEN parameter is medium.
- IF parameter is within this range (35 and above) THEN parameter is high.

In the case of desired price/offered price:

- IF parameter is within this range (0-0.5) THEN parameter is low.
- IF parameter is within this range (0.5-0.9) THEN parameter is medium.
- IF parameter is within this range (0.9 and above) THEN parameter is high.

Negotiation Model

Negotiation is based upon logical combination of desired price of buyer agent P_{db}, offered price of seller P_{os} and the ratio of P_{db} / P_{os}, which helps to decide the resultant logical value Result_lv. If the result of logical combination comes same in more than first negotiation round then we calculate number of higher logical value in all the parameters and which round comes maximum higher logical value that negotiation round will be selected. Here, price depends upon quality and response time, $Price \propto Quality$ and $Price \propto \dfrac{1}{time}$ i.e. $Price \propto \dfrac{Quality}{time}$.

Interaction Among Agents

In a multi-agent system, an agent may need to buy some items from another agent.

There are several seller agents. Each seller agent can sell several types of items. In order to accomplish these items, the agent needs to negotiate with another agent about the appropriate time

and approach to execute selling these items, so that the combined utility can be increased.

The buyer agent queries the broker agent to obtain the list of specification items (quality, time, price etc.) of the seller agents suggest by the broker agent, by propose a particular specification of the items of the buyer agent. According to B2C activities all the stages are described as Figure 1.

1. **Need Identification Support:** As per Figure 1 buyer informs his needs to broker agent. Sellers advertise their items to broker for more potential buyer as possible. In more detail as per Figure 2; a) When buyer agent wants to buy items he has to submit own needs to broker agent and send **informNeed**; b) broker agent inform about the need of buyer agent as message form **informNeed** to seller agent; c) when a seller agent wants to make an offer about items to potential buyers, he has to submit own offer to broker agent in message form **informItems**; d) in the first phase on the basis of the list of items provided by the buyer agents, takes care of sending the offer to the buyer agent by broker agent as **informList**.

2. **Seller Selection Support:** As per Figure 3 this stage occurs when a buyer receive seller agents list which are fully compatible with buyer need, then looks for suitable interest, preferences and cognitive behaviors of seller agents. In detail: a) Buyer agent can request to broker agent in message form **informRequest**; b) all seller agents send details of items profile which contains about their preferences, type of items deal in the previous dealing to broker agent in message **informSellerProfile**; c) broker agent sends cognitive values of each seller agent such as commitment, capability, trust, desire, intention, reputation, index of negotiation information of seller ; he sends a message **informCog_Value+informSeller**; d) buyer agent sends his interests and preference ac-

Figure 1. Communication between Buyer, Broker and Seller

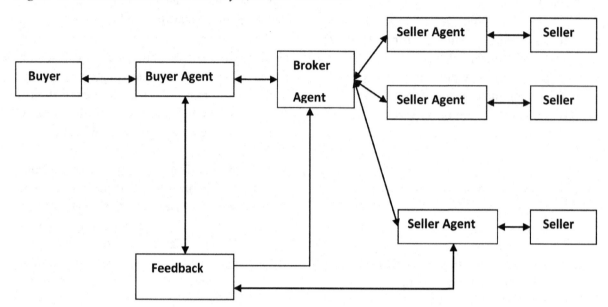

Figure 2. Need Identification Support

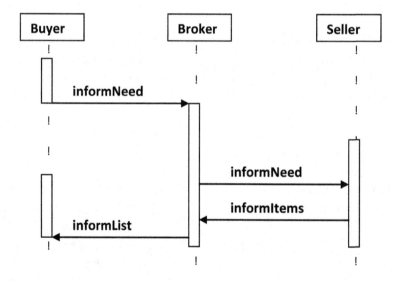

cording to each item such as quality, brand, payment mode in form of message **inform-BusinessPolicy** to broker; e) broker agent inform about the buyer's business policy to seller agent in message form **inform**; f) Seller agent sends his interests and preference according to each item such as quality,

brand, payment mode in form of message **informBusinessPolicy** to broker; g) broker agent Sends Selection Index (SI) along with **informSI** to buyer agent.

3. **Negotiation Support:** As per Figure 4 in this stage a pair of buyer and selected seller agent defines the proposal details. They realize

Figure 3. Seller's Selection Support

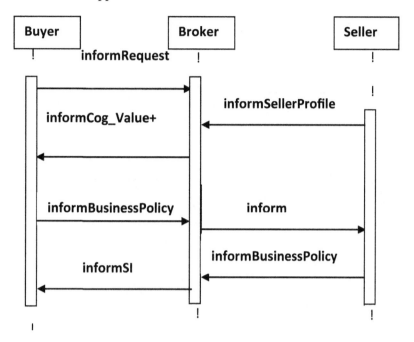

suitable strategies in a multi-round session for their respective proposal by means of messages. In detail: a) buyer agent subscribe with broker agent in form of **subscribe** message; b) selected seller agent subscribe with broker agent in form of **subscribe** message; c) broker agent inform to both buyer and seller agent by send message **inform**; d) Buyer agent build initial proposal and send message to seller through broker agent in **proposeInitialProposal**; e) broker inform to seller agent as an **informInitialProposal**; f) seller agent send message to buyer through broker agent in **generateCounterProposal**; g) broker agent inform the utility to buyer agent in message form **informUtility+informCounterProposal**; h) buyer agent send two type of responses either agree or refuse; in both situation broker inform to seller; in case of agree broker regenerate proposal and send message **informProposal + informUtility**; i) seller agent also send two type of

response either **agree** or **refuse**; j) in both situation broker inform to seller; in case of agree broker refine proposal and send message **informRefineProposal + informUtility**; k) buyer agent can accept the proposal or reject proposal in message **acceptProposal** or **rejectProposal**; l) in both situation broker inform to seller; in case of accept proposal broker send message **inform + informUtility.** Similar message can be communicated from seller through broker to buyer.

4. **Feedback Information Support:** As per Figure 5 buyer agent informs broker agent that to inform the seller for starting his services of items. After getting the information by broker, seller agent will start their services for buyer by direct communication. In more detail, a) Buyer agent can request to broker agent in message form **infReq_Service + Payment** which shows that buyer request to start the services of items as well as pay for it ; b) Broker passes the request of buyer

Figure 4. Negotiation Support

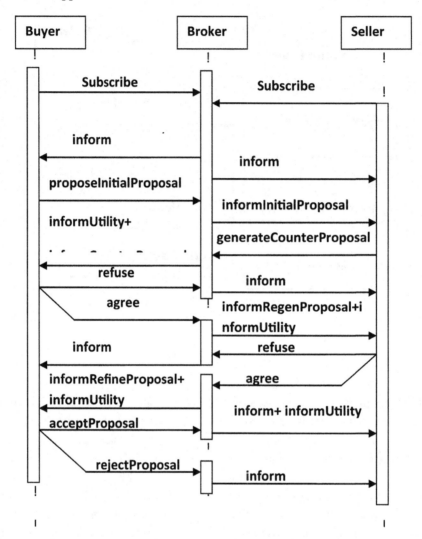

by sending **inform** message to seller ; c) Seller starts his services through the message **infDeliveryItem** by direct communication with buyer ; d) Both seller and buyer inform their service-responses to broker agent in message form **infDeliveryDetail** and **infReceiveDetail** respectively ; e) If any fault is present in the service (delay in time of items, quality and quatity differs etc..) of seller then buyer informs about seller services to feedback agent by using message **infSeller-Feedback**, feedback agent quickly informs the seller's feedback to broker through the message **inform + SellerFeedbackProfile** ; f) Similarly, if any service of buyer (delay in payment time, suddenly change in items etc..) is not considerabled by seller then the seller agent informs (**infBuyerFeedback**) feedback agent and feedback agent sends **message inform + BuyerFeedbackProfile** to broker which informs the feedback of buyer agent.

Figure 5. Feedback Information Support

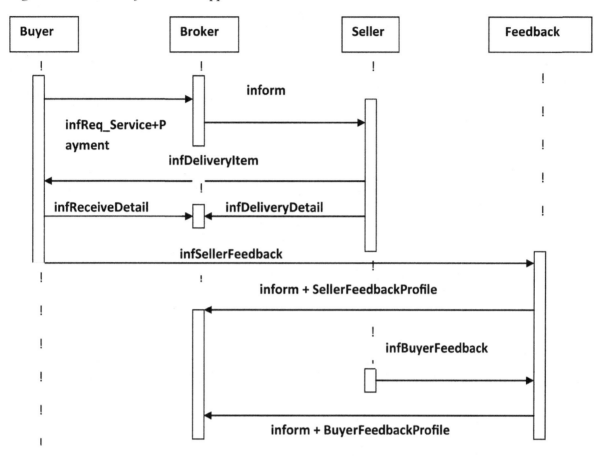

PROTOTYPE IMPLEMENTATION

Various types of experiment are performed earlier; but in this work, we describe only those data by which we can show distinguish type of result and from Table 1, Table 2 and Table 3 calculate various logical values of cognitive parameters. In Table 1, buyer tells his all requirements for the desired items, such as what type of quality, brand he will be preferred, how much quantity he will be needed in particular time of what amount etc. Similarly in Table 2, seller tells his all business profile for particular items i.e. which types of services he has available for particular items and Table 3 shows that his history profiles i.e. the selling record of seller for particular items.

DESCRIPTION OF FLOW-CHARTS AND GUI FORMS

The flow-chart 1 (Figure 6) is used for computing the Selection of maximum trust seller agent. According to flow-chart 1, numerical value of trust for five agents fall in L, L, M, H, H. Using these searching technique, broker agent finds that agent name list whose trust value is high. Ag4 and Ag5 has high trust logical value among all given agents. Now, broker agent search out which agent has highest logical value for all available cognitive parameters, broker finds that Ag5 has all cognitive parameters in high logical range. Thus, Ag5 will be selected for best seller agent for negotiating with buyer agent, i.e. now semi cooperative negotiation perform between seller agent Ag5 and

Table 1. Buyer's business profile

Item Name/Type	Quality	Quantity	Serving Time	Brand	Item Price
Item1	6	100	27	A	6
Item2	6	100	27	A	6
Item3	6	100	27	B	7
Item4	6	100	27	C	8
Item5	6	100	27	C	9

Table 2. Seller's business profile

Item Name/Type	Quality	Quantity	Serving Time	Brand	Item Price
Item1	6	100	32	A	9
Item2	6	100	35	A	8
Item3	6	100	35	A	7
Item4	6	100	42	B	9
Item5	6	100	42	B	9

Table 3. Seller's historical profile

Item Name/Type	Best Selling	Fair Selling	Defective Selling	Preference
Item1	40	40	20	3
Item2	70	20	10	4
Item3	60	40	00	2
Item4	80	10	10	1
Item5	70	20	10	5

buyer agent. After selecting the best seller agent, flow-chart 1 helps to implement the flow-chart 2 which shows the negotiation between selected seller agent and buyer agent. Flow-chat 2 (Figure 7) is further divided into two parts: first one shows that generating of new proposal between buyer and seller agent (Figure 7(a)) and later one show that the selection of maximum cooperative proposal during negotiation (Figure 7(b)). Due to this flow-chart, our experiment introduced the 5-new negotiating proposal are generated between buyer and seller agent and that proposal taking in account whose result value is high. In this experiment, 3-such type of proposal in which result value is high. Thus, the broker agent search

that proposal in which numerical value of desired price, offer price and their ratio value lie in the high logical value. Hence, proposal 2 is selected by broker agent.

Now, the GUI model introduced here which was implemented on Java based application environment. However, the Conceptual Cognitive logical model, negotiation model presented in above is platform independent. Consider the situation where the buyer agent interact with broker agent for fulfill its needs for item 1, item 2, item 3, item 4 and item 5. There are more than one seller agents Ag1, Ag2, Ag3, Ag4, Ag5 with the potential of selling these items interact with broker agent as Figure 1 and Figure 2. Figure 3

Figure 6. Selection of maximum trust Seller Agent

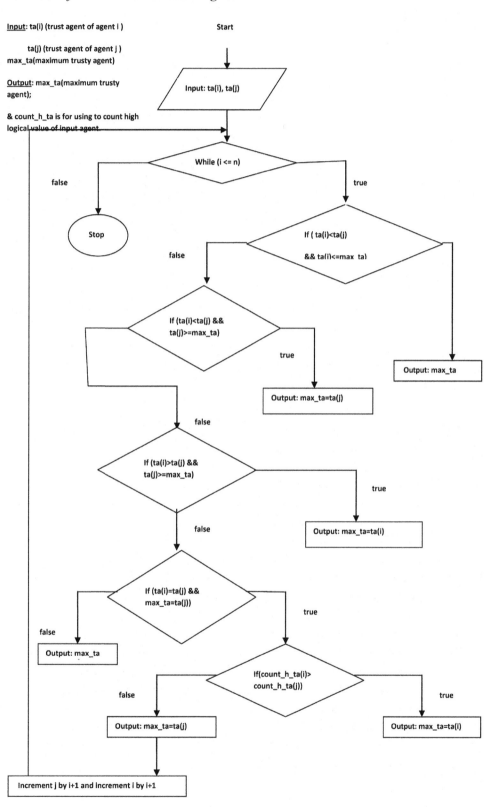

Figure 7(a). Generating new proposal between buyer and seller agent (b). Selection of maximum cooperative proposal during negotiation

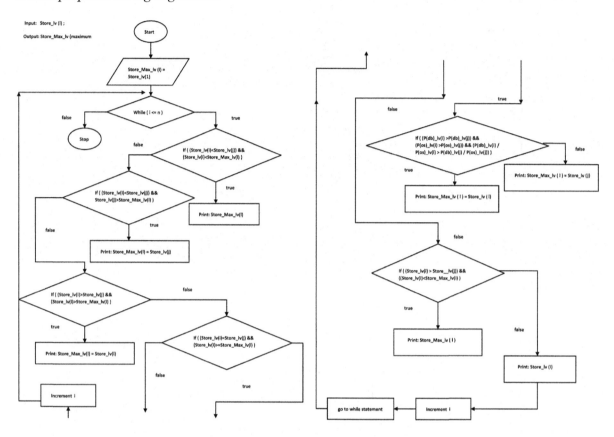

provides a visualization of the selection of a seller agent on the basis of Trust. From the Figure 4 buyer select an agent whose maximum selection index and starting negotiation with him. The trust value of agent depends upon the commitment and capability of the agent. Due to the above concept, GUI Forms are defined as: Figure 8 and Figure 10 are registration form for buyer agent and seller agent respectively, by whom they can register themselves in the site, Figure 9 shows that the entry of all requirements of buyer which he is expected for particular items. Figure 11 defines that the business profile of seller agent i.e. which type of services he is provided for the particular items, i.e. by keeping the good quality and brand of the items and gives the facility of less cost in

items for less serving time. Figure 12 is for the preference of serving items and Figure 13 shows that his all history profiles i.e. the history of selling record of seller for particular items (that shows that how he is balanced the best selling, fair selling and defective selling in their items by which he can convinced the broker agent for selecting himself as a best and trusty seller agent among all five seller agent).

In our experiment, output result shows that the agent Ag5 has maximum trust as per Figure 14. So buyer agent selects agent Ag5 for negotiation. The Figure 15 shows the status of various negotiation steps between the seller and buyer. The new possible negotiation steps control through buyer.

Figure 8. Buyer's Registration Form

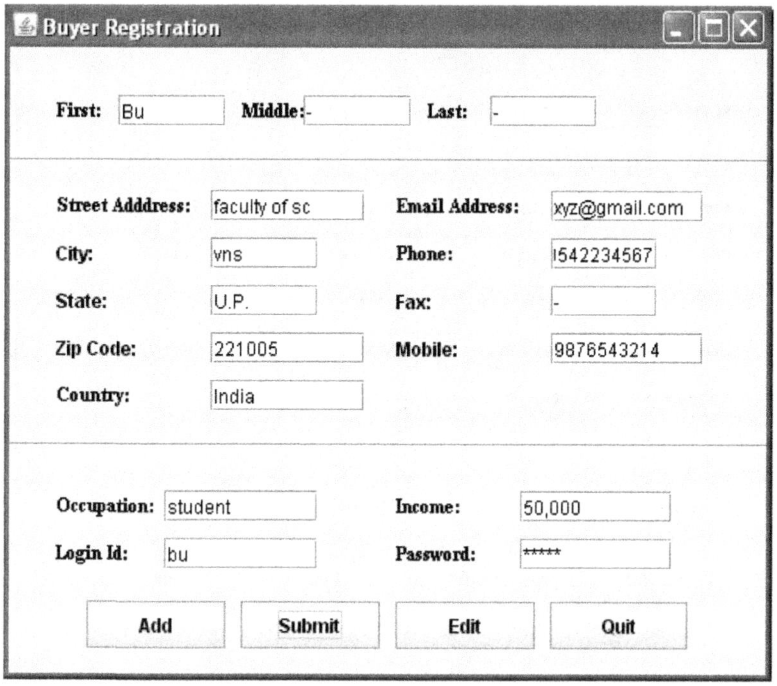

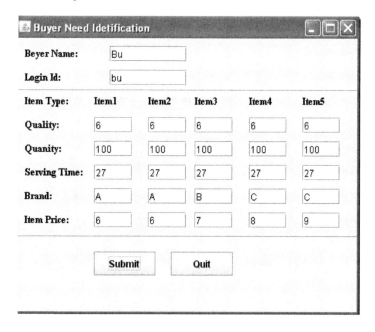

Figure 9. Buyer's Business Profile Form

Figure 10. Seller's Registration Form

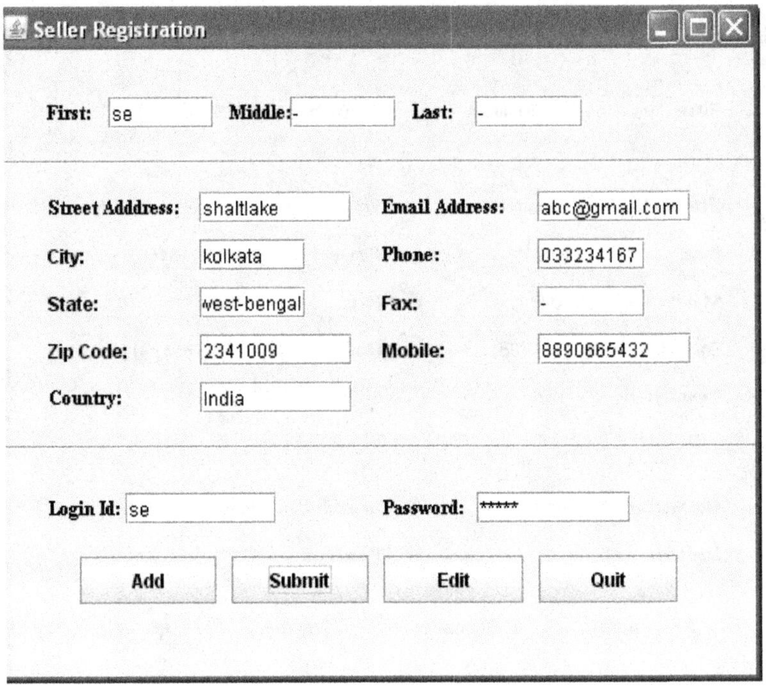

Figure 11. Seller's Business Profile Form

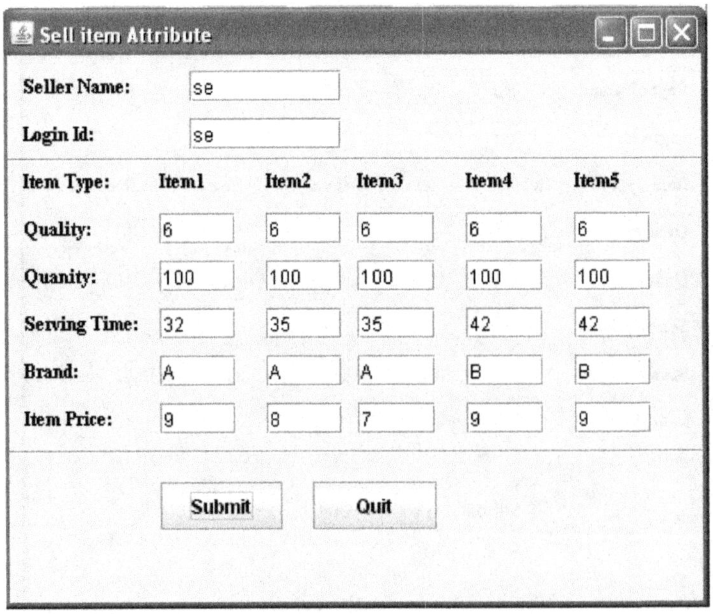

Figure 12. Seller's preference for particular items

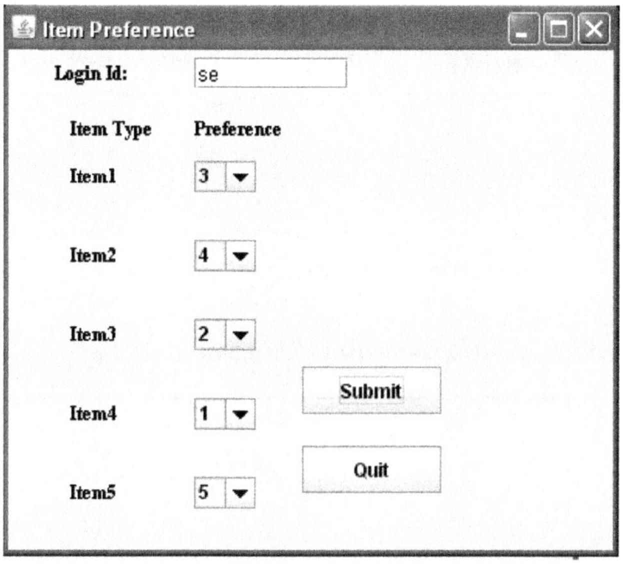

Figure 13. Seller's historical profile Form

Figure 14. Output of Selection of maximum trust seller agent

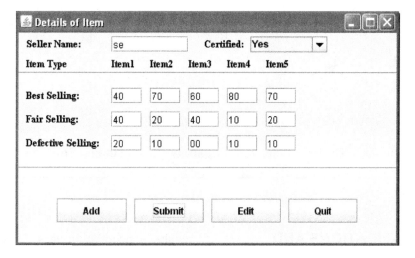

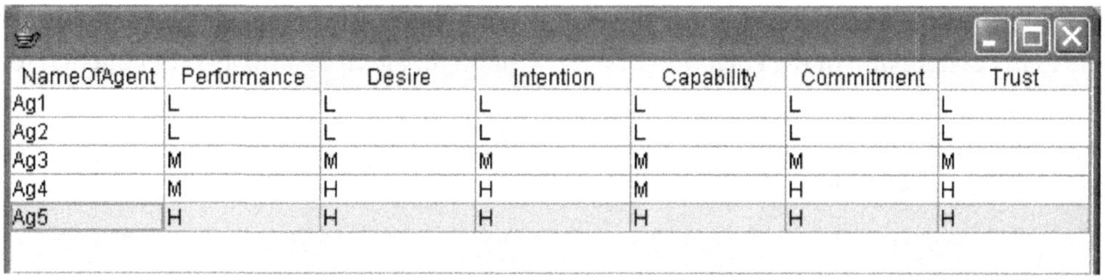

NameOfAgent	Performance	Desire	Intention	Capability	Commitment	Trust
Ag1	L	L	L	L	L	L
Ag2	L	L	L	L	L	L
Ag3	M	M	M	M	M	M
Ag4	M	H	H	M	H	H
Ag5	H	H	H	H	H	H

Figure 15. Output of negotiation between buyer and seller agent

NameOfAgent	DesirePrice	OfferPrice	DesirePrice/OfferPrice	Result
Bu	H	-	-	-
Se	-	M	M	H
Bu	H	-	-	-
Se	-	H	H	H
Bu	M	-	-	-
Se	-	H	M	H
Bu	M	-	-	-
Se	-	M	M	M

Figure 16. Graph for Selection of maximum trust seller agent

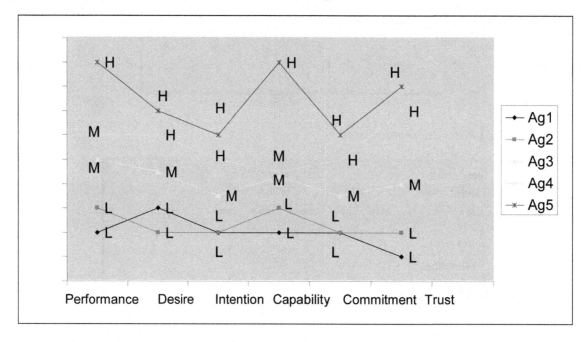

EMPIRICAL VALIDATIONS AND EVALUATION

In the experiment, values were chosen such that they provide both stable behavior of the system and assure a termination property i.e. in most instances lead the conclusion of the selection of a seller agent for negotiation on the basis of selection of maximum trust agent and also lead to the conclusion of the negotiation in a relatively small number of negotiation steps. The importance factors assigned to different categories of supplied items for each seller agent are presented in GUI forms according to Table 1, Table 2, Table 3 entry (as shown) were also chosen to provide a sufficient cover of the space of possible preferences of buyer agent as well as seller agent. Hence from the table it is clear that our approach can fulfill all the necessary features for B2C process. Table 4

Table 4. Comparison of our work with various related works

Feature	(Jonker et al., proposed method)	(Zhang et al., proposed method)	(Makedon et al., proposed method)	(Hsien-Jung Wu proposed method)	(Xiaolong et al., proposed method)	(Stamoulis et al, proposed method)	(Lai et al., proposed method)	(Lai and Sycara, proposed method)	(Paurobally et al., proposed method)	(C.C. Henry Chan Chi-Bin Cheng Chih-Hsiung Hsu proposed method)	(Olmedilla et al., proposed method)	(Gutman, Maes proposed method)	(Lee, Park proposed method)	(Nejdl et al., proposed method)	Our Proposed Approach
Communication model and negotiation environment	Yes	Yes	No	No	Yes	No	No	No	No	No	No	No	No	No	Yes
Cognitive and mental features in customer orientation value for customer relation in e-commerce	Only preferences are predict on the basis of history. Nothing about customer relationship.	No	No	Accumulate customer knowledge without specific cognitive analysis. Generating customer relationship based upon data analysis.	No	No	No	No	No	No	No	No	Survey based profitable customer segmentation system Cognitive parameters are not used for customer analysis.	No	Consider the mental and cognitive features through deterministic computational model. Generating customer relationship.
Business features for customer relation in e-commerce	No	No	No	Yes	No	No	No	No	No	Yes	No	No	Without formulated accounting data used	No	Yes

continued on the following page

181

Table 4. Continued

Computation model for decision-making during negotiation process such as utility model	Yes	Yes	Yes	Not Specify	Yes, but the model does not seems to provide the concrete result for utility, as it represents the utility in the form of other type of utility-values	Yes, but the model does not seems to provide the concrete result for utility, as it represents the utility in the form of other type of utility-values	Yes, but the model does not seems to provide the concrete result for utility, as it represents the utility in the form of other type of utility-values	Yes, but the model does not seems to provide the concrete result for utility, as it represents the utility in the form of other type of utility-values	No	Negotiation, and this transforms the fully competitive price bar-gaining to a cooperative atmosphere.	No	Yes, but no view to provide the concrete utility result	No	No	Yes, Semi-cooperative
Consider interdependence of attributes by considering effect of quality-change over change in price etc.	No	Not specify	Not specify	No	No	No	No	No	No	No	No	No	No	No	Yes
Role of broker agent for seller and buyer	Not specify	Not specify	Not specify	No	Not specify	Not specify	Not specify	Not specify	Not specify	No	Not specify	No	No	Not specify	Act as an advisor or manager (coordinator) for seller agent and buyer agent

shows the comparison of our work with various other related research.

RESULTS AND DISCUSSION

The experiment has been shown number of communications between buyer and various seller agents through broker agent and achieves maximum trust for seller agent Ag5. Ag5 can effectively satisfy the buyer's need (as shown in Figure 16). For long term profits both buyer and selected seller agent tend to compromise their utilities to achieve maximum result gain. The strategies of the model presented here can be used to determine the mental and cognitive features of seller agent through broker. Another important issue discussed in this article is negotiation that sellers often care less about profit on any given transaction and care more about long-term profitability, which implies buyer satisfaction and long-term customer relationships. The proposed method supports the importance of the following factors in our model for B2C process: selection of seller agent on the basis of cognitive and mental parameters, cooperative negotiation, consumer satisfaction, profit, minimal financial margin (profit). Furthermore, our finding that cooperative negotiation is based upon combined utility supported by the buyer and sellers with multi-attribute profile (importance factors, evaluation descriptions) is remarkable. It also influences the outcome of the negotiation aiming to satisfy both parties. The limitation of our work is not providing a learning module which keeps for further work.

CONCLUSION

We propose the agent selection and negotiation method for the purchase domain in a cooperative system in B2C E-Commerce; the buyer agent has a set of requirements of items for which it needs some seller agents. To perform this, the broker agent can choose from several alternatives that produce different qualities and consume different resources. This context requires a negotiation between selected seller agent and buyer agent through the selection of maximum trust seller agent. After selecting a best seller agent from ordering queue, it applies negotiation strategies to find out most profitable proposal by which both buyer and seller can get profit. This mechanism belongs to a semi-cooperative negotiation type. This mechanism also helps to evaluate a good solution for fulfilling the requirements. Our future work involves developing an algorithm for better evaluating the difficulty of a specific negotiation problem in the agents' negotiation process. Prevention from cheating, and maintaining the privacy of seller and buyer agent is attributed to further research in this context. This may be possible by modeling the learning behavior on the part of the negotiating agents.

REFERENCES

Abdul-Rahman, A., & Hailes, S. (2000). Supporting trust in virtual communities. In *Proceedings of the 33rd Annual Hawaii International Conference on Systems Sciences*, Maui, HI (pp. 1-9).

Bell, J. (1995). Changing attitudes in intelligent agents. In *Proceedings of the Workshop on Agent Theories, Architecture and Languages* (pp. 40-50).

Bratman, M. E. (1990). What is intention? In Cohen, P. R., Morgan, J., & Pollack, M. E. (Eds.), *Intentions in communication* (pp. 15–31). Cambridge, MA: MIT Press.

Brazier, F., Dunin-Keplicz, B., Treur, J., & Verbrugge, R. (1997). *Beliefs, Intentions and DESIRE*. Retrieved from http://ksi.cpsc.ucalgary.ca/KAW/KAW96/brazier/default.html

Carter, J., Bitting, E., & Ghorbani, A. (2002). Reputation formalization for an information-sharing multi-agent system. *Computational Intelligence*, *18*(2), 515–534. doi:10.1111/1467-8640.t01-1-00201

Castelfranchi, C., & Falcone, R. (1998). Principles of trust for MAS: Cognitive anatomy, social importance and quantification. In *Proceedings of the International Conference on Multi-Agent Systems*, Paris, France (pp. 72-79).

Chan, H. C., Cheng, C. B., & Hsu, C. H. (2007). Bargaining strategy formulation with CRM for an e-commerce agent. *Electronic Commerce Research and Applications*, *6*, 490–498. doi:10.1016/j.elerap.2007.02.011

Chee, C. N. (2004). *Three critical steps to customer-centric business orientation*. Retrieved from http://www.mcore-asia.com/PDF/Three-2520Critical-2520Steps-2520to-2520Customer-centric-2520Business-2520Orientation.pdf

Esfandiari, B., & Chandrasekharan, S. (2001). On how agents make friends: Mechanisms for trust acquisition. In *Proceedings of the Fourth Workshop on Deception, Fraud and Trust in Agent Societies*, Montreal, QC, Canada (pp. 27-34).

Faratin, P., Sierra, C., & Jennings, N. (2003). Using similarity criteria to make issue trade-offs in automated negotiations. *Journal of Artificial Intelligence*, *142*(2), 205–237. doi:10.1016/S0004-3702(02)00290-4

Fatima, S. S., Wooldridge, M., & Jennings, N. R. (2003, July). Optimal agendas for multi-issue negotiation. In *Proceedings of the Second International Conference on Autonomous Agents and Multiagent Systems*, Melbourne, Australia (pp. 129-136).

Gutman, R., & Maes, P. (1998). Cooperative vs. competitive multi-agent negotiation in retail electronic commerce. In *Proceedings of the Second International Workshop on Cooperative Information Agents*, Paris, France.

Ha, S. H., Bae, S. M., & Park, S. C. (2002). Customer's time-variant purchase behavior and corresponding marketing strategies: An online retailer's case. *Computers & Industrial Engineering*, *43*, 801–820. doi:10.1016/S0360-8352(02)00141-9

Jonker, C. M., Robu, V., & Treur, J. (2007). An agent architecture for multi-attribute negotiation using incomplete preference information. *Autonomous Agents and Multi-Agent Systems*, *15*(2), 221–252. doi:10.1007/s10458-006-9009-y

Kang, N., & Han, S. (2002). Agent-based e-marketplace system for more fair and efficient transaction. *Decision Support Systems*, *34*, 157–165. doi:10.1016/S0167-9236(02)00078-7

Kraus, S., Sycara, K., & Evenchil, A. (1998). Reaching agreements through argumentation: A logical model and implementation. *Artificial Intelligence*, *104*, 1–69. doi:10.1016/S0004-3702(98)00078-2

Krulwich, B. (1996). The bargainfinder agent: Comparison price shopping on the Internet. In Williams, J. (Ed.), *Bots, and other internet beasties* (pp. 257–263). New York, NY: Macmillan.

Lee, J. H., & Park, S. C. (2005). Intelligent profitable customers segmentation system based on business intelligence tools. *Expert Systems with Applications*, *29*, 145–152. doi:10.1016/j.eswa.2005.01.013

Mazumdar, B. D., & Mishra, R. B. (2009). Multiagent paradigm for the agent selection and negotiation in a B2c process. *International Journal of Intelligent Information Technologies*, *5*(1), 61–82. doi:10.4018/jiit.2009010104

Mishra R. B. (2009). Rule based and ANN model for the evaluation of Customer Orientation in CRM, IE(I) 90, 28-33

Panzarasa, P., Jennings, N. R., & Norman, T. J. (2002). Formalizing collaborative decision-making and practical reasoning. *Multi-agent Systems*, *12*(1), 55–117.

Reichheld, F. F. (1996). *The loyalty effect*. Cambridge, MA: Harvard Business School Press.

Sabater, J., & Sierra, C. (2005). Review on computational trust and reputation models. *Artificial Intelligence Review*, *24*, 33–60. doi:10.1007/s10462-004-0041-5

Sandholm, T. W. (1999). Distributed rational decision making. In Weiss, G. (Ed.), *Multiagent systems: A modern approach to distributed artificial intelligence* (pp. 201–258). Cambridge, MA: MIT Press.

Shoham, Y. (1993). Agent oriented programming. *Artificial Intelligence*, *60*(1), 51–92. doi:10.1016/0004-3702(93)90034-9

Sim, K. M., & Chan, R. (2000). A brokering protocol for agent-based e-commerce. *IEEE Transactions on Systems, Man and Cybernetics. Part C, Applications and Reviews*, *30*(4).

Suwu, W., & Das, A. (2001). An agent system architecture for e-commerce. In *Proceedings of the 12th IEEE International Workshop on Database and Expert Systems Applications* (pp. 715-719).

Tang, T. Y., Winoto, P., & Niu, X. (2003). Investigating trust between users and agents in a multi agent portfolio management system: A preliminary report. *Electronic Commerce Research and Applications*, *2*(4), 302–314. doi:10.1016/S1567-4223(03)00039-5

Vieira, A. L. (2008). *An interpersonal approach to modeling business-to-business relationship quality*. Unpublished doctoral dissertation, University of Nottingham, Nottingham, UK.

von Wright, G. H. (1980). *Freedom and determination*. Amsterdam, The Netherlands: North Holland Publishing.

Wilkes, J. (2008). *Utility functions, prices, and negotiation* (Tech. Rep. No. HPL-2008-81). Palo Alto, CA: Hewlett-Packard Labs.

Winer, R. S. (2001). *Customer relationship management: A framework, research directions, and the future*. Retrieved from http://siebel.ittoolbox.com/documents/customer-relationship-management-a-framework-research-directions-and-the-future-16278

Wu, H. J. (2005). An agent-based CRM Model for multiple projects management. In *Proceedings of the IEEE Conference on Engineering Management* (pp. 851-855).

Wu, W., Ekaette, E., & Far, B. H. (2003). Uncertainty management framework for multi-agent systems. In *Proceedings of the ATS Workshop on Refractory Asthma* (pp. 122-131).

Xu, Z. (2008). *Factors which affect the dynamics of privately-owned Chinese firms: An interdisciplinary empirical evaluation.* Unpublished doctoral dissertation, University of St. Andrews, St. Andrews, Scotland.

Yu, B., & Singh, M. P. (2001). Towards a probabilistic model of distributed reputation management. In *Proceedings of the Fourth Workshop on Deception, Fraud and Trust in Agent Societies*, Montreal, QC, Canada (pp. 125-137).

Zacharia, G. (1999). *Collaborative reputation mechanisms for online communities.* Unpublished master's thesis, Massachusetts Institute of Technology, Cambridge, MA.

Zhao, X., Wu, C., Zhang, R., Zhao, C., & Lin, Z. (2004). *A multi-agent system for e-business processes monitoring in a web-based environment.* Beijing, China: Peking University.

This work was previously published in International Journal of Agent Technologies and Systems, Volume 3, Issue 2, edited by Yu Zhang, pp. 33-52, copyright 2011 by IGI Publishing (an imprint of IGI Global).

Chapter 12
The Performance of Grey System Agent and ANN Agent in Predicting Closing Prices for Online Auctions

Deborah Lim
Universiti Malaysia Sabah, Malaysia

Patricia Anthony
Universiti Malaysia Sabah, Malaysia

Chong Mun Ho
Universiti Malaysia Sabah, Malaysia

ABSTRACT

The introduction of online auction has resulted in a rich collection of problems and issues especially in the bidding process. During the bidding process, bidders have to monitor multiple auction houses, pick from the many auctions to participate in and make the right bid. If bidders are able to predict the closing price for each auction, then they are able to make a better decision making on the time, place and the amount they can bid for an item. However, predicting closing price for an auction is not easy since it is dependent on many factors such as the behavior of each bidder, the number of the bidders participating in that auction as well as each bidder's reservation price. This paper reports on the development of a predictor agent that utilizes Grey System Theory GM (1, 1) to predict the online auction closing price in order to maximize the bidder's profit. The performance of this agent is compared with an Artificial Neural Network Predictor Agent (using Feed-Forward Back-Propagation Prediction Model). The effectiveness of these two agents is evaluated in a simulated auction environment as well as using real eBay auction's data.

DOI: 10.4018/978-1-4666-1565-6.ch012

1. INTRODUCTION

Auction markets provide centralized procedures for the exposure of purchase and sale orders to all market participants simultaneously (Lee, 1996). In fact, auctions are not a new topic but have been widely used for centuries (Cassady, 1968). The design and conduct of auctioning institutions has caught the attention of many people over thousands of years. One of the earliest reports of an auction was used to allocate scarce resources in Babylon from about 500 B.C. (Shubik, 1983).

Nowadays, most transactions are conducted online via the Internet. To date, many traditional auction businesses are moving into the online auctions space and joining winners in this market place as a consequence of rapid growth of advance computer technology (Akula & Menasce, 2004). The major difference between these two types is the additional degree of flexibility, multiplicity as well as convenience in the way the online auction is conducted.

Previously, auction has to be conducted face to face. Hence, it requires a venue to gather all auctioneers as well as the auction participants. This requires a fairly high commission since a place needs to be rented, the auction needs to be advertised, and the auctioneer and other employees need to be paid. Since bidders must usually come to the auction site, many potential bidders are excluded. Similarly, it may be difficult for the sellers to move goods to the auction site. However, this does not exist as online auction allows clients to buy and sell items anytime and anywhere they like. Moreover, traditional auction has several limitations and deficiencies on the active period of bid submission. For example, an item only lasts for a few minutes before it is sold. This rapid process gives the bidders little time to make a decision. Online auction removes these deficiencies by providing bidders more flexibility on the time to submit their bids since online auctions are usually active for days or even weeks. Besides that, online auction can be more effective as there is no geographical limitation since both sellers and buyers will be trading in a "virtual" environment and payments can be made via online banking. Having a relatively low price and wider market in products and services, it had made the online auction more successful where it attracts many bidders and sellers as well. Online auctions also allow sellers to sell their goods efficiently and with little action or effort required. With all the benefits and advantages, auctions on the Internet have become a fascinating new type of exchange mechanism as well as an extremely effective way of allocating resources to the individuals who value them most highly.

According to Bapna *et al.* (2001). online auction is one of the most popular and effective ways of trading by bidding for products and services over the Internet. Nowadays, online auctions become an increasingly popular and effective medium for transacting businesses as well, either procuring goods or services, both between individuals over the Internet and between business and their suppliers. According to He *et al.* (2004) online auctions are increasingly being used for a variety of e-commerce applications. Over the last few years, a big number of online auction houses have emerged and the number is still increasing rapidly. According to the Internet auction (http://www.internetauctionlist.com/) there are currently more than 2600 auction company listings over the world. Some examples of popular online auction houses include eBay, Amazon, Yahoo!Auction and UBid. In addition, over 10 million items such as antiques, books, electronic appliances, agricultural products can be found daily for sale at online auctions. For example, in the popular auction house - eBay alone, there are often hundreds or sometimes even thousands of concurrent auctions running worldwide. According to David *et al.* (2005) online auctions continue to attract many customers and currently sell goods worth over $30 billion annually. For example the total revenue of e-Bay increased by more than $4.4 billion from 2004 ($3, 271,309) until 2007 ($7, 672,329).

When bidding in an auction, bidders may face a lot of problems such as picking and monitoring multiple auctions, and making the right bid on an exact time step. A consumer needs to consider how much time is available for him to spend before getting the desired item. Based on the available time, consumers have to select an auction to participate in since all the interested bidders should submit their bids within the given start and end times. Consumer also needs to decide on which auction to bid from among hundreds of auctions offering the same goods concurrently. The consumer can bid in a single auction but he may lose a chance to receive a better price offer in another auction. Besides, in selecting an auction, bidders have to make sure they submit the right bid amount in the auction. Bidder may run into a winner's curse phenomenon in which he may end up paying more for the item.

These problems can be overcome if the bidders can predict the closing price of each auction. If the bidder has an information on the closing price of an auction, he can choose to submit his bid when the auction is about to close giving no time for his opponents to react. The consumer can also make better decisions on the target auction if he knows the closing price for a given auction. There are a lot of popular prediction models in the market such as Neural Network, Fuzzy Logic, Time Series, Evolutionary Computation, Probability Function and Genetic Algorithm. However, predicting a future value is not a simple process. For example, to predict the closing price of an online auction, one has to consider the number of auction selling the same item at the same time, the number of bidders participating in the auction, the behavior of each bidder and each bidder's reservation price. The consideration of all the factors into a prediction model will increase the complexity of the prediction model. Besides that, it is hard to obtain a complete set of data and it is time consuming. Since the auction is dynamic, the prediction model has to make the prediction immediately and accurately in order to ensure that the bidder gains in an auction.

In this paper, we select Grey System Theory as the prediction model. This prediction model is designed for situations with insufficient inputs or incomplete data. Grey System Theory only requires a minimum of four inputs in order to predict the next future value. This is important in online auction situation since it is a burden for the researcher to collect a large set of data in a short span of time. Although Grey System Theory has been successfully applied in a lot of real-time applications such as anthropology, economic, agricultural, ecology and control industry problems, it is not widely used in an online auction. Hence, in order to investigate the suitability of Grey System Theory in predicting the closing price of online auction, we compare the efficiency of Grey System Theory with another famous prediction model which is Artificial Neural Network. Artificial Neural Network is one of the more popular prediction models in the field of Artificial Intelligence as it has long been used by many academicians and has been used numerous times in literatures. As one of the most powerful data modeling tools, it has been widely used to solve problems in machine learning using Feed-Forward Back-Propagation Prediction Model (Fausett, 1994).

The remainder of this paper is as follow. In Section 2, the related work will be discussed. Some case studies which reason why Grey System Theory and Feed-Forward Back-Propagation Neural Network are chosen in predicting online auction closing price will be discussed in Section 3. This is followed by the explanation of the design of the Grey System Theory in Section 4. Section 5 discusses the original Grey Model prediction algorithm. In Section 6, the electronic simulated marketplace that we used in this experiment will be described in detail. The algorithm of the Grey System agent which makes use of the simulated marketplace is discussed in Section 7. The experimental results are elaborated in Section 8. Finally, Section 9 concludes and discusses future work.

2. RELATED WORK

Lin, Chou, Weng, and Hsieh (2011) proposed a final price prediction model for English auction based on the real world data (Yahoo-Kimo Auction) with the help of neuro-fuzzy technique to capture the complicated relationship among the final price and key factors involved in an auction. Three models: regression, neural networks and neuro-fuzzy, were constructed to predict the final prices of these English auctions. Their empirical results showed that neuro-fuzzy performed the best either in the training data sets or in the testing data sets. By using the predicted closing prices, bidders can determine which auction is close to his/her reservation price (the price willing to pay) to avoid the winner's curse (bidder pays a price higher than the true value of the item) phenomenon. On the other hand, the model can also benefit sellers in setting the auction rules to maximize the final price. Hence, through this model, both bidders and sellers can achieve the final price in a more effective way with the maximum utility satisfaction.

Li, Liu, Wu, and Zhang (2006) concentrated on predicting the final prices of online auction items by using Artificial Neural Network Model. This research is concerned with the attributes of the seller and the auction item, the auction's properties and the historical exchange data to make the prediction. Artificial Neural Network and Regression were used to make the prediction. Two approaches were applied to predict discrete price, which are the continuous price prediction that utilized multivariate regression and the logic regression. Although a primary prediction was established in this study, it is still not able to make a generalized prediction model since only one set of data was tested. It is claimed that the accuracy of the prediction model may be increased if more attributes are included such as the seller's experiences in auctioning and online shopping.

He *et al.* (2004) proposed a novel bidding strategy, using the Earliest Closest First heuristic algorithm, for obtaining goods in multiple overlapping English Auctions. The algorithm exploited neuro-fuzzy techniques to predict the expected closing prices of the auctions and to adapt the agent's bidding strategy. The Fuzzy Neural Network (FNN) strategy used neuro-fuzzy techniques to determine which auction the agent should bid in and at what time, to reflect the type of environment in which it is situated. This is done by calculating the auctions that best fit the bidders' preferences and making trade-off in its bidding behavior between the different attributes that characterize the desired good in order to maximize the bidder's satisfaction. This algorithm has been benchmarked against a number of common alternatives available in the literature and the result indicated that it's performance more superior that the others. However the process is complicated and a lot of observational data are required.

Predicting the final closing price of an item being auctioned is very difficult. It is because many factors such as the starting and ending time of an auction and the number of bidders involved can eventually influence the closing price. However, collecting a set of data for online auction is an impossible mission since there is a large number of auctions that start and end everyday in different auction houses. To overcome the problem of gathering hosts of information, a prediction model that use only one parameter seems feasible. This is found in Grey System Theory that only requires one parameter (which is the online auction observational data) to make the prediction.

3. CASE STUDY

A. Grey System Theory Model

In 1982, Deng Julong proposed Grey System Theory which is an evolutionary model of the Simple Exponential Function (Liu & Lin, 2006). This theory applies to the study of unascertained problems with few or poor incoming information

(Lin & Liu, 2004). In other words, only a few of historical data, four until ten data, are required in prediction. In online auction the number of available information are limited and it is often very difficult to predict the outcome of an auction since bidders have different behaviors. Many recent papers in the literature considered Grey System Theory as an efficient prediction model. In this section, various applications of Grey System Theory are discussed.

In order to reduce the probability of the failure of the oil-filled power supply, periodic maintenance is required. One of the methods to examine the condition of the oil-filled transformers is by measuring the gas-in-oil concentration. However, the procedure of measuring these gases is complicated and time consuming. This has led to a desire of an efficient yet fast prediction method so that the condition of the transformer can be analyzed more easily. Yuan Jiwei, Guoqing, and Lei (2000) implemented Grey System Theory to predict the gas-in-oil concentration as a method of maintaining the transformers. By predicting the gas-in-oil concentration in the transformers, it helps engineers and technicians on the timing of the equipments' maintenances. From the experimental results, the prediction models for each dissolved gas could accurately predict the actual amount of dissolved gases found in the insulation oil by utilizing five historical data. In conclusion, by establishing this Grey prediction model, it provides great advantage in evaluating the transformer insulation. It is used to estimate the gas-in-oil concentration timely and data can be further analyzed as an indicator to change parts in a transformer. Besides that, this prediction model is simple, accurate and practical in calculating the concentration of the dissolved gases.

Chiou, Tzeng, Cheng, and Liu (2004) focused on the problem of predicting the quantity of the weapon spare parts used by the Taiwan navy. Due to the irregular time intervals and the relative short life cycle in high technology materials, a prediction model with the simpler requirements can be a better model. In this study, the Grey Prediction Model was applied to forecast the materials spare parts from the year 1999 to 2002. Chiou claimed that for a short term prediction, Grey System Theory is the best model among other prediction models such as Simple Exponential Function, Time Series and regression analysis.

Customer satisfaction is always the ultimate target of total quality management from the companies' point of view. Hence, in order to increase the customer satisfaction, more thorough studies have to be conducted (Wu, Liao, & Wang, 2004). In this study, surveys were conducted periodically and weights were given to the customer requirements, such as the short term need and the long term need, as well as the technical measures. By using Grey System Theory, at least four sets of data are required. Hence, the analysis of the customer requirements and the technical measures can be done conveniently and easily. Four periodical sets of data were collected to predict the fifth set of data. Based on the experimental results, this Grey System Theory produced accurate result in predicting the future set of data. Thus, Grey System Theory is a powerful and dynamic method for evaluating and adjusting the importance of each customer requirement in a very short period of time. To date, Grey System Theory has been successfully applied to agriculture, ecology, economy, meteorology, medicine, history, geography, industry, earthquake, geology, hydrology, irrigation strategy, military affairs, sports, traffic, management, material science environment, biological protection and judicial system (Deng, 1989).

In summary, Grey System Theory is used successfully to analyse uncertain systems that have multi-data inputs, discrete data, and insufficient data. Table 1 shows the Grey Prediction Model compared to other traditional forecasting models (Chiang, Wu, Chiang, Chang, Chang, & Wen, 1998). It can be seen that this model only requires short-term, current and limited data in order to predict a given value. Simple Exponential

Table 1. Attributes of traditional forecasting model

Mathematical Model	Minimum Observations	Mathematical Requirements
Simple Exponential Function	5-10	Basic
Regression Analysis	10-20	Middle
Casual Regression	10	Advanced
Time Series/Box-Jenkins (ARIMA)	50	Advanced
Artificial Neural Network	Large number	Advanced
Grey System Theory (Grey Prediction Model)	4	Basic

Function only requires minimum observations (five to ten) to predict while Grey System Theory requires four observations only. On the other hand, Time Series which has been successfully applied in economical field requires an advance mathematical calculation and a large data set (fifty observations) for prediction. Similarly, Artificial Neural Network which is one of the most powerful data modeling tools in machine learning field also requires a large number of observations and advanced mathematical formulas in the learning and testing steps before it can predict the future value.

Based on the literatures, we can conclude that Grey System Theory has been successfully applied in many areas such as anthropology, military affairs and control industry problems. It requires less input but deliver high accuracy especially in cases where availability of data for prediction is limited. This technique is well suited in predicting the closing price for online auction since the one only requires 4-5 past values to predict the closing price of a given auction. Te predicted value can also be calculated immediately while the auction is progressing.

B. Feed-Forward Back-Propagation Neural Network Model

In order to investigate the accuracy of the Grey System Theory Model, we compare it with the prediction model using Artificial Neural Network

(ANN). We use ANN as a basis for comparison because it is one of the most popular prediction models in the field of Artificial Intelligence, has long been used by many academicians and has been used numerous times in literatures. The development of ANN began approximately fifty years ago (Fausett, 1994). ANN has been successfully applied to a wide variety of problems, such as storing and recalling data or patterns, classifying patterns, performing general mapping from input patterns to output patterns, grouping similar patterns, or finding solutions to constrained optimization problems (Fausett, 1994).

Much work has been done on predicting values using Feed-Forward Back-Propagation Neural Network. Li, Liu, Wu, and Zhang (2006) concentrated on predicting the final prices of online auction items by using Feed-Forward Back-Propagation Neural Network Model. In the Back-Propagation neural network, a feed forward multi layer network based on Back-Propagation algorithm developed by Rumelhart and McCelland in 1986, has become one of the most widely used ANNs in practice. The activation transfer function (ATF) of a Back-Propagation network, usually, is a differentiable sigmoid (S-shape) function, which helps to apply the nonlinear mapping from inputs to outputs. In the paper, they collected a large amount of historical data exchange data from eBay-Eachnet, a famous online auction website in China. Similar to eBay, eBay-Eachnet runs a second price English auction for a variety of consumer goods. In second price English auction the winner only pays the second higher price rather than the original price they bid for. In their experimental dataset, they used 535 value auction records of Nokia mobile telephone data. In their experimental result, they implemented logical regression to investigate the performance of ANN. Based on the results obtained, Feed-Forward Back-Propagation Neural Network Model recorded average accuracy of more than 90% (94%-95%). However, the accuracy of the logistic regression only recorded an average accuracy of 63% - 68%. Based on this finding, we use this model to compare the accuracy of the proposed Grey System Theory.

4. GREY SYSTEM THEORY DESIGN

Grey System Theory is a theory that works based on unascertained systems with partially known and partially unknown information. It works by drawing out valuable information and also by generating and developing the partially known information where it helps in describing correctly and monitors effectively on the systemic operational behavior (Lin & Liu, 2004). Basically, Grey System Theory was chosen based on color (Liu & Lin, 2006). For instance, "black" is used to represent unknown information while "white" is used to represent complete information. Those partially known and partially unknown information is called the "Grey System Theory".

Grey prediction is a quantitative prediction based on grey generating function, Grey Model with first order and only one variable - GM (1, 1) model, which uses the variation within the system to find the relations between sequential data and then establish the prediction model (Liu & Lin, 2006). The Grey Prediction Model is derived from the Grey System, in which one examines changes within a system to discover a relation between sequence and data. After that, a valid prediction

is made to the system. The equation of GM (1, 1) Model is as follow (Liu & Lin, 2006).

$$x^0\left(k\right) + \; az^1\left(k\right) = b,$$

The meaning of the symbol GM (1, 1) is given as (Liu & Lin, 2006):

G M (1, 1)
Grey Model First Order One Variable
Grey Prediction Model has the following advantages (Chiou, Tzeng, Cheng, & Liu, 2004):

a. It can be used in situations with relatively limited data down to as little as four historical data, as stated in Table 1.

b. A few discrete data are sufficient to characterize an unknown system.

c. It is suitable for forecasting in competitive environments where decision-makers have only access to limited historical data.

5. GREY SYSTEM THEORY PREDICTION ALGORITHM

In this section, we describe our predictor agent algorithm which focuses on the Grey generating function, GM used in grey prediction (Deng & David, 1995; Liu & Lin, 2006). The algorithm of GM (1, 1) can be summarized as follows.

Step 1. Establish the initial sequence from historical data. In this case, the data used is the previous values of the online auction closing price observed over time.

$$f^0 = \left\{f_1^0, \; f_2^0, \; f_3^0, \; ..., \; f_n^0\right\}, \qquad where \quad n \geq 2.$$

(1)

Step 2. Generate the first-order Accumulated Generating Operation (AGO) sequence

$$f^1 = \left\{ f_1^1, \ f_2^1, \ f_3^1, \ ..., \ f_n^1 \right\}, \tag{2}$$

where $\quad f_t^1 = \sum_{k=1}^{t} f_k^0 \quad , \quad t = 1, 2, ..., \ n \quad and \quad n \geq 2.$

Step 3. The grey model GM (1,1)

$$f_{t+1}^0 = a \left[-\frac{1}{2} \left(f_{t+1}^1 + f_t^1 \right) \right] + b, \tag{3}$$

where $\forall t \geq 1$.

Step 4. Rewrite into matrix form

$$\begin{bmatrix} f_2^0 \\ f_3^0 \\ \vdots \\ f_n^0 \end{bmatrix} = \begin{bmatrix} -\dfrac{1}{2} \left(f_2^1 + f_1^1 \right) & 1 \\ -\dfrac{1}{2} \left(f_3^1 + f_2^1 \right) & 1 \\ \vdots & \vdots \\ -\dfrac{1}{2} \left(f_n^1 + f_{n-1}^1 \right) & 1 \end{bmatrix} \begin{bmatrix} a \\ b \end{bmatrix} \tag{4}$$

Where a and b=constant value.

Step 5. Solve the parameter a and b

$$\begin{bmatrix} a \\ b \end{bmatrix} = \left(B^T B \right)^{-1} B^T F^0, \tag{5}$$

where $\qquad F^0 = \begin{bmatrix} f_2^0 \\ f_3^0 \\ \vdots \\ f_n^0 \end{bmatrix}$

$$and \quad B = \begin{bmatrix} -\dfrac{1}{2} \left(f_2^1 + f_1^1 \right) & 1 \\ -\dfrac{1}{2} \left(f_3^1 + f_2^1 \right) & 1 \\ \vdots & \vdots \\ -\dfrac{1}{2} \left(f_n^1 + f_{n-1}^1 \right) & 1 \end{bmatrix}$$

Step 6. Estimate AGO value

$$\hat{f}_{t+1}^1 = \left[f_1^0 - \left(\frac{b}{a} \right) \right] e^{-at} + \left(\frac{b}{a} \right), \tag{6}$$

where $\forall t \geq 1$.

Step 7. Get the estimated Inverse Accumulated Generating Operation (IAGO) value or the estimated closing price for a given auction.

$$\hat{f}_t^0 = \hat{f}_t^1 - \hat{f}_{t-1}^1, \qquad where \quad \forall t \geq 2$$

Step 8. Residual Error (RE) is utilized to calculate the accuracy of each time step. The formula for the Residual Error is given as

$$\left(\frac{\left| f_t^0 - \hat{f}_t^0 \right|}{f_t^0} \right) \times 100\%. \tag{7}$$

Where

$f_t^0 = real\,value\,of\,exchange\,rate\,at\,time\,t$

$\hat{f}_t^0 = estimated\,value\,of\,exchange\,rate\,at\,time\,t$

Step 9. Average Residual Error (ARE) for each set of data is used to calculate the accuracy of the predicted data. The formula for ARE is given as

$$ARE = \left(\frac{1}{n} \sum_{t=1}^{n} \frac{\left| f_t^0 - \hat{f}_t^0 \right|}{f_t^0} \right) \times 100\%$$

Where

f_t^0 = real value of exchange rate at time t

$\hat{f}_t^0$ = estimated value of exchange rate at time t

6. THE ELECTRONIC SIMULATED MARKETPLACE

The simulated marketplace environment serves as a model to replicate the real auction scenario where activities of buying and selling are observed among the traders. To date, there are several well-known existing simulated marketplaces available, such as Fishmarket, Minnesota Agent Marketplace Architecture (Magma) and Trading-Agent Competition (TAC's) that have been developed to simulate the real auction environments. Fishmarket only utilized Dutch auction and Magma only involved Vickrey auction. Both are not suitable for the testing this work since it requires auction with different protocols, namely English, Dutch and Vickrey. TAC involves multiple types of auctions with multiple units of goods being offered. However, this research considers a single item only in a single marketplace.

Anthony developed a simulated auction environment that runs multiple heterogeneous protocols: the English, the Dutch, and the Vickrey with multiple protocols (Anthony, 2003). This simulated environment serves as a platform to simulate and replicate the real online auction environment in which there are multiple buyers and

multiple sellers participating in selling and buying. This electronic marketplace is flexible and can be configured to take up any number of auctions and any value of discrete time. Due to the flexibility and suitability of the electronic marketplace, it was decided to use this as the platform to evaluate the accuracy of the predictor agents.

All the auctions running in the marketplace are assumed to be auctioning the item that the consumers are interested in and all auctions are selling the same item. In other words, it is assumed that at all the consumers in the marketplace are interested in the item being auctioned. When the marketplace is activated, multiple English, Dutch and Vickrey auctions are run concurrently with different start and end times. All the auctions have a finite start time and duration generated randomly from a standard probability distribution, except the Dutch auction that has a start time but no pre-determined end time since the closing of the auction is determined by the first bidder who makes the offer to buy.

At the start of each auction (irrespective of the type), a group of random bidders are generated to simulate other auction participants. These participants operate in a single auction and have the intention of buying the target item and possessing certain behaviours. They maintain the information about the item they wish to purchase, their private valuation of the item (reservation price), the starting bid value and their bid increment. These values are generated randomly from a standard probability distribution. Their bidding behaviour is determined based on the type of auction that they are participating in. The auction starts with a predefined starting value; a small value for an English auction and a high value for a Dutch auction. There is obviously no start value for a Vickrey auction as this is a sealed bid and each bidder is required to submit their bid discreetly.

The marketplace announces the current bid values and the current highest bids for English auctions and the current offers for Dutch auctions at each time step. At the end of a given auction, it determines the winning bid and announces the winner.

7. THE GREY SYSTEM PERDICTOR AGENT ALGORITHM

Based on the algorithm of GM (1, 1) which we discuss in Section 4, the Grey System agent algorithm is designed to make use of the simulated marketplace which proposed by Anthony (2003). Firstly, the Grey System Predictor Agent collects the observational data from the simulated marketplace after a particular run. The last eight observational data are reserved for the testing purpose (calculation for the residual error). Predictor Agent then utilizes a number of the latest remaining observational data to generate two constant numbers, a and b in Formula 4 (which are used to build the prediction equation) for GM (1, 1) equation according to a user's requirement. This Predictor Agent predicts the value according to a fixed observational data approach followed by a moving observational data approach. For example, in the case of fixed observational data prediction, ten observational data are collected. They are used to predict the next five future data. It means that these five future values (eleventh to fifteenth data) are predicted based on the same set of ten observational data.

On the other hand, by using the moving observational data prediction, the set of observational data is updated before each prediction and only the latest ten observational data are applied in each prediction. This means that, ten observational data are used to predict the first future value (eleventh data). Then before making the next prediction for the second future value (twelfth data), this set of observational data is updated with the eleventh observational data (obtained from the auction since it is already closed). Since the number of observational data is maintained, the second observational data until the eleventh observational

data are used to predict the second future value (twelfth data). This process is repeated for the third future value and so forth. This is because in the real-time auctions, there will be auctions that close at each time step. Hence, the involvement of the latest or updated observational data is important in order to increase the accuracy of the prediction.

In the fixed situation, the Grey System Agent utilized four latest remaining fixed observations to predict the five future closing prices. The number of fixed observation is increased until eight observations for each particular run. However in the moving stage, four moving observational data are utilized in order to predict the eight future closing prices. As in the previous case, the prediction will loop for seven times. Eight predicted data from each approach would then be compared to the original observational data in order to calculate their residual error. The average residual error would later be calculated from the five observational data in the fixed situation. Finally, the Grey System Predictor Agent selects the result that has the highest accuracy from the fixed observational data and the moving observational data. The optimal number of input data, the result of the fixed observation, the result for the moving observation, the Average Residual Error of fixed stage and the Residual Error for fixed observation as well as moving observation are displayed at the end of a particular run.

8. EXPERIMENTAL EVALUATION

The concept of agent is applied into the prediction model in order to enhance the efficiency. We use two different agents that utilize two different techniques to predict the closing price of the online auctions which are Grey System Agent (GSA) and Artificial Neural Network Agent (ANNA). The experiment is divided into two parts where in the first part the data is taken from the simulated marketplace. In the second part, the performance of the predictor agent will be evaluated using data collected from eBay auctions.

In the real-time auctions, there will be auctions that close at each time step. Thus, the consideration of the latest observational closing price into the prediction is an important issue. In both parts of the experiments, the predictor agent will utilize the fixed observational data as well as the moving observational data. The concept of a fixed observational data is by using a certain number of collected observational data (closing price), several future data are predicted. The latest observational data may not be considered in the prediction. However, the concept of moving observational data means every latest observational data is considered in order to make the next prediction. To investigate the suitability and the performance of this agent, it is a must to apply the moving observation instead of fixed observation for both stages. Moving observational data in this respect means taking into account all the auctions that are closed at every time step.

Here, we would like to compare the performance GSA that uses a minimum number (4 - 8 historical data) of data against ANNA that requires a large number (50 - 100 historical data) of data. These predicted values are then compared with the actual data obtained and the Average Residual Errors are calculated. In the simulated marketplace, we ran the auction from t = 1 until t = 150. We have also set most of auctions to close after t = 30. In one particular run, the closing price history for all auctions running in a marketplace are shown from t = 41 until t = 150.

The GSA which utilizes Grey Prediction Model GM (1, 1) only requires one variable, which is the closing price data from the simulated marketplace. The ANNA utilizes Feed-Forward Back-Propagation Prediction Model (Fausett, 1994) to predict the future values. Two experiments are done for ANNA. In the first experiment, similar to GSA, only the closing price is utilized as the observational data. However, the result obtained

(ARE = 4.61%) is lower than the result obtained by GSA (ARE = 0.77). Hence, to improve the performance of ANNA, three more sets of parameter are plugged in the second experiment consisting of the starting price, the number of bidders and the number of bids. The ANNA is trained to understand the influences of these three parameters (the starting price, the number of bidders and the number of bids) on the closing price. In the experiment, 60% of these observations are for training purpose while the remaining 40% observations are for testing purpose. Using one hidden layer with fifty neurons and one output layer with one neuron produced the lowest ARE. In the experiment, 10000 numbers of epochs, 0.3% learning rate and 0.6% momentum are set. The use of Tangent Sigmoid Transfer Function (Tan-sig) in both hidden layer and output layer produced the best result and hence it was used for prediction.

8.1. Using Electronic Simulated Marketplace Data

A. Experimental Results Using Fixed Data

In the first experiment, five future closing price data are predicted by the agents using 4 - 8 (GSAF) and 50 - 100 (ANNAF) latest historical closing price data. The results of the predictions by the two agents are shown in Figure 1.

In Table 2, the Average Residual Errors (AREs) of Grey System Agent with fixed historical data (GSAF) are between 0.77% to 8.30% and the lowest ARE is obtained by using 6 historical data (ARE = 0.77%). Based on the result, the AREs increase when the number of historical data is increased. The highest ARE is recorded by using 8 historical data with ARE = 8.30%. This shows that GSAF does not perform better if more historical data are utilized due to the nature of GSAF which is designed to perform well in the situation which has less input data.

Figure 1. Results obtained by the four predictor agents by using fixed data over time in simulated auction

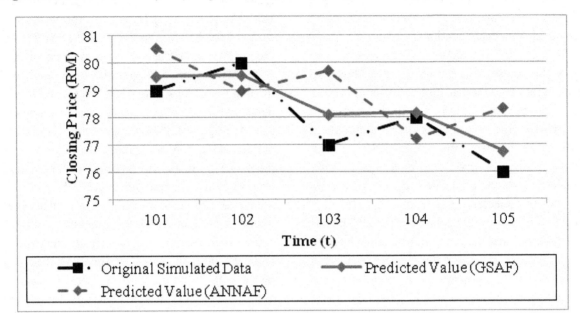

Table 2. Results obtained by using GSAF vs. the original data generated by the simulated auction

No of Observational Data	Time t = 101, Original Data = 79	Time t = 102, Original Data = 80	Time t = 103, Original Data = 77	Time t = 104, Original Data = 78	Time t = 105, Original Data = 76	ARE (%)
4	79.34	79.21	77.59	76.48	74.90	**1.12**
5	78.53	77.09	73.71	71.38	67.13	**5.15**
6	79.52	79.55	78.10	78.17	76.76	**0.77**
7	75.36	74.29	71.62	71.37	69.53	**6.56**
8	80.72	82.40	83.04	86.65	89.23	**8.30**

The AREs for Artificial Neural network with fixed historical data (ANNAF) shown in Table 3 falls between 2.16% and 3.48%. The highest accuracy is using 100 historical data with ARE of 2.16%. Based on the results represent in Table 3, we cannot conclude that when the number of historical data is increased, the accuracy of the predicted value increases as well. However, it can be assumed that, ANNF which requires learning may produce lower ARE value when more historical data are provided.

Figure 1 illustrates the predicted values, from t = 101 until t = 105, by using two predictor agents in the simulated environment against the original data. The best result of each predictor agent have been selected and compared. In this section, instead of ARE, Residual Error (RE) of each predicted value in every time step is also taken into consideration. As shown in Figure 1, GSAF with fewer input (six observational data) data always follows the trend of original simulated data and gives the lowest ARE of 0.77%. This result is expected since the main goal of GSAF is to predict values with minimal number of observational data. t = 104 gives the lowest RE of 0.22%, however t = 103 shows the highest RE (1.43%) within the five predicted values of GSA. ANNAF in this particular run requires 100 historical data. However

Table 3. Results obtained by using ANNAF vs. the original data generated by the simulated auction

No of Observational Data	Time t = 101, Original Data = 79	Time t = 102, Original Data = 80	Time t = 103, Original Data = 77	Time t = 104, Original Data = 78	Time t = 105, Original Data = 76	ARE (%)
50	78.96	80.81	80.47	79.41	79.88	2.50
60	81.26	80.41	81.92	79.00	79.96	3.25
70	81.92	80.13	81.67	79.41	79.31	3.22
80	76.61	78.87	77.21	78.67	80.30	2.25
90	81.79	80.07	80.97	79.53	81.07	3.48
100	80.54	78.98	79.70	77.22	78.33	2.16

ANNAF could not produce better predicted results than GSAF (ARE = 0.77%) and it obtained a higher ARE of 2.16%. This is because the predicted values by using the ANNAF evolved further away from the actual line when compared with GSAF as the time increases. In other words, in each time step, the RE is higher than the RE recorded by using GSAF method even when ANNAF uses a larger set of historical data.

B. Experimental Results Using Moving Data

In the real-time auctions, there will be auctions that close at each time step. Thus, the latest closing price needs to be updated into the prediction process. The next experiment compares the performance of the two predictor agents using moving data from the simulated marketplace.

Table 4 showed the predicted values over time for GSAF and GSAM (moving data). Based on the result of the previous experiment, using 6 data gave the lowest ARE. Hence, 6 moving data are considered in the calculation. The values predicted by using both GSAF and GSAM are still very close to the real value at the beginning time step (t = 102 until t = 106). However, starting from t = 107, it can be noticed that the predicted value by using GSAF started to decrease and deviates from the actual data. However, the GSAM result always followed the trend of the original data until the end as shown in Figure 2. It can be concluded

that when more future data are to be predicted, it is better to use moving data rather than a fixed data. Hence, it can be concluded that the performance of GSA is increased when using moving historical data.

ANNA considers starting price, the number of bidders and the number of bids when predicting the closing price. ANNA predicted the closing price based on one 100 historical data. The results of ANNAF and ANNAM are shown in Figure 3. ANNAM performed better than ANNAF. In Table 5, at t = 108, ANNAF recorded higher RE of 5.54% while ANNAM achieved lower RE of 3.52%. Hence, In this case, ANNAM obtained better result than ANNAF. Based on this experiment it can be concluded that ANNAF is not suitable to be applied in the simulated online auction due to its high value of ARE compared to GSAF and a large historical data set is required.

8.2. Using eBay Data

A. Experimental Results Using Fixed Data

In the first experiment, five future closing price data are predicted by the agents using 4 - 8 (GSAF) and 50 - 100 (ANNAF) latest historical closing price data. The results of the predictions by the two agents are shown in Table 6 and Table 7. In Table 6, the Average Residual Errors (AREs) of the Grey System Agent with fixed historical

Table 4. Results obtained by using Grey System Agent vs. the original data generated by the simulated auction

Time (t)	Original Data	GSAF		GSAM	
		Forecast Using 6 Fixed Observations	RE (%)	Forecast Using 6 Moving Observations	RE (%)
102	80	79.55	0.56	78.86	1.43
103	77	78.10	1.43	78.12	1.45
104	78	78.17	0.22	78.60	0.77
105	76	76.76	1.00	77.41	1.86
106	79	77.88	1.42	78.45	0.70
107	80	75.53	5.59	80.02	0.03
108	82	74.70	8.90	82.24	0.29

data (GSAF) are between 6.21% to 18.31% and the lowest ARE is obtained by using 6 historical data (ARE = 6.21%). Based on the result, the AREs increase when the number of historical data is increased. The highest ARE is recorded by using 8 historical data with ARE = 18.31%. This shows that GSAF does not perform better if more historical data are utilized due to the nature

of GSAF which is designed to perform well in the situation which has less input data.

The AREs for Artificial Neural Network with fixed historical data (ANNAF) shown in Table 7 falls between 6.32% and 9.29%. The highest accuracy is using 100 historical data with ARE of 6.32%. When the number of historical data is increased, the accuracy of the predicted value increases as well. However, when sixty observa-

Figure 2. Results obtained by the grey system agent over time in simulated auction

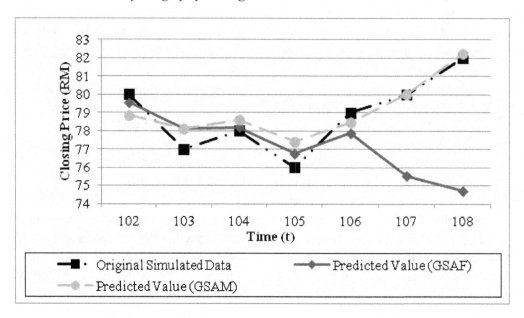

Figure 3. Results obtained by the artificial neural network agent over time in simulated auction

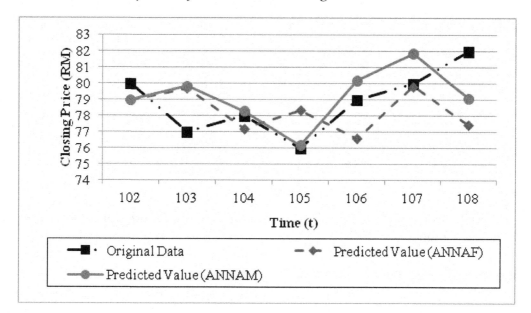

tions are used, ANNAF obtained the highest ARE of 9.29%. Hence, it can be assumed that, ANNF which requires learning may produce lower ARE values when more historical data are provided.

Based on Figure 4, both agents perform well with high accuracy of more than 93.0%. GSAF achieved 93.79% accuracy by using 6 historical data. ANNAF requires a large data set (100 historical data) in order to achieve 93.68% accuracy. However, it is hard to collect a large number of

updated data in a short time during the bidding process. Besides that, GSAF only required 1 variable which is observational closing price in the prediction process compared to ANNAF which consisted of 4 variables (the starting price, the number of bidders, the number of bids and closing price). Hence, with a minimal input data (6 historical data and 1 variable), it can be concluded that GSAF succeeded in predicting online auction

Table 5. Results obtained by using artificial neural network agent vs. the original data generated by the simulated auction

Time (t)	Original Data	ANNAF		ANNAM	
		Forecast Using 100 Fixed Observations	RE (%)	Forecast Using 100 Moving Observations	RE (%)
102	80	78.98	1.28	78.99	1.26
103	77	79.70	3.51	79.84	3.69
104	78	77.22	1.00	78.29	0.37
105	76	78.33	3.07	76.18	0.24
106	79	76.62	3.01	80.20	1.52
107	80	79.83	0.21	81.86	2.33
108	82	77.46	5.54	79.11	3.52

Table 6. Results Obtained by using GSAF vs the original data from the eBay auction (Apple IPhone 8GB)

No of Observational Data	Time t = 101, Original Data = 500	Time t = 102, Original Data = 495	Time t = 103, Original Data = 535	Time t = 104, Original Data = 535	Time t = 105, Original Data = 500	ARE (%)
4	515.24	492.75	498.01	426.62	339.15	12.57
5	516.86	516.88	505.48	438.18	355.51	12.06
6	528.54	545.33	555.57	514.52	462.43	6.21
7	536.57	564.50	588.88	564.87	532.59	8.71
8	547.87	591.04	634.55	633.45	627.78	18.31

closing price with a high prediction accuracy rate by using fixed historical data.

B. Experimental Results Using Moving Data

The next experiment compares the performance of the two predictor agents using moving data from eBay Auction (Apple IPhone 8GB).

Table 8 showed the predicted values over time for GSAF and GSAM (moving data). Based on the result of the previous experiment, GSAF used 6 data that gave the lowest ARE. Hence, 6 moving data are considered in the calculation. The values predicted by using both GSAF and GSAM are still close to the real value at the beginning time step (t = 102 until t = 105). However, starting from t = 106, it can be noticed that the Residual Average (RE) value by using GSAF started to increase.

However, the GSAM result always followed the trend of the original data until the end as shown in Figure 5. It can be concluded that when more future data are to be predicted, it is better to use moving data rather than a fixed data. Hence, it can be concluded GSA's performance improved when moving historical data is used.

ANNA considers the starting price, the number of bidders and the number of bids when predicting the closing price. ANNA predicted the closing price based on 100 historical data. The results of ANNAF and ANNAM are shown in Table 8. In this particular experiment, ANNAM performed better than ANNAF, as expected. It can be observed that at t = 105 and t = 108, ANNAM scored lower RE value than ANNAF.

Based on the result of the experiment, it can be concluded that the moving observational data is highly recommended in the online auction closing

Table 7. Results obtained by using ANNAF vs. the original data from the eBay auction (Apple IPhone 8GB)

No of Observation-al Data	Time t = 101, Original Data = 500	Time t = 102, Original Data = 495	Time t = 103, Original Data = 535	Time t = 104, Original Data = 535	Time t = 105, Original Data = 500	ARE (%)
50	565.21	560.00	514.65	530.60	495.17	6.35
60	560.00	560.00	510.13	560.00	560.00	9.29
70	543.82	510.05	521.30	497.29	560.00	6.68
80	550.60	540.12	527.05	496.25	520.87	6.43
90	552.29	510.33	526.41	490.03	550.01	6.71
100	534.25	537.48	520.75	524.50	557.63	6.32

price. The concept of moving observational data is important and relevant in the closing price prediction as there are many auctions closing within the prediction period. It can also be observed that using GSAM and ANNAM, the predicted values are very close to the original data and performed a consistent prediction results compared to GSAF and ANNAF as shown in Figure 5 and Figure 6. However, GSAM is a better method as it only requires 6 historical data compared to ANNAM that requires 100 historical data.

9. CONCLUSION AND FUTURE WORK

The foremost motivation of this paper is to find out the accuracy of Grey Theory Prediction

Figure 4. Results obtained by the four predictor agents over time in eBay Auction (Apple IPhone 8GB)

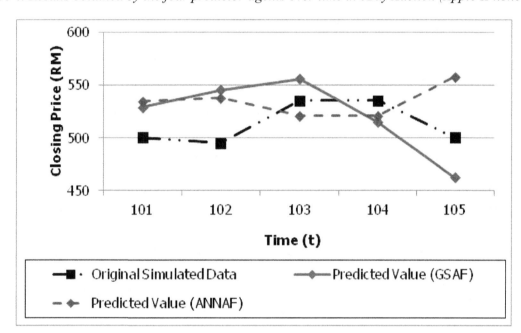

Table 8. Results obtained by using grey system agent vs. the original data from the eBay auction (Apple IPhone 8GB)

Time (t)	Original Data	GSAF		GSAM	
		Forecast Using 6 Fixed Observations	RE (%)	Forecast Using 6 Moving Observations	(RE %)
102	495	545.33	10.17	439.06	11.30
103	535	555.57	3.84	583.16	9.00
104	535	514.52	3.83	490.75	8.27
105	500	462.43	7.51	537.06	7.41
106	535	418.95	21.69	529.93	0.95
107	560	345.86	38.24	533.53	4.73
108	560	237.45	57.60	548.48	2.06

Figure 5. Results obtained by the grey system agent over time in eBay auction (Apple IPhone 8GB)

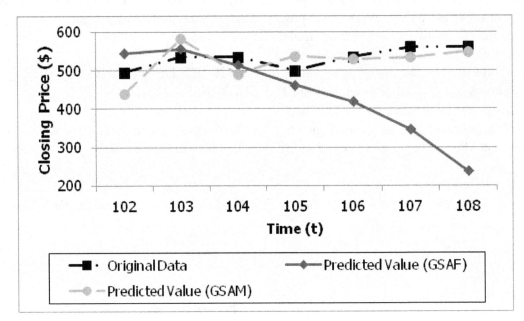

Figure 6. Results obtained by the artificial neural network agent over time in eBay suction (Apple IPhone 8GB)

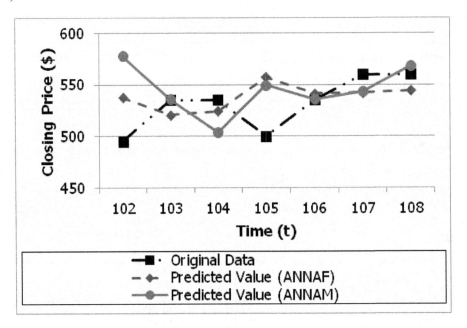

Table 9. Results obtained by using artificial neural network agent vs. the original data from the eBay auction (Apple IPhone 8GB)

Time (t)	Original Data	ANNAF		ANNAM	
		Forecast Using 100 Fixed Observations	RE (%)	Forecast Using 100 Moving Observations	(RE %)
102	495	537.48	8.58	578.00	16.77
103	535	520.75	2.66	536.18	0.22
104	535	524.5	1.96	503.85	5.82
105	500	557.63	11.53	549.72	9.94
106	535	541.21	1.16	536.10	0.21
107	560	542.32	3.16	543.42	2.96
108	560	544.47	2.77	568.09	1.44

Model GM (1, 1) in predicting online auction closing price by comparing its accuracy with the prediction technique using ANN Feed-Forward Back-Propagation Prediction Model. The main concern of this research is to establish an autonomous predictor agent that can predict the online auction closing price instantly at any given time and also in situations where there is insufficient information. These two algorithms had been tested for their scalability by using simulated auctions data and real eBay auctions data. The prediction model predicts the future value by exploiting the past auction history. Besides the comparison against the two predictor agents, two approaches had been introduced, namely using a fixed data prediction approach and a moving data prediction approach. These two approaches had been applied to each of those prediction agents and the ARE and the evolving trend of the predicted results had been discussed.

The experimental results obtained show that using both types of data for both methods, the accuracy rate always exceeds more than 90%. The Grey System Agent gives better result when less input data are used while the Artificial Neural Network Agent can only be used with the availability of a lot of information as well as many input parameters. The experimental results also showed that using moving historical data produces higher accuracy rate than using fixed historical data for both agents. This is important since, bidders in an online auction need to take into accounts all the auctions that are going to close within the prediction period. For future work, we would like to investigate the applicability of the Grey System Theory to predict the bidder's arrival and their bids in a given auction. Besides that, the study should extend the existing model GM (1, 1) to GM (1, N) in order to take into account more auction parameters or variables. This will improve the efficiency and functionality of the predictor agent.

REFERENCES

Akula, V., & Menasce, D. A. (2004). Contrasting grey system theory to probability and fuzzy. *ACM SIGICE Bulletin, 20*(3), 3–9.

Anthony, P. (2003). *Bidding agents for multiple heterogeneous online auctions*. Unpublished doctoral dissertation, University of Southampton, Southampton, UK.

Bapna, R., Goes, P., & Gupta, A. (2001). Insights and analyses of online auctions. *Communications of the ACM, 44*(11), 43–50. doi:10.1145/384150.384160

Cassady, R. J. R. (1968). Review. *Auctions and Auctioneering, 58*(4), 959–963.

Chiang, J. S., Wu, P. L., Chiang, S. D., Chang, T. L., Chang, S. T., & Wen, K. L. (1998). *Introduction to grey system theory.* Taipei, Taiwan: Gao-Li.

Chiou, H. K., Tzeng, G. H., Cheng, C. K., & Liu, G. S. (2004). Grey prediction model for forecasting the planning material of equipment spare parts in navy of Taiwan. In *Proceedings of the IEEE World Automation Congress, 17,* 315–320.

David, E., Rogers, A., Schiff, J., Kraus, S., & Jennings, N. R. (2005). Optimal design of English auctions with discrete bid level. In *Proceedings of the Sixth ACM Conference on Electronic Commerce,* Vancouver, BC, Canada (pp. 98-107).

Deng, J. (1989). Introduction to grey system theory. *Journal of Grey System, 1,* 1–24.

Deng, J., & David, K. W. N. (1995). Control problem of grey system. *Systems & Control Letters, 1*(1), 288–294.

Fausett, L. (1994). *Fundamentals of neural networks (architectures, algorithms & applications).* Melbourne, FL: Florida Institute of Technology.

He, M., Jennings, N. R., & Prugel-Bennett, A. (2004). An adaptive bidding agent for multiple English auctions: A neuro-fuzzy approach. In *Proceedings of the IEEE Conference on Fuzzy Systems,* Budapest, Hungary (pp. 1519-1524).

He, M., Leung, H., & Jennings, N. R. (2003). A fuzzy logic based bidding strategy for autonomous agents in continuous double auctions. *IEEE Transactions on Knowledge and Data Engineering, 15*(6), 1345–1363. doi:10.1109/TKDE.2003.1245277

Lee, H. G. (1996). Electronic brokerage and electronic auction: The impact of IT on market structures. In *Proceedings of the 29th HICSS Conference on Information Systems – Organizational Systems and Technology,* Los Alamitos, CA (pp. 397-406).

Li, X., Liu, L., Wu, L., & Zhang, Z. (2006). Predicting the final price of online auction items. *Expert Systems with Applications, 31*(3), 542–550. doi:10.1016/j.eswa.2005.09.077

Lin, C.-S., Chou, S., Weng, S.-M., & Hsieh, Y.-C. (2011). *A final price prediction model for English auctions: a neuro-fuzzy approach.* New York, NY: Springer Science & Business Media.

Lin, Y., & Liu, S. (2004). A historical introduction to grey systems theory. In *Proceedings of the IEEE International Conference on Systems, Man and Cybernetics* (Vol. 3, pp. 2403-2408).

Liu, S., & Lin, Y. (2006). *Grey information: Theory and practical application with 60 figures.* London, UK: Springer.

Shubik, M. (1983). *Auctions, biddings, and markets: An historical sketch.* New York, NY: New York University Press.

Wu, H. H., Liao, A. Y. H., & Wang, P. C. (2004). Using grey theory in quality function deployment to analyse dynamic customer requirement. *International Journal of Advanced Manufacturing Technology, 25*(11-12), 1241–1247. doi:10.1007/s00170-003-1948-8

Yuan, B., Jiwei, G., Guoqing, T., & Lei, W. (2000). Using grey theory to predict the gas-in-oil concentrations in oil-filled transformer. In *Proceedings of the Sixth International Conference on Properties and Applications of Dielectric Materials,* Xi'an, China (pp. 217-219).

This work was previously published in International Journal of Agent Technologies and Systems, Volume 3, Issue 4, edited by Yu Zhang, pp. 37-56, copyright 2011 by IGI Publishing (an imprint of IGI Global).

Chapter 13
Price Rigidity and Strategic Uncertainty:
An Agent-Based Approach

Robert Somogyi
Paris School of Economics, France

János Vincze
Corvinus University of Budapest and Institute of Economics of the Hungarian Academy of Sciences, Hungary

ABSTRACT

The phenomenon of infrequent price changes has troubled economists for decades. Intuitively one feels that for most price-setters there exists a range of inaction, i.e., a substantial measure of the states of the world, within which they do not wish to modify prevailing prices. Economists wishing to maintain rationality of price-setters resorted to fixed price adjustment costs as an explanation for price rigidity. This paper proposes an alternative explanation, without recourse to any sort of physical adjustment cost, by putting strategic interaction into the center-stage of the analysis. Price-making is treated as a repeated oligopoly game. The traditional analysis of these games cannot pinpoint any equilibrium as a reasonable "solution" of the strategic situation. Thus, decision-makers have a genuine strategic uncertainty about the strategies of other decision-makers. Hesitation may lead to inaction. To model this situation, the authors follow the style of agent-based models, by modeling firms that change their pricing strategies following an evolutionary algorithm. In addition to reproducing the known negative relationship between price rigidity and the level of general inflation, the model exhibits several features observed in real data. Moreover, most prices fall into the theoretical "range" without explicitly building this property into strategies.

DOI: 10.4018/978-1-4666-1565-6.ch013

1. INTRODUCTION

Everyday observations tell us that some prices are changing almost continuously. Financial asset prices, of foreign exchange or of stocks, are obvious examples. Though most people do not buy commodities regularly, it is also well-known that the prices of crude oil, gold, or grain behave similarly. On the other hand most prices we meet in shops or kiosks seem familiar, we expect that they do not move from one day to another.

Infrequent price adjustment has troubled economists for decades. The problem is not the lack of change in itself, but the conviction that prices are kept fixed for much longer than market conditions, costs, and competitors' prices would justify. Intuitively, there exists a range of inaction for most price-setters, i.e., a substantial range of "the states of the world", where they do not wish to modify prevailing prices. Meanwhile basic economic theory instructs us that, at least, when marginal costs change it is rational to adjust prices, even in not fully competitive markets.

According to the prevailing wisdom the stickiness of money prices is the root of the ability of monetary policy to affect (significantly) real - as opposed to merely nominal - variables. It is perhaps less in evidence, but the same phenomenon is a concern for competition authorities, too, as it may signal collusion among market participants.

Economists wishing to maintain the rationality assumption for price-setters resorted to price adjustment costs ("menu costs") as an explanation of price rigidity. The basic idea is that, for instance, the everyday reprinting of an elegant menu for a restaurant is not a reasonable option, being too costly. Certainly, similar issues may be relevant for many other businesses. However, what about meal prices written on a blackboard at a pub's entrance? These prices appear to exhibit the same stickiness, despite the fact that overwriting them each day does not entailing any additional cost. Magazine prices have been one of the foremost examples of unreasonably strong price inflexibility, but printing a different price on each new edition would not entail even a negligible extra cost.

It must be the case that the rigidity of prices has more than one reason. In this paper we propose an alternative, though admittedly partial, explanation, without having recourse to any sort of physical adjustment cost. Rather, we focus on the possible role of strategic uncertainty, and put strategic interaction into the center-stage in our analysis.

The main idea of our approach can be summarized as follows. Price-making can be considered a repeated game, as firms usually act in markets where there exist identifiable competitors. The traditional analysis of these games cannot pinpoint any equilibrium as a reasonable "solution" of the strategic situation. Thus there is genuine strategic uncertainty, a situation where decision-makers cannot know for sure the strategies of other decision-makers. Strategic uncertainty may cause hesitation. If I cut the price would it be interpreted as a signal for a "price-war"? Or if I raise the price shall I lose market-share? Hesitation may lead to inaction, as we all know too well. To model this situation we follow the style of agent-based models. While traditional economics rely on full rationality and on an equilibrium concept, we model boundedly rational agents, thus must assume something about learning. To achieve our goal we adopted an evolutionary algorithm.

In Section 2 we give a survey of the price rigidity literature, followed by notes on agent-based modeling as applied to economics problems. In Section 3 a traditional approach to oligopoly pricing is surveyed. In Section 4 the agent-based oligopoly model is set up, and the learning algorithm is discussed. Section 5 presents the analysis of the model, and the concluding Section summarizes, pointing out paths to further research.

2. LITERATURE SURVEY

The Rigidity of Prices

The most salient fact conflicting with price flexibility this presumption has been termed the PPP (Purchasing Power Parity) puzzle (Rogoff, 1996), this is the general observation that there are large variations across currencies in purchasing power parity, induced by nominal exchange rate changes. Due to this and similar empirical findings, price rigidity has become a fundamental assumption in New-Keynesian macroeconomic models, that are sometimes called the "workhorse" of modern macroeconomics (Gali, 2008). New-Keynesian Phillips curves are derived from individual profit maximization, whereby prices are set by monopolistically competitive firms that face costs of price adjustment. As not all prices are raised immediately following a positive money injection demand increases, and output becomes - temporarily - higher than normal (the same with opposite signs happens after a monetary contraction). Prices follow suit eventually resulting in a positive correlation between growth and inflation. Price adjustment costs imply – in contrast to some former theories - that even foreseeable monetary policy changes have real effects. However, a recent, surprising, finding is that prices posted on the Internet, which can be changed very easily, are not necessarily more flexible than traditional brick-and-mortar prices (Lünnemann & Wintr, 2006). This, in itself, shows that adjustment costs cannot be the only explanation for price rigidity.

Several types of price adjustment costs models have been proposed in the literature. The aggregate implications of these models are similar, though in no case identical (Roberts, 1995) Researchers have frequently shown a lack of concern for looking for the "right" pricing model, as long as the implications seemed to be in line with macroeconomic data, and one should say, with *a priori* beliefs.

In the last decade a series of systematic studies was launched to find out from microdata how firms "in reality" set their prices. This literature is surveyed by Mackowiak and Smets (2008). One of the studies (Fabiani et al., 2007) was conducted by nine Eurosystem central banks, through standardized surveys. It covered more than 11,000 firms. Of the conclusions we refer to those pertinent to our paper. First, it seems that most markets can be characterized as monopolistically competitive (p. 34). Though the authors talk of monopolistically competitive markets we believe that the evidence cannot really distinguish between monopolistic competition and oligopoly. Second: "Markup pricing over costs is the dominant approach to price setting", (p. 8, Fact 7). Third: "According to the surveys, implicit and explicit contracts, cost-based pricing, and coordination failure are the most important reasons underlying price stickiness" (p. 8, Fact 8). In this paper we do not address customer relationship, but emphasize coordination failure in a framework where firms mark up their unit costs. Indirectly this verdict vindicates our previous claim with respect to oligopolistic versus monopolistic competition. To wit: there is no reason for coordination in monopolistically competitive markets. Fourth, in environments with high competitive pressure price reviews appear to be more frequent (p. 205). Below in the sensitivity analyses we check whether our model exhibits a negative relationship between the degree of competition and price rigidity.

As a response to the failure of adjustment cost models Rotemberg (2011) proposed an alternative in the behavioral economics style. Essentially he made intelligible the idea that price stickiness can be caused by a concern for fairness (customer relationships). Spiegler (2011) also analyzes the question of price-setting by a behavioral economics approach. In his model consumers are antagonized by unexpected price hikes, i.e., facing a higher price than their "sampling-based" reference price reduces their utility. He finds that this kind of loss aversion, manifested solely in the price dimension of the product, as opposed to the previous studies he heavily relies on (Kőszegi

& Rabin, 2006; Heidhues & Kőszegi, 2008) can reduce a monopolist's optimal price range thus implying price rigidity.

It is an interesting question to ask what makes prices change if anything. Papers that have addressed this issue usually found that cost changes are more likely to be responsible for price change than variation in demand (Bils & Klenow, 2004).

Recent research has yielded quantitative results as well. Several authors calculated price-rigidity statistics for different time-periods, and areas. On a consumer-price data base for the US Klenow and Krystov (2008) found that 36% of all prices are changed in every month, and that the mean duration of prices is 6.9 months. More substantial price rigidity was detected by Dhyne et al. (2005) for the Euroregion. The respective statistics are 15%, and 13 months. These studies have found substantial heterogeneity across sectors, and as expected, a negative relationship between the level of overall inflation and the degree of price rigidity.

In our model we use the results of Eichenbaum, Jaimovich, and Rebelo (2008), who analyzed the price and cost data of a large American chain store retailer. They found substantial rigidity for "reference" prices, remaining unchanged on average for a year. What is important for us is the finding that reference prices are adjusted whenever they differ significantly from a target price defined as average cost times a "required" markup. The authors calculate the tolerance level as 20%. We will model exactly this type of pricing strategy.

Agent-Based Modeling in Economics

Agent-based models have been used for some time in economics. General surveys are available (Tesfatsion, 2001, 2006; LeBaron, 2006). The paper by Heath, Hill, and Ciarallo (2009) can be consulted mainly from the methodological point of view. Researchers would, in general, like to resolve two issues of traditional economic analysis with the help of agent-based models. First, economists rather than studying complicated market mecha-

nisms usually resorted to shortcuts, as the idea of the Walrasian auctioneer (Tesfatsion, 2006, pp. 845-853). These shortcuts have been regarded increasingly unpalatable. However, as oligopoly pricing models have a simple exchange structure (prices are posted, then buyers arrive and buy or not), we are only marginally concerned with this branch of the literature. Second, traditionally economic models assumed something that, with some lack of precision, has frequently been called full rationality. This means essentially that agents apply strategies that maximize utilities under constraints, and have an objective (probabilistic) understanding of their environment. Full rationality has been seriously put into doubt both in laboratory environments and on the field. Despite continuing efforts to save the rationality assumption it has become accepted that other research programs have significant promise (Kahneman & Tversky, 1979; Gigerenzer & Selten, 2001). Agent-based economic models share a bounded rationality philosophy, where decisions are "practically computable", excluding thereby behaviors that even the modeler cannot determine. Learning models have a long history in economics (Evans & Honkapohja, 1999). But one may say that learning is, strictly speaking, meaningless in traditional models – excluding Bayesian updating of probabilities. On the other hand agent-based models frequently allow for an endogenous updating of strategies. Learning in the agent-based setting was several times reviewed (Brenner, 2006; Duffy, 2006). Though many types of learning models are in use one of them draw particular attention in economic applications: evolutionary learning (Arifovic, 2000). Our approach belongs to this branch of the literature.

Oligopolistic markets have been studied by agent-based models. The article by Midgley et al. (2007), is an example that addresses the problem from an operations-research perspective. The paper whose approach is the closest to ours was written by Chen and Ni (2000). The authors explore the "ecology" generated by evolutionary learning in repeated oligopoly games. Their focus is on the "cooperation versus price wars" issue, and they constrain the set of feasible prices to high (cooperative) and low (punishing). Thus their findings are only tangential to the problem of price rigidity.

3. THE TRADITIONAL OLIGOPOLY PRICING MODEL

There are N ($i=1,...N$) firms in the industry, where N is a constant. Time is measured in discrete units. Firms produce differentiated goods, and have constant marginal cost in period t, evolving according to $c_{it} = P_t c_{i0}$, where P_t is interpreted as the overall price level in the economy, and let p_{it} be the price chosen by firm i in t. For the demand framework we adopted the logit demand function system (Anderson & de Palma, 1992), which can be written as

$$D_{it} = K \frac{e^{-\frac{p_{it}}{\nu P_t}}}{\sum_{j=1}^{N} e^{-\frac{p_{jt}}{\nu P_t}} + e^{\frac{V}{\nu}}} \qquad \forall i, \forall t. \qquad (1)$$

The formula implies that demand depends on prices relative to the general price level. Here K can be interpreted as the absorption capacity of the market. The parameter ν ($\nu > 0$) controls for the degree of differentiation. When $\nu \to 0$, products become more and more homogenous, and slight differences in prices result in large shifts in demand. Like in Bertand-competition, in the limit buyers purchase only at the lowest price. On the other hand, when $\nu \to \infty$, consumers buy randomly, each firm faces the same demand. To save space in the description below we set $K=1$, and $\nu = 1$, but in the sensitivity exercises we treat the general case. The role of V in the denominator is to make the optimal collusive price finite. In the limit when $V \to -\infty$, total demand is equal

to K whatever the prices are, therefore cooperating firms could set "infinitely" large prices. On the other hand, with finite V total demand is bounded even when all prices are set arbitrarily close to 0.

Then the per-period profit functions are given by:

$$\pi_{it} = (p_{it} - c_{it})D_{it}. \qquad (2)$$

These data define in every period a Bertrand-Chamberlin oligopoly game, for which there exists a static Nash-equilibrium. For the case of common costs Anderson and de Palma (1992) established the following relationship:

$$p_t^* = c_t + P_t + \frac{P_t}{N - 1 + e^{\frac{p_t^*}{P_t} + V}}, \qquad (3)$$

where p_t^* is the (common) Nash-equilibrium price. Though there does not exist an explicit solution, this equation is easy to solve numerically. Furthermore one can derive the following relationship for the optimal (static) collusive price:

$$p_{k,t}^* = c_t + P_t + \frac{NP_t}{e^{\frac{p_{k,t}^*}{P_t} + V}}. \qquad (4)$$

These formulas show that as N increases the non-cooperative price monotonically decreases, whereas the collusive price monotonically increases. The non-cooperative and collusive prices will be important benchmarks during the analysis of the agent-based model in the following section.

The analysis of the repeated oligopoly game is potentially very complicated (Abreu, Pearce, & Stacchetti, 1985). It depends largely on the assumptions made on the exogenous processes (marginal costs and general price level). Analytic results are usually available for specific and simple driving processes. To summarize results briefly: sub-game perfect supergame (repeated game) equilibria lie between the static Cournot-Nash equilibrium, and the collusive (joint profit maximizing) outcomes. In general there exists a bewildering variety of Nash-equilibria, if strategies are allowed to be any function of the observable history of the market. While repeated oligopolistic pricing games can produce "collusive" equilibria with rigid prices in peculiar circumstances (Athey, Bagwell, & Sanchirico, 2004). In the next section we approach the problem from the perspective of boundedly rational agents.

4. OLIGOPOLY PRICING BY BOUNDEDLY RATIONAL AGENTS

We model firms as boundedly rational agents that do not pretend to find out what an optimal pricing strategy would be, as optimality depends heavily on the reaction of competitors, as well as on the uncertainties of the marginal cost process. They know their current costs, but otherwise they have only vague ideas on their rivals' behavior. Thus they know that they can "mark up" costs, in other words in a differentiated oligopoly setting prices can be profitably set above marginal cost, even if competitors would remorselessly maximize profits. They also know that there is a remote possibility to collude tacitly, and by effectively forming a powerful cartel prices can be set "high enough" above marginal costs to achieve maximal profits for the whole industry. Furthermore, they know that there is an upper limit, even the omniscient cartel would not set infinitely high prices. On the other hand they are skeptical, and are aware of strategic uncertainty, i.e., they are uncertain about how their competitors behave and react. This reasoning leads these firms to formulate pricing strategies in the following way.

1. Start with a target markup range, where the lowest markup is higher than 1.

2. Observe the marginal cost and calculate the target price range.
3. Check whether your latest price falls into the target range or not.
4. If yes, do not change the price.
5. If no, set the new price as a weighted average of your latest price and the middle of the target range.
6. Observe how strategies work in the market over several periods (any strategy consists of the target markup range (two parameters) and the weight of the old price). Then try to imitate successful strategies, or maybe experiment with a new one.

First, these assumptions reflect the minimally sensible idea that prices have to relate to, and set above, marginal cost. Second, they are implied by the, also, plausible notion that prices may be "too high". Third, they leave room for skepticism, as the markup range is allowed to be non-degenerate. (As it will be seen below, under certain conditions, the length of the range may become 0.)

The firms in our model have a basically rational "worldview" without being too much knowledgeable. They are not supposed to know the demand function quantitatively, and cannot precisely forecast the behavior of their competitors. Observing only their own costs and profits they modify their initial guesses. The change of strategies is based on a specific evolutionary algorithm, i.e., on a generic learning mechanism that has been applied in several contexts within, and, mostly, without economics. The learning mechanism used in this study has certain specific features. We call it evolutionary, because in spirit it is very similar to the class of algorithms surveyed for instance in Arifovic (2000). More precisely it is a modified form of a standard genetic algorithm (Haupt & Haupt, 2004).

For the formulation of such an agent based-setup we have to develop strategies, evaluation functions, and evolutionary operators. We must start with the definition of strategies. Decisions must depend on current marginal costs as a minimum, therefore we can transform the pricing problem into a markup-determination problem (price equals marginal cost times markup). Based on the informal argument presented in the Introduction we limit the strategy space to three dimensions:

1. Setting the lower limit of the markup, μ_{it}^{l} (a positive real number)
2. Setting the upper limit of the markup, μ_{it}^{u} (a positive real number)

In fact it is more convenient to work with a transformation of the two real variables: setting a markup target, and a percentage deviation from the markup target. In any case for given marginal costs and markup limits one can determine a range of prices, whose lower and upper bounds are $p_{it}^{l} = c_{it}\mu_{it}^{l}$, and $p_{it}^{u} = c_{it}\mu_{it}^{u}$, respectively.

3. Setting the weight of the latest price (β) in the calculation of the new price when it is not between the lower and upper bounds for the markup (a real number between *0* and *1*).

Then the strategy (decision function) is the following.

If the prevailing price is between the lower and the upper bounds the price is not changed.

$$p_{it} = p_{i,t-1}. \tag{5}$$

If the prevailing price is below the lower bound, or above the upper bound:

$$p_{it} = \beta p_{i,t-1} + (1-\beta)\frac{p_{it}^{l} + p_{it}^{u}}{2}. \tag{6}$$

It must be emphasized that this strategy set is obviously "much smaller", than the set of all feasible strategies. It is also more restricted than the set of available Markov-strategies. Still, these are

not overly simplistic strategies, either. As we have argued in the previous subsection due reflection can lead someone to opt for these strategies in an oligopolistic situation with strategic uncertainty, thus they are far from being naive.

We start by giving more or less reasonable initial values to the three strategic variables. The initial values of the lower and upper limit of the markup are set to be equal in order to avoid the suspicion of building price rigidity into the model. These values are uniformly distributed among firms between *0* and *0.5,* while the initial weight of the latest price ranges from *0.2* to *0.8.* In the initial period firms act according to these (almost) random strategies. However, the evaluation phase of each run is preceded by a warm-up phase, exactly in order to minimize the noise caused by these initial values.

Evolution requires a measure of fitness. An obvious candidate is actual profits, however, intuitively measuring fitness by a single run of profits would be unreasonable. Thus we define fitness as the average of profits obtained by a strategy with exponentially declining weights.

$$\Phi_{it} = \lambda\Phi_{i,t-1} + (1-\lambda)\pi_{it} \tag{7}$$

We assume that after period 1 firms calculate the fitness of all strategies (not only their own). However, the evaluation phase of each run is preceded by a warm-up phase, exactly in order to minimize the noise caused by these initial values. At the beginning of period 2 the strategy of each firm possibly undergoes changes, according to evolutionary operations. The first operation is selection or reproduction. We define the survival probability of the *i*th strategy by the Boltzmann-selection criterion as

$$Pr_{it} = \frac{e^{\Phi_{it}/H}}{\sum\limits_{j=1}^{N} e^{\Phi_{jt}/H}}, \quad i = 1,2..N, \tag{8}$$

where H is the Boltzmann-constant, frequently referred to as "temperature". At high temperatures the selection pressure is low, whereas at low temperatures it is high (i.e., "only the best can survive"). Notice, that survival depends on the relative fitness of a strategy in the population, thus we model a sort of social learning process. For this purpose, we use the fitness-proportionate method, also referred to as roulette wheel sampling. Thus chance determines if a strategy survives or not. A possible interpretation is noise in observation, i.e., the selection probability comes about from two reasons: firms can observe the fitness of strategies existing in the market only imperfectly, but tend to choose those that are perceived more successful.

Then the surviving strategies may undergo mutation: each of the three elements can be changed randomly. To implement mutation all variables are given a transition probability, called the mutation rate. In addition, we specify a continuous probability distribution for the mutation. We assume that it is normal, with mean *0*, and variance σ^2. Thus here we must only specify the variance. All mutation parameters are exogenous, and they do not change over time.

After disposing of the problem of strategies surviving selection one has to deal with firms whose previous strategy was dropped after the selection process. Our approach is to form a convex combination of the old (dropped) strategy, and one of those that have been selected repeatedly. This operation is not customary in the literature, one can interpret it as giving a certain individual and conservative flavor to the learning process. The weight of the dropped strategy is an exogenous parameter of our model.

5. SIMULATIONS

The Baseline Scenario

In this section, first, we report the baseline scenario values of parameters. Then we describe the results

of this benchmark model which is followed by a sensitivity analysis in which the effect of changes in individual parameter values is checked.

1. Number of firms (N): In the baseline model there are 10 competing firms.
2. Degree of product differentiation (ν): 1
3. Scale of demand (K): 1
4. V in the demand system. In the baseline model its value is $-1.5c$.
5. Boltzmann-constant (H): In the baseline model H is set to 1.
6. Fitness function: In the baseline model its quotient is $\lambda = 0.5$.
7. Mutation parameters: The mutation rate is 5% for all the variables. The standard deviation of the mutation is 0.01 for the markup target, 0.02 for the weight of the old strategy and the deviation from the markup target.
8. Weight of the repeatedly selected strategy: The baseline weight of the latter is 0.55.
9. Inflation environment: The overall annual inflation rate is a normally distributed random variable with an expected value of 3% and a 1 percentage point standard deviation.

Baseline Results

For each parameterization we report statistics based on 100 runs, each with 756 periods. In each run the first 36 periods ("warm-up" phase) was dropped, so the statistics were calculated with an effective sample size of 720 periods in each run. By visual inspection, convergence was not always achieved in single runs of this size, but we never met explosive instability, even when we performed long (100000 periods) simulations. Initial values for strategies did not seem to affect the model's behavior in the long run systematically. In very long simulations sometimes large, but transitory, deviations could be observed. Increasing the mutation rate did not seem to alter the behavior qualitatively, except that large transitory deviations occurred more frequently, and thereby variance and skewness were higher.

An important question was how prices generated by the model are related to "theoretical" prices, the Cournot-Nash and collusive equilibrium prices. Using the baseline parameterization described above in the 100 test runs all prices our model produced fell within the interval defined by those two values.

Another test of the model is to compare its results to actual statistics. This exercise can also be regarded as a first attempt to externally validate the model. With the baseline parameters the average duration of prices is 6.39 months, and its standard deviation is 2.88. We were able to compare these figures with actual inflation data for three different regions.

Table 1 shows the average and standard deviation of monthly inflation for the USA, the Eurozone and Hungary. The sources of these statistics are Klenow and Kryvstov (2008) (Table I and VI, pp. 871 and 886) for the US data and Dhyne et al. (2008) (Table 2, p. 12) for the European data, and Bauer, 2008 for the Hungarian data.

When we replaced the inflation environment parameters with the figures shown in Table 1 we obtained the results presented in Tables 2 and 3.

These show average results of 100 runs, for the percentage of prices changed, and average duration of prices. Average duration is a standard and intuitive measure of price rigidity, it is simply defined as the average time lag between two price changes of the products in the sample. The actual statistics ("Facts") themselves are only broad averages of substantially different sectoral data (Nakamura & Steinsson, 2008, Table 2, p. 1433). We also calculated the percentage of prices falling between the theoretical bounds in these three "real" scenarios. The figures are: 94.7% (USA), 98.8% (Eurozone), 98.2% (Hungary). Taking account of these figures and comparing the columns in Tables 2 and 3 one can conclude that the model's estimates are broadly realistic.

Another interesting question is the model's behavior at different levels of inflation. When the inflation rate is 0, almost total price rigidity arises, i.e., after on average 255 periods, none of the firms change their price for very long. On the other hand, in a hyperinflation environment, using the Hungarian inflation data of July 1946, the model produced full price flexibility. These two experiments accidentally prove that the model is not "empty", price stickiness is not a "built-in" feature of it, but can arise in reasonable scenarios.

Sensitivity Analysis

The number of firms (Table 4) is frequently regarded as one facet of the competition on a given market. Somewhat surprisingly increasing the number of firms causes less variability, but average rigidity is left unaffected.

Table 1. Inflation data

	Monthly Inflation (%)	Standard Deviation. of Inflation
USA	0.27	0.36
Eurozone	0.16	0.20
Hungary	0.40	0.69

Table 2. Percentage of prices changed

	Facts	Model Results
USA	36.2	19.8
Eurozone	15.3	12.7
Hungary	24.7	29.8

Table 3. Average duration (months)

	Facts	Model Results
USA	6.8	5.7
Eurozone	13.0	9.5
Hungary	3.8	3.7

Increasing the size of the market produces more flexible prices. This finding can be considered as the missing "extreme" of the previous exercise. Since the model is defined only for N>1, K/N (the per firm size of the market) can be made arbitrarily large only if $K \rightarrow \infty$. Indeed, increasing K beyond the levels shown in Table 5 further reduces price rigidity, whereas decreasing it do not change rigidity too much.

Another interesting parameter is the degree of differentiation (Table 6). In traditional oligopolistic models less differentiation means more intense competition, and one can see that in this agent-based model with strategic uncertainty this translates into more hesitation, and more price rigidity.

Low temperature (Table 7) is equivalent to high selection pressure. Apparently selection pressure affects price rigidity only marginally.

The weight in the fitness function (Table 8) can be considered as "memory". The memory parameter does not seem highly relevant, which is good, since this lends some robustness to our results.

Increasing the mutation rates (Table 9) partly raises uncertainty, partly can help adaptation. Its effect on price rigidity is unequivocal, it makes prices more rigid.

To sum up the sensitivity analysis one can say that the model makes two interesting predictions: larger markets and those with more differentiated products should exhibit less price rigidity. The model appears to be robust with respect to the

Table 4. Sensitivity analysis – number of firms (N)

Number of Firms	Average Duration	Standard Deviation of Duration
5	6.40	3.27
50	6.48	1.39
100	6.10	1.19

Table 5. Sensitivity analysis – scale of demand (K)

Scale of Demand	Average Duration	Standard Deviation of Duration
0.5 times baseline	6.54	2.92
10 times baseline	5.63	2.18
100 times baseline	3.39	0.80

Table 6. Sensitivity analysis – degree of differentiation

Degree of Differentiation	Average Duration	Standard Deviation of Duration
0.1 times baseline	11.07	6.22
0.5 times baseline	7.25	3.08
10 times baseline	6.13	2.84

Table 7. Sensitivity analysis – temperature

Temperature	Average Duration	Standard Deviation of Duration
0.5	6.99	2.98
2	6.61	3.93
5	6.44	2.65

Table 8. Sensitivity analysis – fitness weights

Fitness Weights	Average Duration	Standard Deviation of Duration
9/10	5.95	2.99
3/4	6.24	3.01
1/3	6.07	2.18
1/10	6.29	2.72
1/100	6.11	2.21

Table 9. Sensitivity analysis – mutation rates

Mutation Rates	Average Duration	Standard Deviation of Duration
0.01	3.31	1.09
0.1	7.62	2.97
0.2	10.07	4.91

details of learning process. Uncertainty, as represented by the mutation rates, seems to increase price rigidity.

CONCLUSION

Microeconomic research has, in general, had a dim conclusion for adjustment costs models: each of them seems to be irreconcilable with some salient features of microdata. Our attempt to explain price rigidity by strategic uncertainty of boundedly rational agents is new in the literature. We wish to make sense of the idea that "coordination failure" is a major, though certainly not unique, source of price rigidity

The oligopoly model in which we tried to substantiate our claim is fairly standard, and can be generalized in several directions. For example we made the simple assumption of common marginal costs, but we have checked that individually different marginal costs would not change the results qualitatively.

It is quite promising to see that the model produces sensible results, along several dimensions. First, it reproduces the negative relationship between the level of overall inflation and price rigidity. Second, most prices fall into the theoretical "range" without explicitly building this feature into strategies. Third, price rigidity statistics are even quantitatively similar to actual data.

Obviously, this simple model cannot explain all phenomena concerning oligopolistic price setting. Its extension into several directions would test its robustness. There remains one important feature of data that the model cannot replicate: price wars. To address this issue should be our next concern.

ACKNOWLEDGMENT

The authors would like to thank Dr. Shu-Heng Chen, anonymous referees and participants of the EUMAS 2010 conference, Eastern Economic Association 37th Annual Conference, Agent-Directed Simulation 2011, 16th Annual Workshop on Economic Heterogeneous Interacting Agents, 17th International Conference on Computing in Economics and Finance and SING 7 conference for their comments and suggestions. Robert Somogyi thanks the support of the Hungarian Academy of Sciences under its Momentum program (LD-004/2010).

REFERENCES

Abreu, D., Pearce, D., & Stacchetti, E. (1985). Optimal cartel equilibria with imperfect monitoring. *Journal of Economic Theory*, *39*, 251–269. doi:10.1016/0022-0531(86)90028-1

Anderson, S. P., & de Palma, A. (1992). The logit as a model of product differentiation. *Oxford Economic Papers*, *44*(1), 51–67.

Arifovic, J. (2000). Evolutionary algorithms in macroeconomic models. *Macroeconomic Dynamics*, *4*, 373–414. doi:10.1017/S1365100500016059

Athey, S., Bagwell, K., & Sanchirico, C. W. (2004). Collusion and price rigidity. *The Review of Economic Studies*, *71*(2), 317–349. doi:10.1111/0034-6527.00286

Bauer, P. (2008). Price rigidity on microdata: stylized facts for Hungary [in Hungarian]. *Statisztikai Szemle*, *86*(3), 39–69.

Bils, M., & Klenow, P. (2004). Some evidence on the importance of sticky prices. *The Journal of Political Economy*, *112*(5), 947–985. doi:10.1086/422559

Brenner, T. (2006). Agent learning representation: Advice on modelling economic learning. In Tesfatsion, L., & Judd, K. L. (Eds.), *Handbook of computational economic* (Vol. 2, pp. 895–947). Amsterdam, The Netherlands: Elsevier.

Chen, S. H., & Ni, C. C. (2000). Simulating the ecology of oligopolistic competition with genetic algorithms. *Knowledge and Information Systems, 2*(3), 285–309. doi:10.1007/PL00011644

Dhyne, E., Álvarez, L. J., Bihan, H. L., Veronese, G., Dias, D., & Hoffmann, J. (2005). *Price setting in the euro area: some stylized facts from individual consumer price data.* Frankfurt am Main, Germany: European Central Bank.

Duffy, J. (2006). Agent-based models and human subject experiments. In Tesfatsion, L., & Judd, K. L. (Eds.), *Handbook of computational economics* (*Vol. 2*, pp. 941–1011). Amsterdam, The Netherlands: Elsevier.

Eichenbaum, M., Jaimovich, N., & Rebelo, S. (2011). Reference prices, costs, and nominal rigidities. *The American Economic Review, 101*(1), 234–262. doi:10.1257/aer.101.1.234

Evans, G. W., & Honkapohja, S. (1999). Learning dynamics. In Taylor, J. B., & Woodford, M. (Eds.), *Handbook of macroeconomics I* (*Vol. A*). Amsterdam, The Netherlands: Elsevier.

Fabiani, S., Loupias, C., Martins, F., & Sabbatini, R. (Eds.). (2007). *Pricing decisions in the Euro area.* New York, NY: Oxford University Press. doi:10.1093/acprof:oso/9780195309287.001.0001

Gali, J. (2008). *Monetary policy, inflation, and the business cycle: An Introduction to the new Keynesian framework.* Princeton, NJ: Princeton University Press.

Gigerenzer, G., & Selten, R. (Eds.). (2001). *Bounded rationality: The adaptive toolbox.* Cambridge, MA: MIT Press.

Haupt, R. L., & Haupt, S. E. (2004). *Practical genetic algorithms* (2nd ed.). Hoboken, NJ: John Wiley & Sons.

Heath, B., Hill, R., & Ciarallo, F. (2009). A survey of agent-based modeling practices. *Journal of Artificial Societies and Social Simulation, 12*(4), 9.

Heidhues, P., & Kőszegi, B. (2008). Competition and price variation when consumers are loss averse. *The American Economic Review, 98*, 1245–1268. doi:10.1257/aer.98.4.1245

Kahneman, D., & Tversky, A. (1979). Prospect theory: An analysis of decisions under risk. *Econometrica, 47*(2), 263–291. doi:10.2307/1914185

Klenow, P. J., & Kryvtsov, O. (2008). State-dependent or time-dependent pricing: Does it matter for recent U.S. inflation? *The Quarterly Journal of Economics, 123*(3), 863–904. doi:10.1162/qjec.2008.123.3.863

Kőszegi, B., & Rabin, M. (2006). A model of reference-dependent preferences. *The Quarterly Journal of Economics, 121*, 1133–1166.

LeBaron, B. (2006). Agent-based computational finance. In Tesfatsion, L., & Judd, K. L. (Eds.), *Handbook of computational economics* (*Vol. 2*, pp. 1187–1233). Amsterdam, The Netherlands: Elsevier.

Lünnemann, P., & Wintr, L. (2006). *Are internet prices sticky?* Frankfurt am Main, Germany: European Central Bank.

Mackowiak, B., & Smets, F. (2008). *On implications of micro price data for macro models.* Frankfurt am Main, Germany: European Central Bank.

Midgley, D. F., Marks, R. E., & Cooper, L. G. (1997). Breeding competitive strategies. *Management Science, 43*(3), 257–275. doi:10.1287/mnsc.43.3.257

Nakamura, E., & Steinsson, J. (2008). Five facts about prices: A reevaluation of menu cost models. *The Quarterly Journal of Economics, 123*(4), 1415–1464. doi:10.1162/qjec.2008.123.4.1415

Roberts, J. M. (1995). New Keynesian economics and the Phillips curve. *Journal of Money, Credit and Banking, 27*(4), 975–984. doi:10.2307/2077783

Rogoff, K. (1996). The purchasing power parity puzzle. *Journal of Economic Literature, 34,* 647–668.

Rotemberg, J. J. (in press). Fair pricing. *Journal of the European Economic Association.*

Spiegler, R. (in press). Monopoly pricing when consumers are antagonized by unexpected price increases: A cover version of the Heidhues-Koszegi-Rabin model. *Economic Theory.*

Tesfatsion, L. (2001). Introduction to the special issue on agent-based computational economics. *Journal of Economic Dynamics & Control, 25*(3-4), 281–293. doi:10.1016/S0165-1889(00)00027-0

Tesfatsion, L. (2006). Agent-based computational economics: A constructive approach to economic theory. In Tesfatsion, L., & Judd, K. L. (Eds.), *Handbook of computational economics* (*Vol. 2*, pp. 831–880). Amsterdam, The Netherlands: Elsevier.

This work was previously published in International Journal of Agent Technologies and Systems, Volume 3, Issue 4, edited by Yu Zhang, pp. 57-69, copyright 2011 by IGI Publishing (an imprint of IGI Global).

Section 5
Simulation in Health Sciences

Chapter 14
A Spatial Agent–Based Model of Malaria:
Model Verification and Effects of Spatial Heterogeneity

S. M. Niaz Arifin
University of Notre Dame, USA

Gregory J. Davis
University of Notre Dame, USA

Ying Zhou
University of Notre Dame, USA

ABSTRACT

In agent-based modeling (ABM), an explicit spatial representation may be required for certain aspects of the system to be modeled realistically. A spatial ABM includes landscapes in which agents seek resources necessary for their survival. The spatial heterogeneity of the underlying landscape plays a crucial role in the resource-seeking process. This study describes a previous agent-based model of malaria, and the modeling of its spatial extension. In both models, all mosquito agents are represented individually. In the new spatial model, the agents also possess explicit spatial information. Within a landscape, adult female mosquito agents search for two types of resources: aquatic habitats (AHs) and bloodmeal locations (BMLs). These resources are specified within different spatial patterns, or landscapes. Model verification between the non-spatial and spatial models by means of docking is examined. Using different landscapes, the authors show that mosquito abundance remains unchanged. With the same overall system capacity, varying the density of resources in a landscape does not affect abundance. When the density of resources is constant, the overall capacity drives the system. For the spatial model, using landscapes with different resource densities of both resource-types, the authors show that spatial heterogeneity influences the mosquito population.

DOI: 10.4018/978-1-4666-1565-6.ch014

INTRODUCTION

Agent-based modeling (ABM) can be applied to a domain with or without an explicit representation of *space*. In some cases, however, an explicit spatial representation may be required for certain aspects of the ABM to be modeled more realistically. For example, in a spatial ABM of malaria, events like obtaining a successful bloodmeal (host-seeking) or finding an aquatic habitat to lay eggs (oviposition) can be modeled by utilizing the distribution of corresponding resources in the landscape.

Malaria is one of the top three pathogen-specific causes of global mortality, causing an estimated one million deaths per year, mainly in children (WHO, 2011). Only female mosquitoes of the genus *Anopheles* transmit human malaria, and as such are known as *malaria vectors*. The species *Anopheles gambiae* is the most important malaria vector in Sub-Saharan Africa, and one of the most efficient vectors (in terms of malaria transmission) in the world. Earlier, we developed an agent-based model derived from a conceptual entomological model of the *A. gambiae* lifecycle (Zhou et al., 2010; Arifin et al., 2010a; Gentile, Davis, StLaurent, & Kurtz, 2010). The model, however, was non-spatial: none of the agents and/or environments possessed any spatial attributes.

In this study, we describe a spatial extension of the previous model. Though in both models, all mosquito agents are represented individually, in the new spatial model, the agents also possess explicit spatial information. We show how the previous model and the current spatial model yield consistent results with identical parameter settings (whenever applicable), and hence are docked. We also show how spatial heterogeneity affects some results in the spatial model.

Spatial heterogeneity is considered as one of the most important factors for an effective representation of the environment being modeled. In the discipline of spatial epidemiology (also known as landscape epidemiology), in most cases, the probability of disease transmission significantly declines with distance from an infected host. Thus, the spatial locations of pathogens, hosts and vectors are fundamentally important to disease dynamics (Ostfeld, 2005).

In modeling malaria with ABMs, representation of space may be crucial (Gu, 2009a, 2009b; Menach, 2005). The dynamics of malaria can be subject to substantial local variations that result from various spatial differences (Vries, 2001). Examples of local variations may include locations of aquatic habitats and bloodmeal events, characteristics of mosquitoes, etc. For malaria models, space can be represented as mosquito world, aquatic habitats, etc. for the mosquito agents; and as houses, huts, etc. for the human agents.

In our malaria simulation, some events (e.g., host-seeking, oviposition) by nature require spatial attributes. The underlying spatial heterogeneity defines the spatial distribution of resources, and controls how easily adult female mosquitoes may find resources that are necessary to complete their gonotrophic cycle (the cycle of obtaining bloodmeals and ovipositing eggs). This, in turn, directly affects the mosquito population in the ABM (Arifin, Davis, & Zhou, 2011).

In the previous non-spatial model, the resource-seeking events were modeled with separate probability distributions (to account for travel and search times incurred by adult female mosquitoes), simply because it did not have any explicit *space* (Zhou et al., 2010; Arifin et al., 2010a; Gentile, Davis, StLaurent, & Kurtz, 2010). For example, host-seeking and oviposition events were modeled with 25% probability of success in each hour of searching (the value of 25% was chosen as a baseline and not meant to be absolute). The spatial model, however, provides opportunities to spatially model these events by coupling them with the corresponding locations of resources in the landscape. This concept can be generalized whenever an agent needs to seek for a resource.

One of the primary goals of this study is model verification, which is achieved in part by *docking* of the non-spatial and spatial models. Docking, also known as *alignment, replication, cross-model validation*, or *model-to-model comparison*, is a form of verification & validation (V&V) that tries to align multiple models (Kennedy et al., 2006; Xiang, Kennedy, Madey, & Cabaniss, 2005). In the past, we showed how to obtain a successful dock between separate implementations of our malaria ABMs (Arifin, Davis, Zhou, & Madey, 2010b; Arifin et al., 2010a). In this study, we show that docking significantly helps in model verification.

In spatial ABMs, space can be represented in a variety of ways. For example, Bian (2003) categorized *grid* and *patch* as the two fundamentally different data models to represent space. A grid consists of a finite number of regular cells. In the patch model, space is partitioned according to landscape features (e.g., patches, corridors, and nodes). We represent space with a discrete, finite-sized grid model.

We broadly categorize the ABMs of malaria into non-spatial and spatial models. The non-spatial models do not model space explicitly (e.g., Janssen & Martens, 1997). These models either represent space abstractly (e.g., a *point* space), or assume various statistical distributions to model various spatial features (e.g., 25% probability of successful completion of a specific event). We emphasize that some models in this category may include abstract spatial representation in various (non-trivial) forms, but agents (in these models) do not possess explicit spatial attributes, and/or the choices made by the agents, i.e., the effects of actions performed by the agents, do not reflect the direct use of any spatial feature. The spatial models, on the other hand, explicitly model space, and the agents, as well as their environments, have explicit spatial coordinates.

The organization of this paper is as follows: we begin by discussing some of the previous works involving non-spatial and spatial ABMs of malaria. Then, we briefly describe our non-spatial and spatial malaria models. For the spatial model, we describe the mosquito agents and their spatial movement, the landscapes in which the agents move, the modeling aspects of the resource-seek-ing events, and a graphical user interface named *AnophGUI*. We compare simulation results from the two models, and present additional results from the spatial model. We also demonstrate the effects of spatial heterogeneity. Finally, we discuss future directions and present some concluding remarks.

NON-SPATIAL ABMS OF MALARIA

Janssen and Martens (1997) describe a model that simulates the adaptation of mosquitoes and parasites to available pesticides and drugs. They couple genetic algorithms with the model to simulate the evolving processes within the mosquito and parasite populations.

McKenzie, Wong, and Bossert (1998) develop a discrete-event simulation model using a single timeline variable to represent the parasite lifecycle in individual hosts and vectors within interacting host and vector populations. That work is further advanced by embedding a differential-equation model of parasite-immune system interactions within each of the individual humans represented in the discrete-event model (McKenzie & Bossert, 2005).

Depinay et al. (2004) present an individual-based simulation model of African malaria vectors that incorporates knowledge of the mechanisms underlying *Anopheles* population dynamics and their relations to the environment. Results show that the model can reproduce some broad, diverse patterns found in the field, allowing detailed analyses and explanations of vector population dynamics. Though the model represents individual locations in space, the choices (e.g., of selecting an oviposition or bloodmeal site) made do not reflect relative distance, attractiveness, wind or other features, i.e., the spatial features remain unused.

Menach, McKenzie, Flahault, and Smith (2005) describe a mathematical model for malaria epidemiology on heterogeneous landscapes. It demonstrates that oviposition is one potential factor explaining heterogeneous biting and vector distribution in a landscape with a heterogeneous distribution of larval habitats, concluding that larval density may be a misleading indicator of a habitat's importance for malaria control.

SPATIAL ABMS OF MALARIA

Vries (2001) presents a spatially-explicit individual-based malaria model that relates various factors to transmission and disease risks, and examines the disease dynamics in human population in the spatial context (the term *individual-based model* is used almost interchangeably with *agent-based model*; individual-based models are simulations based on the global consequences of local interactions of members (agents) of a population). Gu and Novak (2009a) develop a spatial agent-based model to track the status and movement of individual mosquitoes in heterogeneous landscapes. They represent mosquito foraging as a two-stage process: random flight when the resource is not within the mosquito's perception range and directional flight to the resource once the resource is detected. Designing different landscapes, with different arrangements of houses and aquatic habitats and scenarios of source reduction, they conclude that mosquito foraging might be a promising target for malaria control using source reduction, and distance to the nearest houses can be the primary measure for habitat targeting. They extend the spatial model to predict the impact of insecticide-treated bed nets (ITNs) on malaria transmission (Gu & Novak, 2009b). Results show that applications of ITNs could give rise to varying impacts on population-level metrics, highlighting the fact that increased ITN coverage led to significant reduction in risk exposure and malaria incidence only when treated nets yielded high killing effects.

THE AGENT-BASED MODELS

In this section, we briefly describe our malaria ABMs. A detailed description of the non-spatial model (that this study extends), including the description of relevant constants and concepts, and the origin of the functional forms of the equations, can be found in Zhou et al. (2010), Arifin et al. (2010a), and Gentile, Davis, Laurent, and Kurtz (2010). Here, we only describe a subset of the concepts and equations, which are especially relevant for this study.

The mosquito agents, represented individually in both models, go through several states in their lifecycle, as shown in Figure 1. Aquatic mosquitoes live in the aquatic habitats (also known as *breeding sites* in the literature). They go through *Egg, Larva* and *Pupa* states before they turn into adults (this event is known as *emergence*).

Adult mosquitoes live in the mosquito world. They emerge into the *Immature Adult* state. In the *Mate Seeking* state, a male and female pair mates. Adult males spend the rest of their lives in this state until they die. Adult females go out in search of human bloodmeals (the *Bloodmeal Seeking* state). Once an adult female finds a bloodmeal, she rests until her eggs are developed (the *Bloodmeal Digesting* state). In the *Gravid* state, the female tries to lay her eggs. Once all her eggs are laid, she transitions to the *Bloodmeal Seeking* state again, and this cycle (known as the *gonotrophic cycle*) of obtaining bloodmeals and ovipositing eggs continues until the female dies.

At each state, the mortality of mosquito agents is modeled using either constant or variable (age-specific) mortality rates (for details, see Arifin et al., 2010a). Thus, mosquito agents may die out in any of the lifecycle states (Figure 1). Traditionally, some ABMs depict the death events by adding appropriate *sinks* to the corresponding states. In our model, agents may die in any of the states. For simplicity, we chose not to add the sinks with the states in Figure 1.

Figure 1. Lifecycle of mosquito agents (both males and females) in the ABM. Each oval represents a state in the model. The rectangles represent durations for the fixed-duration states. The symbol 'h' denotes hour. States with temperature-dependent duration are described in Table 1. Permissible time transition windows (from one state to another) are shown next to the corresponding state transition arrows as rounded rectangles. We assume that 'death' sinks capture the agents that die out in each state, and omit these sinks from the figure for simplicity. Note that adult males, once reaching the Mate Seeking state, remain forever in that state until they die; adult females, on the other hand, cycle through obtaining bloodmeals (in Bloodmeal Seeking state), developing eggs (in Bloodmeal Digesting state), and ovipositing these eggs (in Gravid state) until they die

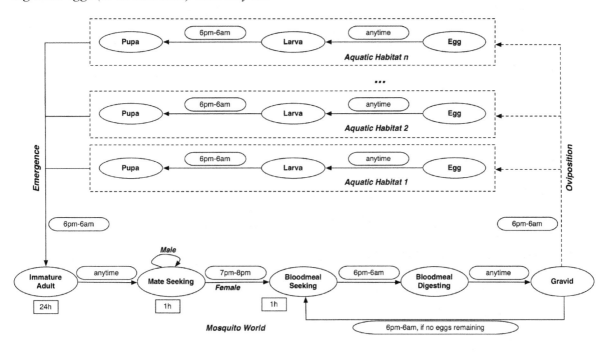

Egg, Larva, Pupa, and *Bloodmeal Digesting* are considered as states with temperature-dependent duration because the state-durations (in hours) depend on the hourly temperature T (in °C). For durations of these states, we define some linear functions that closely resemble the biology of *A. gambiae*:

$$\text{duration}_{\text{incubation}} = -0.923 * T + 60.923$$

$$\text{duration}_{\text{hatch}} \in [1, 240]$$

The state-durations are shown in Table 1. Larval development follows a stochastic thermodynamic model (Depinay et al., 2004):

$$\text{development}_{\text{hour}} = T * 0.000305 - 0.003285$$

where the hourly temperature T (in °C) is restricted in the range [14, 37].

Bloodmeal Seeking and *Gravid* are also considered variable-duration states. However, the state-durations (in hours) of these states do not depend on temperature. They depend on successfully finding a host for a bloodmeal and an aquatic habitat for laying eggs, respectively.

Table 1. Temperature-dependent durations for some of the states

State	Duration (in hours)
Egg	$duration_{incubation} + duration_{hatch}$
Pupa	$duration_{incubation}$
Bloodmeal Digesting	-1.231 * T + 77.231

In the remainder of this section, we describe some terms that are relevant to the spatial ABM, and are used throughout the rest of the paper.

Biomass: the biomass of an aquatic habitat is defined as the sum of the number of eggs, $Eggs_{habitat}$, the one-day old equivalent larval population, N_e, and the number of pupae, $Pupae_{habitat}$, in the habitat:

$$biomass = Eggs_{habitat} + N_e + Pupae_{habitat} \qquad (1)$$

- **Carrying Capacity (CC):** in population biology, carrying capacity is defined as the environment's maximal load (Hui, 2006). It represents the population size of a biological species that the environment can sustain indefinitely, given the available resources (food, water etc.) in the environment. In our models, the carrying capacity (CC), measured in units of *biomass* sustainable by the aquatic habitat, is defined similarly. It is used to model the *Gravid* female mosquito agents' inclination to avoid less suitable aquatic habitats. It limits the number of eggs she may oviposit in that habitat, and is not treated as a hard limit. As suggested by Equation 2, the *biomass* and the CC together determine soft limits on larval density in the aquatic habitat.

- **Combined Carrying Capacity (CCC):** for a given landscape with multiple aquatic habitats, the combined carrying capacity (CCC) is defined as the sum of the CCs of all aquatic habitats. Since the combined aquatic population (controlled by CC in each aquatic habitat) eventually limits the extent of adult population, CCC effectively represents the overall capacity of the system.

- **Resource Density:** for a given landscape with multiple resources, resource density of a particular resource-type is defined as the percentage of total area in the landscape occupied by objects of that resource-type. For example, considering aquatic habitats as the resource-type, a 5 * 10 landscape with 25 AHs have 50% AH-Density.

- **Average Travel Time (ATT):** for a given landscape, the average travel time (ATT) is defined as the average time (in hours) taken by an adult female mosquito to successfully find a resource (of a particular resource-type). In this study, though we do not explicitly measure ATT, it reflects a statistically-expected measure, and affects the simulation results (as described later).

- **Oviposition:** when an adult female finds an aquatic habitat to lay eggs, the potential number of eggs, $Eggs_{potential}$, that she may preferentially lay, is regulated by both the carrying capacity CC and the biomass already present in the habitat:

$$Eggs_{potential} = Eggs_{max} * \left(1 - \frac{biomass}{i*CC}\right) \qquad (2)$$

where $Eggs_{max}$ is the maximum number of eggs she may lay, and i is the oviposition attempt number. For details, see Arifin, Davis, Zhou, and Madey (2010b).

- **Vector Abundance (VA):** it denotes the total number of adult female mosquito (vector) agents in a simulation. For all simulations in this study, we consider VA as the primary output of interest. For each simulation timestep (measured in hours), we keep track of VA by counting the aggregate total of adult female agents across every cell in the landscape.

THE NON-SPATIAL MODEL

In the non-spatial model (Zhou et al., 2010; Arifin et al., 2010a; Gentile, Davis, Laurent, & Kurtz, 2010), the resources (bloodmeal locations and aquatic habitats) and the agents (mosquitoes) have *no* spatial locations. Adult female mosquitoes find resources at random. To model this random behavior, we use uniform statistical distributions generated by Repast pseudo-random numbers generator library (Repast, 2011). All simulation events, including emergence, host-seeking and oviposition, occur without any spatial context.

For example, oviposition is probability-based. During each (simulation) hour, a *Gravid* female tries to find an aquatic habitat with 25% probability of success. As long as the female has remaining eggs to lay, she is allowed to make at most 3 attempts per 12 hours (each night). This, in turn, translates to 25% chance of finding an aquatic habitat per hour.

THE SPATIAL MODEL

The spatial model provides an extension in space of the previous non-spatial model. In this section, we describe the model, and its main features, which include the mosquito agents, the landscapes, the movement and resource-seeking events of adult female mosquito agents across the landscapes, and a graphical user interface (GUI) that facilitates the specification of resources within the landscapes.

Figure 2 depicts a simplified class diagram of the spatial ABM, illustrating its four major classes and attributes. An instance of the MosquitoAgent class represents an individual mosquito agent. An instance of the SimulationModel class runs the

simulation, keeps track of the simulation time, instantiates initial mosquito agents (and places them to different spatial locations), and writes data to output files. It also contains a reference to the spatial grid (landscape), and instantiates the resource objects by interpreting the locations (and other properties) of the resources as specified in an input xml file. Instances of the Bloodmeal-Location and AquaticHabitat classes represent both resource-types (bloodmeal locations and the aquatic habitats, respectively), each instance having its spatial location and other attributes (e.g., carrying capacity of an aquatic habitat). In addition, the SimulationModel instance contains an adultAgentList, which has references to all adult agents.

As stated before, the aquatic agents are born and developed in the aquatic habitats. Each AquaticHabitat instance contains an aquaticAgentList, which is used to reference the aquatic agents in that specific aquatic habitat. When (a subset of) aquatic agents turn into adult agents (via emergence, see Figure 1), they are transferred from the respective aquaticAgentList to the adultAgentList (of the SimulationModel instance).

Agents

In the spatial model, all agents (mosquitoes and resources) possess explicit spatial information. Each mosquito agent is represented individually. The movement, lifecycle, and resource-seeking events (primarily host-seeking and oviposition for adult female mosquitoes) for the agents are also tracked individually. At any given timestep, the location of each individual agent (male or female, adult or aquatic) can be tracked.

The adult female mosquito agents also exhibit *mobility*: in order to seek resources, they move around from one cell to another within the environment (landscape). The locations of resources are specified within different spatial patterns, or landscapes. However, the adult male mosquitoes, as well as the aquatic mosquitoes (both male and

Figure 2. A simplified class diagram of the spatial agent-based model. The ABM consists of four major classes: SimulationModel, AquaticHabitat, BloodmealLocation and MosquitoAgent. Only major attributes and operations are shown. Aggregation relationships are indicated by hollow diamonds on the containing class end. The star represents multiplicity value (zero or more). A bi-directional association is indicated by a line (between the two classes). A uni-directional association is indicated by a line with an arrowhead

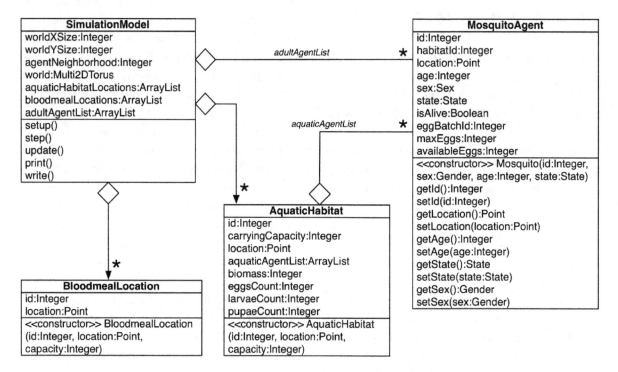

Movement of Adult Female Agents

female, being born and developed in different aquatic habitats), do not move. We prefer to avoid their movements in order to exclude unnecessary details from the ABM. As described before, once the adult males reach the *Mate Seeking* state (Figure 1), they rest forever in the state until they die.

The primary reason for movement of adult female mosquito agents is to seek for resources (bloodmeal locations or aquatic habitats) in order to complete the gonotrophic cycle. For reasons of both simulation speed and biological reality, in our spatial model, adult female mosquitoes move only while they are in *Bloodmeal Seeking* and *Gravid* states. New agents, in the form of eggs,

possess the same spatial location as that of the aquatic habitat in which they are oviposited. Each *Gravid* female may travel one cell per hour and reach one out of eight possible neighboring cells (a Moore neighborhood) or remain in the current cell. For the purpose of this study, the direction of movement into one of the cells of the Moore neighborhood is assumed as random.

In some studies, the mosquito foraging behavior (i.e., the search for hosts and oviposition sites) has been modeled using a combination of methods (rather than using a pure random walk). For example, Gu and Novak (2009a) modeled foraging as a two-stage process: a random flight when the resource site is not within the mosquito's perception range, and a directional flight to the resource site once it is detected. However, the physical distance at which mosquitoes may locate and thus respond to a certain resource site is not well understood, and the limited available field data points to short ranges of mosquito perception (e.g., Gillies, & Wilkes, 1969; Bidlingmayera & Hem, 1980). The inadequate perception of resources suggests that mosquitoes, with reference to their current physical location, have limited ability to explore resource sites, and thus, a random walk through the landscape is a good approximation of the mosquito foraging behavior. Motivated by these, we chose to employ a pure random walk for the mosquito agents when they move through the landscape in search for resource sites.

Landscape

A landscape is used to represent the grid space necessary for the locations and movement of adult female mosquito agents. Resources, in the forms of bloodmeal locations and aquatic habitats, are contained within the landscape. The density and spatial distribution of both types of resources inherently define the spatial heterogeneity of resources within the landscape.

Denoted by its dimensions m * n, a landscape is defined as a collection of m horizontal rows and n vertical columns, and has m * n number of cells. Each cell, with its spatial attributes, may represent a specific resource (an aquatic habitat or a bloodmeal location) or be part of the (adult)

mosquito world. We model landscapes as 2D torus objects, allowing agents to re-appear once they hit the boundaries. For simplicity, we assume that each resource can occupy *exactly* one cell in a landscape.

Resource density of a landscape is regulated by using different dimensions. For example, considering aquatic habitats (AHs), placing 25 AHs in a 10 * 10 landscape produces 25% AH-Density; and placing the same number of AHs in a 5 * 10 landscape produces 50% AH-Density.

We report results that use three types of landscapes (Figure 3):

- **Regular:** the spatial distribution of resources within the entire landscape follows a regular, well-defined pattern; every (non-empty) row and column, which has resources, contains the *same* number of resources. Horizontal and vertical distances between any two neighboring resources always remain the same.
- **Random:** resources are placed randomly following a uniform *random* distribution.
- **Hybrid:** a blend of the previous two; every (non-empty) row contains the same number of resources; within a (non-empty) row, however, they are placed randomly, thus allowing control to both density and randomness.

*Figure 3. Different landscapes used for the spatial model. Each black circle represents a spatial resource (e.g., an aquatic habitat), and each white (empty) rectangle represents a cell in the mosquito world. Sub-figures (a), (b), and (c) depict examples of regular, random, and hybrid landscapes, respectively. Dimension of each landscape is 4 * 8. (a) and (b) has 25% resource density each; (c) has 37.5% resource density*

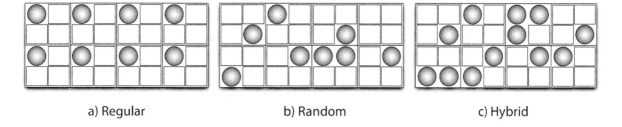

a) Regular   b) Random   c) Hybrid

Resource-seeking Events

The resource-seeking behavior of adult female mosquito agents encompasses two frequent events in our ABMs, namely, host-seeking and oviposition. One primary purpose of this study is to *spatially* model these resource-seeking events, and then to compare results from different models. To model these events, we replace probability-based measures by spatial, distance-based measures. The 25% probability of finding a resource site (in the non-spatial model) is replaced by specifying the adult female mosquito's speed of movement as well as the density distributions of the resources in the corresponding landscape.

In this study, we pay special attention in modeling oviposition. According to Menach (2005), oviposition is one potential factor explaining heterogeneous biting and vector distribution in a landscape with a heterogeneous distribution of habitats. Female mosquitoes tend to aggregate around places where they oviposit, thereby increasing the risk of malaria there, regardless of the suitability of the habitat for larval development (Menach, 2005). Thus, even if an aquatic habitat is unsuitable for mosquito emergence, it can be a significant source for malaria.

AnophGUI: a Graphical User Interface

To facilitate the specification of parameters to the spatial model, we have built a graphical user interface (GUI), named AnophGUI. For a specific landscape composed of hundreds of resources, it automates the task of generating spatial attributes (e.g., location, capacity, etc.) for these resources. Figure 4 shows a screenshot of AnophGUI, and the landscape generated according to the specified parameters.

AnophGUI allows the user to specify the simulation parameters (e.g., length of run) and the relevant weather parameters (e.g., temperature). For spatial models, the user may also select different landscapes, and modify the spatial attributes of a resource. Once the user selects a particular landscape, the resource table, as shown at the bottom-right corner of Figure 4(a), is automatically populated, depending on the number of resources and the size of the landscape.

Simulations: Assumptions and Notation

In all simulation runs, we assume the following convention: **AH** denotes an aquatic habitat, **BML** denotes a bloodmeal location (bloodmeal host), **CC** denotes individual carrying capacity of an aquatic habitat, **CCC** denotes the combined carrying capacity, and **VA** denotes vector abundance. The x-axis denotes simulation time (in days), and the y-axis denotes VA. In describing figures, we refer to a specific graph by the legend used (e.g., Non-Spatial, 25%). All simulations are run for at least 365 days (though in most cases we present only relevant portions of the results) with 1000 initial adult mosquitoes (500 males and 500 females), and no initial eggs in any AH. Male-female ratio of new mosquitoes is assumed to be 1:1.

MODEL VERIFICATION

One of the primary goals of this study is to perform model verification by comparing outputs of the non-spatial model to the spatial model. Model validation, however, is not a significant part of this study; for details about model validation that we performed on these ABMs, see Arifin, Davis, Zhou, and Madey (2010a) and Arifin et al. (2010b).

In this section, we present results of model verification, which is done primarily by means of docking. As stated before, docking is a method for V&V that tries to align multiple models. Kennedy et al. (2006) achieved V&V through docking in two separate case studies involving both agent- and equation-based models. Xiang, Kennedy, Madey, and Cabaniss (2005) performed V&V

Figure 4. AnophGUI: Sub-figure (a) shows a screenshot of the GUI. Sub-figure (b) shows the generated landscape. In the landscape, each black circle represents an aquatic habitat, and each gray rectangle represents a bloodmeal location. For both resource-types (AH and BML), the same number of resource objects is generated. This example resembles a landscape with contiguous water bodies (e.g., a marsh or wetland) in the center, surrounded by human habitats at random distances from the water bodies

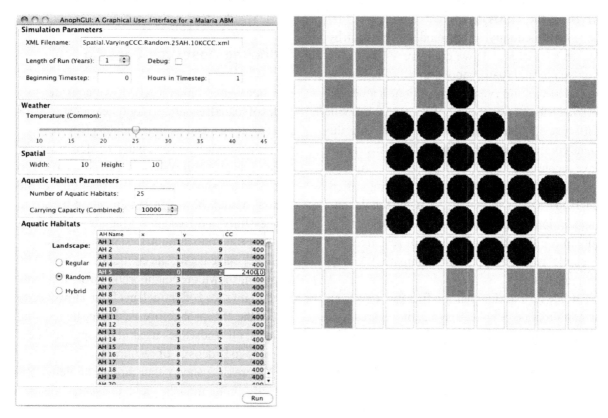

a) AnophGUI screenshot   b) the generated landscape

on an agent-based stochastic model involving the behavior of NOM (natural organic matter), highlighting the use of docking.

For our malaria ABMs, we presented a three-phase docking process that produced agreement in models' output and served the dual purpose of increasing confidence to the core malaria model and revealing errors in model implementations (Arifin, Davis, Zhou, & Madey, 2010b). Later, following a *Divide and Conquer* paradigm, we obtained a successful dock between four separate implementations that sprung from the same core model (Arifin et al., 2010a).

The process of model verification, as described in our earlier studies mentioned required substantial evaluations and re-evaluations of all ABMs (including the non-spatial and spatial models). However, with iterative refinements performed in several phases, the ABMs successively produced more *similar* outputs, which were in increasing agreement among themselves. Hence, the close agreement in model verification results presented in this section (between the non-spatial and spatial models, and between different but comparable scenarios of the spatial model itself) reflects successful cases of model verification performed on the

ABMs (as opposed to potential inadvertent biases introduced by poor experimental or setup design in obtaining *similar* outputs from the ABMs).

In this study, we conduct several experiments, all of which compare outputs (vector abundance, VA) from the ABMs in different settings. The first two experiments investigate model verification by means of docking: 1) we compare VA from the non-spatial and spatial models in which one of the resource-seeking events, oviposition, is modeled in two different ways; and 2) we compare VA with different number of aquatic habitats having the same combined carrying capacity CCC in order to investigate the effect of relative sizes of resources.

Then, to investigate the effect of using different landscapes, we compare VA using regular and random landscapes for the spatial model. Lastly, to explore the effect of density of resources (of a single resource-type), we compare VA with increasing CCC.

It is worth noting that the first few dips seen in adult female populations (e.g., in Figures 5, 6, and 7) can be attributed as artifacts of the simulation warm-up period. For example, the first dip (at around days 10 to 15) is due to deaths of the initial cohort of adults (all of which started with the same age). The second dip (at around days 25 to 30) is due to deaths of the first cohort of

surviving adults (that emerged from immature states), followed by a rise caused by the next cohort. The subsequent dips, diminished successively in magnitude, reflect deaths and emergence of subsequent cohorts as the system approaches to the steady state.

Modeling Resource-Seeking

For our spatial malaria ABM, we consider two types of spatial resources: bloodmeal locations (for host-seeking), and aquatic habitats (for oviposition). In the (earlier) non-spatial model, resource-seeking is probability-based: a female mosquito may find a resource with 25% probability. In the spatial model, however, it is location-based: to successfully find a resource, a female has to search for it by traveling through the landscape. Starting from her current cell, she continues the search by exploring the Moore neighborhood around the cell, with flight speed of one cell per hour. However, to match the 25% probability used in the non-spatial models, all landscapes used in the spatial model possess 25% density of resources.

Figure 5(a) shows that though modeled differently, both models yield consistent results: the 25% probability of finding resources in the non-spatial model is accurately transformed to

Figure 5. Model verification: Sub-figure (a) shows the results of modeling oviposition in two different ways (probability-based in the non-spatial model vs. distance-based in the spatial model). Both models yield consistent results with identical parameter settings. Sub-figure (b) shows that the use of different landscapes (regular and random) in the spatial model does not significantly alter the population levels. Each graph represents the average of 40 simulation runs, and shows only portions of the one-year simulation results

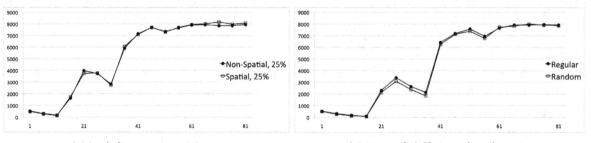

a) Modeling oviposition   b) Use of different landscapes

25% density of resources in the spatial model. To some extent, this helps in model verification, confirming that given other parameters unaltered, with the frequent events modeled in different ways, both models produce similar results, and hence are *docked*.

Relative Sizes of Resources

Next, for both the non-spatial and spatial models, we vary the relative sizes of the AHs in landscapes that all have the same CCC. Size of an AH is determined by its carrying capacity CC. For the spatial model, we use landscapes composed of one large AH vs. many smaller AHs. To construct different cases, the numbers of AHs are increased as squares of the first 10 integers (1 through 10). In all cases, for both models, we use the same AH-Density.

In Figure 6, we compare results for only 1, 16, 49, and 100 AHs in both models (other results show similar trends). As evident from the mean VA level (~8000), once CCC is kept constant, VA does not change significantly if the number of AHs is varied. Also, in all cases, a larger AH can produce n times adult population than the (individual) adult population produced by n smaller AHs.

We also find that in Figure 6(b), until the systems reach equilibrium at around day 60, the non-spatial models ($VA_{Non-spatial, 49 AH}$ and $VA_{Non-spatial, 100 AH}$) always have equal or higher abundances than the spatial models ($VA_{Spatial, 49 AH}$ and $VA_{Spatial, 100 AH}$). We attribute this to the travel time required by adult female agents in the spatial models: the need to search for resource sites, and hence the additional time delays incurred to complete the host-seeking and oviposition events, cause the spatial models to produce less abundances than the non-spatial models (in which agents do not require to travel in space to complete these events, as explained before). After equilibrium, the AHs gradually become *fuller* by new aquatic agents. Thus, governed by Equation (2), in an AH, the

competition perceived by the *Gravid* females (to find a chance to lay their eggs in that AH) increases, and $Eggs_{potential}$ decreases (as the biomass of the AH successively increases). This does not impact the overall abundance of the system, however, which is already in equilibrium and hence has a steady, saturated flow of newly-emerged adult agents from the AHs. Thus, after equilibrium, the models yield *similar* abundances.

Regular vs. Random Landscapes

For the spatial model, we compare VA using two different landscapes, *regular* and *random*. Both landscapes have the same number (100) and density (25%) of AHs, and the same CCC. As shown in Figure 5(b), in these settings, different landscapes do *not* affect the mean (stabilized) abundance (~8000).

It should be noted that in this experiment, due to the use of relatively small landscapes (all having dimensions 20 * 20) and relatively high resource densities (with 25% densities of aquatic habitats), we obtained statistically averaged similarities between landscapes with different distributions (regular vs. random). However, this may change with relatively larger landscapes having relatively lower resource densities, in which cases, the different (and sparser) distributions of the resources, and hence the spatial heterogeneity, may yield radically different abundances in these landscapes. Consider, for example, 100 * 100 landscapes with only 5% AH-Density (i.e., with 500 aquatic habitats), in which the random landscape contains some isolated aquatic habitats having none or very few bloodmeal locations within their proximity. In this case, VA_{random} is expected to be much lower than $VA_{regular}$, since, in the random landscape, the adult female agents, originating from the isolated aquatic habitats, have to travel much longer to find bloodmeal locations (and thus to complete their gonotrophic cycles).

Density of Resources

For the spatial model, we consider the density of a single resource-type: the aquatic habitats. We compare VA with varying number of AHs in 10 * 10 hybrid landscapes. In this setting, as the number of AHs increase in a landscape, so does its AH-Density. In all cases, the same CCC (100K)

is used. The numbers of AHs are increased from 10 to 80, in increments of 10.

Figure 7 shows the results for 10%, 30%, 50%, and 80% AH-Density cases (other cases show similar trends), highlighting the fact that with the same CCC, varying the AH-Density does not affect mean population significantly. However, two interesting observations are made:

Figure 6. Model verification: exploring the effects of relative sizes of resources. Results from non-spatial and spatial models are shown as solid and dashed lines, respectively. Once CCC is kept constant, the relative sizes of multiple AHs do not affect the results. Each graph represents the average of 40 simulation runs, and shows only portions of the one-year simulation results

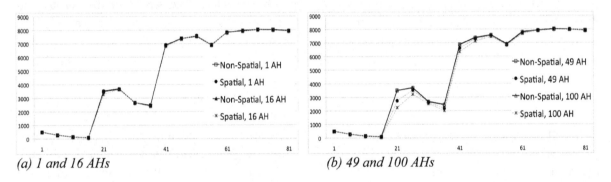

(a) 1 and 16 AHs   *(b) 49 and 100 AHs*

*Figure 7. Results of varying density of resources: once CCC is kept constant (100K), increasing the number of AHs (thus also increasing the AH-Density) only slightly increases the mean population. In all cases, 10 * 10 hybrid landscapes are used. Each graph represents the average of 40 simulation runs, and shows only portions of the one-year simulation results*

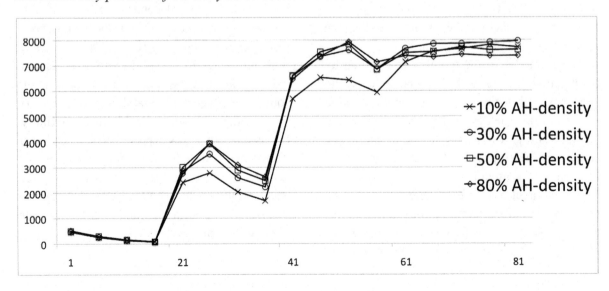

- Until the population reaches equilibrium (at around day 60), $VA_{10\%}$ is less than $VA_{30\%}$, $VA_{50\%}$ and $VA_{80\%}$: due to lower AH-Density, ATT (Average Travel Time) increases, and becomes a limiting factor. For example, in $VA_{10\%}$, a *Gravid* female agent has to search larger number of cells (on average) to find a resource than in the other three higher-density cases. Thus, in $VA_{10\%}$, less number of females may find a chance to lay eggs.

- After equilibrium, $VA_{30\%} > VA_{50\%} > VA_{80\%}$: as AH-Density increases, CC (per AH) and ATT decrease. However, with increasing AH-Density, even though *Gravid* females find opportunities to visit AHs more frequently, they are *more restricted* to lay eggs, as governed by Equation (2). In this case, ATT no longer being a factor in successfully finding a resource, smaller capacities (CCs) of larger number of AHs (higher AH-Densities) dominate in restricting the abundances.

Varying System Capacity

For the spatial model, we vary CCC with same-sized AHs in 10 * 10 random landscapes. In this setting, the AH-Density remains the same (25%) across all landscapes. As the results indicate in Figure 8, CCC indeed drives abundance: in all cases, as CCC is gradually increased from 10K to 80K, mean VA increases at a steady rate.

SPATIAL HETEROGENEITY

In our spatial malaria ABM, spatial heterogeneity encompasses the distribution and relative distances between various resources sought by the adult female mosquito agents within a given landscape. As shown by the following results, spatial heterogeneity, in some cases, may directly influence the mosquito population level. For each resource-type, it is controlled by two parameters: *resource density* and *resource distribution*. In this section, we only analyze how *resource density* affects the population. We use landscapes with different resource-densities of both resource-types

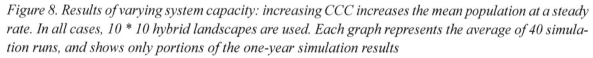

*Figure 8. Results of varying system capacity: increasing CCC increases the mean population at a steady rate. In all cases, 10 * 10 hybrid landscapes are used. Each graph represents the average of 40 simulation runs, and shows only portions of the one-year simulation results*

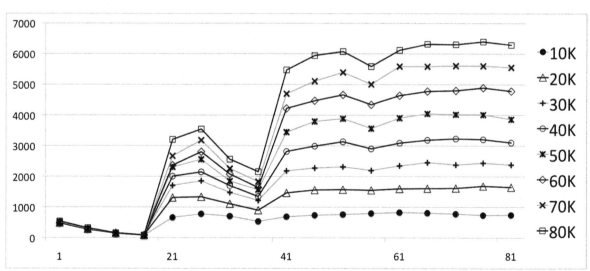

(BMLs and AHs), and also with varying CCCs. For this section, we denote each landscape by the tuple *(#AH, #BML, CCC)*, where *#AH* and *#BML* denote the number of AHs and BMLs in the landscape, respectively.

We found that VA in our spatial model is eventually driven by two parameters: 1) ATT (Average Travel Time) and 2) CCC. ATT is inversely proportional to resource-densities. Since female mosquitoes must travel through the landscape in order to search for resources, ATT can increase or decrease with decreasing or increasing resource-densities, respectively. Thus, considering two (hypothetical) landscapes L_{sparse} and L_{dense} (both having the same dimensions), where L_{dense} has more resource-densities than L_{sparse}, adult females in L_{sparse} would incur higher ATT than that incurred in L_{dense}. In terms of the mosquito population, this translates to the degree of ease with which adult female mosquitoes may find resources. Thus, in landscapes with the same dimensions, as we increase resource-densities, ATT gradually declines until resource-densities reaches a critical level, which we call the *critical resource-densities*.

Until the landscape possesses enough resources to reach the critical resource-densities, the abundance depends on both resource-densities and CCC. The less are the resource-densities, the higher is the ATT (and vice versa). However, if the landscape has resource-densities that exceed the critical levels, ATT may no longer affect the resource-seeking behavior.

However, if the landscape possesses enough resources at or above the critical resource-densities, abundance is driven primarily by CCC; and does not change significantly until CCC is changed (irrespective of increasing the resource-densities at that point as long as it remains at or above the critical level).

In this study, though we do not empirically measure the average travel times or the critical resource-densities for different landscapes, our preliminary simulation results confirm to the above insight. We start with different landscapes that all

possess resource-densities at or above the critical level. As the resource-densities of both resource-types are increased (keeping the same dimensions and the same CCC), we found that abundance remains unchanged until the CCC is changed. For example, using 10 * 10 landscapes with 20K CCC each, and denoting each landscape (as mentioned above) by the tuple *(#AH, #BML, CCC)*, we found that *(10, 10, 20K)*, *(10, 20, 20K)*, *(20, 10, 20K)*, and *(20, 20, 20K)* all yield the same VA (~3000). In these cases, increasing the resource-densities (by increasing the number of resources, e.g., from 10 to 20 AHs) does not affect VA (note that these landscapes already had resource-densities above the critical level). Abundance, in these cases, is primarily controlled by CCC. Similarly, using the same dimensions, as CCC is increased to 40K, landscapes *(20, 10, 40K)* and *(20, 20, 40K)* also yield the same VA (~6000). Again, abundance is limited by CCC and not by resource-densities. We omit these results for space constraints.

Given these initial results, we decided to explore the effect of resource-densities in a larger landscape (30 * 30). In Figure 9, we show two sample landscapes with resource-densities beyond and above the critical level, which are used for the results presented in Figure 10.

First, we explore the case with resource-densities beyond the critical level. As shown in Figure 10(a), as we increase the AH-density (keeping BML-density and CCC unchanged, i.e., with 20 BMLs and 30K CCC in all cases), VA increases and eventually reaches ~4500. This substantiates the first part of our previous claim: as resource-density is increased and is kept *beyond* the critical level, ATT gradually declines, and, as a result, VA successively increases.

We also make two observations in Figure 10(a): 1) the rate of rise in VA is *always* faster with higher resource-density cases; and 2) with a single aquatic habitat, the population dies out – due to the fact that it is too insufficient to maintain a sustainable mosquito population within the relatively larger dimensions (30 * 30) of the landscape.

Figure 9. Two sample 30 * 30 landscapes with variable resource-densities. Each black circle represents an aquatic habitat, and each gray rectangle represents a bloodmeal location. Sub-figure (a) shows a landscape with resource-densities beyond the critical level (with 50 AHs and 20 BMLs). Sub-figure (b) shows a landscape with resource-densities above the critical level (with 100 AHs and 100 BMLs). Similar landscapes are used for results presented in Figure 10

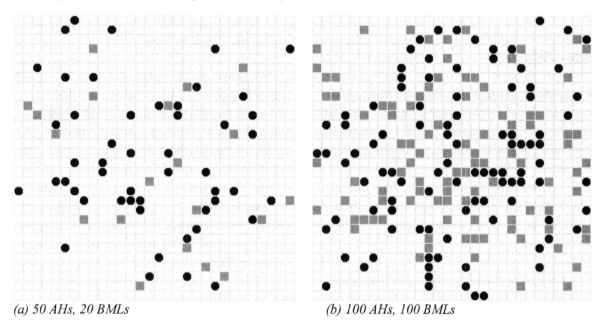

(a) 50 AHs, 20 BMLs   *(b) 100 AHs, 100 BMLs*

Figure 10. Effect of resource density in 30 * 30 landscapes with 30K CCC. Two sample landscapes (with resource-densities beyond and above the critical level) used for these results are shown in Figure 9. Each graph represents a single simulation run, and shows only portions of the one-year simulation results

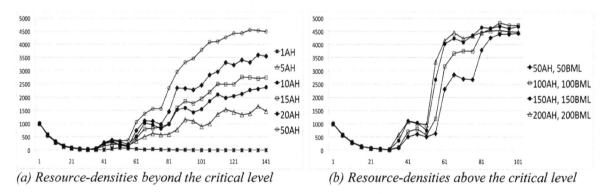

(a) Resource-densities beyond the critical level   *(b) Resource-densities above the critical level*

Next, we explore the case with resource-densities above the critical level. We investigate whether higher density of both resource-types affects the upper limit of sustainable population within the same landscape. Figure 10(b) shows the results: all cases with higher resource-densities reach equilibrium with VA ~4500. This substantiates the second part of our previous claim: as resource-density is increased *above* the critical level (keeping the same dimensions and the same CCC), VA remains unchanged, and is eventually limited by CCC.

However, in Figure 10(b), the rate of rise after the second dips (between days 45 to 76) is *always* faster with higher resource-density cases, because, in these cases, adult female mosquito agents are able to find resources more frequently.

DISCUSSION

In this study, we describe the spatial extension of a previous non-spatial agent-based model of malaria. We also performed model verification by showing that with identical parameter settings, both models yield similar results. The spatial extension provides unique opportunities to investigate the effects of various spatial characteristics of the ABM. Some potential future directions include the following:

- **Cell resolution:** in this study, we do not make any explicit assumption about the cell resolution (size of each cell). In other studies, for example, the cell resolution was set as 50 m to reflect the limited perceptual range of *A. gambiae* (Gu & Novak, 2009a). We plan to investigate results with variable cell resolutions.
- **Movement of agents:** as explained before, in our ABM, the direction of movement (of adult female mosquito agents) is purely random, as opposed to a directional flight when a resource is detected. We plan to explore other methods (e.g., directional) of movements. Also, in our model, the adult female mosquito agents move only while they are in *Bloodmeal Seeking* and *Gravid* states. However, the spatial heterogeneity of the underlying landscape may also affect other states of the model (e.g., *Mate Seeking*), which we plan to model in future.
- **Average Travel Time (ATT):** as described before, ATT reflects the travel time required to successfully find a resource by an adult female mosquito. We use the

notion of ATT as a statistically-expected measure, and do not explicitly calculate it for a given landscape. Once the cell resolution is determined in future, we plan to explicitly calculate ATT, and quantitatively measure any potential effect it may have on resource-seeking.

We also plan to explore the applicability of Zipf's law (Zipf, 1949) in landscapes that simultaneously possess variable-sized AHs. Zipf's law states that the frequency of occurrence of some event is inversely proportional to its rank (with some ranking scheme). Our goal is to analyze and compare the extent of potential biomass that can be sustained in larger AHs than those in smaller AHs (in the same landscape). We also plan to integrate the spatial model with a geographic information system (GIS) module.

ACKNOWLEDGMENT

We would like to thank Frank H. Collins, George and Winifred Clark Chair of Biological Sciences, and Gregory R. Madey, Research Professor of Department of Computer Science and Engineering at the University of Notre Dame, for their continuous support.

REFERENCES

Arifin, S. M. N., Davis, G. J., Kurtz, S., Gentile, J. E., Zhou, Y., & Madey, G. R. (2010a, December). Divide and conquer: A four-fold docking experience of agent-based models. In *Proceedings of the Winter Simulation Conference*, Baltimore, MD.

Arifin, S. M. N., Davis, G. J., & Zhou, Y. (2011, April). Modeling space in an agent-based model of malaria: Comparison between non-spatial and spatial models. In *Proceedings of the Agent-Directed Simulation*, Boston, MA.

Arifin, S. M. N., Davis, G. J., Zhou, Y., & Madey, G. R. (2010b, July). Verification & validation by docking: A case study of agent-based models of Anopheles gambiae. In *Proceedings of the Summer Computer Simulation Conference*, Ottawa, ON, Canada.

Bidlingmayera, W. L., & Hem, D. G. (1980). The range of visual attraction and the effect of competitive visual attractants upon mosquito (Diptera: Culicidae) flight. *Bulletin of Entomological Research*, *70*, 321–342. doi:10.1017/S0007485300007604

Depinay, J., Mbogo, C., Killeen, G., Knols, B., Beier, J., & Carlson, J. (2004). A simulation model of African Anopheles ecology and population dynamics for the analysis of malaria transmission. *Malaria Journal*, *3*(1), 29. doi:10.1186/1475-2875-3-29

Gentile, J. E., Davis, G. J., StLaurent, B., & Kurtz, S. (2010, July). A framework for modeling mosquito vectors. In *Proceedings of the Summer Computer Simulation Conference*, Ottawa, ON, Canada.

Gillies, M. T., & Wilkes, T. J. (1969). A comparison of the range of attraction of animal baits and of carbon dioxide for some West African mosquitoes. *Bulletin of Entomological Research*, *59*(3), 441–456. doi:10.1017/S0007485300003412

Gu, W., & Novak, R. J. (2009a). Agent-based modelling of mosquito foraging behaviour for malaria control. *Transactions of the Royal Society of Tropical Medicine and Hygiene*, *103*(11), 1105–1112. doi:10.1016/j.trstmh.2009.01.006

Gu, W., & Novak, R. J. (2009b). Predicting the impact of insecticide-treated bed nets on malaria transmission: the devil is in the detail. *Malaria Journal*, *8*(1), 256. doi:10.1186/1475-2875-8-256

Hui, C. (2006). Carrying capacity, population equilibrium, and environment's maximal load. *Ecological Modelling*, *192*(1-2), 317–320. doi:10.1016/j.ecolmodel.2005.07.001

Janssen, M. A., & Martens, W. J. M. (1997). Modeling malaria as a complex adaptive system. *Artificial Life*, *3*(3), 213–236. doi:10.1162/artl.1997.3.3.213

Kennedy, R. C., Xiang, X., Cosimano, T. F., Arthurs, L. A., Maurice, P. A., Madey, G. R., et al. (2006, April). Verification and validation of agent-based and equation-based simulations: A comparison. In *Proceedings of the Agent-Directed Simulation Conference*, Huntsville, AL.

McKenzie, F. E., & Bossert, W. H. (2005). An integrated model of Plasmodium falciparum dynamics. *Journal of Theoretical Biology*, *232*(3), 411–426.

McKenzie, F. E., Wong, R. C., & Bossert, W. H. (1998). Discrete-event simulation models of plasmodium falciparum malaria. *Simulation*, *71*(4), 250–261. doi:10.1177/003754979807100405

Menach, A. L., McKenzie, F. E., Flahault, A., & Smith, D. L. (2005). The unexpected importance of mosquito oviposition behaviour for malaria: Non-productive larval habitats can be sources for malaria transmission. *Malaria Journal*, *4*(1), 23. doi:10.1186/1475-2875-4-23

Ostfeld, R. S., Glass, G. E., & Keesing, F. (2005). Spatial epidemiology: An emerging (or re-emerging) discipline. *Trends in Ecology & Evolution*, *20*(6), 328–336. doi:10.1016/j.tree.2005.03.009

Recursive Porous Agent Simulation Toolkit (Repast). (2011). *The repast suite*. Retrieved from http://repast.sourceforge.net

Vries, P. (2001, May 16-17). Modelling malaria risk: An individual based and spatial explicit approach. In *Proceedings of the Workshop on Spatial Aspects of Demography*, Rostock, Germany.

World Health Organization (WHO). (2011). *Malaria facts.* Retrieved from http://www.who.int/mediacentre/factsheets/fs094/en/

Xiang, X., Kennedy, R., Madey, G. R., & Cabaniss, S. (2005, April). Verification and validation of agent-based scientific simulation models. In *Proceedings of the Agent-Directed Simulation Conference*, San Diego, CA.

Zhou, Y., Arifin, S. M. N., Gentile, J., Kurtz, S. J., Davis, G. J., & Wendelberger, B. A. (2010, July). An agent-based model of the Anopheles gambiae mosquito life cycle. In *Proceedings of the Summer Computer Simulation Conference*, Ottawa, ON, Canada.

Zipf, G. K. (1949). *Human behavior and the principle of least effort.* Reading, MA: Addison-Wesley.

This work was previously published in International Journal of Agent Technologies and Systems, Volume 3, Issue 3, edited by Yu Zhang, pp. 17-34, copyright 2011 by IGI Publishing (an imprint of IGI Global).

Chapter 15
Assessing the Impact of Temperature Change on the Effectiveness of Insecticide–Treated Nets

Gregory J. Davis
University of Notre Dame, USA

ABSTRACT

Malaria is a vector-borne illness affecting millions of lives annually and imposes a heavy financial burden felt worldwide. Moreover, there is growing concern that global climate change, in particular, rising temperature, will increase this burden. As such, policy makers are in need of tools capable of informing them about the potential strengths and weaknesses of intervention and control strategies. A previously developed agent-based model of the Anopheles gambiae mosquito is extended, one of the primary vectors of malaria, to investigate how changes in temperature influence the dynamics of malaria transmission and the effectiveness of a common malaria intervention: insecticide-treated nets (ITNs). Results from the simulations suggest two important findings. Consistent with previous studies, an increase in mosquito abundance as temperature increases is observed. However, the increase in mosquito abundance reduces the effectiveness of ITNs at a given coverage level. The implications and limitations of these findings are discussed.

DOI: 10.4018/978-1-4666-1565-6.ch015

INTRODUCTION AND BACKGROUND

Malaria is a vector-borne illness infecting over 500 million people and directly causing over one million deaths each year (WHO, 2004). The primary vectors of malaria are *Anopheline* mosquitoes and the risk of infection is largely dependent on the abundance of these mosquitoes. As such, huge efforts have been made at reducing the transmission of malaria by developing interventions that directly target vector populations. The most common of these interventions in use today are insecticide-treated nets (ITNs), indoor residual spraying of insecticides (IRS) on the walls of human dwellings, the development of chemical and biological larvicides, and reducing the availability of mosquito breeding sites through effective land-use and management strategies. However, in areas where malaria continues to be endemic, vector abundance exceeds resources necessary and available to implement effective control strategies.

There is growing concern that the difficulties in controlling malaria transmission may be exacerbated by environmental changes such as increasing temperature (Chaves & Koenraadt, 2010; Hay et al., 2002; Lindsay & Martens, 1998; Rogers & Randolph, 2000). Empirical evidence in these studies suggests that rising temperatures may not only influence transmission rates, but also increase the spatial distribution of malaria. These concerns arise because temperature can influence the abundance of mosquitoes in a number of important ways.

First, the development rate of aquatic mosquitoes (those in the egg, larva, and pupa developmental stages) is directly related to temperature within feasible ranges necessary for development (16-40°C) with mosquitoes reaching adulthood more quickly at higher temperatures (Bayoh & Lindsay, 2004; Depinay et al., 2004; Hoshen & Morse, 2004; Impoinvil, Cardenas, Gihture, Mbogo, & Beier, 2007). Second, the exoskeleton of newly emerging adults may harden more quickly, thus facilitating development to reproductive viability. Finally, female mosquitoes develop batches of eggs more quickly at higher temperatures once they have successfully obtained a bloodmeal (Hoshen & Morse, 2004). Combined, these temperature-driven effects not only shorten the time it takes a female mosquito to lay eggs for the first time, but also potentially allows for more reproduction attempts across an individual mosquito's lifespan.

The importance of these temperature-drive effects becomes even more apparent when considering that only a subset of the mosquito population is actually capable of transmitting malaria. The transmission of malaria from human to human begins when a female mosquito takes a bloodmeal from an infectious human, thus acquiring gametocytes of the malaria-causing parasite. The mosquito must then survive long enough for the gametocytes to develop into sporozoites, which then migrate to the salivary glands of the mosquito (the extrinsic incubation period, EIP). The sporozoites are then transmitted to humans upon subsequent bloodmeals. The parasite EIP is also temperature dependent with development occurring more rapidly as temperature increases. Thus, changes in vector abundance due to temperature should, in theory, be accompanied by a shift in the proportion of mosquitoes that can potentially transmit malaria.

The goal of the present study is two-fold. First we attempt to characterize how temperature can alter the abundance and structure of mosquito populations. Subsequently, we investigate whether changes in temperature impact the effectiveness of intervention strategies involving ITNs. ITNs function by killing mosquitoes as they attempt to gain a bloodmeal from humans that are covered by them. Given that both the duration of time between bloodmeals for a mosquito and the length of the EIP varies with temperature, it seems reasonable that the effectiveness of a control strategy employing a given distribution of ITNs may also vary. This question is particularly important to policy makers as they contemplate the allocation of intervention resources across a variety of climactic conditions throughout malaria endemic regions.

Related Work

Modeling and simulating populations of mosquitoes to understand malaria transmission dynamics is growing in popularity (McKenzie, 2000). Classical approaches to modeling malaria transmission dynamics have been in the form of equation-based models (Macdonald, 1957; Dietz, Molineaux, & Thomas, 1974) that are some variation of the standard SIR model (see also McKenzie, Wong, & Bossert, 1998, for a discrete-event model). While these models have provided invaluable insight into the epidemiology of malaria transmission, they typically focus on the macro-level relationships among humans, mosquitoes, and parasites. Out of necessity these models often reduce the complexity of transmission dynamics by simplifying micro-level variation (such as assuming population homogeneity) or assuming that micro-level relationships mirror those at the macro-level. As a result, extending these models to describe or explain multiple phenomena can be cumbersome.

Agent-based modeling and simulation (ABMS; sometimes referred to as individual-based modeling) offers an alternative approach to understanding malaria transmission dynamics. Instead of trying to encode broadly scoped population dynamics, the ABMS approach focuses on encoding the basic behavior of individual agents (in this case individual mosquitoes) as well as defining how agents interact with each other and their environment (Auchincloss & Diez-Roux, 2008). Then, by simulating many individual agents, researchers can investigate how interactions among the agents give rise to population-level characteristics. The ABMS approach has been recently used to investigate mosquito populations with the intent of investigating malaria transmission dynamics (Carnahan, Song-gang, Constantini, Touré, &

Taylor, 1997; Gu et al., 2003; Gu & Novak, 2009a). However, the focus of these studies has been to study the spatial behavior of mosquitoes (dispersal patterns while foraging for bloodmeals, breeding sites, etc.) and how that behavior is potentially influenced by various environmental properties (i.e., population density or the spatial structure of the environment). While some extensions to this work involve investigating the impact ITNs on malaria transmission (Gu & Novak, 2009b), they fail to address the complexities that variations in temperature can induce.

However, we have developed an entomological agent-based model of the *Anopheles gambiae* mosquito (Zhou et al., 2010). The novelty of this model is that it was developed to form a biologically realistic representation of the developmental and behavioral stages of *A. gambiae*, the primary vector of malaria in sub-Saharan Africa. In this model, agents (the mosquitoes) progress through a series of developmental and behavioral states defining how they interact with each other and the environment (Figure 1). Importantly, this model does account for the influence of temperature throughout the entire life of the mosquito. As such, this model is an ideal candidate for extending to address the questions of the present study.

THE MODEL

For clarity and brevity, many of the details of the original model will not be fully described here (see Zhou et al., 2010, for a more detailed description of the model and its parameters). Instead, we briefly describe agent behavior and environment, then focus discussion on the portions of the model that are temperature-sensitive in addition to model extensions necessary to assess the intervention effectiveness as a function of temperature. It is also important to note that the original model was described where each time step of the simulation occurred with a resolution of one day. However, the model was implemented to be flexible enough

Figure 1. Lifecycle of the Anopheles gambiae mosquito

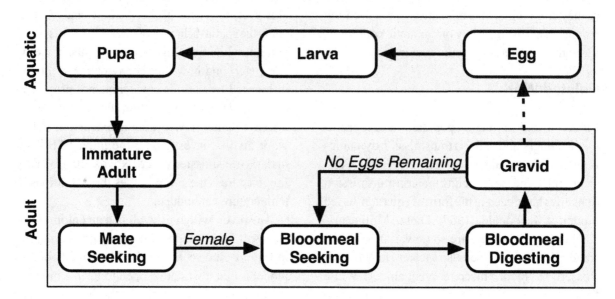

to allow an arbitrary number of hours in each time step and mathematical equivalence between a single daily time step and 24 hourly time steps. The work presented here focuses on time steps that represent one hour.

Agent Behavior and the Environment

As shown in Figure 1, the agents in the original model developed by Zhou et al. (2010) begin their life as an egg in an aquatic breeding site. They remain in the breeding site while they hatch to become larvae and eventually pupae. When pupation is complete, the agent emerges from the breeding site as an immature adult mosquito, and they rest while their exoskeleton hardens. Once the hardening process is complete, they progress to the mate seeking state. Upon a successful mating, female agents begin their search for a bloodmeal (males remain in the mate seeking state indefinitely until death). Upon acquiring a bloodmeal, the female agent digests the bloodmeal to form a batch of eggs from the proteins contained within the blood. Once the batch of eggs has been formed, the gravid agent searches

for a suitable breeding site to oviposit her eggs. Once all eggs have been deposited (creating new agents in the breeding site), the female returns to seek another bloodmeal. The female agents repeat these last three stages (known as the gonotrophic cycle) indefinitely until they die and are removed from the system. It is important to note that only the environment and individual mosquitoes are used within this model. Humans are not explicitly included in the model but instead are represented as a mathematical probability that mosquitoes will find a host when in the bloodmeal seeking state. Furthermore, the malaria causing parasites are also not explicitly modeled. Instead, the EIP is a property of each agent denoting the critical age at which a mosquito has the potential to transmit the parasite.

Throughout the simulation, agents are subject to a baseline daily mortality of 10%. However, this baseline rate is increased in two cases. First, agents in the adult states experience an age-adjusted mortality that increases as they get older (Zhou et al., 2010; Equation 2). This adjustment is made to reflect the physiological hazards due to aging. Second, aquatic agents in the larva state experience increased mortality that dependent on the density of aquatic mosquitoes in their environment (Zhou et al., 2010; Equation 1) with additional mortality assigned as the density increases. This adjustment is made to reflect the effect of predation and competition for food resources in the environment.

The environment is modeled in a two-tiered non-spatial manner. It is important to note that this representation of the environment differs from the one used by Zhou et al. (2010) and is described more fully by Gentile, Davis, and St. Laurent (2010). Semantically and computationally, the representations are equivalent, but differ in their structural implementation to improve maintainability and scalability. The first tier represents the terrestrial environment where the adult agents operate. The terrestrial environment is responsible for updating the adult agents and meteorological factors such as temperature. The second tier operates as a sub-environment of the terrestrial environment and represents the breeding sites in which the aquatic stage mosquitoes operate. This tier has an additional carrying capacity attribute to reflect the overall environment's capacity to support aquatic life. This capacity value influences the density-dependent larval mortality rate described above. Additionally, it regulates the number of eggs a gravid adult can lay in the environment (Zhou et al., 2010; Equation 6).

Because the environment is non-spatial, all agents operate in a "point universe" where actions that involve movement are abstracted as mathematical probabilities that those actions can occur. For instance, female mosquitoes are assumed to be mobile in the mate-seeking, bloodmeal-seeking and gravid states. For each of these states, a likelihood of successful action for agents in these states during a given time step of the simulation is 1.0, 0.25, and 0.25, respectively. Thus, females will always find a successful mate, find a bloodmeal host 25% of the time, and find a suitable breeding site for oviposition 25% of the time. Because mosquitoes are active only during the evening hours (a 12-hour span from 6pm to 5am; agents are assumed to be inactive and resting during the remaining 12 hours of each day), the mosquitoes will, on average find a host for a bloodmeal or a breeding site to lay eggs 3 times per evening. While these probabilities suggest that mosquitoes will successfully perform their associated actions within a given 24-hour period, they allow the ability to account for variation in travel time while still allowing the possibility that these events may span more than a single day.

Temperature Sensitivities

In the original model, an agent's progression from one state to the next is limited by certain criteria. In five of the states (egg, larva, pupa, immature adult, and bloodmeal digesting), those criteria represent a development time (DT; all expressed in hours), which is temperature-dependent. Figure 2 illustrates the relationship between temperature and these DTs. In four of the states, DT has an inverse linear relationship with temperature defined by the following equations:

$$DT_{egg} = -0.923*T+60.923 \qquad (1)$$

$$DT_{pupa} = -0.923*T+60.923 \qquad (2)$$

$$DT_{immatureAdult} = -2.667*T+120.0 \qquad (3)$$

$$DT_{bloodmealDigesting} = -1.231*T+77.231 \qquad (4)$$

where T is the temperature when the agent enters the state which can range from 14-40°C. These equations are continuous approximations derived from the coarsely defined discrete values used in the original model and fit to a linear model (F. Collins, personal communication, September 2011).

The fifth DT, for the larva state, has a more complex relationship with temperature. The relationship is defined using the following formula:

Figure 2. Relationships between development time and temperature for (A) egg, pupa, immature adult, and bloodmeal digesting states, and (B) larva state and for the parasite P. falciparum

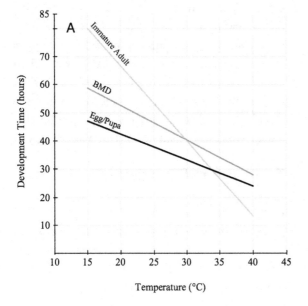

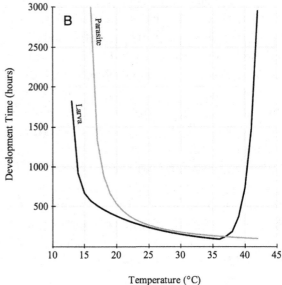

$$DT_{larva} = \cfrac{1}{\rho_{25°C} * \cfrac{T}{298} * \exp\left[\cfrac{\Delta H_A^{\neq}}{R} * \left(\cfrac{1}{298} - \cfrac{1}{T}\right)\right]}$$

$$1 + \exp\left[\cfrac{\Delta H_L}{R} * \left(\cfrac{1}{T_{\frac{1}{2}L}} - \cfrac{1}{T}\right)\right] + \exp\left[\cfrac{\Delta H_H}{R} * \left(\cfrac{1}{T_{\frac{1}{2}H}} - \cfrac{1}{T}\right)\right]$$

$$(5)$$

w h e r e $\rho_{25°C} = 0.00415$, $\Delta H_A^{\neq} = 15684$, $\Delta H_L = 229902$, $\Delta H_H = 822285$, $T_{\frac{1}{2}L} = 310.3$, $T_{\frac{1}{2}H} = 286.4$, and $R = 1.987$ (Zhou et al., 2010; Depinay et al., 2004). Note that the DT for larva below 15°C and above 40°C is longer than 700 hours (~31 days). At these levels of development, the mortality for agents in the larva state (a minimum of 10% daily mortality) outpaces development resulting in agent extinction. Transitions out of the other three states (mate-seeking, bloodmeal-seeking, and gravid) are dependent on the occurrence of a successful event that is not directly influenced by temperature (successful mating event, successful bloodmeal event, and the completion of all eggs being laid, respectively), and thus will not be discussed further (see Zhou et al., 2010, for more details).

Extension 1: Potentially Infectious Mosquitoes

The original model, by default, reports the abundance of mosquitoes at each simulated time step. While an increase in mosquito abundance is expected with increasing temperatures (given the DTs described previously), abundance numbers alone give little insight to the structure of the population actually capable of transmitting malaria. Furthermore, abundance is difficult to correlate to populations occurring in real-world scenarios because, in our model, it is sensitive to other parameters (such as the availability and capacity of breeding sites). Thus, it is important to define another measure that can be compared across simulations.

A more informative metric would be to report the number of mosquitoes that are potentially capable of transmitting malaria (potentially infectious females; PIFs). As stated above, such a measure is dependent on the agent successfully obtaining a bloodmeal (presumably acquiring the malaria causing parasite) and then surviving long enough for the parasite to develop and migrate into the salivary gland so that it can be transferred during a subsequent bloodmeal. To that end, we can approximate this portion of the population by incorporating the parasite development time as a property of each agent.

Plasmodium falciparum (one malaria-causing parasite transmitted by *A. gambiae*) development has been characterized using the Detinova method (Detinova, 1962; Hosen & Morse, 2004; Macdonald, 1957):

$$DT_{parasite} = \frac{DD}{T - T_{min}} * 24 \qquad (6)$$

where DD is the number of degree-days needed for the parasite to develop (111 for *P. falciparum*), *T* is the air temperature (in °C), and T_{min} is the minimum temperature at which the parasite is capable of developing (16°C for *P. falciparum*). The relationship between temperature and $DT_{Parasite}$ is shown in Figure 2. When the agent survives beyond this DT (which begins after its initial bloodmeal), it is marked as potentially infectious. The abundance of PIFs per time step is reported in the output of the model. Additionally, our simulation reports the number of bloodmeals taken by PIFs at each time step.

It is important to reiterate that PIF metrics do not *fully* capture malaria transmission dynamics because neither humans nor the parasite itself are explicitly modeled. Instead, these metrics are approximations of the mosquito population that has the potential to transmit malaria. Actual transmission events will likely vary as a function of the prevalence malaria cases in humans within a given region. However, in regions where malaria is holoendemic, these approximations should mirror actual transmission events.

Extension 2: Interventions

The original model had no provision for simulating interventions targeting the specific stages of the mosquito lifecycle. However, extending the model to incorporate these interventions is relatively straightforward and is accomplished by modeling their effect as a state-dependent mortality. Although ITNs can be encountered in all adult stages, we implemented their effects in the state where mosquitoes are most likely to encounter them, during the bloodmeal seeking state. Figure 3 shows the logic of agents in the bloodmeal seeking state.

There are three parameters that govern the state-dependent mortality ITNs have on mosquitoes the bloodmeal seeking state. The first is ITN effectiveness, which describes the probability that a mosquito will die when it encounters (lands on) an ITN. This parameter could vary from 0.0 (no mortality) to 1.0 (100% mortality). The second parameter necessary is ITN coverage. This parameter represents the proportion of the population owning and using an ITN during the period when mosquitoes are actively seeking a bloodmeal. This parameter varied from 0.0 (no ITNs in use) to 1.0 (entire human population covered by ITNs). The third parameter, host density, describes the probability of encountering a suitable host for a bloodmeal. This parameter was present in the original model and could vary from 0.0 to 1.0.

SIMULATION RESULTS

The original model was implemented using two programming languages (C++ and Java; see Gentile, Davis, & St. Laurent, 2010, for a complete description of the simulation structure and classes used). The Java implementation was modified

Figure 3. Logic for agents in the bloodmeal seeking state

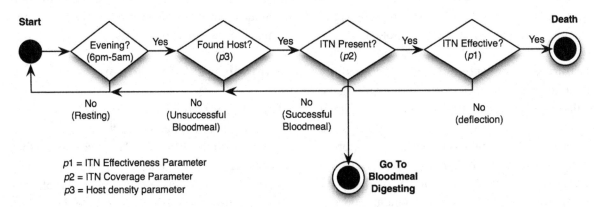

p1 = ITN Effectiveness Parameter
p2 = ITN Coverage Parameter
p3 = Host density parameter

as described above and used to generate our results. Each individual simulation ran with a fixed temperature value (ranging from 10-50°C). All other parameters in the simulation were remained unaltered from the default values used listed in Table 1. Because many portions of the original model contain stochastic elements (probabilities of mortality, number of eggs generated, etc.), 72 replication simulations for each condition were run. Initial test simulations suggest that this number of replications is sufficient to reproduce patterns with less than 1% variability. Additionally, each run of the simulation approaches a steady state population (with some variability) after 1000 steps of the simulation. Thus, ending population estimates for each simulation were derived by averaging results obtained over the last 1000 time steps for each simulation, and then averaging those values across all 72 replications.

Varying Temperature Only

Simulations were run with a fixed temperature value ranging from 10-50°C in two-degree increments. To establish a baseline estimate of how temperature influences population abundance and

Table 1. Default simulation parameter values used

Parameter	Value
Initial number of eggs in simulation	1000
Initial number of adults in simulation	0
Aquatic environment carrying capacity	10,000
Probability of finding a mate while mate seeking	1.0
Probability of finding host while bloodmeal seeking	0.25
Probability of finding aquatic habitat during while gravid	0.25
Baseline daily mortality rate	0.1
Adult mortality parameter s	0.1
Adult mortality parameter b	0.04
Larval mortality rainfall coefficient	1.0 (no effect of rain)
Number of eggs generated while bloodmeal digesting	Random sample from N(170, 30)

structure, the effects of ITNs were excluded by setting their coverage and effectiveness parameters to 0. Figure 4 shows output obtained from these simulations.

From Figure 4A, we observe an increase in the overall abundance of female mosquitoes as temperature increases (for temperatures at or below 38°C). This was an expected result given all developmental delays decreased as temperature increased. Also as expected, all agents in the simulation died when temperatures were below 15°C or above 40°C due to extremely long larval development times at those temperatures (see Equation 4 and Figure 3).

More importantly, there was an increase in the number PIFs with rising temperatures, similar to the pattern of overall abundance. However, the proportion of PIFs continually increased. This can be more clearly seen in Figure 4B and indicates that the structure of the population, specifically the proportion of mosquitoes capable of transmitting malaria, changes as a function of temperature. We suspect the reason for this continual increase is

due to how temperature differentially influences the length of the gonotrophic cycle and the EIP. In our model, the length of the gonotrophic cycle is dominated by the time it takes for the mosquito to form a batch of eggs once a bloodmeal has been acquired. For instance, at 26°C, the mosquito will remain in the bloodmeal digesting state for approximately 45 hours (see Equation 4). At 28°C, this time is reduced to approximately 43 hours. By comparison, the length of the EIP is reduced from 218 hours at 26°C to 181 hours at 26°C. Thus, female mosquitoes become PIFs at a faster rate than they are able to reproduce (increasing abundance) suggesting the shift in population structure outpaces the increase in abundance as temperature increases.

Of critical interest, these results suggest that the prevalence and incidence of malaria may be greater in areas with higher temperatures. Furthermore, these findings mirror those observed by other researchers arriving at similar conclusions (Chaves & Koenraadt, 2010; Hay et al., 2002; Lindsay & Martens, 1998; Rogers & Randolph,

Figure 4. Simulation results observed as a function of temperature. (A) Abundance of females and PIFs. (B) Proportion of female population that are PIFs

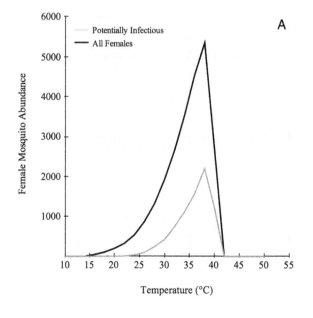
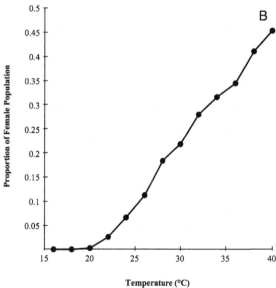

2000), thus adding some qualitative support for the validity of our model and its extensions.

Characterizing ITN Effectiveness as a Function of Temperature

To investigate whether the effectiveness of ITNs varies as a function of temperature, we manipulated the intervention coverage parameter between 0% coverage (replicating the baseline condition above) to 100% coverage in 10% increments. As stated above, the coverage parameter represents the proportion of the population with ownership of an ITN and assumes that all who own an ITN use it when mosquitoes are actively seeking bloodmeals. Furthermore, we assumed that ITNs were 100% effective in killing mosquitoes that encounter them, and accordingly, set the effectiveness parameter to 100%. Simulations across these various ITN parameter values were run using temperatures that varied from 20°C to 40°C (where the abundance of PIFs was non-zero). The results of these simulations are shown in Figure 5 (left panel).

Figure 5A re-illustrates the increase in the abundance of female agents as temperature increases. Furthermore, using ITNs, regardless of the amount of coverage, is effective in reducing the abundance of female agents. However, increasing ITN coverage disproportionately reduces the number of agents across temperature scenarios with larger reductions generally occurring at higher temperatures. This can be seen in Figure 5A where the reduction of female mosquitoes, denoted by the slope of each temperature line, decreases more rapidly as temperature increases. This might be expected considering ITNs were implemented in the simulations to increase the likelihood of mortality for agents seeking a bloodmeal. Because the length of the gonotrophic cycle of an agent is reduced at higher temperatures (due to a decreased DT for the bloodmeal seeking state,

see Figure 2A and Equation 3), these mosquitoes return to the bloodmeal seeking stage more often. As a result, a given mosquito has an increased probability of encountering an ITN across its life span when temperatures are increased.

Female abundance numbers alone, however, only provide part of the necessary information to gain insight into the underlying malaria transmission dynamics. When considering the proportion of PIFs and their biting rates (where the real threat of malaria transmission lay), a number of important patterns emerge. First, Figure 5B reveals that the proportion of PIFs is generally larger at higher temperatures (replicating the previous group of simulations). More importantly, as the investment in ITN coverage increases, the PIF population's response to that increase varies as a function of temperature. At low temperatures, each 10% increase in coverage beyond an initial 10% investment results in diminishing returns with respect to reducing proportion of PIFs. At high temperatures, this pattern is reversed with greater reductions for each additional 10% added. Inspecting of the number of bites from PIFs (Figure 5C) follows a similar pattern where the reduction in bites increases at higher temperatures; however, greater coverage is still necessary to achieve equal biting rates.

Together, these results suggest that malaria control strategies employing ITNs alone will only be effective at high coverage rates. Furthermore, if local temperatures change, an additional deployment of ITNs will be necessary to maintain previous strategy efficacies.

Varying ITN Effectiveness

Using an ITN effectiveness parameter value of 100% in the previous group of simulations represents a best-case scenario characterization of the intervention's effectiveness. However, this is unrealistic in most real world conditions for a

Figure 5. Simulation results observed as a function of temperature and ITN coverage. (A) Overall female abundance with 100% effective ITNs. (B) Proportion of female population that is potentially infectious with 100% effective ITNs. (C) Average number of bites per day from potentially infectious mosquitoes with 100% effective ITNs. (D)(E) and (F) are similar to (A) (B) and (C), respectively, but with 50% effective ITNs

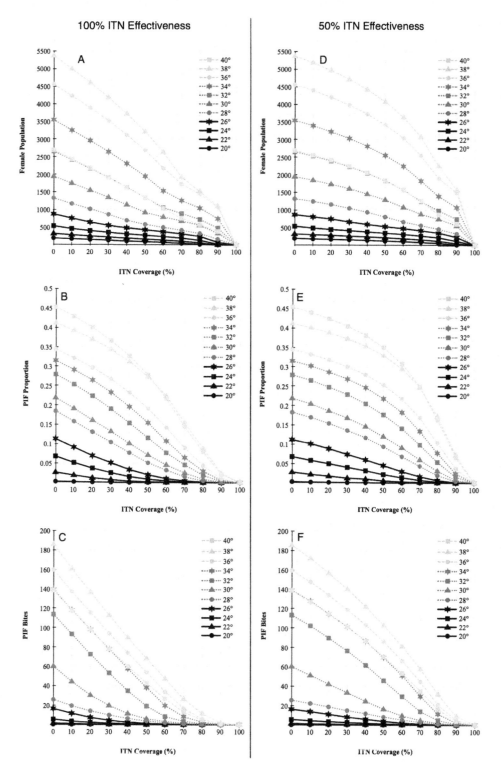

number of reasons. Recall that the coverage parameter reflects ownership *and* usage combined during hours of the day when mosquitoes are active. Thus, to truly achieve 100% coverage, not only would everyone in a malaria endemic region need an ITN, but also they must be covered by it during the entire span of time when mosquitoes are active. While this may be possible for infants and small children, it seems unreasonable that adults would willingly spend the entire evening (from 6pm to 5am) under them. Second, the insecticides used to impregnate the net typically degrade and lose effectiveness over time. Additionally, mosquitoes have evolved to develop at least a minor resistance to insecticides in use today. As such, it seems prudent to examine the whether the transmission dynamics observed previously have a similar pattern when the ITNs are less than 100% effective.

There is reason to suspect that this alteration will produce a different pattern of results. Namely, when ITNs are 100% effective, there is only one outcome that can occur when mosquitoes encounter them, mortality. However, if the effectiveness is less than 100%, the mosquitoes that encounter an ITN may not be killed but instead delayed in achieving a successful bloodmeal. Thus, we expect ITNs to be less effective at killing the mosquitoes, which would result in a smaller reduction in abundance numbers. However, the expected impact on the population structure and prevention of bites from PIFs is unclear.

Simulations were run in the same fashion as the previous group of simulations. However, instead of 100% effectiveness parameter values for the ITNs, that value was changed to 50%. Simulations across these various ITN parameter values were run using the same temperature parameters in the previous simulations. The results of these simulations are shown in Figure 5 (right panel).

There are a number of critical differences between the results of this group of simulations and the previous group. The first is, as expected, increasing ITN coverage is less effective at reduc-

ing the overall abundance of female mosquitoes (Figure 5D vs. Figure 5A). This is due to the fact that some mosquitoes encountering the ITNs are not killed; but rather, mosquitoes avoiding mortality are merely prevented from successfully obtaining a bloodmeal. Additionally, along with decreased killing efficacy, the ITNs are less effective at reducing the proportion of PIFs (Figure 5E vs. Figure 5B). As a result, the number of bites from PIFs is not reduced as efficiently (Figure 5F vs. Figure 5C). Again, these results indicate that ITNs may be a more effective intervention at lower temperatures. However, as ITNs lose effectiveness in killing mosquitoes, the benefits afforded by ITNs become smaller and require a larger investment just to maintain a given level of protection.

These results further illustrate that vector targeted intervention strategies employing only ITNs will have limited effectiveness without sufficiently high coverage rates. Furthermore, strategies involving a given ITN coverage rate will be less effective at targeting the critical PIF sub-population at higher temperatures. While these findings mirror those observed with 100% effective ITNs, they suggest that maintaining intervention effectiveness is a critical consideration for any vector-targeted malaria control strategy.

DISCUSSION

The work presented here used an ABMS approach to characterize how mosquito populations and the effectiveness of intervention strategies involving ITNs might vary as a function of temperature. The general finding emerging from these simulations is that increasing temperature, even by a relatively small amount, not only increases mosquito population size, but also alters the structure of the population such that a larger proportion of the population has the potential to transmit malaria. Furthermore, these changes in population structure have non-trivial effects on the efficacy of intervention strategies involving ITNs.

When considering the influence of temperature on mosquito population structure in the absence of any interventions, we observed two important findings. First, as temperature increases, the abundance of mosquitoes increases (both males and females, although only females were discussed). This is largely due to the shortened development times at higher temperatures. Second, the structure of the mosquito population changes such that a larger proportion of the population survives to become potentially infectious. This too was an expected result given the known effects of temperature on the EIP of malaria causing parasites. Replication of these two effects provides some qualitative validation of the current model given similar findings by other researchers (Chaves & Koenraadt, 2010; Hay et al., 2002; Lindsay & Martens, 1998; Rogers & Randolph, 2000).

To assess how intervention strategies might also be affected by temperature, we replicated the previous experiments with the addition of a state-dependent mortality for mosquitoes in the bloodmeal seeking state. This manipulation was intended to model the effects of ITNs with varying coverage levels (0 to 100% in 10% increments) and two different effectiveness values (100% and 50% effectiveness in killing mosquitoes that came in contact with them). There were two sources of evidence that ITNs appeared to be more effective at higher temperatures. First, relative to a baseline condition in which ITNs were not present, all three metrics (abundance, proportion of PIFs, and bites from PIFs) showed a larger reduction, at higher temperatures. Second, as coverage increased from one coverage level to the next, the reduction in all three metrics were larger as temperature increased. The notable exception to these observations was when temperature was 40°C. At this temperature setting, larval development time is sufficiently long to allow natural mortality to begin outpacing development resulting in an overall reduction of mosquitoes. However, at higher temperatures,

extraordinarily high coverage levels were necessary to reduce potential transmission events to levels where those events would be infrequent enough to prevent the spread of malaria. In contrast, while ITNs were less effective in reducing all three metrics, transmission event reduction to unsustainable levels could be achieved with lower coverage rates. This is likely due to the slower EIP at these temperatures.

Perhaps the most compelling finding in this study is that, regardless of temperature, control strategies relying only on ITNs seem insufficient for eradicating malaria transmission. In fact, a total reduction in the number of transmission events seems possible only when the temperature is below 24°C (without >90% coverage). Thus, malaria control policies may need to be rethought in light of temperature change. Although they are rarely used in isolation, ITNs are the most widely used vector-targeted intervention. If temperatures increase slightly, the effectiveness of ITNs appears to drop and control strategies may need to employ additional interventions to counteract this change. These results do, however, suggest that policy makers need not target 100% coverage of ITNs across all areas. Where the boundaries of malaria prevalence are thought to be constrained by climatic effects (i.e., the highlands of Kenya and Uganda), a small investment in ITNs (i.e., distributing ITNs to a low percentage of residents) can potentially be reasonable strategy for preventing these areas from becoming malaria endemic.

In considering the conclusions being drawn from this study, there are a number of assumptions and limitations that our work is subject to. While many of these apply to the original model as well, we will focus on the issues directly related to the work presented here. First and foremost, the model needs to be more rigorously validated. While we have presented a number of equations characterizing the development times various life cycle stages that can be influenced by temperature, all but one of these are based on one expert's estimations. That said, the model is still useful as it serves to generate hypotheses for these gaps in knowledge that can be empirically tested and refined.

Another limitation of this work is that it only characterizes the steady state estimations of the mosquito populations for fixed parameter values. In particular, the temperature was held constant throughout the simulation. As a result, the inferences drawn from these results are only applicable to particular instances in time. If this model were to be used as basis for making decisions regarding malaria control resources, it would need to be extended to accept fluctuating parameter values to account for seasonality, variability in breeding site capacity and availability due to rainfall, and so forth. Future work is necessary to address these issues.

ACKNOWLEDGMENT

The author wishes to thank Dr. Gregory Madey and Dr. Frank Collins for their guidance and support during the development of this work. Additionally, we would like to acknowledge S. M. Niaz Arifin, James E. Gentile, Ying Zhou, who contributed greatly to the development of the original model and helped verify the extensions described the present study.

REFERENCES

Auchincloss, A., & Diez Roux, A. (2008). A new tool for epidemiology: The usefulness of dynamic-agent models in understanding place effects on health. *American Journal of Epidemiology, 168*, 1–8. doi:10.1093/aje/kwn118

Bayoh, M., & Lindsay, S. (2004). Temperature-related duration of aquatic stages the Afrotropical malaria vector mosquito Anopheles gambiae in the laboratory. *Medical and Veterinary Entomology, 18*, 174–179. doi:10.1111/j.0269-283X.2004.00495.x

Carnahan, J., Song-gang, L., Costantini, C., Touré, Y., & Taylor, C. (1997). Computer simulation of dispersal by Anopheles gambiae s.l. in West Africa. In *Proceedings of the Fifth International Workshop on the Synthesis and Simulation of Living, Complex Adaptive System*s (pp. 387-394).

Chaves, L., & Koenraadt, C. (2010). Climate change and highland malaria: Fresh air for a hot debate. *The Quarterly Review of Biology, 85*, 27–55. doi:10.1086/650284

Depinay, J., Mbogo, C., Killeen, G., Knols, B., Beier, J., & Carlson, J. (2004). A simulation model of African Anopheles ecology and population dynamics for the analysis of malaria transmission. *Malaria Journal, 3*, 29. doi:10.1186/1475-2875-3-29

Detinova, T. (1962). *Age grouping methods in Diptera of medical importance*. Geneva, Switzerland: World Health Organization.

Dietz, K., Molineaux, L., & Thomas, A. (1974). A malaria model tested in the African savannah. *Bulletin of the World Health Organization, 50*, 347–357.

Gentile, J. E., Davis, G. J., & St. Laurens, B. (2010) Modeling mosquito vectors. In *Proceedings of the Summer Computer Simulation Conference*, Ottawa, ON, Canada.

Gu, W., Killeen, G., Mbogo, C., Regens, J., Githure, J., & Beier, J. (2003). An individual-based model of Plasmodium falciparum malaria transmission on the coast of Kenya. *Transactions of the Royal Society of Tropical Medicine and Hygiene, 97*, 43–50. doi:10.1016/S0035-9203(03)90018-6

Gu, W., & Novak, R. (2009a). Agent-based modeling of mosquito foraging behaviour for malaria control. *Transactions of the Royal Society of Tropical Medicine and Hygiene, 103*, 1105–1112. doi:10.1016/j.trstmh.2009.01.006

Gu, W., & Novak, R. (2009b). Predicting the impact of insecticide-treated bed nets on malaria transmission: The devil is in the detail. *Malaria Journal, 8*, 256. doi:10.1186/1475-2875-8-256

Hay, S., Cox, J., Rogers, D., Randolph, S., Stern, D., & Shanks, G. (2002). Climate change and the resurgence of malaria in the East African highlands. *Nature, 415*, 905–909. doi:10.1038/415905a

Hoshen, M., & Morse, A. (2004). A weather-driven model of malaria transmission. *Malaria Journal, 3*, 32. doi:10.1186/1475-2875-3-32

Impoinvil, D., Cardenas, G., Gihture, J., Mbogo, C., & Beier, J. (2007). Constant temperature and time period effects on Anopheles gambiae egg hatching. *Journal of the American Mosquito Control Association, 23*, 124–130. doi:10.2987/8756-971X(2007)23[124:CTATPE]2.0.CO;2

Lindsay, S., & Martens, W. (1998). Malaria in the African highlands: Past, present, future. *Bulletin of the World Health Organization, 76*, 33–45.

Macdonald, G. (1957). *The epidemilogy and control of malaria*. Oxford, UK: Oxford University Press.

McKenzie, F. (2000, January) Why model malaria? *Parasitology Today*.

McKenzie, F., Wong, R., & Bossert, W. H. (1998). Discrete-event simulation models of Plasmodium falciparum malaria. *Simulation, 71*, 250–261. doi:10.1177/003754979807100405

Rogers, D., & Randolph, S. (2000). The global spread of malaria in a future, warmer world. *Science, 289*, 1763–1766.

World Health Organization. (2004). *Changing history*. Geneva, Switzerland: World Health Organization.

Zhou, Y., Arifin, S., Gentile, J., Kurtz, S., Davis, G., & Wendelberger, B. (2010). An agent-based model of the Anopheles gambiae mosquito life-cycle. In *Proceedings of Summer Simulation Multiconference* (pp. 1-8).

This work was previously published in International Journal of Agent Technologies and Systems, Volume 3, Issue 3, edited by Yu Zhang, pp. 35-48, copyright 2011 by IGI Publishing (an imprint of IGI Global).

Chapter 16
A Framework for Modeling Genetically–Aware Mosquito Vectors for Sterile Insect Technique

James E. Gentile
University of Notre Dame, USA

Samuel S. C. Rund
University of Notre Dame, USA

ABSTRACT

Vector-borne diseases account for 16% of the global infectious disease burden (WHO, 2004). Many of these debilitating and sometimes fatal diseases are transmitted between human hosts by mosquitoes. Mosquito-targeted intervention methods have controlled or eliminated mosquito-borne diseases from many regions of the world but regions of constant transmission (holoendemic areas) still exist (Molineaux et al., 1980). To eliminate these illnesses, researchers need to understand how interventions impact a mosquito population so as to identify potential avenues for new intervention techniques. This paper presents a software architecture that allows researchers to simulate transgenic interventions on a mosquito population. The authors present specifications for a model that captures these transgenic aspects and present a software architecture that meets those needs. The authors also provide a proof of concept and some observations about sterile insect technique strategies as simulated by this architecture.

DOI: 10.4018/978-1-4666-1565-6.ch016

1. INTRODUCTION

Vector-borne illnesses are transmitted between hosts by an intermediate organism fever, and lymphatic filariasis are mosquitoes. Vector-borne illnesses account for around 16% of the infectious disease burden globally. Malaria is the most serious as it infects 500 million people a year and kills over a million, mostly children under five years of age (WHO, 2004). Malaria occurs throughout the tropics but particularly plagues sub-Saharan Africa, where it is considered a holoendemic disease. Many studies have focused on the mortality of the disease on populations under 5 years of age (Crawley, 2004; Omumbo et al., 2004; Greenwood & Mutabingwa, 2002). In Africa, malaria causes 18% of childhood deaths (Bryce et al., 2005). Eradication of diseases like malaria will save the lives of countless children throughout the world. The United Nations has been successful at local eradication by targeting the mosquito population. Despite these efforts, holoendemic areas of transmission require a different intervention strategies (Gabaldon, 1978). Recently, there has been focus on using multiple, con- current interventions and research into new intervention avenues. Of these, sterile insect technique (SIT) is arising as a promising method based on its success at controlling other insect populations. In SIT, males are lab-reared to be sterile or carry a dominant lethal gene. Females inseminated by these males pass the lethal gene to her eggs. Those progeny cease development at certain life-stages and die. Modeling and simulation can assist in the effort of looking into new intervention strategies be they combining existing interventions for a complementary effect or looking into avenues of new interventions. Many interventions can be modeled as a behavioral interruption of the insect. For instance, repellent could deflect a mosquito when it seeks a bloodmeal. However, other intervention forms, like SIT, require models to be aware of the populations phenotypes and adjust agent behavior accordingly. Breakthroughs are being made in modeling the transmission of these diseases, their

active members and their dynamics (Gu & Novak, 2009; Bomblies et al., 2009), (Craig et al., 1999; Killeen et al., 2003). Among the various modeling techniques available, agent-based methods (Macal & North, 2008) show the most promise. In these models, each member of an interaction or system is treated as an individual with a set of rules dictating their behavior (Macal & North, 2008). By observing the interaction between agents and probing the system at choice times, system-level properties can emerge providing insight into the engine of disease transmission (Bomblies et al., 2008). This approach to modeling is conducive to evaluating the benefit of certain intervention methods and to anticipating possible behavior changes of the mosquitoes.

In this paper, we introduce a software architecture for modeling genetically- aware agents. Though the paper's scope is the vector for malaria, this architecture can be expanded to other forms of agents by describing their own behavior and attributes. The system is capable of accurately encoding a mosquito's life cycle and behavior in a structure we call a strategy. The strategy is flexible and can be adapted to accurately characterize a new genus, species or variation within one species. The architecture is designed such that there can be an arbitrary number of nested sub-environments which the agents can interact with when egg-laying and when they are in the aquatic stage of their life cycle. The movement of agents between environments is handled through message passing making this system ideal for parallelization across many cores or many computers with existing tools like OpenMP (Chapman et al., 2007) and MPI (Gabriel et al., 2004). Finally, agents are able to inherit phenotypes from their parents and these attributes can define their behavior.

We discuss the complexity of mosquito vectors first then outline the dynamics needed to capture genetic heredity. Section 4 introduces a software architecture that is capable of simulating genetically-aware agents. Finally, a proof of concept is presented along with a closing discussion.

2. COMPLEXITY OF MOSQUITOES

The majority of species that act as vectors of human disease are flies (order Diptera), primarily mosquitoes (family Culicidae). Mosquitoes are able to exploit resources quickly as they become available, have short generation times, and lay many eggs per brood.

Mosquitoes spend the immature stages of their life in an aquatic habitat and emerge as adults into the open-air environment (illustrated in Figure 1). A female mosquito lays a clutch of eggs in a pool or other collection of water. These eggs hatch and go through several stages of larval development before turning into a pupa and eventually emerging from that pupa as a fully formed adult. When mosquitoes emerge, they take some time to harden their exoskeleton and then seek a mate. Once mated, females of certain species need to take a bloodmeal in order to obtain the protein and nutrients required to develop a batch of eggs. The female seeks out a blood host, obtains a blood meal and takes some time to digest the blood and develop her batch of eggs. When the eggs are fully developed, the female seeks out a suitable aquatic habitat and lays her eggs on the surface. The length of time between consecutive bloodmeals is known as the gonotrophic cycle and is an important parameter in estimating the length of time between when a vector takes an infected blood meal and when it can transmit that disease.

This mosquito life cycle can be partitioned into basic aquatic and adult stages The different stages of aquatic development can be simplified to the egg, larvae, and pupal states. The adult life stage can be subdivided into the different types of adult behavior. Though genera and species of mosquitoes might differ in the time spent in different stages, a flexible model that accounts for the basic biology of a vector would be applicable to many different types of disease vectors. For example, even non-mosquito vectors like sand-flies, whose larvae develop in the soil, still have distinct immature and mature life stages and adult behavioral patterns that are common to blood-feeding insect (Sharma & Singh, 2008).

Changes in the density of a mosquito population and mosquito survivor- ship can be dramatically influenced by environmental variables such as temperature and precipitation. Shifts in temperature can influence the development time of immature stages, the flight activity and survival of adults. Precipitation in a region determines the number and quality of breeding habitats available. Since many vector-borne diseases occur over a large geographical range, a model that allows for changes in environmental variables and accurately represents a vector population's response to those variables is critical for predicting disease risk. In a time when people are reconsidering the prospect of worldwide malaria eradication, it is increasingly important to examine many different transmission scenarios for the possibility of disease intervention.

3. INTERVENTION BY HEREDITY

Genetic differences underlie an array of mosquito behaviors and traits including preference for biting indoors versus outdoors, patterns of circadian flight activity, preference for blood feeding on animals versus humans, resistance to insecticide, ability for larvae to grow in polluted aquatic habitats, ability to be infected by the malaria parasite, and properties that confer reproductive isolation on a population. As these traits can dramatically

Figure 1. The life cycle of mosquitoes

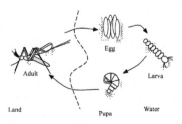

affect the transmission of malaria, as well as their response to interventions, the ability to model these genetic differences, their transmission through a mosquito population, and their resulting success is of high epidemiological value. A genetically-aware entomological model (GAEM) has the ability to facilitate mosquito agents responding to the environment based on their own individual traits, which may ultimately prove more or less favorable under differing conditions. Such a system would, for example, allow for the exploration of the usefulness of genetic modifications to mosquitoes, predict the selective pressure on various mutations, compare competition among various strains and species under differing conditions and scenarios, and model the emergence of reproductively isolated species.

In order to develop a GAEM, we need to understand how exploiting heredity can control malaria. Malaria is transmitted between hosts through a female mosquito. The male mosquitoes do not bloodfeed. The mosquito picks up the *Plasmodium* parasite from an infected host. Upon entering the mosquito, the parasite undergoes a transition where it moves from the insect's gut into the salivary glands. This incubation period takes ten to twelve days (Beier, 1998). It is transmitted to a new host through mosquito subsequent bites.

Some of the most effective strategies to control malaria is to interfere directly with the vector's ability to inoculate hosts. In other words, a goal is to reduce the occurrences of bites a human experiences from mosquitoes that have survived the parasite's incubation period. The number of these bites per person is a good estimator of vectorial capacity, the vector population's ability to transmit the disease between hosts. One way to reduce vectorial capacity is to reduce the number of mosquitoes. The sterile insect techniques (SITs) in this work do just that. Using lab-reared males, they inject a dominant lethal gene or males with compromised genetic material into the population. Females mate with these altered males. Progeny that receive the corrupted gene in one allele cease

developing and die. This method exploits heredity and the vector's mating behavior through the injection of altered males.

Anopheline mosquitoes mate at dusk in large swarms in a variety of locations such as over wells or grassy open areas (Manoukis et al., 2009). The swarms are formed entirely by males in what is called a lek, a non-resource- based aggregation (Manoukis et al., 2009). Females enter the swarms to mate because they are possibly attracted by the sound produced by the beating of the males' wings (Manoukis et al., 2009). Male mosquitoes swarm when they mate to access females easily and to reduce risk when seeking a mate (Charlwood & Jones, 1979). The object of SIT is to infiltrate the swarms with males that are genetically compromised or carry a lethal gene. Because females mate only once and males may mate with several females, the effect of SIT should significantly reduce the offspring population.

SIT has been successful in reducing the population of agricultural pests and some vectors. The most well known example is the eradication of the New World screwworm, Cochliomyia americana, which burrows into warm-blooded animals, including humans (Klassen & Curtis, 2005). Noted as responsible for the development of the SIT concept, Edward Fred Knipling noticed that female screwworms mated only once and that males were very aggressive in seeking females (Klassen & Curtis, 2005). He concluded that if sterility could be induced in the males, the population would decrease dramatically. With SIT, the New World screwworm was successfully eradicated from the USA, Mexico, Central America, and North Africa in the 1980s and 1990s (Klassen & Curtis, 2005). SIT also successfully eliminated the cotton crop pest, the boll weevil Anthonomous grandis grandis, from the USA in the 1970s and the tsetse fly, which carries trypanosome parasites, from Zanzibar (Klassen & Curtis, 2005).

Though traditional SIT has been successful in reducing the population of agricultural pests and some disease vectors, SIT has not been widely implemented in the eradication of malaria or the suppression of mosquito populations in general. Most releases of sterile male mosquitoes were conducted to answer specific research questions rather than effectively reduce a population (Benedict & Robinson, 2003). A few SIT population reduction programs have been attempted, but these programs were not of a sufficient scale to be implemented in non-isolated areas (Benedict & Robinson, 2003). The most successful attempt to reduce the population of an Anopheline mosquito was the elimination of an albimanus from a 15 km² area in El Salvador (Lofgren et al., 1974). Attempts were then repeated on a larger scale along the Pacific coast of El Salvador, but this effort failed due to the immigration of female mosquitoes from neighboring regions into the targeted region (Benedict & Robinson, 2003). Another complication of SIT is the possible loss of male fitness, which would render the sterilized males less competitive than the wild males (Benedict & Robinson, 2003).

We explore three possible SIT strategies. The first is the introduction of non-viable males (NVM). Lab-reared males carry sperm with compromised genetic material that halts offspring as eggs. The other two methods are the late-acting and early-acting "release of insects carrying a dominant lethal" (RIDL) in which the lethal gene halts female offspring but enables the male offspring to survive and pass on the lethal gene to subsequent generations (Thomas et al., 2000). With the RIDL method, males homozygous for a female-only lethal gene would be released. In the first generation of offspring, all offspring are heterozygous for the lethal gene. All male offspring can carry the lethal gene, and no females survive (Figure 2). For the second generation of offspring, only the male parent is heterozygous for the gene and the wild female parent does not carry it. Thus for the second generation, only half of the male offspring will be heterozygous for the lethal gene and only half of the females will die. This transgenic trend will continue to future generations. RIDL has been demonstrated in the fruit fly, Drosophila melanogaster, but its development is far less progressed for mosquito applications (Windbichler et al., 2008).

The lethal gene may cease development of the female offspring at two different stages, so the lethal gene is defined as either late-acting or early-acting. Late-acting lethality allows several days of larval development. Larvae compete for resources, and so allowing the larvae to live as

Figure 2. We investigate two intervention methods which involve the release of genetically-altered males. NVM releases males with depreciated genes whose eggs cannot hatch. RIDL targets female mosquitoes as eggs (early) or pupae (late)

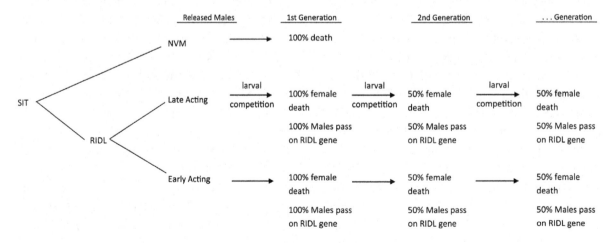

long as possible helps to crowd out natural populations of non-transgenic mosquito larvae (Paaijmans et al., 2009). Early-acting lethality may prevent the eggs from ever hatching and thus does not affect larval competition from the native population. Because the effect of RIDL is propagated throughout successive generations without continued human intervention, RIDL may yield a greater reduction in vectorial capacity per released male than NVM.

Although a promising intervention for malaria, the implementation of SIT is challenging. Mosquitoes must be mass-reared and separated by sex. Sterilized males must also be carefully transported to the release site. Helinski et al. (2008) tested the release of NVM mosquitoes in Sudan and cited mass-rearing and transportation as difficulties in the implementation of SIT. SIT could also be expensive to implement. Because SIT is challenging, modeling the effect of this intervention will enable public health workers to implement SIT in an effective, efficient matter. This genetically-aware entomological model could provide beneficial information to those working to eradicate malaria.

This section described the need for modeling heredity dynamics for mosquito vectors. We choose an agent-based model for capturing the transgenic characteristics of these methods because these types of models give every acting member its own unique set of attributes. We chose to extend an existing architecture for agent-based models. This is presented in Gentile et al. (2010) and allows developers to write simulations quickly by extending six abstract classes that describe the agents' environment and behavior. Our architecture is presented in Figure 3.

4. MOSQUITO VECTOR MODELING

The previous sections outlined the needs of an entomological, genetically aware software architecture for simulation. Such an architecture would be able to characterize complex and variable mosquito behavior. It would also need to capture the genetic dynamics of heredity to explore gene transmission across a mosquito population.

We use an agent-based discrete-time simulation to design an architecture to capture genetics and behavior in an entomological simulation. This allows agents to have there own genotypes which will govern their behavior and development. We have designed an agent-based modeling framework with the following specifications. There is a flexible time resolution for discrete events. Environments can contain sub-environments. Complex agent behavior is built using simple building blocks forming a coherent strategy. Agents have phenotypes which are inherited from their parents. Finally, our frame- work makes use of message passing and was structured to be parallelized.

4.1. Structure

Our framework defines six building blocks that make up the architecture. The structure of these components is displayed in Figure 3 and has a clear hierarchy. The remaining content in this section describes the responsibilities for each component in the framework from the top down. Each class is an abstraction allowing this model architecture to be extended beyond entomological applications despite the context of this paper.

At the root of the hierarchy is the simulation. This object is responsible for maintaining time and other variables relevant to all objects. The simulation class also contains a listing of environments and an inbox. The inbox object will be described in the next section when the method for passing agents is discussed. It is the simulation's responsibility to be the heartbeat for the system.

Contained within the simulation is a set of discrete environments. Multiple environments provide a mechanism for the partitioning of the simulated world into manageable sections (both conceptually and pragmatically). Environments interface with their parent containers to access

Figure 3. The software architecture we used in the model. The six base classes are on the left while the extensions for this work are presented on the right. We describe each element in Section 4

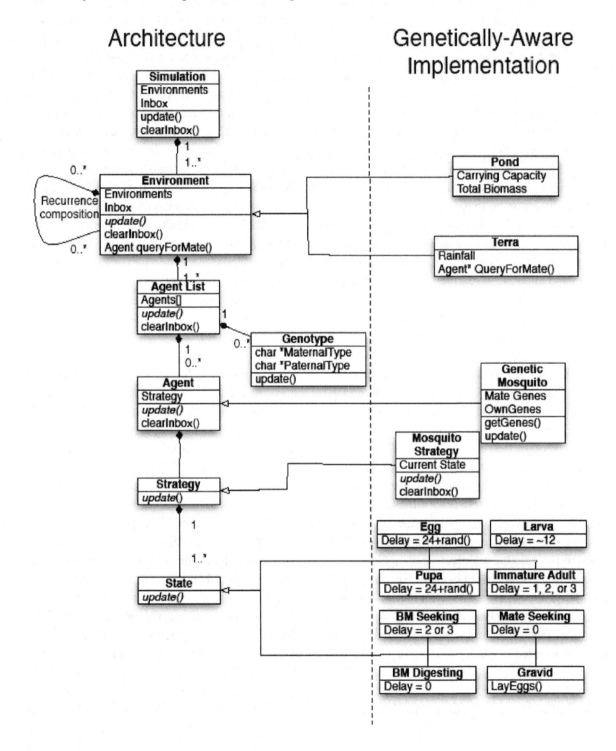

and inherit variables but can also contain their own local variables. Within an environment is a list of sub-environments which can be discrete elements (ponds, puddles, houses, etc.) or territories. Another critical member of an environment is its agent list.

Agent lists are containers holding all the agents within an environment. An agent list for a given environment does not contain agents existing in sub-environments. At their most simple, they are an array of agents but they can be reimplemented to perform population-wise functions. Agent lists can be easily extended to perform more advanced queries on the agent population within a given environment.

Agents are the autonomous entities, which operate, in a given environment. They consist of a set of variables describing their attributes. The behavior of an agent is affected by environmental variables and its own characteristics. The operations of an agent are encoded into a structure known as a strategy.

A strategy determines the agent's development, behaviors and interactions. It is collection of discrete, connected states. An agent moves through the states given a collection of rule sets.

States are distinct elements describing an agent's action or inaction at any moment in time. States are connected to others through edges. States consist of an entry point, a time delay,

behavioral decision rules and pathways to other states. The entry point sets initial conditions for the state. The time delay pauses the agent for a given period. This can be a relative time (1 hour) or an absolute time (3:05 P.M. or next Thursday). After the delay, behavioral decisions are made. The decision is an algorithm defined by the programmer which can take into account both environmental and agent-specific variables. The algorithm determines which state the agent moves to next. States can probe the environment through interfaces mimicking sensors or interact with the environment when moving or finding other agents or other environments.

4.2. Agent Routing Through Message-Passing

It is very common for an agent to move between environments in an entomological simulation (Figure 4). When an aquatic pupa emerges as a mosquito, it moves out of a pond and into a terra environment. When an agent flies across a spatial boundary between two environments, it passes from one to another. This section describes how this movement is performed.

Every environment has knowledge about its parent container (the simulation or another environment) and its own sub-environments. When an agent's strategy decides the agent is to pass

Figure 4. Communication diagram to illustrate the message passing during one simulation timestep

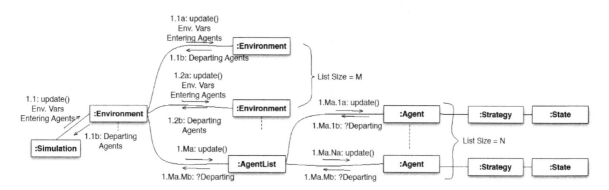

between environments, it addresses the agent to the appropriate environment and places it in the parent container's inbox. The address is a descriptor for the environment so it knows where to route the agent.

In an entomological simulation, there are three common ways for an agent to pass from one environment to another: injection, emergence and movement. Injection happens when an adult inserts an egg into a pond. In emergence, a pupa has matured into an adult and goes from a pond (sub-environment) to a terra (parent container). Movement is the passing of an agent between two terras.

When a mosquito is laying eggs, new agents are created and injected into a pond (sub-environment). Programmatically, this is done by the mosquito strategy querying the terra for a pond. Eggs are created by the mosquito via the strategy and placed into the pond's inbox.

For emergence, the agent's strategy decides that it is time to transition from the pond to the terra. The strategy interfaces with the pond informing it of the change. The pond removes the agent from its agent list and places it into the terra's inbox through a message. The agent, strategy and all, is received by terra and waits in its inbox.

When an agent moves between terras, it is going between two environments of equal rank in the hierarchy. This is allowed in the simulation through implemented routing. The strategy detects the transition between two environments by checking the agent's position against the terra's bounds. The strategy informs its terra of this event. The terra removes that agent from itself and sends it to the parent object (the simulation). The agent waits for routing in the simulation's inbox.

Inboxes, seen in the class diagram, contain agents that are being inserted into an environment. For each agent in the inbox, the address is checked. Addresses are descriptions as to where the agent needs to go. If it is determined the containing

object is the agent's new home, it is added to the environment's agent list. If it is determined that the agent is bound for a sub-environment in that object, it is added to that sub-environment's inbox and awaits processing. Messages can be passed internally through shared memory or they can be sent between computers. Internal messages will allow for one simulation to be threaded in one machine using a tool like OpenMP. The simulation can be distributed over a cluster using MPI. These methods will allow simulations to take better advantage of multi-core machines and computing clusters.

4.3. Updates

An update refers to the actions the of simulation objections during and the calculation of variables for one time step. Every element of the simulation has an update function and these are called in a recursive fashion. The call traverses the hierarchy in a depth-first fashion.

The first update pulse is handled by the simulation. Upon receiving this instruction, the simulation updates all the independent, global variables and then clears its inbox. All the agents within the simulation's inbox are routed to other environments. When the inbox is clear, the simulation calls the update function for each environment.

For all environments, updates happen in the following manner. First, the environmental variables are refreshed. Next the agents in its inbox are added to its agent list or routed to an appropriate sub-environment. Then the agent list is told to update.

The agent list updates by first performing any list-specific operations. Finally, the agents are updated. The agents tell their strategies to update which, in turn, tell their current state to do so. An update to an agent's state can either have the agent remain in that state if it is delayed or have the agent transfer to a new state.

4.4. Capturing Genetics

In order for some intervention methods to be simulated, genetics need to be captured in the agent population. For every gene to capture, an agent needs to store phenotypes, one from its mother and one from its father.

A reproductive female stores the gene set of her mate and passes his and her phenotype to progeny upon instantiation. In the progeny's constructor, it selects one phenotype from each parent at random (similar to a Punnet Square). That agent's genetic makeup is stored and passed on to its progeny if it reproduces. As agent's makeup, behavior or development can thus be dependent on its phenotype.

Gene transfer between reproductive agents is performed by a series of messages (Figure 5). The female agent queries the environment for a reproductive male and gets a response. If a male is found, the female asks for the male's genes and get a response.

4.5. Design Benefits

There are several major benefits to this design. First, agent behavior is easy to conceptualize and encode. Second, behavior is easy to alter and extend. Third, changes to objects in the simulation have a known scope. Forth, every agent sees the environment the same way. Next, the method for transferring agents and for updating is conducive to parallelization. Finally, genetic information is inherited from parents and affect an agent.

This architecture presents a clear and concise method for encoding an agent's behavior. This is done by having a strategy consist of an implemented state diagram that interfaces with the agent and the environment. States within the strategy are responsible for one discrete action of the mosquito and it is easy to isolate and alter that behavior because of its narrow scope.

Every agent owns a unique version of its strategy. Therefore, it is trivial to add behavioral variation even within agents of the same species. Since behavior has a finite scope, code-level adjustments are simple. Likewise, novel strategies can be easily created for new agent types.

Figure 5. The genes are transferred during mating. This is all performed through message passing. First, the female queries her environment for a mate. She then retrieves the mate's genotype

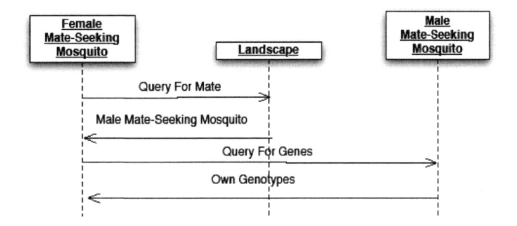

The framework clearly defines the arrangement of objects and how those objects are updated. This ensures the program is broken into manageable bits whose scope is very well defined within the simulation as a whole. This is desirable as more complex scenarios are devised and experimental results hinge on how the changes made to the simulation propagate through to all the agents. Our framework guarantees that only changes visible to the agent affect the agent.

In the real world, all agents are working in parallel. This means that they are all sensing the same world at the same time. This idea is replicated in the simulation by locking the environmental variables before the agents are updated. This way all agents see the same snapshot of the world. Therefore, simulation results are not affected by the order in which agents are updated.

The hierarchical design, the message passing and updating processes make this system easily parallelizable. Every environment on the same tier can be processed concurrently. Furthermore, the updating of all the agents within an environment can be threaded. Agents can move between environments either through shared memory or between machines through message passing. All communication is performed vertically in the hierarchy and is designed so that deadlocks are impossible.

An agent inherits genotypes through parental lines. Certain transgenic features can be modeled by adding new phenotypes which govern behavior and those genes will be passed on to progeny. The genetic makeup of a new agent is dependent on its familial line and is implemented with a Punnet-Square style algorithm.

An emerged female remains in a mate-seeking state until 6 P.M. (dusk) when she is randomly paired with a mate. This is performed through a series of messages passed between her and the environment, simulating her observation of and attraction to the male swarm and her response to climatic conditions. After receiving a mate, the female queries for the male's genetic information. This is illustrated in Figure 5. The female passes the genotype to her offspring.

When a new agent is generated in our system (Table 1), it is given one copy (an allele) for each trait from each parent. The constructor randomly selects one from each parent and defines the new combination as the agent's genotype. Alleles from this new genotype are passed to subsequent generations if the agent reproduces.

The encoded genetic information governs the mosquito's behavior. In the architecture, state transitions are dependent on environmental attributes (e.g., time) and agent specific characteristics (e.g., sex or empty egg batch). We extend

Table 1. Our model is a series of behavioral and developmental states. This table summarizes the model by time in state and exit condition. The topology of the states is presented in Figure 7. rnd() is a random process which represents the observed distribution of egg hatch and adult emergence times

State	Duration	Exit Condition
Egg	1 day + rnd()	None
Larva	about 12 days	Nighttime
P upa	1 day + rnd()	Nighttime
I mmature Adult	53 hours	None
M ate Seeking	-	6 P.M. & Female
Bloodmeal Seeking	-	Meal Success & Night
Bloodmeal Digesting	36 hours	Nighttime
Gravid	-	Empty Egg Batch & Night

these rules to account for more agent attributes (genes). New egg and pupa conditions were made for each of the three sterile insect technique methods we investigated (shown in Figure 6). Nonviable males generate offspring that never progress past the egg stage. Early-acting RIDL halts development of females in the egg state but allows males to develop fully and pass on the lethal gene. Late-acting RIDL ceases female development at the pupa state and allows males to fully develop as in early-acting RIDL.

It is important to touch on several possible design constraints. First, this architecture requires the system to operate on a time step which can be anchored to the real world (i.e., hourly or daily). The time step does not have to be constant however, it can change from courser to finer detail given the scope of the simulation. For instance, an hourly time step might be required at night but a 12 hour step through the day may be sufficient for insects whose behavior is mostly nocturnal. The system is also memory intensive given that each agent holds its own strategy. Therefore, the number of agents it can represent is largely dependent on the computational resources provided to the model.

5. PROOF OF CONCEPT

We used the genetically-aware model to model the possible the effects of three SIT interventions in an Anophelene population. These were the release of non-viable males (NM) and the release of genetically modified males carrying a dominant lethal gene (RIDL) in both the early and late-acting stages. The release of NVMs results in zero progeny of females that mate with non-viable males. Early-acting RIDL prevents female eggs from hatching, and late-acting RIDL terminates growth of females in the larval stage. RIDL results in a first generation in which all offspring

inherit the gene, causing the females to die and the males to become heterozygous for the lethal trait (meaning there is one copy of the gene in the agent) that can be passed on to offspring. When these heterozygous males mate with wild females, half of the offspring will inherit the gene while the other half will be wild-type. In this second generation, half of the females will die and half of the males will pass on the lethal gene. The pattern of the second generation continues for subsequent generations.

The transgenic dynamics of RIDL make this technique more effective than NVM since RIDL enables the propagation of the gene throughout several generations of mosquitoes without further intervention. Furthermore, late- acting RIDL is hypothesized to be more effective than early-acting RIDL due to the effect of larval competition on the population (recall that larvae compete for resources in ponds and older larva are favored). Our model should report this general trend to show validity. For further testing, we asked two key questions for these techniques, How many? and How often?. In asking "how many?", we hope to determine how many NVM or RIDL males should be released in comparison to the number of wild males in a particular region.

These ratios have been shown to range from 2:1 to 15:1 of sterile-to-wild males in a variety of other insects (Dame et al., 2009; Feldmann & Hendrichs, 2001), though no study looks at malaria vectors specifically (Lofgren et al., 1974). We hope to find an appropriate altered-to-wild male ratio for the malaria vector for each of the SIT methods. Another important question is how often should SIT males be released? Public health workers should understand the effects of releasing the insects daily, weekly, or monthly. Infiltrating the male swarms more frequently may be more effective than waiting for long periods between releases.

Figure 6. Our model allows for genetic traits to directly affect the state transitions of agents. We capture three sterile insect technique strategies. The first involves releasing non-viable males into the population. All their progeny will cease developing as eggs. The other two strategies target females through a dominant lethal gene. Females with this gene will cease development as eggs or pupa. Males with 'K' will survive and mate

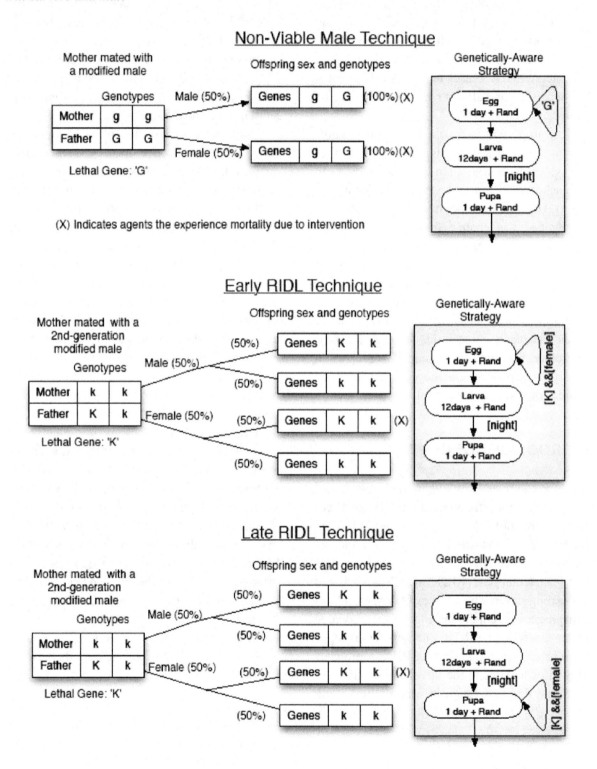

Figure 7. We model the mosquito lifecycle in the pond and in terra. Our simulation structure maintains a global clock which is used to determine the times in state and the exact time of day. This is the topology of the state's linked in the agent's strategy. The time in states are presented at one temperature (25 degrees Celsius)

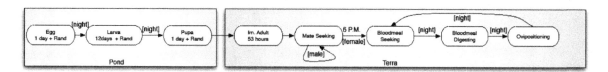

5.1. How Many?

To evaluate the effectiveness of SIT under different release proportions we constructed our simulation to release various ratios of SIT males to wild-type males. The system started with all wild-type mosquitoes until the population was constant. Then, SIT males were counted in our simulation. Every 14 days, the number of SIT males was released based on the established proportion. The release happened every 14 days because we considered this a feasible time scale for those who would be working to eradicate malaria by releasing SIT males. Ten simulations were averaged for each release pro- portion, which ranged from 1:1 to 9:1 for NVM to wild-type males. The effectiveness of these various proportions was measured by their reduction of vectorial capacity (shown in Figure 8). We report our findings in measures of potentially infectious night bites and reduction in vectorial capacity. Vectorial capacity is the count of bites from insects that have fed, survived the period of time Plasmodium takes to develop in the insect, and have fed again. The reduction amount was generated by dividing by the night bites in a control simulation that did not experience any intervention. Ten simulation runs were averaged for all the presented numbers in all the plots including the control simulations.

As expected, late-acting RIDL was the most effective SIT intervention while the release of NVM was the least effective. Late-acting RIDL yielded the greatest reduction in vectorial capac-

ity. The surprising result was the impact of a transgenic reservoir in the mosquito population. The trend of the RIDL curves differs greatly from that of the NVM. Recall that RIDL passes the dominant lethal gene through the paternal line and NVM does not. This passage generates a population of males in successive generations that are potentially lethal. This indicates that the release of NVM needs the male population to be nearly saturated with altered males. These results qualitatively align with those found by Phuc et al. (2007) when modeling SIT for another disease vector however, these models and SIT deployment is not reported in Anopheles gambiae.

5.2. How Often?

In addition to experimenting with the various proportions at which SIT males were released, we also varied the frequency at which they were released. Mosquitoes were injected at various intervals ranging between 1 day and 29

Figure 9 suggests that releasing smaller numbers more frequently has a better effect than releasing large batches every 20 or 25 days, especially for the release of late-acting RIDL mosquitoes. In contrast, the reduction in vectorial capacity when early-acting and NVM mosquitoes are released is not greatly affected by the frequency of release days. The same proportion of mosquitoes (4:1 SIT to wild-type males) was released each 29-day period, so the periods between releases did not affect the total number of mosquitoes released. In

Figure 8. The release proportion of sterile males has an effect on vectorial capacity (1 being the vectorial capacity without intervention). More sterile males lead to more retarded agents and less vectorial capacity. The release of early-acting and late-acting RIDL mosquitoes yields reductions in vecto- rial capacity at various proportions. The release of NVM requires a critical saturation of population to take effect on vectorial capacity. The vectorial capacity is presented as a proportional reduction in this plot

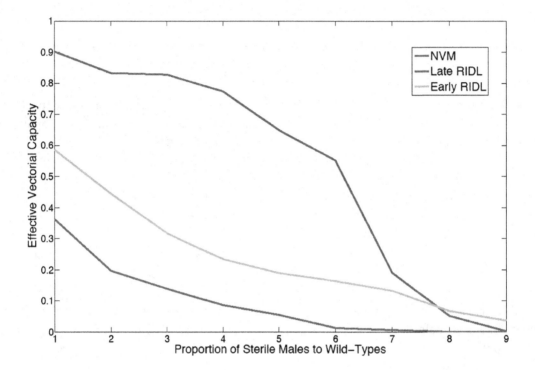

this experiment, we found that late-acting RIDL was not only again the most effective SIT method but also most affected by changes in frequency (shown in Figure 9). The late-acting RIDL method reduced vectorial capacity more effectively when released more frequently. The vectorial capacity was reduced by 200 potentially infectious night bites when late-acting RIDL mosquitoes were released every day com- pared to when they were released once every month. When the late-acting RIDL males were released at periods ranging from 1 day to 14 days, there were roughly 300 infectious night bites. After about 14 days, the infectious night bites increased. The late-acting RIDL is probably more effective with higher frequency of release because the effect of larval competi-

tion is maximized. The larvae produced by the transgenic males maintain a relatively constant presence in the larval habitats when the frequency of release is high. They maintain competition with the non-transgenic larvae and effectively reduce the population. When the transgenic males are not released as frequently, the transgenic larvae exist in one large cohort before dying from the lethal trait. They are not quickly replaced by more transgenic larvae and therefore cause barely any competition for the wild-type larvae. This trend is not exhibited in the release of early-acting RIDL and NVM mosquitoes, which reduced vectorial capacity by only 100 or less infectious night bites when released more frequently (every 14 days) rather than once a month.

Figure 9. The period between male release can have an effect on vectorial capacity (night bites)

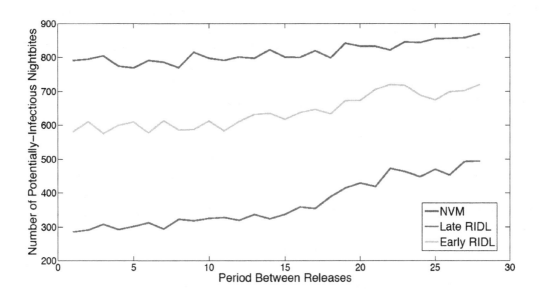

By simulating genetics with our model, we are able to determine the relative differences in effectiveness and efficiency of various SIT interventions of malaria. As we expected, late-acting RIDL appears to be the most effective in all scenarios. Therefore, taking advantage of larval competition may be the most effective in the implementation of SIT. We were also able to determine which proportions of release and which frequencies would be the most influential in the field. The release of early and late-acting RIDL mosquitoes was effective at any release proportion while the release of NVM was effective only when the proportion reached 7:1 NVM males to wild-type males. Late-acting RIDL's efficacy depended on the release period while NVM and early-acting did not. Using our GAEM, we predict that an efficient SIT method is late-acting RIDL released at a 6:1 proportion to the native population and at a period of no more than 14 days

6. DISCUSSION

This paper presented a framework for modeling genetically-aware mosquito vectors. Simulations are constructed using six building blocks arranged in a hierarchy. Mosquito biology and associated behavior is encoded into a structure known as a strategy. Strategies are composites of fundamentally simple states. Strategies are easily extended allowing for variation and complexity. Structure and order is maintained by giving every object its own specific and finite scope. Every agent has the same view so the order in which agents are processed does not matter. The framework has built-in mechanisms for message passing allowing for the framework to be parallelized.

Genetic differences lead to alternative behaviors, susceptibilities, and vectorial capacities that require a model that responds accordingly. We discussed several real-world situations in which this is important including allowing for the exploration of the usefulness of genetic modifications to mosquitoes, pre- diction of the selective pressure on various mutations, comparing competition among various strains and species under differing conditions and scenarios, and modeling the emergence of reproductively isolated species. We designed an agent-based model to simulate genetic inheritance and allowed behavior to depend on an agent's genes. As a proof-of-concept, we simulated implementations of sterile insect technique for malaria intervention, both late and early-acting RIDL and the release of non-viable males. Within the limits of our model, our results show late-acting RIDL to be superior to release of non-viable males in reducing vectorial capacity. Additionally, improved reductions in vectorial capacity may be achieved through the increase in frequency of releasing males. Late-acting RIDL was shown to be most sensitive to this release frequency. Releases may be most effective at 14 day intervals, but there are also complications to consider, such as the expense of creating transgenic males and transporting them to release sites. The conclusions of this paper as well as further consideration of these logistical issues may aid public health workers in their efforts to eradicate malaria.

Though our model demonstrates that the most effective SIT strategy is the release of late-acting RIDL, success of this strategy may only be proven in field experiments. Our model is not sensitive to several unknown mosquito behavior dynamics that may alter the results of our SIT modeling experiments. For example, we assume that female mosquitoes do not have a preference for any type of males. In the field, irradiated or genetically modified males may not compete well, and females might more frequently mate with wild-type males. Competition among the larvae may also be affected.

RIDL larvae may not be as competitive as wild-type larvae and therefore contribute less to density-dependent mortality (Phuc et al., 2007). Also, the RIDL gene may not cause lethality in 100% of the females that acquire the gene, as is assumed in our model. RIDL lethality proved approximately 95-97% effective in Aedes aegypti, the vector of dengue fever (Phuc et al., 2007). Furthermore, genetic modification is not entirely predictable. Mutations may develop and propagate as mosquitoes are reared for release. These mutations may alter mosquito behavior. The model also assumes a closed system. Possible migration of mosquitoes from other habitats may alter the effectiveness of SIT strategies. Furthermore, genetically altered males may not remain localized and may migrate away from the target eradication area. Field experimentation would yield further insight about these concerns and would enable the construction of more accurate model.

REFERENCES

Beier, J. (1998). Malaria parasite development in mosquitoes. *Annual Review of Entomology*, *43*(1), 519–543. doi:10.1146/annurev.ento.43.1.519

Benedict, M., & Robinson, A. (2003). The first releases of transgenic mosquitoes: An argument for the sterile insect technique. *Trends in Parasitology*, *19*(8), 349–355. doi:10.1016/S1471-4922(03)00144-2

Bomblies, A., Duchemin, J., & Eltahir, E. (2008). Hydrology of malaria: Model development and application to a Sahelian village. *Water Resources Research*, 44.

Bomblies, A., Duchemin, J., & Eltahir, E. (2009). A mechanistic approach for accurate simulation of village scale malaria transmission. *Malaria Journal*, 8, 223. doi:10.1186/1475-2875-8-223

Bryce, J., Boschi-Pinto, C., Shibuya, K., & Black, R. (2005). WHO estimates the causes of death in children. *Lancet*, 1147–1152. doi:10.1016/S0140-6736(05)71877-8

Chapman, B., Jost, G., & Pas, R. d. (2007). *Using OpenMP: Portable shared memory parallel programming (Scientific and engineering computation)*. Cambridge, MA: MIT Press.

Charlwood, J., & Jones, M. (1979). Mating behavior in the mosquito *Anophe-les gambiae sl.* close range and contact-behavior. *Physiological Entomology, 4*, 111–120. doi:10.1111/j.1365-3032.1979. tb00185.x

Craig, M., Snow, R., & Sueur, D. L. (1999). A climate-based distribution model of malaria transmission in sub-Saharan Africa. *Parasitology Today (Personal Ed.), 15*(3), 105–110. doi:10.1016/S0169-4758(99)01396-4

Crawley, J. (2004). Reducing the burden of anemia in infants and young children in malaria-endemic countries of Africa: From evidence to action. *The American Journal of Tropical Medicine and Hygiene, 71*(2), 25.

Dame, D., Curtis, C., Benedict, M., Robinson, A., & Knols, B. (2009). Historical applications of induced sterilisation in field populations of mosquitoes. *Malaria Journal, 8*(2), 2. doi:10.1186/1475-2875-8-S2-S2

Feldmann, U., & Hendrichs, J. (2001). *Integrating the sterile insect technique as a key component of area-wide tsetse and trypanosomiasis intervention* (p. 66). New York, NY: Food & Agriculture Organization of the United Nations.

Gabaldon, A. (1978). What can and cannot be achieved with conventional anti-malaria measures. *The American Journal of Tropical Medicine and Hygiene, 27*(4), 653–658.

Gabriel, E., Fagg, G., Bosilca, G., & Angskun, T. (2004). Open MPI: Goals, concept, and design of a next generation MPI implementation. In *Proceedings of the 11ᵗʰ European PVM/VPI Users' Group Meeting Conference*, Budapest, Hungary (pp. 97-104).

Gentile, J. E., Davis, G. J., Laurent, B. S., & Kurtz, S. (2010). A framework for modeling mosquito vectors. In *Proceedings of the Summer Simulation* (pp. 1-8).

Greenwood, B., & Mutabingwa, T. (2002). Malaria in 2002. *Nature, 415*(6872), 670–672. doi:10.1038/415670a

Gu, W., & Novak, R. (2009). Agent-based modelling of mosquito foraging behaviour for malaria control. *Transactions of the Royal Society of Tropical Medicine and Hygiene, 103*(11), 1105–1112. doi:10.1016/j.trstmh.2009.01.006

Helinski, M., Hassan, M., El-Motasim, W., Malcolm, C., & Knols, B., & El- Sayed, B. (2008). Towards a sterile insect technique field release of Anophe-les arabiensis mosquitoes in Sudan: Irradiation, transportation, and field cage experimentation. *Malaria Journal, 7*(1), 65. doi:10.1186/1475-2875-7-65

Killeen, G., Knols, B., & Gu, W. (2003). Taking malaria transmission out of the bottle: implications of mosquito dispersal for vector- control interventions. *The Lancet Infectious Diseases, 3*(5), 297–303. doi:10.1016/S1473-3099(03)00611-X

Klassen, W., & Curtis, C. (2005). *History of the sterile insect technique. Sterile insect technique: Principles and practice in area-wide integrated pest management.* New York, NY: Springer.

Lofgren, C., Dame, D., Breeland, S., Weidhaas, D., Jeffery, G., & Kaiser, R. (1974). Release of chemosterilized males for the control of Anopheles albimanus in El Salvador: III. Field methods and population control. *The American Journal of Tropical Medicine and Hygiene, 23*(2), 288.

Macal, C., & North, M. (2008). Agent-based modeling and simulation: ABMS examples. In *Proceedings of the 40th Conference on Winter Simulation* (pp.101-112).

Manoukis, N., Diabate, A., Abdoulaye, A., Diallo, M., & Dao, A. (2009). Structure and dynamics of male swarms of Anopheles gambiae. *Journal of Medical Entomology, 46*(2), 227. doi:10.1603/033.046.0207

Molineaux, L., Gramiccia, G., & WHO. (1980). *The Garki project: Research on the epidemiology and control of malaria in the Sudan savanna of west Africa.* (p. 311). Retrieved from http://www.cabdirect.org/abstracts/19812901070.html;jsessionid=329ED17B0C4FCD0D9EB971E95BABC593

Omumbo, J., Hay, S., Guerra, C., & Snow, R. (2004). The relationship between the Plasmodium falciparum parasite ratio in childhood and climate estimates of malaria transmission in Kenya. *Malaria Journal, 3,* 17. doi:10.1186/1475-2875-3-17

Paaijmans, K., Huijben, S., Githeko, A., & Takken, W. (2009). Competitive interactions between larvae of the malaria mosquitoes Anopheles arabiensis and Anopheles gambiae under semi-field conditions in western Kenya. *Acta Tropica, 109*(2), 124–130. doi:10.1016/j.actatropica.2008.07.010

Phuc, H., Andreasen, M., Burton, R., Vass, C., Epton, M., & Pape, G. (2007). Late-acting dominant lethal genetic systems and mosquito control. *BMC Biology, 5*(1), 11. doi:10.1186/1741-7007-5-11

Sharma, U., & Singh, S. (2008). Insect vectors of leishmania: Distribution, physiology and their control. *Journal of Vector Borne Diseases, 45.*

Thomas, D., Donnelly, C., Wood, R., & Alphey, L. (2000). Insect population control using a dominant, repressible, lethal genetic system. *Science, 287*(5462), 2474. doi:10.1126/science.287.5462.2474

WHO. (2004). *Changing history.* Geneva, Switzerland: World Health Organization.

Windbichler, N., Papathanos, P., & Crisanti, A. (2008). Targeting the X chromosome during spermatogenesis induces Y chromosome transmission ratio distortion and early dominant embryo lethality in Anopheles gambiae. *PLOS Genetics, 4*(12). doi:10.1371/journal.pgen.1000291

This work was previously published in International Journal of Agent Technologies and Systems, Volume 3, Issue 3, edited by Yu Zhang, pp. 49-65, copyright 2011 by IGI Publishing (an imprint of IGI Global).

Section 6
Simulation in Ecosystem

Chapter 17
Quasi–PSO Algorithm for Modeling Foraging Dynamics in Social Mammals

Marco Campenní
Institute of Cognitive Sciences and Technologies (ISTC), Italy

Federico Cecconi
Institute of Cognitive Sciences and Technologies (ISTC), Italy

ABSTRACT

In this paper, the authors present a computational model of a fundamental social phenomenon in the study of animal behavior: the foraging. The purpose of this work is, first, to test the validity of the proposed model compared to another existing model, the flocking model; then, to try to understand whether the model may provide useful suggestions in studying the size of the group in some species of social mammals.

INTRODUCTION

The Foraging Theory is a branch of behavioral ecology that studies the behavior of foraging animals in response to a (more or less) complex environment in which they live. The Optimal Foraging Theory (*OFT*) (see MacArthur & Pianka, 1966; Emlen, 1966) is a refined version of this theory which establishes that animals must find, capture and consume food with more calories as possible, using the shortest possible time.

DOI: 10.4018/978-1-4666-1565-6.ch017

Essentially, there are three main versions of the *OFT*:

- The optimal diet model that describes the behavior of a forager that meets with different types of prey and must decide which one to attack;
- The patch selection theory describing the behavior of a forager whose prey is concentrated in small areas, but one far from the other so that the forager must spend a significant amount of time (and energy) to over from one to another;

- The central place foraging theory, which describes the behavior of a forager who must return to a particular place (usually always the same) to consume is/her own food or to give it to his/her offspring.

The research field that deals with developing models of behavior related to foraging and hunting has a long and established tradition and has worked for more than thirty years; since from the mid seventies, many aspects of the dynamics and behaviors related to the activity of foraging and hunting were investigated.

Some authors (Caraco & Wolf, 1975) have proposed to investigate the influence of ecological factors in determining the size of a group of (social) foragers (rather than to adopt the traditional analytical approach to model this type of phenomenon); other researchers (Nudds, 1978) have attempted to extend the research on determining the size of a social group of carnivorous mammals from the case of lions to that of wolves. Others (Caraco, 1980) have presented models of foraging in stochastic environment; incorporating the responses of forager to environmental unpredictable changes, these models may be useful to make different predictions from those obtained with traditional deterministic models. Analytical models (Rodman, 1981) have been proposed to explain the dynamics and behaviors related to foraging (such as a simple model that expresses the inclusive fitness in function of the group size, when social groups contain relative and the individual fitness varies with the size of the group). Some researchers (Clark & Mangel, 1984) have theorized that i) the group foraging (or group flocking) may increase the rate of individual feeding as a result of information sharing among group members, and also ii) the group foraging reduces the variation in the rate of the feeding for its members. Both of these benefits grow with decreasing amounts of food and if it is patchy distributed. Finally, some models of foraging dynamics based on rules (Rands, Cowlishaw,

Pettifor, Rowclife, & Johnstone, 2003; Rands, Pettifor, Rowclife, & Cowlishaw, 2004; Rands, Pettifor, Rowclife, & Cowlishaw, 2006) and evolutionary optimization algorithms (Cecconi & Campenni', 2010; Campenni' & Cecconi, 2009) have been proposed in recent years.

MATERIAL AND METHODS

Particle Swarm Optimization *(PSO)*

Our model, agent-based (Cecconi, 2008) and created using NetLogo (n.d.), is strongly inspired by PSO algorithm. The PSO algorithm is a stochastic optimization population-based algorithm that derives from Evolutionary Optimization (EO). The goal of EO is to determine values for parameters or state variables of a model that will provide the best possible solution to a predefined cost function or objective, or a set of functions, in the case of two or more competing objectives (Goldberg, 1989; Fonseca & Fleming, 1996; Back, 1996; Ravindran, Phillips, & Solberg, 2001; Taha, 2011; Sarker, Mohammadian, & Yao, 2002). Several approaches have been proposed for efficiently finding i) the best solutions to problems with single objective function and ii) Pareto-optimal solutions to complex problems of multi-objective optimization. In particular, evolutionary algorithms have shown a powerful approach to solving search and optimization problems that consider multiple conflicting objectives. Although the class of multi-objective optimization problems has been sufficiently investigated (see Parsopoulos & Vrahatis, 2002; Hu, Eberhart, & Shi, 2003; Radicchi, Castellano, Cecconi, Loreto, & Parisi, 2004), the evolutionary algorithms today available, typically implement a single algorithm for the evolution of the population. However, existing theories (see Wolpert & Macready, 1997) and numerical experiments have shown that it is impossible to develop a single algorithm for population evolution that could be always efficient for a set of different optimization problems. Thus, in the last years memetic algorithms (also called hybrid genetic algorithms) have been proposed to increase the efficiency of optimization population-based algorithms. These methods are inspired by models of adaptation in natural systems and use genetic algorithms for global exploration of the space of combining them with local heuristic search for exploitation of the most promising areas. The original version of PSO was introduced by Kennedy et al. (2001) (see Kennedy, Eberhart, & Shi, 2001; Kennedy & Eberhart, 1995); in the PSO (see also Engelbrecht, 2005) a swarm of particles move in the n-dimensional space of solutions to a problem (multi-objective), trying to find the best solution. This algorithm can be used to model and predict social behavior in the presence of different objectives. The swarm is generally modeled by particles with a position and a speed in a multidimensional space. These particles fly" in this hyperspace and have two main cognitive abilities (very simple): i) they have the memory of his best position; ii) they know the best position and iii) the better positions of nearby particles. The members of the swarm can instantly communicate each other their positions and they can adjust their position and speed as a result of such information flow. In this way, a particle has the following information:

- Overall best is known to each particle and is immediately updated whenever a new better position is found by any particle in the swarm;
- Local best that refers to the best solution found by the single particle;
- Best of neighbors that the particle obtained by communicating with a subset of the particles swarm.

To implement a model of foraging behavior, the traditional Particle Swarm Optimization algorithm (PSO) has limitations which prevent its use. The model we present in this work attempts to overcome these limitations and to understand the key elements that contribute to the emergence of social behavior, under certain conditions; to test the excellence of the proposed model we compared our results with those obtained with a traditional flocking algorithm.

Quasi-Particle Swarm Optimization (Q-*PSO*)

In our model agents (particles) have as well:

- Local information (which derives from their perception of the environment) and
- (Indirect) information arising from the neighbors (produced by interaction with other agents);
- Moreover, they change their position and speed (on the basis of information they receive).

However, in our model there is no information about a global best; in fact, assuming that in our simulated world there is no qualitative difference between a unit of food and the other, it makes no sense to speak of the global best. In our model there are units of food, qualitatively equal to one another, which are distributed in the environment so as to form little islands full of food (as the *OFT* and more precisely in its meaning of patch selection theory). We have also implemented a proto-form of communication: agents exchange signals when they find a source of food and these signals propagate in the environment (degrading the intensity) as acoustic waves. Classic *PSO* algorithm is not useful to model the phenomenon of interest, because:

- In the foraging behavior in question (patch selection theory), it makes no sense to speak of global best;
- Furthermore, in such social behavior it is implausible to speak of instantaneous information (such as that modeled by the *PSO*);

- In foraging behavior modeling where the food is modeled by discrete patches[1] we cannot define any gradient for the objective function.

To overcome these major limitations of *PSO,* in our model there is no information about the overall best and a proto-form of stigmergic communication (physically plausible) is implemented.

The world consists of a two-dimensional toroidal grid on which the agents move. The task of the agents (simulated robots, see Nolfi & Floreano, 1978; Patel, Honavar, & Balakrishnan, 2001) is to explore the world to find all the units of available food in the shortest time possible.

Each agent is characterized by some individual properties:

- Velocity $v1$ (basic);
- Velocity $v2$ (less than $v1$, to be adopted in an area where there is food);
- Direction;
- Rotation speed (indicating how abruptly agent changes its direction);
- Flag indicating that the agent is in a particular area (i.e., where a source of food is).

The model also contains simple rules that allow us to implement the behavior of agents:

i.   If an agent A is close to an agent B, both change their direction in order to get away as possible from each other (this is a big difference from the *PSO* and other swarm algorithms, e.g., flocking);
ii. When an agent finds food, it changes its speed (from $v1$ to $v2$) and
iii. Changes its direction in order to make more circular movements,
iv. Emits a signal that propagates in the environment as an acoustic wave.
v.   When an agent receives a signal (which may be the result of the sum of different signals), it tries to follow the gradient of the signal.

In our model (see the interface of the simulator in Figure 1), the signal is different from the chemical signal emitted by termites to indicate to other members of the colony the presence of a food source (see stigrefs, n.d.); in our model, the signal is subject to evaporation (as in the case of termites), but (a) it spreads concentrically from the origin in the environment and it is not deposited in the environment as a chemical trace and (b) each signal can be added to other signals produced in other parts of the world; (c) moreover, the signal is emitted only if the agent modifies its speed. Once the signal is emitted, the agents can follow the gradient of the signal (indirectly reaching information about the position of the source of food).

PSO Dynamics

As mentioned, *PSO* is, in origin, an optimization technique, deriving from the evolutionary optimization (*EO*): its main features are the natural inspiration (like evolutionary techniques) and the possibility to implement *PSO* onto different levels, from the agent's level (like a search problem in a physical environment), to solutions' space level. Reliance on a single biological model of natural selection and adaptation presumes that a single method exists that efficiently evolves a population of potential solutions through the parameter space. However, existing theory and numerical experiments demonstrated that it is impossible to develop a single algorithm for population's evolution that is always efficient for a diverse set of optimization problems.

In recent years, memetic algorithms (also called hybrid genetic algorithms) have been proposed to increase the search efficiency of population-based optimization algorithms. These methods are inspired by models of adaptation in natural systems, and use a genetic algorithm for global exploration of the search space, combined with a local search heuristic for exploitation. Memetic algorithms have been shown to significantly speed

Figure 1. The simulator interface. Agents, small blue robots, move in the environment searching food (brown patches). When an agent finds a unit of food, it emits a signal that propagates in the environment (inside the dashed circle).

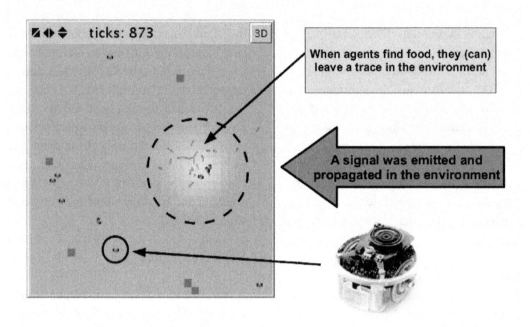

up the evolution toward the global optimal solution for a variety of real-world optimization problems.

However, our conjecture is that a search procedure adaptively changing the way by means of which is generated the offspring and based on the shape and local peculiarities of the fitness landscape, will further improve the efficiency of evolutionary search. This approach is likely to be productive because the nature of the fitness landscape (objective functions mapped out in the parameter space, also called the response surface) often varies considerably between different optimization problems, and dynamically changes en route to the global optimal solutions[2].

To defend these assumptions, we start the description of dynamics of *PSO from* another bio-inspired group behavior model, the Ant colony optimization, a technique for combinatorial optimization, inspired from ant behavior. Ant colony optimization was introduced as a technique for combinatorial optimization. The inspiring source of ant colony optimization model is the foraging behavior of real ant colonies. At the core of this behavior is the indirect communication between ants by means of chemical pheromone trails, which enables them to find short paths between their nest and food sources. This characteristic of real ant colonies is exploited in ant colony optimization algorithms in order to solve, for example, discrete and continuous optimization problems, and to manage tasks such as routing and load balancing in telecommunication networks and, more recently, in mobile ad hoc networks such as sensor networks. The swarm optimization and the ant optimization have certain characteristics in common. In fact, could we image a swarm of agents not only looking for resources but imitating behaviors each other too? The advantage using this approach is the flexibility and the scalability of algorithm.

In *PSO we* define $\mathbf{x}_k$ a vector with the position of particle k, $\mathbf{v}_k$ the current velocity of particle k and the heading for particle k, $\mathbf{p}_k$ (in other words $\mathbf{p}_k$ is the best position found by particle k). We compute g, the index (the ID) of the particle that has found the best position. We define $Q(\mathbf{x})$ the quality of position $\mathbf{x}$. In other words, Q is the value of objective functions.

$$g = \arg \max x_k Q(p_k)$$

Now we write down the velocity dynamics in this form

$$v_k^{t+1} = \left[w v_k + \phi_1 \left(p_k - x_k \right) + \phi_2 \left(p_g - x_k \right) \right]_{\text{at time } t}$$

The equation is, essentially, the description of an acceleration dynamics: i) in $w\mathbf{v}_k$ $w \in [0, 1]$ is an inertial factor: particle tends to maintain direction. ii) $\varphi_1(\mathbf{p}_k - \mathbf{x}_k)$ is the so-called *cognition* factor: particle should go toward private best; φ_1 is a random uniform variable distributed over $[0, 2]$. iii) $\varphi_2(\mathbf{p}_g - \mathbf{x}_k)$ is the social part of the dynamics: particle should go toward public best.

Obviously, we update position with

$$\dot{x}_k = v_k$$

In a Word, What is *PSO*?

It is a simple, population based, stochastic optimization method. From the point of view of final users, the main question is twofold: how can we make sure that we have convergent trajectories? and do we really understand the behavior of *PSO* in terms of guaranteed convergence on global minima?

We can resume the main result: it has been proved that particles converge to stable points. This result derives from the dynamics-style of *PSO formulation*[3]. Trajectories of particles are trajecto-

ries in the classical sense used for dynamics. But, for the question of convergence on minima, the answers are much messier. In this work we use an empirical approach to this problem; anyway we would try to sketch some general point about *PSO minima* searching properties.

What are the Origins of *PSO*?

The initial objective was to simulate the choreography of birds in a flock. Then, the flock's simulation becomes the simulation of a biased flock, with birds that know where the *best* position to catch is. In this context, we talk about i) cognitive components to indicate the capacity to quantify own performance, and ii) social components to indicate the capacity to quantify the influence of the others on my performance. In this sense, we can use the *Vs exploitation* concept to define (a) the ability to explore, and (b) the ability to concentrate the search around a promising area. We could express this argument in terms of minima search: *PSO has* a great number of parameters which could directly influence the ratio ρ between exploration and exploitation. Thus, if a problem has a structure in such a manner that ρ is a critical parameter; *PSO* is a good candidate to resolve it. We resume this point showing one of the analytic results in Wolpert and Macready (1997).

We may define the velocity update with

$$v_{ij}(t + 1) = \chi \left[v_{ij}(t) + \phi_1(y_{ij}(t) - x_{ij}(t)) + \phi_2(\hat{y}_j(t) - x_{ij}(t)) \right],$$

where $\hat{y}_j(t)$ is the global best position, $y_{ij}(t)$ is the particle best position and χ is

$$\chi = \frac{2k}{\left| 2 - \phi - \sqrt{\phi(\phi - 4)} \right|}$$

and

$$\phi = \phi_1 + \phi_2,$$

$$\phi_1 = c_1 r_1,$$

and

$$\phi_2 = c_2 r 2$$

With these assumptions, Berg finds that:

- With $\varphi \geq 4$ and $\kappa \in [0, 1]$ the swarm is guaranteed to converge
- κ controls the exploration-exploitation; with κ near zero we have fast convergence and local exploitation; with κ near 1 we observe a global search.

This direct link between searching and parameters is a chief asset of *PSO*.

Q – *PSO* Dynamics

As seen before, we define a modified version of *PSO with* some original features: i) the influence between agents is implemented by a *discrete angular moment r* ($\mathbf{R} = 0, 1, -1, r \in \mathrm{R}$) applied on the direction of the agent ($h_{t+1} = h_t r \kappa$ with κ a small factor); ii) the agents emit signals when they reach sources of food.

Now, we recall the *PSO* formulation for a bi-dimensional word, using *h* to indicate the heading of the agents and *v* their velocities:

$$\dot{v}_{x,k}(t) = \overbrace{\rho(v_{x,k}(t))}^{Inertial\ Factor} + \overbrace{\varphi_1\left(\vec{P}_k, \vec{x}_k(t)\right)}^{Individual} + \overbrace{\varphi_2\left(\vec{P}_g, \vec{x}(t)\right)}^{Social},$$

and

$$\dot{v}_{y,k}(t) = \rho(v_{y,k}(t)) + \varphi_1\left(\vec{P}_k, \vec{x}_k(t)\right) + \varphi_2\left(\vec{P}_g, \vec{x}(t)\right),$$

and

$$\dot{\vec{x}} = \vec{v}_k,$$

where *Individual* indicates the influence of local valuation about the quality of the solution, *Social* indicates the effect of the best valuation about the solution. For the reasons stated above, we modify the dynamics: i) deleting the inertial factor; ii) substituting the individual valuation with the avoiding rule: to modify the angular moment as a function of the presence of other agents in the interacting area; iii) substituting the social valuation with sensitivity about signaling.

The *Q−PSO dynamics* is described in Figure 2.

The rotation of agent ($\dot{r}$) is controlled by the interaction with other agents.

If there is at least one agent in the radius of interaction, agents invert their angular moment. The heading of the agent ($\dot{h}$) is computed by three factors:

- The heading of the agent changes considering the direction indicated by *r*. We use a factor $1/\eta_1$ to weight the influence of this factor;
- The heading changes clock-wise (or anti-clockwise) when the agent reaches a food patch; and
- The heading is sensible to the gradient of the field *S* (we will describe the concept of field below).

Each agent has two different scalar velocity, v_1 and v_2. When an agent reaches a food patch, it changes its velocity, decreasing the movement.

The main assumptions about the convergence and the stability mentioned above for the *PSO* are the same for $Q−PSO$. The substitution of global best with field's interaction is a more critical point. The origin of the field is the interaction between agents and food: in analogy with electromagnetism, when agents arrive on foods, they modify their velocity (decreasing it and modifying their heading) and they emit a field. For the foraging

Figure 2. The dynamics of Q-PSO

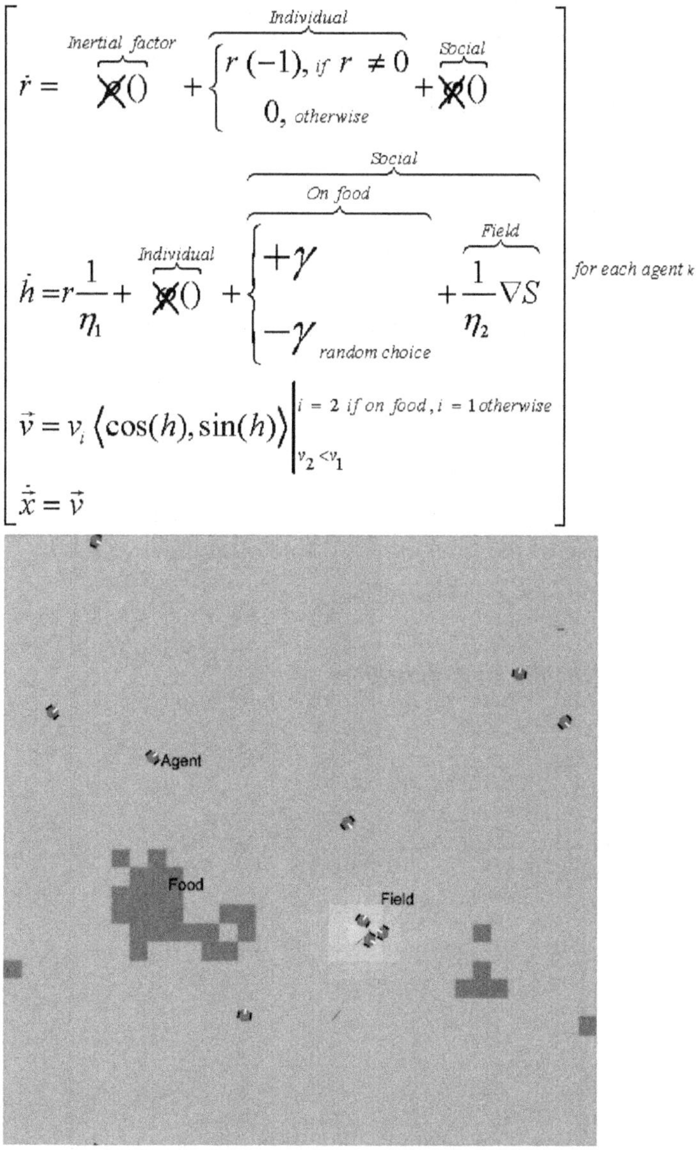

models, the perception of a communicative signal is almost instantaneous (but not exactly instantaneous): this is the reason because we implemented a physically plausible kind of signal emitted by agents that propagates in the environment and decreases its intensity during the time.

RESULTS AND DISCUSSION

To test the excellence of results obtained using our model, we decided to compare them with those obtained by a classical model of flocking, already used to model foraging behavior (Clark & Mangel, 1984) and more plausible than the traditional *PSO*. As it can be seen in Figure 3 and

Figure 4, the time needed to find all units of food is different in the two cases. The biggest differences are represented by the surface that relates to the results obtained by simulating few dozen of agents (from 10 to 20) populating a world where they can find a limited source of food (from 10 to 60 units of food this means that the percentage varies from 0.009182736 to 0.055096419, 1089 being the overall number of cells constituting the world).

In particular, our model (Figure 4) gives better results especially in the zone few agents-few units of food (in Figure 3 and Figure 4, the zone close to the vertical axis showing the needed time). In Fig. 3 and Fig. 4 the surface of responses (expressed in terms of time needed to find all the units of food) is represented, in the case of the flocking algorithm (Figure 3) and that of Q-*PSO* (Figure 4), while we vary the number of agents and units of food very slowly (from 10 to 100 with step = 1) using a single run for each combination of the parameters.

Figure 5 shows the difference of performance between Q-*PSO* and Flocking algorithm: we calculated the difference of time units needed to find all the patches of food available in the world; when the result is a negative number, this means that Q-*PSO* algorithm better performed than the Flocking; when this is a positive number, the performance of Q-*PSO* is worse. As we can appreciate in the figure, for a particular combination of parameters (number of agents ranging from 10 to 20 and units of food ranging from 10 to 60) in most cases Q-*PSO* algorithm takes less time to find all sources of food.

Figure 3. Results obtained by the flocking algorithm

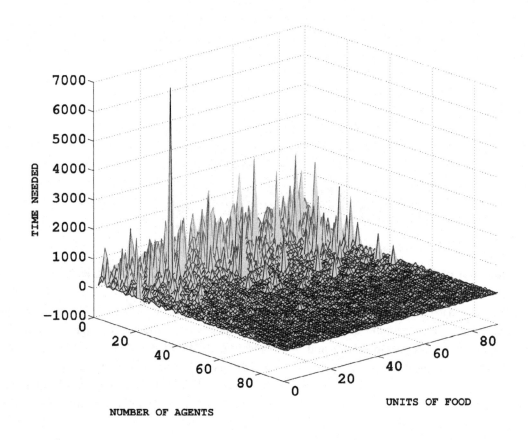

Figure 4. Results obtained by the Q-PSO algorithm

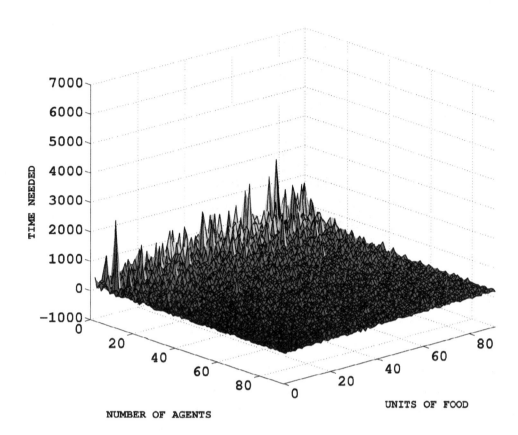

Figure 6 confirms the same results, in the multirun approach as well. As we can appreciate, our model is more efficient than the flocking one, given few agents (10) and independently of the unit of food (for this set of parameters).

CONCLUSION

The results obtained with both approaches (single run-slow change of the number of agents and number of units of food vs. multirun approach) are particularly interesting given certain conditions. Indeed, above a certain threshold on the number of agents (number of agents more than 30), the two models (Q-PSO and flocking) are substantially equivalent.

The interesting results are obtained simulating a world in which few agents (few dozen) have to find a small amount of food patchy distributed in the environment. This result, though preliminary, seems to provide encouraging indications for what happens in nature for large mammalian carnivores (like wolves and lions), that are organized in groups (packs of wolves and pride of the lions) of 10 and 30 individuals, respectively. We think that the dynamics of foraging in populations of mammalian carnivores can be usefully studied using algorithms Q-PSO-based because it considers i) individual learning, ii) collective learning and iii) speed, and all these elements are crucial in the foraging behaviors. Beyond the specific hunting strategies adopted by animals, the model seems to capture some features (probably, derived from evolutionary pressures) that have lead up some

Figure 5. Difference of performance between Q-PSO and Flocking algorithm

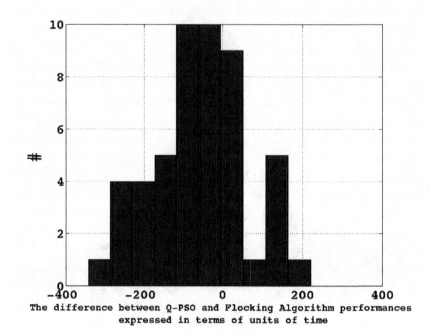

Figure 6. Results obtained with Q-PSO and Flocking algorithms. The solid lines show the results obtained by Q-PSO algorithm. The dotted lines show the results obtained by a traditional algorithm, the flocking. Our model shows better performance (the shortest time to find all the units of food) when the group is formed by very few agents (10) for each of the experimental conditions about the number of units of food (10, 30, 50); in this second approach we made a more abrupt change in the number of agents (10 to 30 with step of 10) and in units of food in the world (10 to 50 with step of 20), and repeated the simulations with the same set of parameters for different runs (20), so we took the average values.

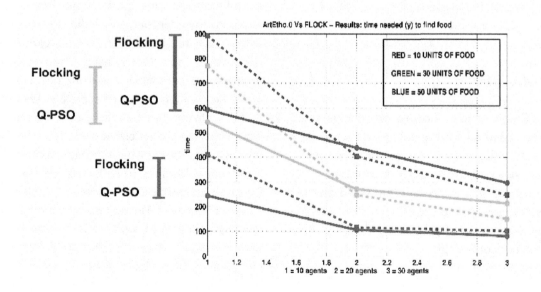

species to socially organize themselves in small groups. Future studies oriented to the implementation of social structures (such as hierarchies and the presence of alpha individuals) and more complex cognitive skills (such as real predatory strategies) may provide further evidence about the usefulness of the proposed model to study animal behavior.

REFERENCES

Bäck, T. (1996). *Evolutionary Algorithms in Theory and Practice: Evolution Strategies, Evolutionary Programming, Genetic Algorithms*. New York: Oxford University Press.

Campenni', M., & Cecconi, F. (2009). Collective foraging vs. distributed foraging dilemma in evolutionary robotics framework: an embodied and situated implementation of *PSO* (particle swarm optimization) algorithm. In *Proceedings of the 7th European conference on Computing and Philosophy*.

Caraco, T. (1980). On foraging time allocation in a stochastic environment. *Ecology, 61*, 119–128. doi:10.2307/1937162

Caraco, T., & Wolf, L. L. (1975). Ecological determinants of group sizes of foraging lions. *American Naturalist, 109*, 343–352. doi:10.1086/283001

Cecconi, F. (2008). *Agent based simulation for social studies* (Tech. Rep.). In *Proceedings of the 10th European Agent Systems Summer School*, Lisbon, Portugal.

Cecconi, F., & Campenni', M. (2010). *PSO* (particle swarm optimization): One method, many possible applications. In R. Sarker & T. Ray (Eds.), *Agent Based Evolutionary Search* (pp. 229-254). Berlin: Springer Verlag.

Clark, C. W., & Mangel, M. (1984). Foraging and flocking strategies: Information in an uncertain environment. *American Naturalist, 123*, 626–664. doi:10.1086/284228

Emlen, J. M. (1966). The role of time and energy in food preference. *American Naturalist, 100*, 611–617. doi:10.1086/282455

Engelbrecht, A. P. (2005). *Fundamentals of Computational Swarm Intelligence*. New York: John Wiley & Sons.

Fonseca, C., & Fleming, P. (1996). An overview of evolutionary algorithms in multiobjective optimization. *Evolutionary Computation, 3*, 1–16. doi:10.1162/evco.1995.3.1.1

Goldberg, D. (1989). *Genetic Algorithms in Search, Optimization and Machine Learning*. Reading, MA: Addison-Wesley.

Hu, X., Eberhart, R. C., & Shi, Y. (2003). Particle swarm with extended memory for multi-objective optimization. In *Proceedings of the Swarm Intelligence Symposium*. Washington, DC: IEEE.

Kennedy, J., & Eberhart, R. (1995). Particle swarm optimization. In *Proceedings of the IEEE Int. Conf. on Neural Networks*, Piscataway, NJ.

Kennedy, J., Eberhart, R., & Shi, Y. (2001). *Swarm Intelligence*. San Francisco: Morgan Kaufman.

MacArthur, R. H., & Pianka, E. R. (1966). On the optimal use of a patchy environment. *American Naturalist, 100*, 603–609. doi:10.1086/282454

netlogo. (n.d.). Retrieved from www.ccl.northwestern.edu/netlogo/

Nolfi, S., & Floreano, D. (2000). *Evolutionary Robotics*. Cambridge, MA: MIT Press.

Nudds, T. D. (1978). Convergence of group size strategies by mammalian social carnivores. *American Naturalist, 112*, 957–960. doi:10.1086/283336

Parsopoulos, K. E., & Vrahatis, M. N. (2002). Particle swarm optimization method in multi-objective problems. In *Proceedings of the 2002 ACM symposium on applied computing*.

Patel, M., Honavar, V., & Balakrishnan, K. (Eds.). (2001). *Advances in the Evolutionary Synthesis of Intelligent Agents*. Cambridge, MA: MIT Press.

Radicchi, F., Castellano, C., Cecconi, F., Loreto, V., & Parisi, D. (2004). Defining and identifying communities in networks. *Proceedings of the National Academy of Sciences of the United States of America, 101*(9), 2658–2663. doi:10.1073/pnas.0400054101

Rands, S. A., Cowlishaw, G., Pettifor, R. A., Rowclife, J. M., & Johnstone, R. A. (2003). The spontaneous emergence of leaders and followers in foraging pairs. *Nature, 423*, 432–434. doi:10.1038/nature01630

Rands, S. A., Pettifor, R. A., Rowclife, J. M., & Cowlishaw, G. (2004). State-dependent foraging rules for social animals in selfish herds. In *Proceedings of the Royal Society, 271*, 2613–2620. doi:10.1098/rspb.2004.2906

Rands, S. A., Pettifor, R. A., Rowclife, J. M., & Cowlishaw, G. (2006). Social foraging and dominance relationships: the efects of socially mediated interference. *Behavioral Ecology and Sociobiology, 60*, 572–581. doi:10.1007/s00265-006-0202-4

Ravindran, A., Phillips, D. T., & Solberg, J. J. (2001). *Operations Research Principle and practice*. New York: John Wiley & Sons.

Rodman, P. S. (1981). Inclusive fitness and group size with a reconsideration of group sizes in lions and wolves. *American Naturalist, 118*, 275–283. doi:10.1086/283819

Sarker, R., Mohammadian, M., & Yao, X. (Eds.). (2002). *Evolutionary Optimization*. Boston: Kluwer Academic Publishers.

stigrefs. (n.d.). Retrieved from www.stigmergic-systems.com/stig_v1/stigrefs/article1.html

Taha, H. A. (2011). *Operations Research: An Introduction*. Upper Saddle River, NJ: Prentice Hall.

van den Bergh, F., & Engelbrecht, A. P. (2006). A study of particle swarm optimization particle trajectories. *Information Sciences, 176*(8), 937–971. doi:10.1016/j.ins.2005.02.003

Wolpert, D. H., & Macready, W. G. (1997). No free lunch theorems for optimization. *IEEE Transactions on Evolutionary Computation, 1*, 67–77. doi:10.1109/4235.585893

ENDNOTES

[1] We imagine that no kind of information about particular features of sources of food is accessible to the agents, e.g., the smell.

[2] We will call global *minima* the points of the fitness landscape with maximum values.

[3] A complete review about *PSO* dynamics is in van den Bergh and Engelbrecht (2006).

This work was previously published in International Journal of Agent Technologies and Systems, Volume 3, Issue 1, edited by Yu Zhang, pp. 27-38, copyright 2011 by IGI Publishing (an imprint of IGI Global).

Compilation of References

Abdul-Rahman, A., & Hailes, S. (2000). Supporting trust in virtual communities. In *Proceedings of the 33rd Annual Hawaii International Conference on Systems Sciences*, Maui, HI (pp. 1-9).

Abraham, A., Grosan, C., & Ramos, V. (Eds.). (2006). *Stigmergic optimization. Studies in computational intelligence (Vol. 31)*. Heidelberg, Germany: Springer-Verlag.

Abreu, D., Pearce, D., & Stacchetti, E. (1985). Optimal cartel equilibria with imperfect monitoring. *Journal of Economic Theory, 39*, 251–269. doi:10.1016/0022-0531(86)90028-1

Acquisti, R., & Gross, R. (2006). Imagined communities: Awareness, information sharing, and privacy on the facebook. In *Proceedings of the 6th Workshop on Privacy Enhancing Technologies* (pp. 36-58).

Adamic, L. A., Lukose, R. M., Puniyani, A. R., & Huberman, B. A. (2001). Search in power law networks. *Physics Review Letters E, 64*(4), 046135.

Ahmed, M., Ahmad, M. S., & Mohd Yusoff, M. Z. (2009). A review and development of agent communication language. *Electronic Journal of Computer Science and Information Technology, 1*(1), 7–12.

Akula, V., & Menasce, D. A. (2004). Contrasting grey system theory to probability and fuzzy. *ACM SIGICE Bulletin, 20*(3), 3–9.

Albert, R., & Barb'asi, A. L. (2002). Statistical Mechanics of Complex Networks. *Modern Physics*, 47-97.

Albert, R., Jeong, H., & Barabasi, A. (2000). Error and attack tolerance of complex networks. *Nature, 406*, 378–382. doi:10.1038/35019019

Alrawagfeh, W., Brown, E., & Mata-Montero, M. (2011, April 3-7). Identifying norms of behaviour in open multi-agent societies. In *Proceedings of the Agent-Directed Simulation Symposium as part of the Spring Simulation Multi-conference*, Boston, MA.

Amaral, L. A. N., Scala, A., Barthelemy, M., & Stanley, H. E. (2000). Classes of small-world networks. *Proceedings of the National Academy of Sciences of the United States of America, 97*(21), 11149–11152. doi:10.1073/pnas.200327197

Anderson, J. R. (2007). Animal Behavior: Tolerant Primates Cooperate Best. *Current Biology, 17*(7). doi:10.1016/j.cub.2007.02.005

Anderson, S. P., & de Palma, A. (1992). The logit as a model of product differentiation. *Oxford Economic Papers, 44*(1), 51–67.

Andrighetto, G., Campenni, M., Cecconi, F., & Conte, R. (2008). The complex loop of norm emergence: A simulation model. In *Proceedings of the Second World Congress on Simulating Interacting Agents and Social Phenomena* (pp. 17-33).

Anthony, P. (2003). *Bidding agents for multiple heterogeneous online auctions*. Unpublished doctoral dissertation, University of Southampton, Southampton, UK.

Arentze, T., van den Berg, P., & Timmermans, H. (2009). Modeling social networks in geographic space: Approach and empirical application. In *Proceedings of the Workshop on Frontiers in Transportation: Social Networks and Travel*.

Arentze, T. A., & Timmermans, H. (2006). Social networks, social interactions and activity-travel behavior: A framework for micro-simulation. *Environment and Planning. B, Planning & Design, 35*(6), 1012–1027. doi:10.1068/b3319t

Arentze, T. A., & Timmermans, H. J. (2004). A learning-based transportation oriented simulation system. *Transportation Research Part B: Methodological, 38*, 613–633. doi:10.1016/j.trb.2002.10.001

Arifin, S. M. N., Davis, G. J., & Zhou, Y. (2011, April). Modeling space in an agent-based model of malaria: Comparison between non-spatial and spatial models. In *Proceedings of the Agent-Directed Simulation*, Boston, MA.

Arifin, S. M. N., Davis, G. J., Kurtz, S., Gentile, J. E., Zhou, Y., & Madey, G. R. (2010a, December). Divide and conquer: A four-fold docking experience of agent-based models. In *Proceedings of the Winter Simulation Conference*, Baltimore, MD.

Arifin, S. M. N., Davis, G. J., Zhou, Y., & Madey, G. R. (2010b, July). Verification & validation by docking: A case study of agent-based models of Anopheles gambiae. In *Proceedings of the Summer Computer Simulation Conference*, Ottawa, ON, Canada.

Arifovic, J. (2000). Evolutionary algorithms in macroeconomic models. *Macroeconomic Dynamics, 4*, 373–414. doi:10.1017/S1365100500016059

Arora, M., & Syamala, D. M. (2009). Weight Based Funds Allocation Algorithm. In *Proceedings of the Advance Computing Conference (IACC-2009)* (pp. 413-417). Washington, DC: IEEE.

Athey, S., Bagwell, K., & Sanchirico, C. W. (2004). Collusion and price rigidity. *The Review of Economic Studies, 71*(2), 317–349. doi:10.1111/0034-6527.00286

Auchincloss, A., & Diez Roux, A. (2008). A new tool for epidemiology: The usefulness of dynamic-agent models in understanding place effects on health. *American Journal of Epidemiology, 168*, 1–8. doi:10.1093/aje/kwn118

Axelrod, R. M. (1997). *The Complexity of Cooperation: Agent-Based Models of Competition and Collaboration*. Princeton, NJ: Princeton University Press.

Axhausen, K. (2006). *Social networks, mobility biographies and travel: The survey challenges* (Tech. Rep. No. 343). Zurich, Switzerland: Institut für Verkehrsplanung und Transportsysteme.

Backstrom, L., Dwork, C., & Kleinberg, J. (2007). Wherefore art thou? Anonymized social networks, hidden patterns, and structural steganography. In *Proceedings of the 16th International Conference on World Wide Web* (pp. 181-190).

Bäck, T. (1996). *Evolutionary Algorithms in Theory and Practice: Evolution Strategies, Evolutionary Programming, Genetic Algorithms*. New York: Oxford University Press.

Bădică, C., Ganzha, M., Gawinecki, M., Kobzdej, P., & Paprzycki, M. (2006). Towards trust management in an agent-based e-commerce system – initial considerations. In A. Zgrzywa (Ed.), *Proceedings of the MISSI 2006 Conference* (pp. 225-236). Wroclaw, Poland: Wroclaw University of Technology Press.

Bapna, R., Goes, P., & Gupta, A. (2001). Insights and analyses of online auctions. *Communications of the ACM, 44*(11), 43–50. doi:10.1145/384150.384160

Bass, F. (1969). A new product growth model for consumer durables. *Management Science, 15*, 215–227. doi:10.1287/mnsc.15.5.215

Bauer, P. (2008). Price rigidity on microdata: stylized facts for Hungary [in Hungarian]. *Statisztikai Szemle, 86*(3), 39–69.

Bayoh, M., & Lindsay, S. (2004). Temperature-related duration of aquatic stages the Afrotropical malaria vector mosquito Anopheles gambiae in the laboratory. *Medical and Veterinary Entomology, 18*, 174–179. doi:10.1111/j.0269-283X.2004.00495.x

Beier, J. (1998). Malaria parasite development in mosquitoes. *Annual Review of Entomology, 43*(1), 519–543. doi:10.1146/annurev.ento.43.1.519

Bell, J. (1995). Changing attitudes in intelligent agents. In *Proceedings of the Workshop on Agent Theories, Architecture and Languages* (pp. 40-50).

Bellifemine, F. L., Caire, G., & Greenwood, D. (2007). *Developing Multi-Agent Systems with JADE*. New York: John Wiley & Sons Ltd. doi:10.1002/9780470058411

Benedict, M., & Robinson, A. (2003). The first releases of transgenic mosquitoes: An argument for the sterile insect technique. *Trends in Parasitology*, *19*(8), 349–355. doi:10.1016/S1471-4922(03)00144-2

Benenson, J. F., Markovits, H., Fitzgerald, C., Georoy, D., Flemming, J., Kahlenberg, S. K., & Wrangham, R. W. (2009). Males' Greater Tolerance of Same-Sex Peers. *Psychological Science*, *20*(2). doi:10.1111/j.1467-9280.2009.02269.x

Bhattacharya, I., & Getoor, L. (2006). A latent dirichlet model for unsupervised entity resolution. In *Proceedings of the SIAM Conference on Data Mining*.

Bhattacharya, I., & Getoor, L. (2007). Collective entity resolution in relational data. *ACM Transactions on Knowledge Discovery from Data*, *1*(1), 1–36. doi:10.1145/1217299.1217304

Bianchi, L., Dorigo, M., Gambardella, L. M., & Gutjahr, W. J. (2009). A survey on metaheuristics for stochastic combinatorial optimization. *Natural Computing*, *8*, 239–287. doi:10.1007/s11047-008-9098-4

Bidlingmayera, W. L., & Hem, D. G. (1980). The range of visual attraction and the effect of competitive visual attractants upon mosquito (Diptera: Culicidae) flight. *Bulletin of Entomological Research*, *70*, 321–342. doi:10.1017/S0007485300007604

Bils, M., & Klenow, P. (2004). Some evidence on the importance of sticky prices. *The Journal of Political Economy*, *112*(5), 947–985. doi:10.1086/422559

Blei, D. M., Ng, A. Y., & Jordan, M. I. (2003). Latent dirichlet allocation. *Journal of Machine Learning Research*, *3*, 993–1022. doi:10.1162/jmlr.2003.3.4-5.993

Blum, C., Aguilera, M. J. B., Roli, A., & Sampels, M. (Eds.). (2008). *Hybrid metaheuristics: An emerging approach to optimization. Studies in computational intelligence (Vol. 114)*. Heidelberg, Germany: Springer-Verlag.

Boella, G. Pigozzi, & van der Torre, L. (2009). Five guidelines for normativemulti-agent systems. In *Proceedings of the Symposium on Normative Multi-agent Systems*.

Boella, G., Gabriella, P., Munindar, P., & Harko, V. (2010). Normative multiagent systems: Guest editors' introduction. *Logic Journal of IGPL*, *18*(1), 1–3. doi:10.1093/jigpal/jzp079

Boella, G., & van der Torre, L. (2007). Norm negotiation in multiagent systems. *International Journal of Cooperative Information Systems*, *16*(1), 97–122. doi:10.1142/S0218843007001585

Boella, G., van der Torre, L., & Verhagen, H. (2006). Introduction to normative multiagent systems. *Computational & Mathematical Organization Theory*, *12*(2-3), 71–79. doi:10.1007/s10588-006-9537-7

Boella, G., van der Torre, L., & Verhagen, H. (2008). Introduction to the special issue on normative multiagent systems. *Journal of Autonomous Agents and Multi-Agent Systems*, *17*, 1–10. doi:10.1007/s10458-008-9047-8

Boman, M. (1999). Norms in artificial decision making. *Artificial Intelligence and Law*, *7*(1), 17–35. doi:10.1023/A:1008311429414

Bomblies, A., Duchemin, J., & Eltahir, E. (2008). Hydrology of malaria: Model development and application to a Sahelian village. *Water Resources Research*, *44*.

Bomblies, A., Duchemin, J., & Eltahir, E. (2009). A mechanistic approach for accurate simulation of village scale malaria transmission. *Malaria Journal*, *8*, 223. doi:10.1186/1475-2875-8-223

Bonabeau, E., Guérin, S., Snyers, D., Kuntz, P., & Theraulaz, G. (2000). Three-dimensional architectures grown by simple 'stigmergic' agents. *Bio Systems*, *56*, 13–32. doi:10.1016/S0303-2647(00)00067-8

Borenstein, E., & Ruppin, E. (2003). Enhancing Autonomous Agents Evolution with Learning by Imitation. *Journal of Artificial Intelligence and Simulation of Behavior*, *1*(4), 335–348.

Bramley, I. (2005). *SOA takes off – New WebSphere SOA foundation extends IBM's lead with new system z9 mainframes as the hub of the enterprise* (2nd ed.). Armonk, NY: IBM.

Bratman, M. E. (1987). *Intention, plans and practical reason*. Cambridge, MA: Harvard University Press.

Bratman, M. E. (1990). What is intention? In Cohen, P. R., Morgan, J., & Pollack, M. E. (Eds.), *Intentions in communication* (pp. 15–31). Cambridge, MA: MIT Press.

Brazier, F., Dunin-Keplicz, B., Treur, J., & Verbrugge, R. (1997). *Beliefs, Intentions and DESIRE.* Retrieved from http://ksi.cpsc.ucalgary.ca/KAW/KAW96/brazier/default.html

Brenner, T. (2006). Agent learning representation: Advice on modelling economic learning. In Tesfatsion, L., & Judd, K. L. (Eds.), *Handbook of computational economic* (*Vol. 2*, pp. 895–947). Amsterdam, The Netherlands: Elsevier.

Brown, J., & Reinegen, P. (1987). Social ties and word-of-mouth referral behavior. *The Journal of Consumer Research, 14*(3), 350–362. doi:10.1086/209118

Bryce, J., Boschi-Pinto, C., Shibuya, K., & Black, R. (2005). WHO estimates the causes of death in children. *Lancet,* 1147–1152. doi:10.1016/S0140-6736(05)71877-8

Campenni', M., & Cecconi, F. (2009). Collective foraging vs. distributed foraging dilemma in evolutionary robotics framework: an embodied and situated implementation of *PSO* (particle swarm optimization) algorithm. In *Proceedings of the 7th European conference on Computing and Philosophy.*

Campenni, M., Andrighetto, G., Cecconi, F., & Conte, R. (2008, September 1-5). Normal = normative? The role of intelligent agents in norm innovation. In *Proceedings of the Fifth Conference of the European Social Simulation Association.*

Caraco, T. (1980). On foraging time allocation in a stochastic environment. *Ecology, 61,* 119–128. doi:10.2307/1937162

Caraco, T., & Wolf, L. L. (1975). Ecological determinants of group sizes of foraging lions. *American Naturalist, 109,* 343–352. doi:10.1086/283001

Carnahan, J., Song-gang, L., Costantini, C., Touré, Y., & Taylor, C. (1997). Computer simulation of dispersal by Anopheles gambiae s.l. in West Africa. In *Proceedings of the Fifth International Workshop on the Synthesis and Simulation of Living, Complex Adaptive Systems* (pp. 387-394).

Carter, J., Bitting, E., & Ghorbani, A. (2002). Reputation formalization for an information- sharing multi-agent system. *Computational Intelligence, 18*(2), 515–534. doi:10.1111/1467-8640.t01-1-00201

Cassady, R. J. R. (1968). Review. *Auctions and Auctioneering, 58*(4), 959–963.

Castelfranchi, C., & Falcone, R. (1998). Principles of trust for MAS: Cognitive anatomy, social importance and quantification. In *Proceedings of the International Conference on Multi-Agent Systems,* Paris, France (pp. 72-79).

Castelfranchi, C. (2004). Formalizing the informal? Dynamic social order, bottom-up social control, and spontaneous normative relations. *Journal of Applied Logic, 1*(1-2), 47–92. doi:10.1016/S1570-8683(03)00004-1

Cecconi, F. (2008). *Agent based simulation for social studies* (Tech. Rep.). In *Proceedings of the 10th European Agent Systems Summer School,* Lisbon, Portugal.

Cecconi, F., & Campenni', M. (2010). *PSO* (particle swarm optimization): One method, many possible applications. In R. Sarker & T. Ray (Eds.), *Agent Based Evolutionary Search* (pp. 229-254). Berlin: Springer Verlag.

Chan, M., Campo, E., & Estève, D. (2003). PROSAFE: a multisensory remote monitoring system for the elderly or the handicapped. In *Proceedings of the 1st International Conference on Smart homes and health Telematics (ICOST 2003),* Paris (pp. 89-95).

Chandler, D. (1987). *Introduction to modern statistical mechanics.* New York, NY: Oxford University Press.

Chang, E., Hussain, F., & Dillon, T. (2006). *Trust and Reputation for Service-Oriented Environments: Technologies for Building Business Intelligence and Consumer Confidence.* New York: John Wiley & Sons, Ltd. doi:10.1002/9780470028261

Chan, H. C., Cheng, C. B., & Hsu, C. H. (2007). Bargaining strategy formulation with CRM for an e-commerce agent. *Electronic Commerce Research and Applications, 6,* 490–498. doi:10.1016/j.elerap.2007.02.011

Chan, M., Estève, D., Escriba, C., & Campo, E. (2008). A review of smart homes—Present state and future challenges. *Computer Methods and Programs in Biomedicine, 91*(1), 55–81. doi:10.1016/j.cmpb.2008.02.001

Chapman, B., Jost, G., & Pas, R. d. (2007). *Using OpenMP: Portable shared memory parallel programming (Scientific and engineering computation).* Cambridge, MA: MIT Press.

Charlwood, J., & Jones, M. (1979). Mating behavior in the mosquito *Anophe-les gambiae sl.* close range and contact-behavior. *Physiological Entomology, 4*, 111–120. doi:10.1111/j.1365-3032.1979.tb00185.x

Chaves, L., & Koenraadt, C. (2010). Climate change and highland malaria: Fresh air for a hot debate. *The Quarterly Review of Biology, 85*, 27–55. doi:10.1086/650284

Chavez, A., & Maes, P. (1996). Kasbah: An agent marketplace for buying and selling goods. In *Proceedings of the 1st International Conference on the Practical Application of Intelligent Agents and Multi-Agent Technology*, London, UK.

Chavez, A., Moukas, A., & Maes, P. (1997). Challenger: A Multi Agent System for Distributed Resource Allocation. In *Proceeding of First International Conference on Autonomous Agents (Agent97)*, Marina Del Ray, CA (pp. 323-331). New York: ACM Press.

Chee, C. N. (2004). *Three critical steps to customer-centric business orientation.* Retrieved from http://www.mcore-asia.com/PDF/Three-2520Critical-2520Steps-2520to-2520Customer-centric-2520Business-2520Orientation.pdf

Chen, J. R., Wolfe, S. R., & McLean, S. D. W. (2000). A distributed multi-agent system for collaborative information management and sharing. In *Proceedings of the 9th International Conference on Information and Knowledge Management* (pp. 382-388).

Chen, W., Manikonda, V., & Durfee, E. (2008). A flexible human agent collaboration (HAC) framework for human-human activity coordination. In *Proceedings of the AAAI Fall Symposium*.

Cheng, J., Bai, H., & Li, Z. (2008). Quantification of Non Quantitative Indicators of Performance Measurement. In *Proceedings of the Wireless Communications, Networking and Mobile Computing (WiCOM '08), 4th International Conference* (pp. 1-5).

Chen, S. H., & Ni, C. C. (2000). Simulating the ecology of oligopolistic competition with genetic algorithms. *Knowledge and Information Systems, 2*(3), 285–309. doi:10.1007/PL00011644

Chiang, J. S., Wu, P. L., Chiang, S. D., Chang, T. L., Chang, S. T., & Wen, K. L. (1998). *Introduction to grey system theory.* Taipei, Taiwan: Gao-Li.

Chiou, H. K., Tzeng, G. H., Cheng, C. K., & Liu, G. S. (2004). Grey prediction model for forecasting the planning material of equipment spare parts in navy of Taiwan. In. *Proceedings of the IEEE World Automation Congress, 17*, 315–320.

Chung, K. L. (1974). *A course on probability theory.* New York, NY: Academic Press.

Clark, A. F., & Doherty, S. T. (2008). Examining the nature and extent of the activity-travel preplanning decision process. *Transportation Research Record, 2054*, 83–92. doi:10.3141/2054-10

Clark, C. W., & Mangel, M. (1984). Foraging and flocking strategies: Information in an uncertain environment. *American Naturalist, 123*, 626–664. doi:10.1086/284228

Conte, R., Castelfranchi, C., & Dignum, F. (1999). Autonomous norm acceptance. In J. P. Müller, A. S. Rao, & M. P. Singh (Eds.), *Proceedings of the 5th International Workshop on Intelligent Agents: Agents, Theories, Architectures, and Languages* (LNCS, 1555, pp. 99-112).

Corchado, J. M., Bajo, J., & Abraham, A. (2008). GerAmi: Improving Healthcare Delivery in Geriatric Residences. *IEEE Intelligent Systems*, 19-25. *GERHOME project.* (2005). Retrieved August 20, 2010, from gerhome.cstb.fr

Cordella, L., Foggia, P., Sansone, C., & Vento, M. (2004). A (sub)graph isomorphism algorithm for matching large graphs. *IEEE Transactions on Pattern Analysis and Machine Intelligence, 26*(10), 1367–1372. doi:10.1109/TPAMI.2004.75

Cowan, R., & Jonard, N. (2004). Network structure and the diffusion of knowledge. *Journal of Economic Dynamics & Control, 28*(8), 1557–1575. doi:10.1016/j.jedc.2003.04.002

Craig, M., Snow, R., & Sueur, D. L. (1999). A climate-based distribution model of malaria transmission in sub-Saharan Africa. *Parasitology Today (Personal Ed.), 15*(3), 105–110. doi:10.1016/S0169-4758(99)01396-4

Crawley, J. (2004). Reducing the burden of anemia in infants and young children in malaria-endemic countries of Africa: From evidence to action. *The American Journal of Tropical Medicine and Hygiene, 71*(2), 25.

Culotta, A. (2003). *Maximizing cascades in social networks*. Amherst, MA: University of Massachusetts.

da Silva, V. T., et al. (2004). A UML Based Approach for Modeling and Implementing MultiAgent Systems. In *Proceedings of 3rd International Joint Conference on Autonomous Agents and Multi Agent Systems*, New York (pp. 914-921).

Dame, D., Curtis, C., Benedict, M., Robinson, A., & Knols, B. (2009). Historical applications of induced sterilisation in field populations of mosquitoes. *Malaria Journal, 8*(2), 2. doi:10.1186/1475-2875-8-S2-S2

Dastani, M., Grossi, D., Meyer, J.-J. C., & Tinnemeier, N. (2008). Normative multi-agent programs and their logics. In *Proceedings of the Workshop on Knowledge Representation for Agents and Multi-Agent Systems* (pp. 236-243).

David, E., Rogers, A., Schiff, J., Kraus, S., & Jennings, N. R. (2005). Optimal design of English auctions with discrete bid level. In *Proceedings of the Sixth ACM Conference on Electronic Commerce*, Vancouver, BC, Canada (pp. 98-107).

Davidsson, P. (2002). Agent-Based Social Simulation: A Computer Science View. *Journal of Artificial Societies and Social Simulation, 5*(1).

Dean, J., & Ghemawat, S. (2008). MapReduce: Simplified data processing on large clusters. *Communications of the ACM, 51*(1), 107–113. doi:10.1145/1327452.1327492

Delgado, J. (2002). Emergence of Social Convenetions in Complex Networks. *Artificial Intelligence*, 171–185. doi:10.1016/S0004-3702(02)00262-X

DeLoach, S. A. (1999). Multi-agent systems engineering - A methodology and language for designing agent systems. In *Proceedings of the Conference on Agent Oriented Information Systems* (pp. 45-57).

Deng, J. (1989). Introduction to grey system theory. *Journal of Grey System, 1*, 1–24.

Deng, J., & David, K. W. N. (1995). Control problem of grey system. *Systems & Control Letters, 1*(1), 288–294.

Depinay, J., Mbogo, C., Killeen, G., Knols, B., Beier, J., & Carlson, J. (2004). A simulation model of African Anopheles ecology and population dynamics for the analysis of malaria transmission. *Malaria Journal, 3*, 29. doi:10.1186/1475-2875-3-29

Detinova, T. (1962). *Age grouping methods in Diptera of medical importance*. Geneva, Switzerland: World Health Organization.

Dhyne, E., Álvarez, L. J., Bihan, H. L., Veronese, G., Dias, D., & Hoffmann, J. (2005). *Price setting in the euro area: some stylized facts from individual consumer price data*. Frankfurt am Main, Germany: European Central Bank.

Dietz, K., Molineaux, L., & Thomas, A. (1974). A malaria model tested in the African savannah. *Bulletin of the World Health Organization, 50*, 347–357.

Dignum, F. (1999). Autonomous agents with norms. *AI and Law, 7*, 69–79.

Domingos, P., & Richardson, M. (2001). Mining the network value of customers. In *Proceedings of the 7th ACM SIGKDD International Conference on Knowledge Discovery and Data Mining* (pp. 57-66).

Donath, J. (1999). *Identity and deception in the virtual community*. London, UK: Routledge.

Duffy, J. (2006). Agent-based models and human subject experiments. In Tesfatsion, L., & Judd, K. L. (Eds.), *Handbook of computational economics* (Vol. 2, pp. 941–1011). Amsterdam, The Netherlands: Elsevier.

Edmonds, B., Norling, E., & Hales, D. (2009). Towards the Evolution of Social Structure. *Computational & Mathematical Organization Theory, 15*.

Eichenbaum, M., Jaimovich, N., & Rebelo, S. (2011). Reference prices, costs, and nominal rigidities. *The American Economic Review, 101*(1), 234–262. doi:10.1257/aer.101.1.234

Elster, J. (1989). Social norms and economic theory. *The Journal of Economic Perspectives, 3*(4), 9–117.

Emlen, J. M. (1966). The role of time and energy in food preference. *American Naturalist, 100*, 611–617. doi:10.1086/282455

Engelbrecht, A. P. (2005). *Fundamentals of Computational Swarm Intelligence*. New York: John Wiley & Sons.

Epstein, J. (1999). Agent-Based Computational Models and Generative Scoail Science. *Complexity, 4*(5). doi:10.1002/(SICI)1099-0526(199905/06)4:5<41::AID-CPLX9>3.0.CO;2-F

Esfandiari, B., & Chandrasekharan, S. (2001). On how agents make friends: Mechanisms for trust acquisition. In *Proceedings of the Fourth Workshop on Deception, Fraud and Trust in Agent Societies*, Montreal, QC, Canada (pp. 27-34).

Evans, G. W., & Honkapohja, S. (1999). Learning dynamics . In Taylor, J. B., & Woodford, M. (Eds.), *Handbook of macroeconomics I* (*Vol. A*). Amsterdam, The Netherlands: Elsevier.

Fabiani, S., Loupias, C., Martins, F., & Sabbatini, R. (Eds.). (2007). *Pricing decisions in the Euro area*. New York, NY: Oxford University Press. doi:10.1093/acprof:oso/9780195309287.001.0001

Fararo, T. J., & Sunshine, M. H. (1964). *A Study of a Biased Friendship Net*. Syracuse, NY: Syracuse University Press.

Faratin, P., Sierra, C., & Jennings, N. (2003). Using similarity criteria to make issue trade-offs in automated negotiations. *Journal of Artificial Intelligence, 142*(2), 205–237. doi:10.1016/S0004-3702(02)00290-4

Fasli, M. (2007). *Agent Technology for E-Commerce*. New York: John Wiley & Sons.

Fatima, S. S., Wooldridge, M., & Jennings, N. R. (2003, July). Optimal agendas for multi-issue negotiation. In *Proceedings of the Second International Conference on Autonomous Agents and Multiagent Systems*, Melbourne, Australia (pp. 129-136).

Fatima, S. S., Wooldridge, M., & Jennings, N. R. (2006). Multi-issue negotiation with deadlines. *Journal of Artificial Intelligence, 27*, 381–417.

Fausett, L. (1994). *Fundamentals of neural networks (architectures, algorithms & applications)*. Melbourne, FL: Florida Institute of Technology.

Feldmann, U., & Hendrichs, J. (2001). *Integrating the sterile insect technique as a key component of area-wide tsetse and trypanosomiasis intervention* (p. 66). New York, NY: Food & Agriculture Organization of the United Nations.

Ferber, J. (1999). *Multiagent systems*. Reading, MA: Addison-Wesley.

FIPA. (2001). *Ontology service specification: XC00086D*. Geneva, Switzerland: Author.

FIPA. (2002a). *ACL message structure specification: SC00061G*. Geneva, Switzerland: Author.

FIPA. (2002b). *Communicative act library specification: SC00037J*. Geneva, Switzerland: Author.

Fleurke, M., Ehrler, L., & Purvis, M. (2003). JBees – An adaptive and distributed framework for workflow systems. In *Proceedings of the IEEE/WIC International Conference on Intelligent Agent Technology*, Halifax, NS, Canada.

Fonseca, C., & Fleming, P. (1996). An overview of evolutionary algorithms in multiobjective optimization. *Evolutionary Computation, 3*, 1–16. doi:10.1162/evco.1995.3.1.1

Foued, B., Ait-Kadi, D., Mellouli, S., & Ruiz, A. (2009). A reputation-based model for semicompetitive multi-agent systems. *International Journal of Intelligent Information and Database Systems, 3*, 146–162. doi:10.1504/IJIIDS.2009.025160

Foundation for Intelligent Physical Agents. (2002). *FIPA ACL message structure specification* (Tech. Rep. No. SC00061G). Geneva, Switzerland: Foundation for Intelligent Physical Agents.

Foundation for Intelligent Physical Agents. (2002). *FIPA contract net interaction protocol specification* (Tech. Rep. No. SC00029H). Geneva, Switzerland: Foundation for Intelligent Physical Agents.

Gabaldon, A. (1978). What can and cannot be achieved with conventional anti-malaria measures. *The American Journal of Tropical Medicine and Hygiene, 27*(4), 653–658.

Gabriel, E., Fagg, G., Bosilca, G., & Angskun, T. (2004). Open MPI: Goals, concept, and design of a next generation MPI implementation. In *Proceedings of the 11th European PVM/VPI Users' Group Meeting Conference*, Budapest, Hungary (pp. 97-104).

Gali, J. (2008). *Monetary policy, inflation, and the business cycle: An Introduction to the new Keynesian framework*. Princeton, NJ: Princeton University Press.

Ganzha, M., Gawinecki, M., Kobzdej, P., Paprzycki, M., & Bădică, C. (2006). Functionalizing trust in a model agent based e-commerce system. In M. Bohanec et al. (Eds.), *Proceedings of the 2006 Information Society Multiconference* (pp. 22-26). Ljubljana, Slovenia: Josef Stefan Institute Press.

Gentile, J. E., Davis, G. J., & St. Laurens, B. (2010) Modeling mosquito vectors. In *Proceedings of the Summer Computer Simulation Conference*, Ottawa, ON, Canada.

Gentile, J. E., Davis, G. J., StLaurent, B., & Kurtz, S. (2010, July). A framework for modeling mosquito vectors. In *Proceedings of the Summer Computer Simulation Conference*, Ottawa, ON, Canada.

Gigerenzer, G., & Selten, R. (Eds.). (2001). *Bounded rationality: The adaptive toolbox*. Cambridge, MA: MIT Press.

Gilby, I. C., & Wrangham, R. W. (2008). Association patterns among wild chimpanzees (Pan troglodytesschweinfurthii) reflect sex differences in cooperation. *Behav Eloc Sociobiol, 62*(11).

Gillies, M. T., & Wilkes, T. J. (1969). A comparison of the range of attraction of animal baits and of carbon dioxide for some West African mosquitoes. *Bulletin of Entomological Research, 59*(3), 441–456. doi:10.1017/S0007485300003412

Gladwell, M. (2000). *The tipping point*. Boston, MA: Little Brown.

Goldberg, D. (1989). *Genetic Algorithms in Search, Optimization and Machine Learning*. Reading, MA: Addison-Wesley.

Goldenberg, J., Libai, B., & Muller, E. (2001). Talk of the network: A complex systems look at the underlying process of word-of-mouth. *Marketing Letters, 3*(12), 211–223. doi:10.1023/A:1011122126881

Gorodetski, V., Karsaev, O., & Konushy, V. (2003). Mulit Agent System for Resource Allocation and Scheduling. In *Proceeding of 3rd International Workshop of Central and East European conference on Multi Agent System*, Prague, Czech Republic (pp. 236-246).

Goundan, P. R., & Schulz, A. S. (2007). *Revisiting the greedy approach to submodular set function maximization*. Retrieved from http://www.optimization-online.org/DB_FILE/2007/08/1740.pdf

Granovetter, M. (1978). Threshold models of collective behavior. *American Journal of Sociology, 83*(6), 1420–1443. doi:10.1086/226707

Greenwood, B., & Mutabingwa, T. (2002). Malaria in 2002. *Nature, 415*(6872), 670–672. doi:10.1038/415670a

Grimmelmann, J. (2008). *Facebook and the social dynamics of privacy*. Retrieved from http://www.scribd.com/doc/9377908/Facebook-and-the-Social-Dynamics-of-Privacy

Grossi, D. (2007). *Designing invisible handcuffs: Formal investigations in institutions and organizations for MAS*. Unpublished doctoral dissertation, Utrecht University, Utrecht, The Netherlands.

Grossi, D., Aldewereld, H., & Dignum, F. (2007). Designing norm enforcement in e-institutions. In P. Noriega, J. Vázquez-Salceda, G. Boella, O. Boissier, V. Dignum, N. Fornara, & E. Matson (Eds.), *Proceedings of the International Workshop on Coordination, Organizations, Institutions, and Norms in Agent Systems II* (LNCS 4386, pp. 101-114).

Grushin, A., & Reggia, J. A. (2006). Stigmergic self-assembly of prespecified artificial structures in a constrained and continuous environment. *Integrated Computer-Aided Engineering, 13*, 289–312.

Gutman, R., & Maes, P. (1998). Cooperative vs. competitive multi-agent negotiation in retail electronic commerce. In *Proceedings of the Second International Workshop on Cooperative Information Agents*, Paris, France.

Gu, W., Killeen, G., Mbogo, C., Regens, J., Githure, J., & Beier, J. (2003). An individual-based model of Plasmodium falciparum malaria transmission on the coast of Kenya. *Transactions of the Royal Society of Tropical Medicine and Hygiene, 97*, 43–50. doi:10.1016/S0035-9203(03)90018-6

Gu, W., & Novak, R. (2009). Agent-based modelling of mosquito foraging behaviour for malaria control. *Transactions of the Royal Society of Tropical Medicine and Hygiene, 103*(11), 1105–1112. doi:10.1016/j.trstmh.2009.01.006

Gu, W., & Novak, R. (2009b). Predicting the impact of insecticide-treated bed nets on malaria transmission: The devil is in the detail. *Malaria Journal, 8*, 256. doi:10.1186/1475-2875-8-256

Hackney, J., & Marchal, F. (2007). Model for coupling multi-agent social interactions and traffic simulation. In *Proceedings of Annual Meeting on Frontiers in Transportation.*

Hare, B., Melis, A. P., Woods, V., Hastingsn, S., & Wrangham, R. (2007). Tolerance Allows Bonobos to Outperform Chimpanzees on a Cooperative Task. *Current Biology, 17*(7). doi:10.1016/j.cub.2007.02.040

Ha, S. H., Bae, S. M., & Park, S. C. (2002). Customer's time-variant purchase behavior and corresponding marketing strategies: An online retailer's case. *Computers & Industrial Engineering, 43*, 801–820. doi:10.1016/S0360-8352(02)00141-9

Haupt, R. L., & Haupt, S. E. (2004). *Practical genetic algorithms* (2nd ed.). Hoboken, NJ: John Wiley & Sons.

Hay, S., Cox, J., Rogers, D., Randolph, S., Stern, D., & Shanks, G. (2002). Climate change and the resurgence of malaria in the East African highlands. *Nature, 415*, 905–909. doi:10.1038/415905a

He, M., Jennings, N. R., & Prugel-Bennett, A. (2004). An adaptive bidding agent for multiple English auctions: A neuro-fuzzy approach. In *Proceedings of the IEEE Conference on Fuzzy Systems*, Budapest, Hungary (pp. 1519-1524).

Heath, B., Hill, R., & Ciarallo, F. (2009). A survey of agent-based modeling practices. *Journal of Artificial Societies and Social Simulation, 12*(4), 9.

Heidhues, P., & Kőszegi, B. (2008). Competition and price variation when consumers are loss averse. *The American Economic Review, 98*, 1245–1268. doi:10.1257/aer.98.4.1245

Helinski, M., Hassan, M., El-Motasim, W., Malcolm, C., & Knols, B., & El- Sayed, B. (2008). Towards a sterile insect technique field release of Anophe-les arabiensis mosquitoes in Sudan: Irradiation, transportation, and field cage experimentation. *Malaria Journal, 7*(1), 65. doi:10.1186/1475-2875-7-65

He, M., Leung, H., & Jennings, N. R. (2003). A fuzzy logic based bidding strategy for autonomous agents in continuous double auctions. *IEEE Transactions on Knowledge and Data Engineering, 15*(6), 1345–1363. doi:10.1109/TKDE.2003.1245277

Henderson, M. (1996). *The Forgiveness Factor – Stories of Hope in a World of Conflict*. Saint Paul, MN: Grosvenor Books USA.

Hoshen, M., & Morse, A. (2004). A weather-driven model of malaria transmission. *Malaria Journal, 3*, 32. doi:10.1186/1475-2875-3-32

Hu, X., Eberhart, R. C., & Shi, Y. (2003). Particle swarm with extended memory for multi-objective optimization. In *Proceedings of the Swarm Intelligence Symposium*. Washington, DC: IEEE.

Huang, G., & Bryden, K. M. (2005). Introducing virtual engineering technology into interactive design process with high-fidelity models. In *Proceedings of the Winter Simulation Conference*, Orlando, FL (pp. 1958-1967).

Hui, C. (2006). Carrying capacity, population equilibrium, and environment's maximal load. *Ecological Modelling, 192*(1-2), 317–320. doi:10.1016/j.ecolmodel.2005.07.001

Huynh, T. D., Jennings, N. R., & Shadbolt, N. R. (2004). Fire: An integrated trust and reputation model for open multi-agent systems. In *Proceedings of the 16th European Conference on Artificial Intelligence* (pp. 18-20).

Huynh, T. D., Jennings, N. R., & Shadbolt, N. R. (2006). An integrated trust and reputation model for open multi-agent systems. *Autonomous Agents and Multi-Agent Systems, 13*(2), 119–154. doi:10.1007/s10458-005-6825-4

Impoinvil, D., Cardenas, G., Gihture, J., Mbogo, C., & Beier, J. (2007). Constant temperature and time period effects on Anopheles gambiae egg hatching. *Journal of the American Mosquito Control Association, 23,* 124–130. doi:10.2987/8756-971X(2007)23[124:CTATPE]2.0.CO;2

Janilma, A. R., Peres, D. V., & Bergmann, U. (2005). Experiencing AUML for MAS Modeling: A critical View. In *Proceedings of the First Workshop on Software Engineering for Agent Oriented System, Seas.*

Janssen, M. A., & Martens, W. J. M. (1997). Modeling malaria as a complex adaptive system. *Artificial Life, 3*(3), 213–236. doi:10.1162/artl.1997.3.3.213

Jin, Y., Matsuo, Y., & Ishizuka, M. (2007). Extracting social networks among various entities on the web. In *Proceedings of the 4th European Conference on the Semantic Web* (pp. 251-266).

Jin, E. M., Girvan, M., & Newman, M. E. J. (2001). The Structure of Growing Social Networks. *Physical Review E: Statistical, Nonlinear, and Soft Matter Physics, 64*(4). doi:10.1103/PhysRevE.64.046132

Jones, C., & Matarić, M. (2003). From local to global behavior in intelligent self-assembly. In *Proceedings of the IEEE International Conference on Robotics and Automation*, Taipei, Taiwan (pp. 721-726).

Jonker, C. M., Robu, V., & Treur, J. (2007). An agent architecture for multi-attribute negotiation using incomplete preference information. *Autonomous Agents and Multi-Agent Systems, 15*(2), 221–252. doi:10.1007/s10458-006-9009-y

Jøsang, A., Keser, C., & Dimitrakos, T. (2005). Can we manage trust? In P. Herrmann, V. Issarny, & S. Shiu (Eds.), *Trust Management, Third International Conference, iTrust'2005* (LNCS 3477, pp. 93-107). New York: Springer.

Jøsang, A., Ismail, R., & Boyd, C. (2007). A survey of trust and reputation systems for online service provision. *Decision Support Systems, 43,* 618–644. doi:10.1016/j.dss.2005.05.019

K4CARE project. (2006). Retrieved August 20, 2010, from www.k4care.ne

Kahneman, D., & Tversky, A. (1979). Prospect theory: An analysis of decisions under risk. *Econometrica, 47*(2), 263–291. doi:10.2307/1914185

Kang, N., & Han, S. (2002). Agent-based e-marketplace system for more fair and efficient transaction. *Decision Support Systems, 34,* 157–165. doi:10.1016/S0167-9236(02)00078-7

Kempe, D., Kleinberg, J., & Tardos, E. (2003). Maximizing the spread of influence through a social network. In *Proceedings of the 9th ACM SIGKDD International Conference on Knowledge Discovery and Data Mining* (pp. 137-146).

Kempe, D., Kleinberg, J., & Tardos, E. (2005). Influential nodes in a diffusion model for social networks. In L. Caires, G. F. Italiano, L. Monteiro, C. Palamidessi, & M. Yung (Eds.), *Proceedings of the 32nd International Colloquium on Automata, Languages and Programming* (LNCS 3580, pp. 1127-1138).

Kennedy, J., & Eberhart, R. (1995). Particle swarm optimization. In *Proceedings of the IEEE Int. Conf. on Neural Networks*, Piscataway, NJ.

Kennedy, R. C., Xiang, X., Cosimano, T. F., Arthurs, L. A., Maurice, P. A., Madey, G. R., et al. (2006, April). Verification and validation of agent-based and equation-based simulations: A comparison. In *Proceedings of the Agent-Directed Simulation Conference*, Huntsville, AL.

Kennedy, J., Eberhart, R., & Shi, Y. (2001). *Swarm Intelligence.* San Francisco: Morgan Kaufman.

Killeen, G., Knols, B., & Gu, W. (2003). Taking malaria transmission out of the bottle: implications of mosquito dispersal for vector- control interventions. *The Lancet Infectious Diseases, 3*(5), 297–303. doi:10.1016/S1473-3099(03)00611-X

Klassen, W., & Curtis, C. (2005). *History of the sterile insect technique. Sterile insect technique: Principles and practice in area-wide integrated pest management.* New York, NY: Springer.

Kleinberg, J. (2000). The small-world phenomenon: An algorithmic perspective. In *Proceedings of the 32nd ACM Symposium on Theory of Computing* (pp. 163-170).

Klenow, P. J., & Kryvtsov, O. (2008). State-dependent or time-dependent pricing: Does it matter for recent U.S. inflation? *The Quarterly Journal of Economics, 123*(3), 863–904. doi:10.1162/qjec.2008.123.3.863

Klügl, F., Bazzan, A. L. C., Ossowski, S., & Chaib-Draa, B. (Eds.). (2010, May 11). *Sixth Workshop on Agents in Traffic and Transportation*, Toronto, ON, Canada.

Koch, J. B. (2008). *Autonomous construction agents: An investigation framework for large sensor network self-management* (Master's thesis). Available from ProQuest Dissertations and Theses database (UMI No. 1461866)

Koeppen, J., & Lopez-Sanchez, M. (2010). Generating new regulations by learning from experience. In P. Noriega, J. Vázquez-Salceda, G. Boella, O. Boissier, V. Dignum, N. Fornara, & E. Matson (Eds.), *Proceedings of the International Workshop on Coordination, Organizations, Institutions, and Norms in Agent Systems II* (LNCS 4386, pp. 72-79).

Kollingbaum, M. J., & Norman, T. J. (2003). Norm adoption and consistency in the NoA agent architecture. In M. M. Dastani, J. Dix, & A. El Fallah-Seghrouchni (Eds.), *Proceedings of the First International Workshop on Programming Multi-Agent Systems* (LNCS 3067, pp. 169-186).

Kőszegi, B., & Rabin, M. (2006). A model of reference-dependent preferences. *The Quarterly Journal of Economics, 121*, 1133–1166.

Kraus, S., Sycara, K., & Evenchil, A. (1998). Reaching agreements through argumentation: A logical model and implementation. *Artificial Intelligence, 104*, 1–69. doi:10.1016/S0004-3702(98)00078-2

Krulwich, B. (1996). The bargainfinder agent: Comparison price shopping on the Internet . In Williams, J. (Ed.), *Bots, and other internet beasties* (pp. 257–263). New York, NY: Macmillan.

Kumar, R., Novak, J., Raghavan, P., & Tomkins, A. (2004). Structure and evolution of blogspace. *Communications of the ACM, 47*(12), 35–39. doi:10.1145/1035134.1035162

Labrou, Y., & Finin, T. (1994). *State of the art and challenges for agent communication languages*. Baltimore, MD: Department of Computer Science and Electrical Engineering, University of Maryland.

Laleci, G. B., Dogac, A., Olduz, M., Tasyurt, I., Yuksel, M., & Okcan, A. (2008). SAPHIRE: A Multi-Agent System for Remote Healthcare Monitoring through Computerized Clinical Guidelines . In Annicchiarico, R., Cortés, U., & Urdiales, C. (Eds.), *Agent Technology and e-Health* (pp. 25–44). Berlin: Birkhäuser Verlag. doi:10.1007/978-3-7643-8547-7_3

Law, A. M. (2007). *Simulation & modeling analysis*. New York, NY: McGraw Hill.

LeBaron, B. (2006). Agent-based computational finance. In Tesfatsion, L., & Judd, K. L. (Eds.), *Handbook of computational economics* (Vol. 2, pp. 1187–1233). Amsterdam, The Netherlands: Elsevier.

Lee, H. G. (1996). Electronic brokerage and electronic auction: The impact of IT on market structures. In *Proceedings of the 29th HICSS Conference on Information Systems – Organizational Systems and Technology*, Los Alamitos, CA (pp. 397-406).

Lee, J. H., & Park, S. C. (2005). Intelligent profitable customers segmentation system based on business intelligence tools. *Expert Systems with Applications, 29*, 145–152. doi:10.1016/j.eswa.2005.01.013

Leskovec, J., Krause, A., & Guestrin, C. (2007). Cost-effective outbreak detection in networks. In *Proceedings of the 13th ACM SIGKDD International Conference on Knowledge Discovery and Data Mining* (pp. 420-429).

Liljeros, F., Edling, C. R., Amaral, L. A. N., Stanely, H. E., & Aberg, Y. (2001). The Web of Human Sexual Contacts. *Nature*, 907–908. doi:10.1038/35082140

Lin, Y., & Liu, S. (2004). A historical introduction to grey systems theory. In *Proceedings of the IEEE International Conference on Systems, Man and Cybernetics* (Vol. 3, pp. 2403-2408).

Lin, C.-S., Chou, S., Weng, S.-M., & Hsieh, Y.-C. (2011). *A final price prediction model for English auctions: a neuro-fuzzy approach*. New York, NY: Springer Science & Business Media.

Lindsay, S., & Martens, W. (1998). Malaria in the African highlands: Past, present, future. *Bulletin of the World Health Organization, 76*, 33–45.

Liu, S., & Lin, Y. (2006). *Grey information: Theory and practical application with 60 figures*. London, UK: Springer.

Li, X., Liu, L., Wu, L., & Zhang, Z. (2006). Predicting the final price of online auction items. *Expert Systems with Applications*, *31*(3), 542–550. doi:10.1016/j.eswa.2005.09.077

Local Programming Associates. (n. d.). *Chimera Agents for WIN-Prolog*. Retrieved from http://www.lpa.co.uk/chi.htm

Lofgren, C., Dame, D., Breeland, S., Weidhaas, D., Jeffery, G., & Kaiser, R. (1974). Release of chemosterilized males for the control *of* Anopheles albimanus in El Salvador: III. Field methods and population control. *The American Journal of Tropical Medicine and Hygiene*, *23*(2), 288.

Lopez, F. (2003). *Social powers and norms: Impact on agent behaviour*. Unpublished doctoral dissertation, University of Southampton, Southampton, UK.

Lopez, F., Luck, M., & d'Inverno, M. (2002). Constraining autonomy through norms. In *Proceedings of the First International Joint Conference on Autonomous Agents and Multi Agent Systems* (pp. 674-681).

Lünnemann, P., & Wintr, L. (2006). *Are internet prices sticky?* Frankfurt am Main, Germany: European Central Bank.

Macal, C. M., & North, M. J. (2006). Tutorial on agent-based modeling and simulation part 2: How to model with agents. In *Proceedings of the Winter Simulation Conference* (pp. 73-83).

Macal, C., & North, M. (2008). Agent-based modeling and simulation: ABMS examples. In *Proceedings of the 40th Conference on Winter Simulation* (pp.101-112).

MacArthur, R. H., & Pianka, E. R. (1966). On the optimal use of a patchy environment. *American Naturalist*, *100*, 603–609. doi:10.1086/282454

Macdonald, G. (1957). *The epidemilogy and control of malaria*. Oxford, UK: Oxford University Press.

Mackowiak, B., & Smets, F. (2008). *On implications of micro price data for macro models*. Frankfurt am Main, Germany: European Central Bank.

Manoukis, N., Diabate, A., Abdoulaye, A., Diallo, M., & Dao, A. (2009). Structure and dynamics of male swarms of Anopheles gambiae. *Journal of Medical Entomology*, *46*(2), 227. doi:10.1603/033.046.0207

Margus, O. J. A. (2001). Agent Based Software Design. In . *Proceedings of Estonian Academy of Sciences and Engineering*, *50*, 5–21.

Mazumdar, B. D., & Mishra, R. B. (2009). Multiagent paradigm for the agent selection and negotiation in a B2c process. *International Journal of Intelligent Information Technologies*, *5*(1), 61–82. doi:10.4018/jiit.2009010104

Mc Morrow, K. (2004). *The Economic and Financial Market consequences of Global Ageing*. New York: Springer.

Mccallum, A., Wang, X., & Corrada-Emmanuel, A. (2007). Topic and role discovery in social networks with experiments on enron and academic email. *Journal of Artificial Intelligence Research*, *30*, 249–272.

McKenzie, F. (2000, January) Why model malaria? *Parasitology Today*.

McKenzie, F. E., & Bossert, W. H. (2005). An integrated model of Plasmodium falciparum dynamics. *Journal of Theoretical Biology*, *232*(3), 411–426.

McKenzie, F., Wong, R., & Bossert, W. H. (1998). Discrete-event simulation models of Plasmodium falciparum malaria. *Simulation*, *71*, 250–261. doi:10.1177/003754979807100405

Melis, A. P., Hare, B., & Tomasello, M. (2006). Engineering cooperation in chimpanzees: tolerance constraints on cooperation. *Animal Behaviour*, *72*(2). doi:10.1016/j.anbehav.2005.09.018

Menach, A. L., McKenzie, F. E., Flahault, A., & Smith, D. L. (2005). The unexpected importance of mosquito oviposition behaviour for malaria: Non-productive larval habitats can be sources for malaria transmission. *Malaria Journal*, *4*(1), 23. doi:10.1186/1475-2875-4-23

Midgley, D. F., Marks, R. E., & Cooper, L. G. (1997). Breeding competitive strategies. *Management Science*, *43*(3), 257–275. doi:10.1287/mnsc.43.3.257

Miller, E. (2005). An integrated framework for modelling short- and long-run household decision-making. In Timmermans, H. (Ed.), *Progress in activity-based analysis* (pp. 175–202). Oxford, UK: Elsevier. doi:10.1016/B978-008044581-6/50012-0

Mishra R. B. (2009). Rule based and ANN model for the evaluation of Customer Orientation in CRM, IE(I) 90, 28-33

Mohamad Noor, N. M., Abdul Samat, N. H., Yazid Saman, M., Suzuri Hitam, M., & Man, M. (2007). iWDSS-Tender: Intelligent Web-based Decision Support System for Tender Evaluation. In *Proceedings of the IEEE International Symposium on Signal Processing and Information Technology* (pp. 1011-1016).

Mokhtarian, P. L., & Salomon, I. (2001). How derived is the demand for travel? Some conceptual and measurement considerations. *Transportation Research Part A, Policy and Practice, 35*, 695–719. doi:10.1016/S0965-8564(00)00013-6

Mokhtarian, P. L., Salomon, I., & Handy, S. L. (2006). The impacts of ICT on leisure activities and travel: A conceptual exploration. *Transportation, 33*, 263–289. doi:10.1007/s11116-005-2305-6

Molineaux, L., Gramiccia, G., & WHO. (1980). *The Garki project: Research on the epidemiology and control of malaria in the Sudan savanna of west Africa.* (p. 311). Retrieved from http://www.cabdirect.org/abstracts/19812901070.html;jsessionid=329ED17B0C4FCD0D9EB971E95BABC593

Mossel, E., & Roch, S. (2007). On the submodularity of influence in social networks. In *Proceedings of the Thirty-Ninth Annual ACM Symposium on Theory of Computing* (pp. 128-134).

Muehlen, M., & Rosemann, M. (2000). Workflow-based process monitoring & controlling – Technical & organizational issues. In *Proceedings of the 33rd Hawaii International Conference on Systems Sciences*, Wailea, HI.

Mumpower, J. L., & Darling, T. A. (1991). Modeling Resource Allocation Negotiations. In *Proceeding of the IEEE Twenty Fourth Annual Hawii International Conference* (Vol. 3, pp. 641-649).

Nakamura, E., & Steinsson, J. (2008). Five facts about prices: A reevaluation of menu cost models. *The Quarterly Journal of Economics, 123*(4), 1415–1464. doi:10.1162/qjec.2008.123.4.1415

Narayanan, A., & Shmatikov, V. (2009). *De-anonymizing social networks.* Retrieved from http://www.cs.utexas.edu/~shmat/shmat_oak09.pdf

Nemhauser, G. L., & Wolsey, L. A. (1978). Best algorithms for approximating the maximum of a submodular set function. *Mathematics of Operations Research, 3*(3), 177–188. doi:10.1287/moor.3.3.177

netlogo. (n.d.). Retrieved from www.ccl.northwestern.edu/netlogo/

Newman, M. E. J. (2003). *The Structure and Function of Complex Networks.* Society for Industrial and Applied Mathematics.

Newman, M. E. J. (2004). Detecting Community Structure in Networks. *The European Physical Journal B, 38*(2). doi:10.1140/epjb/e2004-00124-y

Nolfi, S., & Floreano, D. (2000). *Evolutionary Robotics.* Cambridge, MA: MIT Press.

Noury, N. (2005). AILISA: Experimental platforms to evaluate remote care and assistive technologies in gerontology. In *Proceedings of 7th international workshop on enterprise networking and computing in healthcare industry (HEALTHCOM 2005)*, South Korea (pp. 67-72).

Novak, J., Raghavan, P., & Tomkins, A. (2004). Anti-aliasing on the web. In *Proceedings of the 13th International Conference on World Wide Web* (pp. 30-39).

Nudds, T. D. (1978). Convergence of group size strategies by mammalian social carnivores. *American Naturalist, 112*, 957–960. doi:10.1086/283336

Odell, J., Parunak, V., & Bernhard, D. (2000). Expending UML for Agents. In *Proceeding of The Agent Oriented Information Systems Workshop at 17th National Conference on Artificial Intelligence*, Austin, TX (pp. 3-17).

OLDES project. (2010). Retrieved August 20, 2010, from www.oldes.eu

Omumbo, J., Hay, S., Guerra, C., & Snow, R. (2004). The relationship between the Plasmodium falciparum parasite ratio in childhood and climate estimates of malaria transmission in Kenya. *Malaria Journal, 3*, 17. doi:10.1186/1475-2875-3-17

Ostfeld, R. S., Glass, G. E., & Keesing, F. (2005). Spatial epidemiology: An emerging (or re-emerging) discipline. *Trends in Ecology & Evolution, 20*(6), 328–336. doi:10.1016/j.tree.2005.03.009

Ostrom, E. (2000). Collective action and the evolution of social norms. *The Journal of Economic Perspectives, 14*, 137–158. doi:10.1257/jep.14.3.137

Paaijmans, K., Huijben, S., Githeko, A., & Takken, W. (2009). Competitive interactions between larvae of the malaria mosquitoes Anopheles arabiensis and Anopheles gambiae under semi-field conditions in western Kenya. *Acta Tropica, 109*(2), 124–130. doi:10.1016/j.actatropica.2008.07.010

Padgham, L., & Winikoff, M. (2004). *Developing intelligent agent systems - A practical guide*. New York, NY: John Wiley & Sons. doi:10.1002/0470861223

Panzarasa, P., Jennings, N. R., & Norman, T. J. (2002). Formalizing collaborative decision-making and practical reasoning. *Multi-agent Systems, 12*(1), 55–117.

Parsopoulos, K. E., & Vrahatis, M. N. (2002). Particle swarm optimization method in multi-objective problems. In *Proceedings of the 2002 ACM symposium on applied computing*.

Patel, M., Honavar, V., & Balakrishnan, K. (Eds.). (2001). *Advances in the Evolutionary Synthesis of Intelligent Agents*. Cambridge, MA: MIT Press.

Phuc, H., Andreasen, M., Burton, R., Vass, C., Epton, M., & Pape, G. (2007). Late-acting dominant lethal genetic systems and mosquito control. *BMC Biology, 5*(1), 11. doi:10.1186/1741-7007-5-11

Project Monitoring System. (2006). *Department of Foreign Aid and Budgeting Monitoring, Ministry of Plan Implementation, Sri Lanka*. Retrieved from http://www.fabm.gov.lk

Radicchi, F., Castellano, C., Cecconi, F., Loreto, V., & Parisi, D. (2004). Defining and identifying communities in networks. *Proceedings of the National Academy of Sciences of the United States of America, 101*(9), 2658–2663. doi:10.1073/pnas.0400054101

Rammal, A., Trouilhet, S., Singer, N., & Pécatte, J. M. (2008). An Adaptive System for Home Monitoring Using a Multiagent Classification of Patterns. *International Journal of Telemedicine and Applications*.

Rands, S. A., Cowlishaw, G., Pettifor, R. A., Rowclife, J. M., & Johnstone, R. A. (2003). The spontaneous emergence of leaders and followers in foraging pairs. *Nature, 423*, 432–434. doi:10.1038/nature01630

Rands, S. A., Pettifor, R. A., Rowclife, J. M., & Cowlishaw, G. (2004). State-dependent foraging rules for social animals in selfish herds. In . *Proceedings of the Royal Society, 271*, 2613–2620. doi:10.1098/rspb.2004.2906

Rands, S. A., Pettifor, R. A., Rowclife, J. M., & Cowlishaw, G. (2006). Social foraging and dominance relationships: the efects of socially mediated interference. *Behavioral Ecology and Sociobiology, 60*, 572–581. doi:10.1007/s00265-006-0202-4

Ravindran, A., Phillips, D. T., & Solberg, J. J. (2001). *Operations Research Principle and practice*. New York: John Wiley & Sons.

Recursive Porous Agent Simulation Toolkit (Repast). (2011). *The repast suite*. Retrieved from http://repast.sourceforge.net

Redner, S. (1998). How Popular is Your Paper? An Emprical Study of the Citation Distribution. *Eur. Phys.*, 131-134.

Reichheld, F. F. (1996). *The loyalty effect*. Cambridge, MA: Harvard Business School Press.

Rindt, C. R., Marca, J. E., & McNally, M. G. (2003). An agent-based activity microsimulation kernel using a negotiation metaphor. In *Proceedings of the 82nd Annual Meeting of the Transportation Research Board*.

Riolo, R. L., Cohen, M. D., & Axelrod, R. (2001). Evolution of cooperation without reciprocity. *Nature, 414*, 6862. doi:10.1038/35106555

Roberts, J. M. (1995). New Keynesian economics and the Phillips curve. *Journal of Money, Credit and Banking, 27*(4), 975–984. doi:10.2307/2077783

Rodman, P. S. (1981). Inclusive fitness and group size with a reconsideration of group sizes in lions and wolves. *American Naturalist, 118*, 275–283. doi:10.1086/283819

Rogers, D., & Randolph, S. (2000). The global spread of malaria in a future, warmer world. *Science, 289*, 1763–1766.

Rogoff, K. (1996). The purchasing power parity puzzle. *Journal of Economic Literature, 34*, 647–668.

Rossi, G., Stefano, A., & Hales, D. (2009). Evolving Networks for Social Optima in the Weakest Link Game. *Computational & Mathematical Organization Theory, 15*(2). doi:10.1007/s10588-008-9051-1

Rotemberg, J. J. (in press). Fair pricing. *Journal of the European Economic Association.*

Sabater, J., & Sierra, C. (2001). A reputation model for gregarious societies. In *Regret: A reputation model for gregarious societies* (pp. 61–69). Montreal, Canada: Regret.

Sabater, J., & Sierra, C. (2005). Review on computational trust and reputation models. *Artificial Intelligence Review, 24*, 33–60. doi:10.1007/s10462-004-0041-5

Sakka, E., Prentza, A., Lamprinos, I. E., Leondaridis, L., & Koutsouris, D. (2004). Integration of monitoring devices in the e-Vital service. In *Proceedings of the 26th Annual International Conference of the Engineering in Medicine and Biology Society (EMBC 2004)* (Vol. 4, pp. 3097-3100).

Salehi-Abari, A., & White, T. (2009). Towards con-resistant trust models for distributed agent systems. In *Proceedings of the 21st International Joint Conference on Artifical Intelligence (IJCAI 2009)* (pp. 272-277). San Francisco: Morgan Kaufmann Publishers Inc.

Sandholm, T. (1993). An implementation of the contract net protocol based on marginal cost calculations. In *Proceedings of the 11th National Conference on Artificial Intelligence* (pp. 256-262).

Sandholm, T. W. (1999). Distributed rational decision making . In Weiss, G. (Ed.), *Multiagent systems: A modern approach to distributed artificial intelligence* (pp. 201–258). Cambridge, MA: MIT Press.

Sarker, R., Mohammadian, M., & Yao, X. (Eds.). (2002). *Evolutionary Optimization.* Boston: Kluwer Academic Publishers.

Sathiyamoorthy, E., Iyenger, N., & Ramachandran, V. (2010). Agent based trust management framework in distributed e-business environment. *International Journal of Computer Science & Information Technology, 2*, 14–28.

Savarimuthu, B. T. R., Cranfield, S., Purvis, M., & Purvis, M. (2009). Internal agent architecture for norm identification. In J. Padget, A. Artikis, W. Vasconcelos, K. Stathis, V. T. da Silva, E. Matson, & A. Polleres (Eds.), *Proceeding of the 5th International Workshop on Coordination, Organization, Institutions and Norms in Agent Systems* (LNCS 6069, pp. 241-256).

Savarimuthu, B. T. R., Cranfield, S., Purvis, M., & Purvis, M. (2010). A data mining approach to identify obligation norms in agent societies. In L. Cao, A. L. C. Bazzan, V. Gorodetsky, P. A. Mitkas, G. Weiss, & P. S. Yu (Eds.), *Proceedings of the 6th International Workshop on Agents and Data Mining Interaction* (LNCS 5980, pp. 43-58).

Savarimuthu, B. T. R., Cranfield, S., Purvis, M., & Purvis, M. (2010). Identifying conditional norms in multi-agent societies. In M. De Vos, N. Fornara, J. V. Pitt, & G. Vouros (Eds.), *Proceeding of the 6th International Workshop on Coordination, Organization, Institutions and Norms in Agent Systems* (LNCS 6541, pp. 19-24).

Savarimuthu, B. T. R., Cranfield, S., Purvis, M., & Purvis, M. (2010). *Norm identification in multi-agent societies.* Retrieved from http://otago.ourarchive.ac.nz/handle/10523/1031

Savarimuthu, B. T. R., Purvis, M., & Fleurke, M. (2004). Monitoring and controlling of a multiagent-based workflow system. In *Proceedings of the Australasian Workshop on Data Mining and Web Intelligence*, Dunedin, New Zealand (pp. 127-132).

Scarlat, E., & Maries, I. (2009). Towards an increase of collective intelligence within organizations using trust and reputation models. In N. T. Nguyen, R. Kowalczyk, & S. M. Chen (Eds.), *First International Conference on Computational Collective Intelligence. Semantic Web, Social Networks and Multiagent Systems (ICCCI 2009)* (LNCS 5796, pp. 140-151). New York: Springer.

Sharma, U., & Singh, S. (2008). Insect vectors of leishmania: Distribution, physiology and their control. *Journal of Vector Borne Diseases*, 45.

Shetty, J., & Adibi, J. (2004). *The Enron email dataset database schema and brief statistical report*. Marina del Rey, CA: Information Sciences Institute.

Shoham, Y., & Tennenholtz, M. (1997). On the Emergence of Social Conventions: Modeling, Analysis and Simulations. *AI*, 139-166.

Shoham, Y. (1993). Agent oriented programming. *Artificial Intelligence*, 60(1), 51–92. doi:10.1016/0004-3702(93)90034-9

Shoham, Y., & Tennenholtz, M. (1995). On social laws for artificial agent societies: Off-line design. *Artificial Intelligence*, 73(1-2), 231–252. doi:10.1016/0004-3702(94)00007-N

Shubik, M. (1983). *Auctions, biddings, and markets: An historical sketch*. New York, NY: New York University Press.

Sim, K. M., & Chan, R. (2000). A brokering protocol for agent-based e-commerce. *IEEE Transactions on Systems, Man and Cybernetics. Part C, Applications and Reviews*, 30(4).

Sommerfeld, A. (1956). *Thermodynamics and statistical mechanics*. New York, NY: Academic Press.

SOPRANO project. (2010). Retrieved August 20, 2010, from www.soprano-ip.org

Spiegler, R. (in press). Monopoly pricing when consumers are antagonized by unexpected price increases: A cover version of the Heidhues-Koszegi-Rabin model. *Economic Theory*.

Srinivasan, S. (2004). Role of trust in e-business success. *Information Management & Computer Security*, 12(1), 66–72. doi:10.1108/09685220410518838

Staddon, J., Golle, P., & Zimny, B. (2007). Web-based inference detection. In *Proceedings of 16th USENIX Security Symposium* (pp. 1-16).

Steinfield, C., Jang, C., & Pfaff, B. (1999). Supporting virtual team collaboration: The TeamSCOPE system. In *Proceedings of the International ACM SIGGROUP Conference on Supporting Group Work*, Phoenix, AZ (pp. 81-90).

stigrefs. (n.d.). Retrieved from www.stigmergicsystems.com/stig_v1/stigrefs/article1.html

Suresh, S. (2004). AHP Based System for Formal R & D project Selection. *Journal of Scientific and Industrial Research*, 63, 888–896.

Surowiecki, J. (2004). *The wisdom of crowds*. New York, NY: Random House.

Suwu, W., & Das, A. (2001). An agent system architecture for e-commerce. In *Proceedings of the 12th IEEE International Workshop on Database and Expert Systems Applications* (pp. 715-719).

Tablado, A., Illarramendi, A., Bagüés, M. I., Bermúdez, J., & Goñi, A. (2004). Aingeru: an Innovating System for Tele Assistance of Elderly People. In *Proceedings of the 1st International Workshop on Tele-Care and Collaborative Virtual Communities in Elderly Care (TELECARE)* (pp. 27-36).

Taha, H. A. (2011). *Operations Research: An Introduction*. Upper Saddle River, NJ: Prentice Hall.

Tang, T. Y., Winoto, P., & Niu, X. (2003). Investigating trust between users and agents in a multi agent portfolio management system: A preliminary report. *Electronic Commerce Research and Applications*, 2(4), 302–314. doi:10.1016/S1567-4223(03)00039-5

Tesfatsion, L. (2001). Introduction to the special issue on agent-based computational economics. *Journal of Economic Dynamics & Control*, 25(3-4), 281–293. doi:10.1016/S0165-1889(00)00027-0

Tesfatsion, L. (2006). Agent-based computational economics: A constructive approach to economic theory . In Tesfatsion, L., & Judd, K. L. (Eds.), *Handbook of computational economics* (Vol. 2, pp. 831–880). Amsterdam, The Netherlands: Elsevier.

Theraulaz, G., & Bonabeau, E. (1995). Coordination in distributed building. *Science, 269,* 686–689. doi:10.1126/science.269.5224.686

Theraulaz, G., & Bonabeau, E. (1999). A brief history of stigmergy. *Artificial Life, 5,* 97–116. doi:10.1162/106454699568700

Thomas, D., Donnelly, C., Wood, R., & Alphey, L. (2000). Insect population control using a dominant, repressible, lethal genetic system. *Science, 287*(5462), 2474. doi:10.1126/science.287.5462.2474

Timmermans, H. J., & Zhang, J. (2009). Modeling household activity travel behavior: Examples of state of the art modeling approaches and research agenda. *Transportation Research Part B: Methodological, 43,* 187–190. doi:10.1016/j.trb.2008.06.004

Toivonen, L., Kovanen, L., Kivela, M., Onnela, J.-P., Saramaki, J., & Kaski, K. (2009). A Comparative Study of Social Network Models: Network Evolution Models and Nodal Attribute Models. *Social Networks, 31.*

Tsvetovatyy, M., Gini, M., Mobasher, B., & Wieckowski, Z. (1997). MAGMA: An agent-based virtual marketplace for electronic commerce. *Applied Artificial Intelligence, 11*(6), 501–542. doi:10.1080/088395197118046

Turkle, S. (1997). *Life on the screen: Identity in the age of the Internet.* New York, NY: Simon & Schuster.

Umeyama, S. (1988). An eigendecomposition approach to weighted graph matching problems. *IEEE Transactions on Pattern Analysis and Machine Intelligence, 10*(5), 695–703. doi:10.1109/34.6778

van den Berg, P., Arentze, T., & Timmermans, H. (2008). Social networks, ICT use and activity-travel patterns: Data collection and first analyses. In *Proceedings of the 9th International Conference on Design and Decision Support Systems in Architecture and Urban Planning.*

van den Bergh, F., & Engelbrecht, A. P. (2006). A study of particle swarm optimization particle trajectories. *Information Sciences, 176*(8), 937–971. doi:10.1016/j.ins.2005.02.003

van Laarhoven, P. J. M., & Aarts, E. H. L. (1987). *Simulated annealing: Theory and applications.* Dordrecht, The Netherlands: Reidel.

Verhagen, H. (2000). *Norm autonomous agents.* Unpublished doctoral dissertation, Royal Institute of Technology and Stockholm University, Stockholm, Sweden.

Verykios, V. S., Bertino, E., Fovino, I. N., Provenza, L. P., Saygin, Y., & Theodoridis, Y. (2004). State-of-the-art in privacy preserving data mining. *SIGMOD Record, 33.*

Vieira, A. L. (2008). *An interpersonal approach to modeling business-to-business relationship quality.* Unpublished doctoral dissertation, University of Nottingham, Nottingham, UK.

Virone, G., & Sixsmith, A. (2008). Monitoring Activity Patterns and Trends of Older Adults. In *Proceedings of the 30th IEEE-EMBS (Engineering in Medicine and Biology),* Vancouver, Canada (pp. 20-24).

von Wright, G. H. (1980). *Freedom and determination.* Amsterdam, The Netherlands: North Holland Publishing.

Vries, P. (2001, May 16-17). Modelling malaria risk: An individual based and spatial explicit approach. In *Proceedings of the Workshop on Spatial Aspects of Demography,* Rostock, Germany.

Wainer, J., Ferreira, P. R. Jr., & Constantino, E. R. (2007). Scheduling meetings through multi-agent negotiations. *Decision Support Systems, 44,* 285–297. doi:10.1016/j.dss.2007.03.015

Wang, Y., & Lin, K. J. (2008). Reputation-oriented trustworthy computing in e-commerce environments. *IEEE Internet Computing, 12,* 55–59. doi:10.1109/MIC.2008.84

Watts, D. J. (1999). *Small Worlds.* Princeton, NJ: Princeton University Press.

Watts, D. J. (2002). A simple model of global cascades in random networks. *Proceedings of the National Academy of Sciences of the United States of America, 99*(9), 5766–5771. doi:10.1073/pnas.082090499

Weiser, M. (1991). The Computer for the Twenty-First Century. *Scientific American, 265*(3).

Wen, C.-H., & Koppelman, F. S. (2000). A conceptual and methdological framework for the generation of activity-travel patterns. *Transportation, 27,* 5–23. doi:10.1023/A:1005234603206

Werfel, J., & Nagpal, R. (2006). Extended stigmergy in collective construction. *IEEE Intelligent Systems, 21*, 20–28. doi:10.1109/MIS.2006.25

WHO. (2004). *Changing history*. Geneva, Switzerland: World Health Organization.

Wilkes, J. (2008). *Utility functions, prices, and negotiation* (Tech. Rep. No. HPL-2008-81). Palo Alto, CA: Hewlett-Packard Labs.

Wilson, E. O. (2000). *Sociobiology: The new synthesis*. Cambridge, MA: Harvard University Press.

Windbichler, N., Papathanos, P., & Crisanti, A. (2008). Targeting the X chromosome during spermatogenesis induces Y chromosome transmission ratio distortion and early dominant embryo lethality in Anopheles gambiae. *PLOS Genetics, 4*(12). doi:10.1371/journal.pgen.1000291

Winer, R. S. (2001). *Customer relationship management: A framework, research directions, and the future*. Retrieved from http://siebel.ittoolbox.com/documents/customer-relationship-management-a-framework-research-directions-and-the-future-16278

Wobber, V., Wrangham, R., & Hare, B. (2010). Bonobas Exhibit Delayed Development of Social Behavior and Cognition Relative to Chimpanzees. *Current Biology, 20*(3). doi:10.1016/j.cub.2009.11.070

Wolpert, D. H., & Macready, W. G. (1997). No free lunch theorems for optimization. *IEEE Transactions on Evolutionary Computation, 1*, 67–77. doi:10.1109/4235.585893

Wooldridge, M. (2009). *An introduction to multi-agent systems* (2nd ed.). New York, NY: John Wiley & Sons.

World Health Organization (WHO). (2011). *Malaria facts*. Retrieved from http://www.who.int/mediacentre/factsheets/fs094/en/

World Health Organization. (2004). *Changing history*. Geneva, Switzerland: World Health Organization.

Wortman, J. (2008). *Viral marketing and the diffusion of trends on social networks*. Philadelphia, PA: University of Pennsylvania.

Wu, H. J. (2005). An agent-based CRM Model for multiple projects management. In *Proceedings of the IEEE Conference on Engineering Management* (pp. 851-855).

Wu, W., Ekaette, E., & Far, B. H. (2003). Uncertainty management framework for multi-agent systems. In *Proceedings of the ATS Workshop on Refractory Asthma* (pp. 122-131).

Wu, Y., & Zhang, Y. (2009). Stability Analysis in Dynamic Social Networks. In *Proceedings of the Symposium on Agent-Directed Simulation (ADS'09), the 2010 Spring Simulation Multiconference (SpringSim'10)*, Orlando, FL.

Wu, H. H., Liao, A. Y. H., & Wang, P. C. (2004). Using grey theory in quality function deployment to analyse dynamic customer requirement. *International Journal of Advanced Manufacturing Technology, 25*(11-12), 1241–1247. doi:10.1007/s00170-003-1948-8

Xiang, X., Kennedy, R., Madey, G. R., & Cabaniss, S. (2005, April). Verification and validation of agent-based scientific simulation models. In *Proceedings of the Agent-Directed Simulation Conference*, San Diego, CA.

Xiao, A., Bryden, K. M., & McCorkle, D. S. (2005). VE-suite: A software framework for design-analysis integration during product realization. In *Proceedings of the ASME International Design Engineering Technical Conferences and Computers and Information in Engineering Conference: Vol. 3. 25th Computers and Information in Engineering Conference, Parts A and B*, Long Beach, CA (pp. 859-867).

Xu, L., & Weigand, H. (2001). The evolution of the contract net protocol. In X. S. Wang, G. Yu, & H. Lu (Eds.), *Proceedings of the Second International Conference on Advances in Web-Age Information Management* (LNCS 2118, pp. 257-264).

Xu, Z. (2008). *Factors which affect the dynamics of privately-owned Chinese firms: An interdisciplinary empirical evaluation*. Unpublished doctoral dissertation, University of St. Andrews, St. Andrews, Scotland.

Yu, B., & Singh, M. P. (2000). A social mechanism of reputation management in electronic communities. In *Cooperative Information Agents IV - The Future of Information Agents in Cyberspace (CIA 2000)* (LNCS 1860, pp. 154-165). New York: Springer.

Yu, B., & Singh, M. P. (2001). Towards a probabilistic model of distributed reputation management. In *Proceedings of the Fourth Workshop on Deception, Fraud and Trust in Agent Societies*, Montreal, QC, Canada (pp. 125-137).

Yuan, B., Jiwei, G., Guoqing, T., & Lei, W. (2000). Using grey theory to predict the gas-in-oil concentrations in oil-filled transformer. In *Proceedings of the Sixth International Conference on Properties and Applications of Dielectric Materials*, Xi'an, China (pp. 217-219).

Zacharia, G. (1999). *Collaborative reputation mechanisms for online communities.* Unpublished master's thesis, Massachusetts Institute of Technology, Cambridge, MA.

Zacharia, G., & Maes, P. (2000). Trust management through reputation mechanisms. *Applied Artificial Intelligence, 14*(9), 881–908. doi:10.1080/08839510050144868

Zhang, Y. (2009). A deterministic model for history sensitive cascade in diffusion networks. In *Proceedings of the IEEE International Conference on Systems, Man and Cybernetics* (pp. 1977-1982).

Zhang, Y., & Leezer, J. (2009). Emergence of Social Norms in Complex Networks. In *Proceedings of the Symposium on Social Computing Applications (SCA09), The 2009 IEEE International Conference on Social Computing (SocialCom-09)*, Vancouver, Canada (pp. 549-555).

Zhao, X., Wu, C., Zhang, R., Zhao, C., & Lin, Z. (2004). *A multi-agent system for e-business processes monitoring in a web-based environment*. Beijing, China: Peking University.

Zhou, Y., Arifin, S. M. N., Gentile, J., Kurtz, S. J., Davis, G. J., & Wendelberger, B. A. (2010, July). An agent-based model of the Anopheles gambiae mosquito life cycle. In *Proceedings of the Summer Computer Simulation Conference*, Ottawa, ON, Canada.

Zhou, B., Pei, J., & Luk, W. (2008). A brief survey on anonymization techniques for privacy preserving publishing of social network data. *ACM SIGKDD Explorations Newsletter, 10*(2), 12–22. doi:10.1145/1540276.1540279

Zimmermann, M., & Eguiluz, v. (2005). Cooperation, Social Networks and the Emergence of Leadership in a Prisoners Dilemma with Adaptive Local Interactions. *Physical Review*.

Zipf, G. K. (1949). *Human behavior and the principle of least effort*. Reading, MA: Addison-Wesley.

Zouba, N., Bremond, F., & Thonnat, M. (2010). An Activity Monitoring System for Real Elderly at Home: Validation Study. In *Proceedings of the 7th IEEE International Conference on Advanced Video and Signal-Based Surveillance (AVSS 2010)*, Boston.

About the Contributors

Yu Zhang received her Ph.D. in Computer Science at Texas A&M University in 2005. She is currently Associate Professor in the Department of Computer Science at Trinity University and Director of the Laboratory for Distributed Intelligent Agent Systems. Dr. Zhang's research falls within Agent-Based Modeling and Simulation. Her research is currently supported by three NSF grants. She is in the editorial board for several journals including The Transaction of Simulation, and The International Journal of Agent Technologies and Systems, and in program committee for over 10 conferences and technical groups, such as Autonomous Agents and Multi-Agent Systems. She has regularly reviewed proposals for federal agencies. She is Program Co-Chair of Agent Directed Simulation of SCS SpringSim 2010. She is in the organizing committee of IEEE SMC 2009 and SCS SpringSim 2009. She is Program Chair of IEEE Women In Engineering Central Texas Chapter (CTC), Program Chair of IEEE SMC Society CTC, and Vice Chair of IEEE Computer Society CTC.

* * *

Mohd S. Ahmad received his BS in electrical and electronic engineering from Brighton Polytechnic, UK in 1980. He started his career as a power plant engineer specialising in process instrumentation and control in 1980. After completing his MS in artificial intelligence from Cranfield University, UK in 1995, he joined UNITEN as a principal lecturer and head of dept. of computer science and information technology. He obtained his PhD from Imperial College, London, UK in 2005. He has been an associate professor at UNITEN since 2006. His research interests includes applying constraints to develop collaborative frameworks in multi-agent systems, collaborative interactions in multi-agent systems and tacit knowledge management using AI techniques.

Wagdi Alrawagfeh is a PhD student of Computer Science Department at Memorial Univesity of Canada under supervision of Dr. Edward Brown and Dr. Anrique Mata- Mantero. He received his Master degree in Computer Science from Amman Arab Univeristy-Jordan 2004, and his Bachelor in Computer Science from Al Isra Private University – Jordan 2000. His research interests are in Normative Multi-agent Systems and Autonomous agents. Particularly, he studies the norm identification in open multi-agent society and its effect on the agents' behaviours. He worked as a lecturer from 2005-2008 at Al Isra Private University of Computer Science Dept- Jordan.

Patricia Anthony obtained her PhD in computer science from Southampton University in 2003. She is currently attached with Universiti Malaysia Sabah as a lecturer and researcher. Her research interest is in the applications of agent and semantic technology in various fields such as e-commerce and education. To date, she has published more than 50 articles in the forms of journals and conference proceedings. She also holds several research grants related to semantic agent based computing. She is currently the director for the Center in Excellence in Semantic Agents at the university.

Theo Arentze is an Associate Professor with the Urban Planning Group at the Eindhoven University of Technology

S. M. Niaz Arifin received his B.S. from Bangladesh University of Engineering and Technology (BUET) in 2004 and his M.S. from the University of Texas at Dallas in 2006. He is currently working on his Ph.D. at the University of Notre Dame. His research interests include agent-based simulations, spatial and GIS-based simulation models for malaria, and mathematical modeling in biology. His M.S. research focus was on artificial intelligence and natural language processing. He served as a software developer in the stereotactic breast cancer treatment project at Xcision Medical Systems, California and the Rails online database project at Sabre Holdings Corporation, Texas.

Manish Arora holds MCA (Guru Nanak Dev University, Amritsar), MBA in Operation Management (Indira Gandhi National Open University, New Delhi) and 'C' Level (M. Tech) from DOEACC Society, New Delhi. He has nearly two decades experience in teaching, software development and consultancy. His areas of expertise include Multi agent systems, databases and web technologies. Presently, he is working as Principal Systems Analyst in DOEACC Society, Chandigarh Centre and managing different government projects. He has published 4 papers on multi agent technologies in various international journals and conferences.

Amelia Bădică holds a Ph.D. in Economics and she currently works as Senior Lecturer at the Business Information Systems Department, University of Craiova, Romania. She has a specialization in Management Information Systems at Binghamton University, USA. Her research interests cover the application of expert systems, software engineering and Web technologies in business and management. She co-authored several papers in journals and conference proceedings on these subjects. She was involved as principal investigator in a research project concerning data extraction from the Web.

Costin Bădică holds a Ph.D. in Computer Science and in 2006 he received the title of Professor of Computer Science from University of Craiova. He is currently with the Department of Software Engineering, Faculty of Automatics, Computers and Electronics of the University of Craiova, Romania. During 2001 and 2002 he was Post-Doctoral Fellow with the Department of Computer Science, King's College London, United Kingdom. His research interests are at the intersection of Artificial Intelligence, Distributed Systems and Software Engineering. He authored and co-authored more than 100 publications related to these topics as journal articles, book chapters and conference papers. He prepared special journal issues and co-edited 4 books in Springer's Studies in Computational Intelligence series. He co-initiated and he is co-organizing the Intelligent Distributed Computing -- IDC series of international conferences that is being held yearly. He is member of the editorial board of 4 international journals. He also served as programme committee member of many international conferences.

K. Suzanne Barber is the AT&T Endowed Professor in Engineering and Director of the Center for Identity at The University of Texas, delivering the highest quality identity management discoveries, applications, education and outreach available serving our nation's citizens and our nation's industrial, government, and academic institutions to aggressively combat current, emerging, and future identity management threats and fraud. Dr. Barber has published over 300 articles in refereed publications and garnered over $30M in research sponsorship for innovations in the areas of information assurance, cyber-trust, cyber-security, identity management, intelligent agent-based systems, and software engineering. Dr. Barber has invented and commercialized core technologies that provide unprecedented levels of project/system visibility and knowledge discovery to all stakeholders by keeping contributors fully informed, coordinated and operating at targeted quality levels.

Swati Basak obtained B.Sc (Computrer Science) from BHU, Varanasi. Now studying in M.Sc (Computr Science) from Dept. of Computer Science Faculty of Science, BHU, Varanasi India. Her research interest is Multiagent system

Edward Brown is Head of the Department of Computer Science, Memorial University of Newfoundland, Canada. His principal research interests are software agents, intellectual property, and privacy issues related to technology. Dr. Brown also has a law practice in the area of software technology law. His primary interests intersect under the topic of information privacy, and his most recent work deals with formalizing the monitoring and enforcement of information management policies.

Kenneth "Mark" Bryden is the program director of the simulation, modeling and decision science program in the US Department of Energy's Ames Laboratory. In addition, he heads the Virtual Engineering Research Laboratory within the Virtual Reality Applications Center at Iowa State University. He has an active research and teaching program in the areas of complexity, energy systems, decision science, and design engineering. His research is specifically focused on integrating information technologies, self-organization, and cognition into the engineering processes needed to support decision making for and the realization of complex systems. Dr. Bryden is the recipient of numerous awards including three R&D 100 awards in the past five years for his work on the open source software package VE-Suite.

Suratna Budalakoti holds an MSE degree, and is currently a Ph.D. student, in Electrical and Computer Engineering at the University of Texas at Austin. From 2005 to 2006, he worked for RIACS at the NASA Ames Research Center on the problem of anomaly detection in aviation data. He graduated with a B.E. degree in Computer Science from the National Institute of Technology, Rourkela, India in 2001. His research interests include data mining and multi-agent systems.

Radu Burete is M.Sc. student at Department of Software Engineering, University of Craiova, Romania.

Marco Campennì is assistant researcher at Institute of Cognitive Sciences and Technologies (ISTC)–National Research Council of Italy and received a PhD from the University of Rome "Tor Vergata" where he studied Artificial Intelligence applications to social phenomena. He works on AI applications in social simulations and A-Life approach to animal social behaviour. In cognitive science his interest is on theoretical and computational models of complex behaviours.

Federico Cecconi is researcher at Institute of Cognitive Sciences and Technologies (ISTC) – National Research Council of Italy and associate professor at LUMSA. Its research interests are in the field of dynamics of cellular automata and complex networks, neural networks and cognitive modeling, micro-economic modeling by agent based simulation.

Gregory J. Davis is a graduate student at the University of Notre Dame pursuing a joint Ph. D. within the Psychology and Computer Science & Engineering departments. Professionally, he has developed web-based data collection and reporting software for the Department of Epidemiology & Biostatistics at the University of Texas Health Science Center in San Antonio, developed statistical models of cancer risk and treatment benefits, and developed device drivers for mobile hardware platforms. His research interests in psychology involve understanding and modeling the mechanisms of human visual attention. His research interests in computer science & engineering are in the area of agent-based modeling and simulation applied to biological populations, including simulating disease vectors. Additionally, his interests include developing simulation tools for non-programmers, web- based data collection and reporting, and mobile application development.

David DeAngelis is a Ph.D. candidate in Electrical and Computer Engineering at the University of Texas at Austin. His research focuses on understanding and influencing the behavior of people in online communities. He earned an M.S.E. degree in 2006 from the University of Texas for his work on the security applications of trust in multi-agent systems, and he graduated with a B.S. in Electrical and Computer Engineering from Carnegie Mellon University in 2004.

M. Syamala Devi is a professor in the department of Computer Science & Applications, Panjab University, Chandigarh. She served as Chairperson, Department of Computer Science and Applications for three years. She received her Ph.D degree in Computer Science & Systems Engineering from Andhra University, Visakhapatnam and M. E. in Computer Science & Engineering, from NIT, Allahabad. Before joining Panjab University, she served Indian Space Research Organization, Sriharikota, and National Institute of Technical Teachers' Training & Research, Chandigarh. Her areas of expertise include algorithms, Image Processing, Distributed Artificial Intelligence and Educational Computing. She has guided and has been guiding a number of student projects at Ph.D and post graduate level. She has published about fifty papers in various national and international research journals, proceedings of seminars, and conferences. She has conducted various short-term courses, workshops, seminars and symposia.

Chong Mun Ho is the associate professor at the school of science and technology, Universiti Malaysia Sabah. From 2003-2005 and 2007-2011, he served as the Head of Program Mathematics with Economics, School of Science and Technology, Universiti Malaysia Sabah. He received his BS (mathematics) and MS (mathematics) degree from Universiti Malaya in 1993 and 1995 and his Ph.D. (economics) from Yokohama National University, Japan in 2003. Ho has won a Silver Medal in 32nd International Exhibition of Inventions, Geneva 2004 and enables him to receive an Excellent Scientists Award from Ministry of Higher Education in 2004. Presently, Ho is appointed as Deputy Dean (Academic and International) of Centre for Postgraduate Studies, UMS. His current research has been concerned with the pension systems, theory of incentives, analysis, mathematical education (recreational mathematics) and intelligent agent.

Veermata Jijabai Technological Institute (V.J.T.I), Mumbai, India. He completed his MSE in Electrical and Computer Engineering at the University of Texas at Austin in 2009 while working as a research assistant in the Laboratory for Intelligent Processes and Systems. He currently works at Microsoft Corporation in Sunnyvale, California.

Deborah Lim Phaik Kuan received her BS (software engineering) degree from University Malaysia Sabah in 2003-2006. She is doing her master degree by research in Universiti Malaysia Sabah under supervision of Dr Patricia Anthony, co-supervisor Dr Ho. Cong Mun. She has become a master student in the field of Artificial Intelligent (Intelligent Agent) since 2006. She obtained her MS in computer science at the Universiti Malaysia Sabah in 2009. Deborah current PHD research is concerned with the semantic agent interaction.

Kristen Lund is an undergraduate student at Trinity University majoring in Mathematics and Computer Science. She is from Garland, Texas, and began studying multi-agent systems with Dr. Yu Zhang in the spring semester of her sophomore year. The research in multi-agent systems was continued throughout the summer in a NSF Research Experiences for Undergrads program. Her research interests include the modeling of social networks, category theory, and programming languages.

Moamin A. Mahmoud received his BS in Mmathematics from the college of mathematics and computer science, University of Mosul, Iraq in 2007. Then, he received his MS in information technology at the college of graduate studies, Universiti Tenaga Nasional (UNITEN), Malaysia in 2010. Currently, he is enrolled in the PhD of information and communication technology program at the College of Graduate Studies, Universiti Tenaga Nasional (UNITEN). His current research interests include artificial intelligence, software agent and multiagent systems.

Manrique Mata-Montero is an associate professor at Memorial's department of Computer Science with principal research interests in theoretical computer science, serial and parallel computational complexity and Agent based systems. . He has an undergraduate degree 1978, University of Costa Rica, M.Sc. Computer Science, 1982, Northwestern University, Il., USA. and Ph.D. 1990, University of Victoria, B.C., Canada.

Bireshwar Dass Mazumdar obtained MCA degree from UP Technical University, Lucknow, India in the year of 2005. He has 2 years experience of teaching in the field of computer science and engineering. Presently he is a fulltime research scholar in Department of Computer Engineering, Institute of Technology, BHU, Varanasi India. His research interest is Multiagent system and its application in e-commerce, e-governance.

Neelam Modanwal obtained B.Sc (Computrer Science) from BHU, Varanasi. Now studying in M.Sc (Computr Science) from Dept. Of Computer Science Faculty of Science, BHU, Varanasi India. Her research interest is Multiagent system.

Florin Moraru is M.Sc. student at Department of Software Engineering, University of Craiova, Romania.

Ali Rammal is a PhD in computer science and temporary teacher and researcher at INSA of Toulouse. He is a member of SMAC team (Cooperative multi-agent systems) team at IRIT. He is also a member of ISIS team (Informatique et Système d'Informations pour la Santé: Computer and Information System for Health), University Jean-Francois Champollion. His research is focused on multi-agent systems and distributed classification methods on the domain of homecare, especially on the learning and classification of elderly and dependent people behaviour using multi-agent technologies.

Nicole Ronald is a PhD candidate with the Urban Planning Group at the Eindhoven University of Technology.

Robert Somogyi is currently a PhD student at the department of economics of Ecole Polytechnique (ParisTech) under the supervision of Francis Bloch. After his graduation from the 5-year-long Quantitative Economics program of Corvinus University of Budapest, he studied at a one-year-long Master 2 program of Paris School of Economics called „Analyse et Politique Economiques". His main fields of interests are network theory, agent-based computational economics and theoretical industrial organization.

Nicolas Singer received his Ph.D. degree in computer science, from the University Blaise Pascal at Clermont-Ferrand (France) in 1997. After having worked on multi-agent system and web technology for five years, he was appointed to the school of engineering ISIS in 2001. Since, his researches focus on information systems in the field of e-health, especially those that need to be massively distributed and where multi-agent technologies can bring efficient solutions.

Harry Timmermans is a Professor and Chair of the Urban Planning Group at the Eindhoven University of Technology.

Sylvie Trouilhet received her Ph.D. degree in computer science, from the University of Paul Sabatier at Toulouse in 1993. This is one of the first French theses on the Multi-Agent Systems (MAS). She has been involved especially in interactions and communication between agents. She is a member of the MAS French research group since it foundation in 1995. She is a lecturer in programming engineering in the University of Toulouse. She is working in the area of large scale multi-agents systems for the last ten years. Her current research focus is on deployment of massively distributed systems and on knowledge gathering in the field of health.

Maksim Tsikhanovich is an undergraduate student at Bard College majoring in Computer Science. He participated into the NSF Research Experiences for Undergrads program directed by Dr. Yu Zhang in the summer of 2009. His research interests include the modeling of social networks, multi-agent systems, and theoretical modeling and simulation to massive multi-agent systems.

Aditya Velivelli completed his bachelor's degree in India in 1999. After receiving his master of science degree at the University of Missouri-Rolla in 2001, Dr. Velivelli completed his PhD in mechanical engineering at Iowa State University in 2008. Between 2005 and 2009, Dr. Velivelli worked in industry developing geometry editing and volume grid generation methods, and modeling fluid flow in power plant furnaces. He returned to Iowa State University in 2009 as a postdoctoral researcher where he worked on stigmergic construction as an optimization tool with Professor Mark Bryden. Dr. Velivelli is currently employed as a thermal application engineer at Exa Corporation, USA.

János Vincze is senior research fellow at the Institute of Economics of the Hungarian Academy of Sciences, and Associate Professor at the Department of Mathematical Economics of Corvinus University of Budapest. He holds a PhD from the Corvinus University of Budapest. Formerly he worked at the National Bank of Hungary, and taught at the Central European University. He has participated in several international research projects sponsored by the Commission of the European Union. He has published on diverse aspects of applied micro and macroeconomic theory. In the last few years he has started to apply ideas borrowed from psychology and computer science to traditional economic problems, like pricing, the housing market and tax evasion.

Mohd Z. M. Yusoff obtained his BS and MS in computer science from Universiti Kebangsaan Malaysia in 1996 and 1998 respectively. He started his career as a Lecturer at UNITEN in 1998 and has been appointed as a Principle Lecturer at UNITEN since 2008. His has produced and presented more than 40 papers for local and international conferences. His research interest includes modeling and applying emotions in various domains including educational systems and software agents, modeling trust in computer forensic and integrating agent in knowledge discovery system.

Ying Zhou is a fourth-year Ph.D. student in the Computer Science and Engineering Department at University of Notre Dame. She is working with Dr. Collins and Dr. Madey on the project of Malaria Transmission Consortium, which is funded by the Bill & Melinda Gates Foundation. Ying's research efforts span agent-based modeling the Anopheles mosquito population dynamics, exploration of effectiveness of various vector control interventions, investigating impact of insecticide resistance of mosquitoes on interventions, and PDA-based Malaria Indicator Survey development.

Index